PROBLEM SOLVING AND COMPUTATION FOR SCIENTISTS AND ENGINEERS: AN INTRODUCTION USING C

STEVEN R. LERMAN

Class of 1922 Distinguished Professor
of Civil and Environmental Engineering

Massachusetts Institute of Technology

PRENTICE HALL, Englewood Cliffs, New Jersey 07632

Library of Congress Cataloging-in-Publication Data

Lerman, Steven R.
    Problem solving and computation for scientists and engineers : an
introduction using C / Steven R. Lerman.

        p.   cm.
    Includes index.
    ISBN 0-13-482126-2
    1. Science—Data processing.   2. Engineering—Data processing.
3. Problem solving—Data processing.   4. Algorithms.   5. C (Computer
program language)   I. Title.
Q183.9.L45 1993
502.85—dc20   92-24326
                CIP

Acquisitions editor: MARCIA HORTON
Production editor: IRWIN ZUCKER
Manufacturing buyer: DAVID DICKEY
Prepress buyer: LINDA BEHRENS
Supplements editor: ALICE DWORKIN

Editorial assistant: DOLORES MARS
Cover design: LUNDGREN GRAPHICS
Cover art: "THE THINKER" BY RODIN;
  PARIS, RODIN MUSEUM, VANNI/ART
  RESOURCE

©1993 by Prentice-Hall, Inc.
A Simon & Schuster Company
Englewood Cliffs, New Jersey 07632

Printed in the United States of America

10 9 8 7 6 5 4 3 2 1

ISBN   0-13-482126-2

Prentice-Hall International (UK) Limited, *London*
Prentice-Hall of Australia Pty. Limited, *Sydney*
Prentice-Hall Canada Inc., *Toronto*
Prentice-Hall Hispanoamericana, S.A., *Mexico*
Prentice-Hall of India Private Limited, *New Delhi*
Prentice-Hall of Japan, Inc., *Tokyo*
Simon & Schuster Asia Pte. Ltd., *Singapore*
Editora Prentice-Hall do Brasil, Ltda., *Rio de Janeiro*

To my wife, Lori
and my children,
Deborah, Amy, and David

CONTENTS

2 THE C LANGUAGE AND SOME ELEMENTARY ALGORITHMS   *17*

PREFACE

Philosophy of the Book

The organization and content of this book are based on five educational principles:

- Students need to learn how to apply algorithmic thinking to solve problems in engineering, science, management, and planning. While most of this book is devoted to algorithms which will be implemented as computer programs, the basic cognitive strategies used in devising algorithms are applicable to a wider range of situations.
- Learning a particular computer language should be secondary to learning fundamental algorithms. While the student should learn a programming language in an introductory-level course, the language should be a means of expressing algorithms in a way computers can deal with rather than an end in itself.
- It is important for students to see algorithms in the context of computational problems they will face. This tends to make the approach in this book far more pragmatic than would be typical in a standard course in computer algorithms. This approach is appropriate for undergraduates who will use computation as a tool rather than those who intend to major in computer science.

- Students should see realistic problems solved in complete computer programs as part of their education. The experience of both understanding and writing such programs is crucial to effective pedagogy.

- In a single-semester introductory course, students should see algorithmic solutions to a wide array of problems. Thus, this book deals with many diverse areas of computation rather than any single area in-depth.

As a result of applying these basic principles, the book is organized very differently from most first-level undergraduate textbooks in computation. The vast majority of introductory textbooks treat a particular programming language as their focal point. These books introduce parts of the language's syntax, such as variable declarations, program control, functions, data types, and the other categories of programming statements, in distinct sections, using examples to illustrate the use of these program building blocks. The approach used here is quite different. This book presents different areas of computation, and introduces parts of the programming language on an "as needed" basis. In my view, this provides the student with a much more natural introduction to a programming language. The problems motivate why one might need a particular programming construct.

Organizing an introductory computer course around different problem areas keeps students' attention on the important issues. Different computer languages will come into and out of general usage during a student's working years. It is quite likely that a student who needs to develop computer programs later in life will have to learn different languages over time; no single language will be useful over the span of forty or more years. The object of an introductory course in computation should be to teach an algorithmic style of thinking and problem solving rather than simply to drill students on the details of one particular programming language.

Why Use the C Programming Language?

C is neither the most theoretically appealing nor the best structured computer language. It is also not the easiest language to learn. Moreover, if one desires, C can be used to code truly obscure programs. One might then reasonably ask, "Why do I choose to teach it in this book?"

I have chosen to teach students the C programming language for largely pragmatic reasons. Despite all its shortcomings, C has become a computational *lingua franca* because it serves the needs of general-purpose programming quite well, produces efficient executable code, and is relatively easy to implement on diverse computer architectures. In short, the aesthetic shortcomings of C are outweighed by its proven value and widespread acceptance. Some other programming languages, such as Modula 2, are similar to Esperanto — appealing to theoreticians but little used in practice.

Many of the shortcomings of C as a programming langugae often cited by critics can be counterbalanced by judicious use of common sense in developing programs. In this book I stress a style of program development that leads to clear, concise, well-documented software. The examples use a modular style and avoid obscure syntax whenever possible. Toward this end I have relegated some parts of the C language to the appendix, with the belief that most novice programmers do not need them. For example, the `switch` statement, bit operators, and conditional expressions can readily be avoided in introductory applications.

I have chosen to use the ANSI standard dialect of C. The new ANSI standard is being widely adopted, and virtually all compiler vendors will use it in the next few years. Some of the compilers will retain an "old style" C option to allow pre-ANSI C programs to be compiled. Because there is a great deal of such earlier code still in use, I have included a discussion of the major differences between ANSI and earlier C implementations as part of the appendix. Students who will have to work with pre-ANSI software written in C should find this discussion helpful.

Examples Used in the Book

The book utilizes two types of examples. Many of the algorithms are illustrated by showing an implementation of a particular function in C. These examples appear within the sections that explain the theory of the algorithm. In most cases the use of these functions in actual applications is not illustrated.

The book also includes what I call *programming projects*. These are extended examples that are complete programs which can be compiled and executed on virtually any computer that has an ANSI-compliant C compiler. They are presented in separate sections, often with a discussion of the problem being solved and some sample input data.

The programming projects are drawn from diverse applications in engineering, science, management, and planning. It is my hope that students will find both the programming aspects of these examples and the application areas of interest. I believe that these extended programming examples are essential learning aids for most students. They do far more than demonstrate how a particular problem is solved in a computer program. Through the use of examples, instructors can help students learn a style of programming. Examples that are well-designed programs set a standard for student programmers. Students should be encouraged to model their own programs on these examples, using a similar format and commenting style. In teaching this material at M.I.T., I have found it useful to include style as one of the criteria in evaluating student work, reinforcing the idea that obscure programs that are undocumented are often costly in the long run.

Using this Book

This book is designed for a number of distinct student audiences. Instructors are encouraged to use different portions of the book selectively depending on the type of students they are teaching. The book includes considerably more material than most courses will cover in a single semester. This allows instructors some flexibility in matching the text to the needs of the course.

For example, some sections of the chapter on numerical methods assume that the student has had an introductory course in calculus. This material will be of most value to students in engineering and science. Instructors teaching courses for students from other disciplines may choose to skip these sections. Similarly, some instructors may decide not to cover computer graphics in a single-semester introductory course.

Some of the chapters contain sections that need to be read in order to understand material presented subsequently. For example, all of Chapter 2 should be read by students. Chapters 3 through 6 have some sections that present new features of the C programming language. Most instructors will include these sections as required reading in any syllabus. The notation shown in the margin (a large capital C in a rounded box) to the left of any major section heading denotes that the section contains material about C which should be covered. The integral sign notation (also shown in the left margin) denotes material that requires knowledge of calculus. These notations are provided as guides to the reader to determine which sections must be read to follow later programming examples and which should be skipped by readers not familiar with basic calculus.

About the Exercises

Each chapter is followed by a series of exercises, most of which involve some computer programming. Many of the exercises introduce some new algorithms or ideas that are not covered in the body of the text. Other exercises extend the material in the book, requiring some augmentation of the algorithms already presented. The notion of assigning exercises that are substantial in nature follows the general philosophy that homework should involve students in learning something new, not just drill them on material already covered. It is generally the case that the best way to learn how to use computational methods to solve problems is for students to write, test, and debug complete programs.

The majority of the exercises involve writing computer programs, and many are appropriate for weekly assignments. Students should not be expected to solve all the exercises. Instead, instructors should pick which are most suitable for the particular group of students taking their courses.

In the undergraduate course at M.I.T. upon which this book is based, my colleagues and I encourage students to discuss assignments with each other, sharing ideas about how to solve them. Allowing students to exchange ideas is an excellent means for informal tutoring of some students by others. However, we enforce a "no sharing of code" rule that prohibits students from using each other's programs in their assignments. This makes it possible for us to evaluate students fairly in grading assignments. In another introductory computing subject at M.I.T., with a proportionately larger teaching staff, the instructors do not impose such a rule, relying on weekly small group tutorials (each with three to five students) to make sure that each student understands the material in the assignments. Whether or not the latter approach is feasible varies from university to university.

Finding Elements of the C Programming Language in this Book

Because the introduction of parts of the C programming language are interspersed in this book with the presentation of computational methods, readers may have a little difficulty in locating descriptions of some specific part of the language's syntax. The index provides entries for all parts of C covered in the book. In addition, the following table provides a road map for readers interested in where in the book various parts of the C language are covered.

Component of the C Language	Section
variables	2.4
assignment statements	2.4
arithmetic operators	2.5
variable types	2.6
`limits.h` header file	2.6
constants	2.7
mixed arithmetic	2.8
use of functions	2.9
header files	2.10
`#define` statements	2.10
`stdio.h` header file	2.10
function prototypes	2.12
argument passing	2.13
pointer variables	2.13
`printf()` function	2.14
`scanf()` function	2.15
scope of variables	2.16
external variables	2.16
`if` statements	2.17
control blocks	2.17
`while` loops	2.18
`for` loops	2.18
increment and decrement operators	2.19
precedence of operators	2.22
`float.h` header file	3.2
part of the standard math library	3.3
pointers to functions	3.4
one dimensional arrays	4.2
passing arrays as arguments	4.2
strings in C	4.3
multidimensional arrays	4.6
`struct`s	5.2
passing `struct`s as arguments	5.2
`exit()` function	5.3
dynamic memory allocation and deallocation	5.4
`stdlib.h` header file	5.4

Component of the C Language	Section
ragged arrays	5.5
`argc` and `argv`	5.6
`typedef` statements	5.7
use of multiple source files	5.8
static functions	5.8
file input and output	6.2
`static` variables	8.6
hexadecimal and octal constants	A.1
mixed arithmetic with unsigned quantities	A.2
`register` variables	A.3
`const` qualifier	A.4
`volatile` qualifier	A.4
other control options for `printf()` and `scanf()`	A.5
character input and output functions	A.6
string input functions `gets()` and `fgets()`	A.7
string output functions `puts()` and `fputs()`	A.7
the complete math library	A.8
character library	A.9
`bsearch()` and `qsort()`	A.10
other parts of the standard library	A.11
`size_t` and `ptrdiff_t` types	A.12
enumerations	A.13
conditional compilation (`#if...#elif...#else`)	A.14
`#ifdef` and `#ifndef`	A.14
`do ... while` loops	A.15
`switch` and `break` statements	A.16
`continue` statement	A.17
statement labels and the `goto` statement	A.18
unions	A.19
conditional expressions	A.20
bit operators	A.21
bit fields	A.22
earlier versions of C	A.23

Acknowledgments

This book was prepared with the help of many people who contributed ideas and commented on early drafts. Professor Nigel H. M. Wilson provided initial drafts of much of Chapter 6 and gave detailed comments through several revisions of the book. Other faculty colleagues at M.I.T., particularly Professors Haris Koutsopoulos, Robert Logcher, and John Williams provided comments on specific areas as well as ideas for how material should be presented. James Culbert provided invaluable comments on Chapter 9.

The various teaching assistants who have helped me teach the course at M.I.T. upon which this book is based also provided comments at various stages. These included Nestor Agbayani, Kalidas Ashok, Nikola Deskovic, Clark Frazier, Manuel Garmilla, Sreenivasa Gorti, Yusin Lee, Herve Magnan, and Anil Mukundan. Senior teaching assistants Patrick Kinnicutt and Ruaidhri O'Connor both read and commented on several drafts.

Georgia Taylor helped with many aspects of the manuscript preparation, especially in drawing many of the figures.

Scott Centurino, an M.I.T. undergraduate, labored many hours in developing solutions to all the exercises, writing some original problems, and dealing with reformatting of the text to speed the publishing process. He also checked the code in the book to make sure that it worked on a wide range of computers and C compilers.

The approach to this book was heavily influenced by my discussions with two people, Professor Hal Abelson and Dr. George Kocur.

Professors Richard D. Alpert (Boston University), David B. Ashley (University of California at Berkeley), Joseph Lambert (Pennsylvania State University), Leon Levine (University of California at Los Angeles), and Keith B. Olson (Montana College of Mineral Science and Technology) and an anonymous reviewer all provided valuable comments on an early draft that have been incorporated into this book.

Finally, the author is indebted to the M.I.T. School of Engineering and Department of Civil and Environmental Engineering for their financial support of this book.

Steven R. Lerman
Massachusetts Institute of Technology

PROBLEMS, ALGORITHMS, AND COMPUTER PROGRAMS

1.1 INTRODUCTION

This book is about three things:

- Real-world problems for which computers may be useful tools. These problems come from science, engineering, business, architecture, planning, and other areas.
- Procedural methods, called *algorithms* to solve problems.
- Programs that instruct a computer to execute the algorithms that solve problems.

Like the three legs of a tripod, all of these are essential elements in making effective use of computers. A failure to appreciate the role of any of these three elements can lead to horrifying results.

Pragmatic uses of computers should always begin with an understanding of the problem at hand. For example, one commonplace application of computers is in routine business functions such as accounting and payroll. Without a clear statement of how such functions are done, no one can develop a useful procedure for making a business more cost-effective through computerization. Similarly, in engineering, computers are used to compute the stresses and deformations of elements of complicated structures such as suspension bridges and skyscrapers. Again, unless we first understand the physics of such systems, developing useful computer methods for analyzing them is hopeless.

The need for a clear, unambiguous statement of a problem would seem to be obvious. However, it is astonishing how often both students and professionals will march to a computer seeking answers before the questions are well-formulated.

Assuming that a well-formulated problem statement is in hand, one must formulate a procedure for solving the problem. *Algorithms* are procedures that are well-defined and lead to definite results. The word *algorithm* comes from the name of the Persian mathematician al Khowarzimi who lived circa A.D. 825.[1]

In brief, an algorithm is a finite set of steps, each of which may require one or more operations, that are executed sequentially unless the current step specifies otherwise, and lead to solution of a specific problem. Note that this definition requires that algorithms use a *finite* number of steps; they must eventually terminate on some measurable condition.

The definition of an algorithm does not state how many steps will be required. Other than stating that an algorithm must solve the problem at hand, the definition does not provide any criteria for distinguishing "good" algorithms from "bad" ones. We will often find in our study of algorithms that there are many ways to solve a particular problem, some of which work much better than others. One of the goals of this book is to help the reader understand why some algorithms are better than others for particular problems.

The third "leg of the tripod" is computer programming, the implementation of algorithms on a particular computer. Algorithms have become increasingly important because computers can execute a long but finite series of steps quickly. In a very strong sense, the abstract, mathematical notion of an algorithm was complemented by computer technology, making many procedures practical. Computers became the natural vehicle for implementing many types of algorithms because they are capable of executing certain types of operations with extraordinary speed, thus expanding the range of problems for which algorithms are useful.

1.2 EXAMPLES OF ALGORITHMS

It is useful to consider a few simple examples of algorithms. Consider first the problem of finding a way through a simple maze such as the one shown in Figure 1.1. The route from the entrance of this maze to the exit can found by the simple "right hand on wall" algorithm. To understand this algorithm, imagine that you are walking through the maze. If you place your right hand on the wall to your right when you enter the maze, and *always* keep that hand touching the wall while you walk, you will eventually reach the exit.

The "right hand on wall" method qualifies as an algorithm because it has a finite number of steps. Note, however, that the method can make no claim to being the fastest

[1]His full name was Abu Ja'far Mohammed ibn Musa al Khowarzimi. Readers interested in a further description of the origin of the word algorithm are referred to the first chapter of [Knuth, Donald E. 73a].

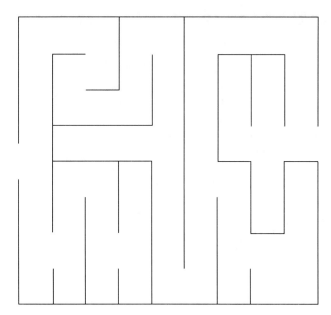

Figure 1.1 Simple maze.

way to get through the maze. In fact, using this algorithm may lead you down a number of dead ends before you find the exit.

Another interesting property of this algorithm is that it requires that you start the maze at the beginning. Imagine that you are blindfolded and led into the maze, and then abandoned there. In this case, the algorithm is of no real use. If you touch the nearest wall with your right hand and apply the algorithm, you may find yourself circling around an interior "island" of the maze forever. Thus, the "right hand on wall" algorithm solves the maze problem only when you apply it upon entering the maze.

The simple operation of multiplying two numbers provides another example. Anyone who has completed grade school has already been taught algorithms. For example, when learning how to multiply, most people are taught to write the two numbers in a column. The standard algorithm taught to elementary school students then proceeds with successively multiplying each of the digits of the second number by the first. The results, appropriately shifted to account for the place of each of the digits, are then added. For example, in solving for the product of 49 and 26, one would construct the following table:

$$
\begin{array}{r}
49 \\
26 \\
\hline
294 \\
98 \\
\hline
1274
\end{array}
$$

This is not, however, the only possible algorithm for multiplication. Another algorithm, called multiplication *a la russe*, proceeds as follows:[2]

- Step 1. Write two numbers in separate columns. If the number in the first column is odd, repeat the second number in a third column.
- Step 2. Halve the first number (forgetting remainders) and double the second. If the number in the first column is odd, record the second number in the third column. Otherwise, leave the third column blank.
- Step 3. Repeat steps 1 and 2 until the number in the first column is 1.
- Step 4. Add the numbers in the third column. The sum is the product of the original two numbers.

When applied to finding the product of 49 and 26, this algorithm produces the following table:

49	26	26
24	52	–
12	104	–
6	208	–
3	416	416
1	832	832
		1274

An interesting aspect of the multiplication *a la russe* algorithm is that it never requires the general multiplication of two numbers. The only basic operations are halving, doubling, and adding. Clearly, while both the grade school and *a la russe* algorithms produce the same results, they use entirely different methods. The existence of totally distinct methods for accomplishing a single task is often encountered in the study of algorithms.

1.3 SOLVING PROBLEMS WITH COMPUTERS

It is possible to implement algorithms as a set of computer instructions in what is called *machine language*. Programs written in machine language require the statement of an algorithm as a series of steps, each corresponding to an instruction that can be executed by the hardware of the computer. Unfortunately, most computers have a very limited set of basic instructions built in, so even relatively simple algorithms require many such steps.

[2]Multiplication *a la russe* is used as an example of an algorithm in [Brassard, G. and Bratley, P. 88].

Machine language programming was almost universal in the 1950s and common-place in the 1960s. However, programs written in machine language have a number of shortcomings. In particular, they are:

- Laborious to write. Machine language programs generally require many state-ments to accomplish even simple tasks.
- Difficult to adapt and maintain. Improving or fixing deficiencies in programs written in machine language requires specialized knowledge.
- Extremely difficult to move to different computers. A machine language program can only execute on the type of computer for which it was written. Thus, such programs may have to be entirely recoded for new computer architectures.
- Relatively expensive to develop. The cost of developing a machine language program is often quite high.

For this reason, most computer algorithms are written in what are called *high-level languages*. Literally hundreds of such languages have been created, often with specialized applications in mind. The best-known high-level languages include BASIC, FORTRAN, COBOL, Algol, Lisp, PL/1, Ada, Modula 2, Pascal, and C. These languages allow programmers to express algorithms in a much more compact way, using more powerful statements that are somewhat closer to human language.

The job of translating these languages into instructions the computer can actually execute is left to a *compiler* or *interpreter*. A compiler is a computer program which accepts as input the algorithm written in some high-level language and produces machine language as output. The output of the compiler can then be executed on the computer. An interpreter reads and executes the high-level language one statement at a time. In general, compilers produce more efficient programs, while interpreters make it easier to find and correct errors in programs.

To be any real use in expressing algorithms, computer languages all provide the following capabilities:

1. Specifying values of data.
2. Recording results.
3. Performing calculations and assigning results to variables.
4. Testing values and selecting alternative courses of actions.
5. Repeating actions.
6. Terminating the algorithm.

In addition, most languages allow the programmer to organize components of a program into subunits. These subunits are often called *abstractions* or *objects*. For example, if part of a program is supposed to get input values from the user and check whether they meet certain tests for validity, this subunit of work might be defined as a *procedure*, or *function*, and given some mnemonic name such as **get_valid_inputs**. Once the subunit has been defined, it might be used in many places in the program. This is called *procedural abstraction*.

A second form of abstraction allows groups of related data items to be "bundled" together into larger units which can be referenced, changed, and managed. This is called *data abstraction*. For example, an algorithm for producing paychecks might require the name, social security number, hourly wage rate, and hours worked for each employee. A programming language might allow you to create a data abstraction that includes all these items, and give it a single name such as `employee_data`.

Thus, we add the following four capabilities to our list of useful features of a programming language:

1. A means of procedural abstraction.
2. A way to invoke a procedural abstraction.
3. A means of data abstraction.
4. A way to access and assign values to elements within a data abstraction.

In this book we use the C programming language to express algorithms. The basics of the language are introduced in Chapter 2. In succeeding chapters we expand the reader's knowledge of C, showing additional features of the language when they are needed to implement particular algorithms.

1.4 WHAT IS A COMPUTER?

There are many types of computers. While it is not a goal of this book to teach the reader the details of computer hardware, some basic knowledge of how computers execute programs often makes understanding computer languages and programs easier.

For this reason, we introduce the essential elements of computers and how they operate. Our description is intentionally general because computers vary widely depending on their vintage and manufacturer. Nevertheless, virtually all computers in widespread use today share certain common elements.

Figure 1.2 is a block diagram showing the major components of a typical computer. The reader should be aware that Figure 1.2 greatly simplifies the elements of a modern computer and that computers vary widely in their detailed implementation of these general elements. In addition, this "model computer" represents a single processor, serial computer of the type first characterized by J. von Neumann [vonNeumann, John 63]. The overwhelming majority of computers now in use are variants of this basic model, and all of the discussions of algorithms in this book assume use of this type of computer.

The figure depicts five key elements of a computer:

- The central processing unit
- Random access memory
- The bus
- Secondary storage
- Displays or terminals

Each of these is considered in a subsection below.

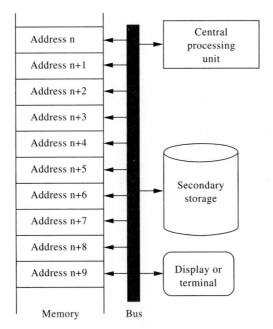

Figure 1.2 Basic elements of a typical computer.

1.4.1 The Central Processing Unit

Every computer has at least one *central processing unit*, or CPU. The CPU is the part of the computer that executes programs. It contains the circuitry needed to execute the instructions. For example, it is generally the CPU that adds two numbers or directs the movement of information from one part of the computer to another. Often, the CPU has a set of *registers*. These are places which can be used to store values or results of computations. The CPU can access values in registers extremely quickly.

The instructions a CPU executes are represented by numbers; each instruction has a corresponding numerical code. Computers may have any number of instructions. Most practical computers have at least on the order of 100 instructions, and rarely have more than a few hundred. The instruction set is the *machine language* for the computer.

1.4.2 Random Access Memory

A second key element of a computer is *random access memory*, or RAM. The memory of the computer is where both programs and data are stored. Each place in memory where something can be stored is called a *location*, and every location has a unique *address*.

All information (including both programs and data) is stored in binary (base 2) form. For example, the decimal value 29 would be represented by the binary value 11101. Each one or zero is called a *bit*. Usually, the bits are organized into larger groups. For example, most computers use groups of 8 bits which together are called a *byte*. A single byte can represent integer values from 0 through 255. A single byte is generally used to represent characters, where each character is encoded in one of the integer values between 0 and 255.

In most computers, a byte is the smallest unit of information which can be stored and operated on. Some computers use even larger groups such as 32 bits (or even 64 bits) as their smallest working units. On machines that use bytes as their smallest unit, each byte in the memory has a unique address.

Figure 1.2 shows a section of a computer's memory starting with location n. Addresses generally are numbered sequentially starting from zero, and actual memory size may range from tens of thousands of bytes through hundreds of millions of bytes. Memory generally comes in units of *kilobytes* and *megabytes*. (Each kilobyte is actually 1024 bytes and a megabyte is 1024 kilobytes.) Typically, personal computers might have from a fraction of a megabyte up to four or eight megabytes. Large mainframe computers can have a hundred or more megabytes of RAM.

A central concept in computers is that the CPU gets its instructions from the computer's memory. Thus, computer programs are stored in memory, with instructions being fetched by the processor on an "as needed" basis. Generally, a CPU has a special register (often called the *instruction register*) which stores the memory address of the next instruction to be executed. Each time an instruction is fetched from memory, this register is advanced to the next memory location. This is called *sequential execution*. However, some instructions change the contents of the instruction register. This is how a computer branches from one part of a program to another. Various machine language instructions reset the value of the instruction register. For example, an instruction might determine the next address to be executed depending on whether another register contains a certain value.

The computer's memory is also used to store the data values used in a program. These may be numerical values (stored in base 2), letters encoded as numerical values, or other information represented in binary form. The computer hardware makes no distinction between the memory locations used for instructions and the locations used for data. The flow of a program's execution is totally controlled through the instruction register.

It is worth noting that since computers store both instructions and data as binary information, it is possible for a computer program to change itself. Such programs are called *self-modifying*.

1.4.3 The Bus

The element in Figure 1.2 labeled the *bus* is the set of interconnections through which data moves from one part of the computer to another. A computer might have a number of buses, each designed to interconnect different portions of the computer. For example, it is not unusual for a computer to have a bus for accessing RAM and another bus for accessing input and output devices.

1.4.4 Secondary Storage

A fourth component on most computers is some form of *secondary storage*. This often takes the form of a removable "floppy" disk, fixed "hard" disk, tape drive, or other device in which information is stored on a series of magnetic charges on some medium. There are several differences between the RAM on a computer and secondary storage, including the following:

- Information cannot be moved directly from secondary storage devices to the CPU. It must first be moved to the computer's random access memory.
- Secondary storage devices are generally several orders of magnitude slower than RAM for storage and retrieval of information.
- Most computers have considerably more secondary storage than they have RAM.
- Information in secondary storage is organized into units called *files*.
- Per unit of storage, secondary storage is considerably less expensive than RAM.
- On most computers, the information in RAM is lost when the computer is shut off. In contrast, secondary storage is generally *persistent*. Information in secondary storage remains unchanged when the computer is turned off.

1.4.5 Displays or Terminals

The fifth component of a typical computer consists of one or more *displays* or *terminals*. Personal computers typically have a single console (a keyboard, a monitor, and sometimes a pointing/selecting device such as a mouse). In contrast, larger, more powerful computers may have hundreds of terminals connected to them, allowing their resources to be shared by many users.

1.5 A HYPOTHETICAL ROBOT

To make the ideas in the preceding sections more concrete, imagine a very simple computer that directs a small robot.[3] The robot/computer is assumed to have a random access memory for holding both a program and data, and a processor that can execute a very small set of instructions. In addition, the robot has a display which can show up to five characters. We assume that there is no secondary storage in the computer, and that programs and data are loaded by attaching some other computer to the robot and moving information directly into the robot's memory.

The central processor of our hypothetical computer will be assumed to have an instruction register and one general register. Execution of a program begins by pushing

---

[3]The idea of using a robot as a pedagogical tool to introduce computer programming was developed in detail in a book by [Pattis, R.E. 81].

a button that sets the value of the instruction register to zero, causing the computer to execute the instruction in memory location zero. The uses of the general register will be made clear below.

The goal of this section is to develop a program for the robot to find the exit from a maze in which the walls are aligned on a grid. Walls are assumed to be either vertical or horizontal, with minimum separation between walls of one unit.

The central processor in our imaginary robot is capable of accepting the following instructions:

- Move the robot forward one step.
- Test if the robot is still inside maze. If the robot is in the maze, the value of the general register is set to one. Otherwise, the value of the general register is set to zero.
- Test if there is a wall of the maze directly in front of the robot. If there is a wall in front of the robot, the value of the general register is set to one. Otherwise, the value of the general register is set to zero.
- Test if the value of the general register is zero. If it is, then the next memory location contains the address of the next instruction to be executed. If not, then the memory location two greater than the current instruction contains the address of the next instruction to be executed.
- Direct the robot to turn right 90 degrees.
- Output a message on the robot's display. The message displayed is encoded in the values of the next five memory locations. The message is coded so that the number 0 is a blank space and the numbers 1 through 26 correspond to the letters A through Z.
- Branch to another instruction. The value in the next memory location will be the address of the next instruction executed.
- Stop the robot.

The following table gives the machine instruction code of each for the eight instructions in our imaginary robot/computer.

ROBOT MACHINE INSTRUCTIONS

Code	Instruction
1	move forward
2	test if still in maze
3	test if wall ahead
4	test for zero
5	turn right
6	output message
7	branch to instruction
8	stop

Note that the robot has no direct way of turning left 90 degrees. In order to make a left turn, the robot will have to make three right turns in succession.

Given this hypothetical automaton, we can now construct a machine language program that implements the "right hand on wall" algorithm. The program would be as shown in the following table.

MACHINE LANGUAGE PROGRAM FOR MAZE

Address	Value	Explanation
0	1	forward one step
1	2	check if in maze
2	4	test for zero
3	18	branch if out of maze
4	5	branch if in maze
5	5	turn right
6	3	test if wall ahead
7	4	test for zero
8	15	branch if no wall ahead
9	10	branch if wall ahead
10	5	right
11	5	right
12	5	right
13	7	branch to ⎫
14	6	location 6 ⎭
15	1	forward
16	7	branch to ⎫
17	1	location 1 ⎭
18	6	display instruction
19	4	letter D
20	15	letter O
21	14	letter N
22	5	letter E
23	0	blank
24	8	stop

The reader can verify that this program will actually get out of the maze in Figure 1.1 by simulating the program's execution on a piece of paper.

Each line in this table is an address in the machine's memory followed by a machine instruction (one through eight), an address in the computer's memory, or a piece of data (one of the letters encoded as a number). Even in this hypothetical computer, our maze-solving program is difficult to follow. Now contrast this with the expression of an algorithm in a hypothetical high-level language. A program might appear as follows:

```
forward
WHILE still_in_maze {
        right
        WHILE wall_ahead {
                left
                    }
        forward
            }
put "DONE "
stop


left
{
  right
  right
  right
}
```

In this high-level language, the statements **forward, still_in_maze, wall_ahead, right, put,** and **stop** correspond to their machine language counterparts. However, the construction using the word **WHILE** causes the program to loop over the instructions enclosed in the "curly braces" (denoted by **{** and **}**) until the value in the general register is zero.

The value enclosed in quotes after the **put** provides a simplified way of presenting characters to the computer. In order to translate this into machine instructions for our hypothetical computer, the compiler would first generate the instruction code for the put operation, and then place the numerical codes for the letters **D, O, N, E** and a space in the following five memory locations.

Even more interesting is the use of the word **left** in the program. In this language, **left** is the name of a procedural abstraction. When used as part of the first section of the program (inside the **WHILE** clause) it instructs the computer to execute the function named **left**. The implementation of **left** follows the **stop** statement, and defines the procedure **left** as a series of three right turns.

Clearly, this expression of the algorithm is vastly easier to understand than is the machine language version. Of course, to use it would require that someone write a compiler for the higher-level language we have informally defined. The great advantage is that once such a compiler has been developed by someone with specialized knowledge of the robot and how it worked, anyone interested in programming our computer to do all sorts of things could make use of it. The compiler serves as a general platform upon which all the robot programmers can build.

1.6 SYSTEM SOFTWARE

Of course, real computers are vastly more complicated than our primitive robot, and useful higher-level languages are considerably more sophisticated than our robot language.

While the principles illustrated here generalize quite well, modern computers generally come with a set of programs that makes programming them considerably easier. These programs are collectively called the *system software*.

The single most important part of the systems software is the *operating system*. This is the software that manages the resources of the computer, including the files on the secondary storage devices, the sessions from the terminals or the display, the use of memory, the division of the CPU's time across various tasks, and many other functions. Operating systems generally come with the computer, and they are often developed by the company that manufactured the computer. When a computer is turned on, it loads the operating system into RAM (usually from secondary storage) before any user can execute a program.

While an operating system is an extraordinarily complicated program, it is nonetheless just another program. It is quite possible to have a number of operating systems available for a single computer, with the customer deciding which one he or she would like. For example, most of the computers manufactured by Digital Equipment Corporation can be run with either the VMS operating system or Ultrix, a particular version of the UNIX operating system.[4] Similarly, there are a number of operating systems available for IBM mainframe computers.

The system software may also include one or more *command shells*. Command shells are programs that direct the interaction with the computer's users. In most cases, when you type the name of a program to be executed, you are interacting with the shell. The shell then directs the operating system to find the program on secondary storage and begin the program's execution.

Shells manage the user's session, providing a "friendly" interface between the operating system services and the user. For example, MS-DOS (the operating system run on most IBM personal computers and compatibles) comes with a standard shell, and you can buy shells from other vendors.[5] Similarly, most UNIX systems come with two or more shells, with each user selecting the shell he or she prefers. While early shells provided a "text" only interface, modern computers (particularly personal computers) often come with *graphical user interfaces* that allow users to express what they want the computer to do by using a pointing device and selecting among things displayed on the screen.

System software may also include various language compilers, text editors, graphics packages, utilities for copying files, and other features. The quantity and quality of these vary widely among computer vendors.

---

[4]VMS and Ultrix are trademarks of the Digital Equipment Corporation. UNIX is a trademark of AT&T Bell Laboratories.

[5]MS-DOS is a trademark of Microsoft, Inc.

1.7 WHERE TO FROM HERE?

The remainder of this book focuses on algorithms and their implementation in the C programming language. For the most part, the book is organized around various algorithmic areas.

The rest of this book consists of the following chapters:

- Chapter 2 provides the foundations of the C programming language as well as a few elementary algorithms. Our goal in this chapter is to provide the reader with a sufficient understanding of C so that small but useful programs can be written.
- In Chapters 3 and 4 we present a range of algorithms for solving numerical problems. Chapter 3 covers topics such as finding the roots of equations, numerical integration, and solving simple differential equations. We also discuss the problem of numerical precision, an important topic that is too often ignored in introductory texts. Chapter 4 explores the uses of computers in matrix algebra and solving simultaneous linear equations.
- Chapter 5 is devoted to the area of data structures. These are ways of organizing data stored in a computer so that certain types of retrieval are fast and reliable. Data structures are often used in implementing algorithms.
- In Chapter 6 we explore algorithms for searching and sorting large volumes of data. This area is crucial to the application of computers for managing data bases.
- Chapter 7 is devoted to graphics. It explores how to manage and operate on geometric information. This is a rapidly expanding field of applications for computers, particularly in engineering, architectural design, and visualization of scientific information.
- In Chapter 8 we explore the use of computers for simulating complicated systems that are subject to randomness. The algorithms covered here include using computers to generate random numbers and the use of randomly generated values to model physical, social, and economic systems.
- In Chapter 9 we introduce *object-oriented programming*, a concept of growing importance in software design. The central ideas in object-oriented programming and C++, an extension of the C language that supports these ideas, are described.

1.8 EXERCISES

1-1. Rewrite the machine language program for solving the maze to implement a "left-hand rule," where upon entering the maze you place your left hand on the wall to your left and keep it there.

1-2. Obtain the following information for at least one computer:
(a) The number of bytes of RAM it has.
(b) The amount of secondary storage available.

(**c**) How many instructions the CPU can execute per second.

(**d**) The name of the operating system running on the computer.

(**e**) Whether there is more than one command shell available.

(**f**) The compilers available on that computer.

(**g**) The name of at least one text editor.

1-3. Write down the steps you use when you perform long division as an algorithm. State the steps and their order precisely enough so that there is no ambiguity about how the procedure works.

1-4. Suppose that you have a stack of cards with the name of a person written on each one. Write the series of steps you would use to put the cards in alphabetical order as an algorithm.

1-5. Imagine a simple computer that is capable of doing the following instructions:

- Read an integer from the keyboard. An integer value is read from the keyboard. This value is placed in the general register. The instruction code for this operation is 1.

- Write an integer to the display. The value in the general register is written to the display. The instruction code for this operation is 2.

- Add two integer values. This adds two integer values stored in memory and places the result in the general register. The values to be added are in the addresses given in the two memory locations after the instruction. The instruction code for this operation is 3. Thus, if the portion of memory where execution is proceeding includes the instruction 3 followed by the values 12 and 14 in the next memory locations, the computer will add the contents of memory locations 12 and 14, placing the result in the general register.

- Store a value. This takes a value from the general register and places it in a memory location. The address where the value is to be placed is given in the memory location immediately following the instruction. The instruction code for this operation is 4. Thus, if the portion of memory where execution is proceeding includes the instruction 4 followed by the value 19 in the next memory location, the computer will store the contents of the general register in memory location 19.

- Load a value. This takes a value from memory and places it in the general register. The address where the value is to be retrieved from is given in the memory location immediately following the instruction. Thus, if the portion of memory where execution is proceeding includes the instruction 5 followed by the value 28, the computer will replace the contents of the general register with the contents of memory location 28.

- Compute half of a value. This instruction computes half of the value in the general register, ignoring remainders. The instruction code is 6. The result replaces the value in the general register. Thus, if the general register contains the value 17 and this instruction is executed, the value in the general register after the instruction executes will be 8.

- Test for zero. This instruction tests if the value of the general register is zero. If it is, then the next memory location contains the address of the next instruction to be executed. If not, then the memory location two greater than the current instruction contains the address of the next instruction to be executed. The instruction code for this operation is 7. Thus, if the portion of memory where execution is proceeding includes the instruction 7 followed by the values 52 and 54 in the next two memory locations, the computer will execute the instruction in memory location 52 next if the general register is zero and the instruction in memory location 54 next if the general register is nonzero.

Write a program in machine code for this computer that reads in two integer values, multiplies these values using the *a la russe* method, and outputs the product. Assume that execution of the program begins at memory location zero.

2

THE C LANGUAGE AND SOME ELEMENTARY ALGORITHMS

2.1 INTRODUCTION

As discussed in Chapter 1, the goal of this book is to teach how to develop computer algorithms for solving problems that arise in science, engineering, management, and planning. Since we will be using the C programming language to express those algorithms, it is essential that the reader become familiar with C. In this chapter we introduce the most important elements of C and describe how they are used in the solution of some simple but interesting problems. We also illustrate how the same basic algorithm can be implemented in very different ways.

We begin with some brief historical background on the C language. We follow this with an exposition of the key "building blocks" the C programmer uses. Our goal in this chapter is to give the reader enough information so that he or she can understand some simple programs as well as code some algorithms. The exposition in this chapter is far from complete, with many aspects of the C language intentionally omitted at this stage. Some features of C which are more advanced will be introduced in later chapters, while other features that are not frequently used are discussed in the appendix.

2.2 HISTORY OF C

The C programming language was developed by Dennis Ritchie of Bell Laboratories in 1972. Its original purpose was to provide a language in which a new operating system he was working on could be written. That operating system was originally developed in a language called B, which in turn was derived from BCPL, a language developed by Martin Richards in 1967. C added some concepts to B that made it a more useful programming language.

The philosophy underlying C's design was that:

- The language should have a small number of components from which programs are developed. C has a set of powerful language elements and operators that allow the programmer to create compact yet highly functional programs.
- The language should empower rather than restrict the programmer. C does not impose the constraints that characterize what are called "structured programming languages." Instead, it provides the programmer a great deal of leeway, allowing semantic and logical constructions not permitted in many other languages.
- C should be machine independent in the sense that C code could be compiled and executed on virtually every computer. Indeed, the broad popularity of C is in part a result of the ease with which C compilers can be written for different computer architectures ranging from supercomputers to the smallest personal computers.
- C should allow the programmer to produce well-organized modular computer programs which can be debugged, augmented, and maintained at reasonable cost.
- The C language should be useful in implementing as broad a range of algorithms as possible. This accounts for the fact that C is used for tasks as diverse as coding computer operating systems, writing spreadsheet programs, doing large-scale numerical analysis, and developing interactive computer graphics software.

The features of C that reflect the above design philosophy make the language very much a "two-edged sword." A C programmer can write programs that fail in almost an infinite number of subtle ways. Overall, experienced C programmers tend to view the language's flexibility and power as one of the things they most like about it. However, the lack of constraints in the language make it possible for beginning programmers to make a wide array of mistakes.

The compact nature of C makes it possible to write working programs that are almost impossible for even experienced programmers to decipher. In this book we explicitly encourage a style of programming that is clear and straightforward. The reader should, however, be aware that many of the C programs they will encounter in other situations may not have been developed with clarity as a prime objective.

The original design of the C language was definitively expressed in a book entitled *The C Programming Language*[Kernighan, Brian W. and Ritchie, Dennis M. 78] by Brian Kernighan and Dennis Ritchie. This book became a *de facto* reference standard for subsequent implementers of the C language. In fact, it was quite common for firms selling C language compilers to advertise that they were "fully compliant with Kernighan and Ritchie" to signify that their compiler had the complete set of useful features.

As C became widely used, a few enhancements were added to the original Kernighan and Ritchie specification. The enhanced versions were almost always upward compatible in the sense that C programs adhering to the original Kernighan and Ritchie specification would still work correctly. However, in the early 1980s it became clear that the enhancements were often incompatible with each other. In addition, there was a growing need for clarity in the specification of both the C language and the wide range of software libraries that programmers had become accustomed to relying upon. This spurred the formation of a committee of the American National Standards Institute (ANSI) in 1983 to specify the C language in a formal way. That committee adopted the pragmatic view that the original Kernighan and Ritchie specification should be changed as little as possible, and that widely used enhancements to C should be codified and preserved whenever feasible. The resulting standard was published in draft form [American National Standards Institute 88], and after the ANSI-mandated period of review and comment, formally adopted as a standard [American National Standards Institute 89].

The version of C used in this text is based on that published standard. While there are still many older, non-ANSI-compliant C compilers in use, it is quite clear that virtually all of them will be replaced by ANSI-compliant versions.

2.3 CONSTITUENTS OF A C PROGRAM

C programs are simply collections of *statements* that are to be executed sequentially in order to accomplish some task. In a sense, a C program is very much like a recipe in which some ingredients are listed and a series of instructions are given to the cook. These instructions are given in the order they are to be executed. In fact, a well-written recipe is an algorithm.

C allows statements in "free format." This means that a statement may be divided into many different lines, and that blank space may be used freely to separate elements within statements. Blank lines are also allowed and are frequently used to separate parts of programs. Horizontal and vertical tabs and the special character used by many printers to denote the beginning of a new page (called a "formfeed") may also be used freely within C programs. In C, blank spaces, tabs, newlines, carriage returns, vertical tabs, and formfeeds are collectively referred to as *white space*.

C also allows comments to be inserted in a program. Any text that begins with the characters **/*** and ends with the characters ***/** is a comment. For example, the text

```
/* This program was written by Jane Doe
         on August 21, 1990  */
```

is a comment. It is totally ignored by the C compiler.

We generally use the free format style of C to make our programs clearer. We strongly encourage students to adopt a standard layout for their programs because it makes them much clearer to readers, including the program's author, who may need to discover the cause of an error.

In the next sections of this chapter we introduce the C statement types that are essential for implementing simple computer algorithms.

2.4 SIMPLE C VARIABLES AND ASSIGNMENT STATEMENTS

 One of the fundamental building blocks of C programs is a *variable*. In its simplest form, a variable has a *name* (also called an identifier) and a *value*. For example, we might use the name **weight** to hold the value of the weight of some object.

C requires that variable names begin with a letter or _ (an underscore), and that they consist entirely of letters, digits, and the underscore character. For example, the following are valid variable names:

```
Test_Value
Go_4_it
my_program
degrees_celsius
x_times_y
```

However, these names are not valid:

1st — invalid because it begins with a number
two?times — invalid because it includes a question mark
high tea — invalid because it includes a space
forty-five — invalid because it includes a hyphen

While variable names may be any length, different C implementations may treat only the first *n* characters as significant in the sense that characters beyond the first *n* in a variable name may be ignored by the C compiler. At an absolute minimum, *n* must be 6 for all variables for a C compiler to comply with the ANSI standard. In most cases, *n* is at least 31.

C treats upper- and lowercase letters as different. Thus, the identifiers **weight**, **Weight**, **WEIGHT**, and **WEiGHT** are four distinct variables. We follow the widely accepted convention of using only lowercase letters for variable names.

C has 32 words that are reserved *keywords*. These words are part of the C language, and you are therefore not allowed to use them for variable names. All keywords in C use only lowercase letters. The full list of C keywords is:

```
auto      double   int       struct
break     else     long      switch
case      enum     register  typedef
```

```
char       extern   return   union
const      float    short    unsigned
continue   for      signed   void
default    goto     sizeof   volatile
do         if       static   while
```

Variables are most often given a value through an *assignment statement* such as

```
weight = 90;
```

Note that the assignment statement ends with a semicolon. This is true for all statements in the C language. After this statement is executed, the variable named `weight` will have a value of 90. The term `90` in the statement above is called a *constant* since its value is fixed.

One way to interpret assignment statements is to think of the equals sign (`=`) as an *operator*, a symbol that causes some action in a computer program. In this context, the equals sign means "compute the value of the expression on the right of the assignment operator and set the value of the variable named on the left-hand side to that value." This idea confuses beginning programmers who are familiar with the use of the equal sign in mathematics. In mathematics, we use the equal sign to denote the fact that two quantities are mathematically identical. In an assignment statement, we use the equal sign as an active operator. The difference is subtle but important. For example, in mathematics, the statement

$$weight = 90$$

is entirely equivalent to the statement

$$90 = weight$$

However, in C, the first statement is a perfectly acceptable assignment statement, while the second statement is simply not valid. This is because the value 90 on the left-hand side of the statement

```
90 = weight;
```

is a constant rather than a variable, so it cannot be assigned a new value.

The difference between the assignment statement and the mathematical use of the equals sign is even clearer when the following C statement is considered:

```
weight = weight + 1;
```

In the conventional mathematical use of the equal sign, this statement is false. However, in C (and many other programming languages), statements of this type are used all the time. In words, this C statement means "take the current value of the variable `weight`, add one to that value, and make the result the new value of the variable `weight`."

2.5 ARITHMETIC OPERATIONS

The assignment statement generalizes in many different ways. The general form is

```
<variable> = <expression>;
```

where the notation **<variable>** means any C variable, and **<expression>** denotes any combination of variables and operations which produce a value. Assignment statements are themselves expressions in C. For example,

```
a = b = c;
```

is a legal statement. The operation of assignment associates from right to left, so that the expression

```
b = c;
```

would be evaluated first. This would assign the value of the variable **c** to **b**; the value of **b** would be the resulting value of the expression. This would in turn be assigned to the variable **a**.

C allows expressions to include a rich variety of operations, including standard arithmetic operations such as addition and multiplication. For example, if **volume**, **density**, and **weight** are variables, then the statement

```
weight = density * volume;
```

is a valid C statement in which the variable **weight** is assigned the product of the values of the variables **density** and **volume**.

The arithmetic operators in C are

+	for addition
-	for subtraction
*	for multiplication
/	for division
%	for modulos (This is the remainder from the division of one integer by another.)

Note that the modulos operator may only be used with integer values.

In an expression, the operators have an "order of precedence," so that multiplication, division, and modulo arithmetic operations are performed before addition and subtraction. Thus, the statement

```
weight = 2 + 5 * 6;
```

results in a value of **weight** equal to 32 ((5*6) + 2) rather than 42 ((2+5) * 6).

Multiplication, division, and modulos operators have the same precedence, as do the addition and subtraction operators.

At least for the five operators listed above, operations *of the same precedence* are performed "left to right," meaning that the statement

```
weight = 11 * 2 % 3;
```

results in **weight** being computed as (11 * 2) %3, which equals 1, rather than 11 * (2 %3), which equals 22.

The minus sign (-) can also be used in C to denote the negative of a quantity. For example, the statement

```
negweight =  -weight;
```

means that the variable **negweight** is assigned the negative of the value of **weight**. When used in this way, the minus sign is called a *unary* operator. (The plus sign can be used in the same way, but it is rarely of any value.) Both the unary minus and plus operators take precedence over the standard arithmetic operators, so the C statement

```
x = y - -z;
```

is perfectly legal, though awkward. In words, the statement means "take the negative of the value of the variable **z**, subtract it from **y**, and assign the result as the value of **x**." It has exactly the same effect as the simpler statement using arithmetic addition:

```
x = y + z;
```

C allows the programmer to use parentheses to override the standard order in which operations are carried out. For example, the statement

```
weight = (2 + 5) * 6;
```

forces the addition operation to be done first, so that weight is assigned the value 42. Parentheses may be nested to any arbitrary level, so that the statement

```
weight = ((((2 + 5) * 6)+7) *3) - 6;
```

is valid. The reader may verify that weight will be assigned the value 141 as a result of this statement.

C also provides some "shorthand" forms for common types of assignment statements. For example, because assignment statements of the form

```
total_weight = total_weight + weight;
```

are so common in computer programs, C provides a convenient shorthand for them. The statement

```
total_weight += weight;
```

is exactly the same as the earlier assignment statement. The notation **+=** can be expressed in words as "increment the left-hand side by the right-hand side."

C provides comparable assignment operators for subtraction, multiplication, division, and modulus. Thus, the C statements

```
weight = weight - 7 * units;
price = price * markup;
count = count/2;
index = index % size;
```

could all be written equivalently as

```
weight -= 7 * units;
price *= markup;
count /= 2;
index %= size;
```

The use of these shorthand assignment operators is entirely a matter of taste. We will use them in situations where their meaning is obvious.

2.6 DEFINITION OF VARIABLES

2.6.1 Integers and Characters

Because most computers store and operate on different types of data in different ways, the C language requires that every variable be defined as having some *type*. The type of a variable must be defined in a C program before that variable is used.

Perhaps the most commonly used type in C is the **int**, which stands for integer. For example, before using the variable **weight** in the examples of the preceding section, we must first have defined its type with a declaration of the form

```
int weight;
```

C allows you to define more than one variable of the same type in a single definition using the comma (**,**) as a separator, as in the example

```
int weight, volume, density;
```

This would define **weight**, **volume**, **density** all to be integer variables.

It is customary for C programs to begin with a series of variable definitions. Putting all the definitions in a single place makes it easy for the reader to find out the type of each variable used in the program.

Most computers provide for a number of different integer types, depending on the magnitude of the integer values in the specific application. Different integer types use different amounts of computer memory and require different amounts of time to retrieve from memory, operate on, and store in memory. C reflects this capability of most computers by allowing the programmer to specify the type of **int** required by including the qualifiers **short** and **long** in a variable's definition. Examples of declarations that use these qualifiers are

```
short int temperature;
long int federal_deficit;
```

Another variable type provided in C is **char**. This type is most often used to store single characters. However, it may also be used to store integers that are small in absolute value.

Because C was designed to run on many different types of hardware, the C standard is not particularly specific about the ranges of values which different types of variables must be able to hold. The only firm rules are as follows:

- Any valid character can be stored in a variable of type **char**.
- Any value that can be stored in a **short int** variable can also be stored in either an **int** or a **long int** variable.
- Any value that can be stored in an **int** can be stored in a **long int**.

In order for programmers to deal with the lack of specificity in the largest and smallest values allowed in the various types of integers, every C implementation is required to have a file that provides more details. This file is named **limits.h,** and it is stored in a standard place on each computer in which a C compiler is installed. *Typical* ranges for most computers are as follows:

- Variables of type **char** can hold integers between -128 and +127.
- Variables of type **short int** can hold integers between -32,768 and +32,767.
- Variables of type **long int** can hold integers between -2,147,483,648 and +2,147,483,647.
- Variables of type **int** are stored as either **short int**s or **long int**s. Which of these is used depends on the type of computer.

C also allows the prefix **unsigned** to be applied to any of the integer data types. This is used for nonnegative quantities to extend their range of representable values. When unsigned data types are stored in the computer's memory, there is no need to store information about the sign of the integer quantity, since it is always positive.

For example, the variable **height** might be declared

```
unsigned short int height;
```

In this case the valid range might be from 0 to 65,535 rather than from -32,768 to 32,767.

2.6.2 Floating-Point Types

C also provides data types for information that spans a much wider range of magnitudes than can be accommodated with integers. This type of information representation is generally referred to as "floating point." Data stored in this format is kept in a binary form of scientific notation, as in the form 1.56323×10^{-22}. Each number is represented by a fraction part (corresponding to the value 1.56323) and an integer exponent (the value -22). This form of data representation is essential for scientific and engineering applications, and most computers are designed with special hardware to speed up numerical operations on data of this type.

C provides three types of floating-point variables:

- **float**, which is often referred to a single precision.
- **double**, which is often referred to as double precision.
- **long double**, a type which was added in the ANSI standard and which is rarely used.

Programmers using floating-point data types must be conscious of the fact that the fraction part has limited precision. For example, on most computers, variables of type **float** are limited to six or seven decimal digits in their fraction parts, and variables of type **double** are limited to about 16 decimal digits. The exponents of **float**s are typically limited to values between -38 and +38. The maximum values for the exponents of **double**s are sometimes (but not always) much greater, often ranging near -128 through 128. The issues of precision and magnitude of floating-point values are discussed in Section 3.2.

2.7 CONSTANTS

We have already introduced the idea of an integer constant. However, C allows for many different types of constants, including the following:

- Character constants. These are most often written as single characters enclosed in single quotes, as in the form **'c'**, **'Q'**, or **'7'**. Note that the character constant **'7'** is entirely different from the integer constant 7. The former defines a single character, while the latter is an integer value. The backslash (\) is used to denote a special character which is not printable. Some special character constants defined in C are the "newline" character (written as **'\n'**), the "tab" character (written as **'\t'**), the apostrophe (written as the **'\' '**), and the backslash itself (written as **'\\'**).
- Integer constants. Any value that can be stored as a regular **int** is an integer constant. If it is too large in absolute value to fit into a regular **int**, it will automatically be stored as a **long int**. The programmer can force any integer constant to be represented as a **long int** value by appending the suffix **L** (or the lowercase **l**) to its value. Thus, the constant **743L** would be stored

as a long integer.[1]   Similarly, the suffix **U** (or **u**) on a constant denotes an **unsigned int** value, as in the example **5412U**. The suffixes **L** and **U** can be combined to denote an **unsigned long** constant, as in the value **3742UL**.

- Floating-point constants. Floating-point constants can have both a decimal point in them and exponents in base ten. For example, the value 1.56323×10^{-22} is written as a constant in C as **1.56323e-22**. Unless the suffix **F** (or **f**) is added to a floating-point constant, C treats it as a **double**.
- String constants. A string constant in C is a series of characters enclosed in double quotes. For example, **"Hello world\n"** is a string constant. It consists of the words **Hello** and **world** followed by the special newline character. Note that the double quote marks *delimit* the string constant; they are not part of it.

2.8 INTEGER AND MIXED ARITHMETIC

2.8.1 Integer Division

One of the rules C (and many other programming languages) follows is that when one integer is divided by another, the remainder is discarded. This means, for example, that if **quotient** is a variable of type **int**, the assignment statement

```
quotient = 14 / 5;
```

will result in **quotient** having a value of 2. The remainder of 4 is discarded.

The rule that the remainder from integer division is always discarded can produce results that may seem odd to the beginning programmer. Mathematically, the quantities

```
6*10 / 5
```

and

```
6 /5 * 10
```

are identical. However, if **quotient** is again of type **int**, the C statement

```
quotient = 6 * 10 / 5;
```

results in **quotient** having the value 12, while the statement

```
quotient = 6 / 5 *  10;
```

results in **quotient** having the value 10. In the first case, because arithmetic operators of equal precedence in C are evaluated from left to right, the quantity 6 * 10 is

---

[1]Use of the lowercase letter "el" to denote long integer constants should be avoided because it appears very similar to the digit 1.

computed first, producing a value of 60, and 60/5 is 12. In the second example, the integer operation 6 / 5 produces a result of 1, with the remainder being discarded, and 1 * 10 = 10.

2.8.2 Conversion of Types in Assignment Statements

Suppose that some variable **d** is defined as a **double** and another variable **i** is defined as an **int**. What happens when the value of **d** is assigned to **i**? This corresponds to the following fragment of C code:

```
double d;
int i;

d = 5.4;
i = d;
```

The rule in C is that after the right-hand side of an assignment statement is computed, the type of the resulting value is converted to the type of the variable on the left-hand side. In the case above, the value of **d** is 5.4, and this is converted to an **int**, truncating the value to the integer 5. Note that C always truncates floating-point values when converting them to integers. If a value of type **double** is assigned to a variable of type **float**, the least significant part of the **double** is rounded off to fit in a **float**.

Some of the conversions C performs automatically when assigning results of one type to another may produce unexpected results. For example, suppose that the variable **c** is of type **char** and the variable **i** is of type **int**. The statement

```
i = c;
```

never loses any information since C guarantees that any integer which can be stored in type **char** must also fit into an **int**. However, an assignment statement such as

```
c = i;
```

can produce seemingly strange results if the value of **i** is too large to be represented in a **char**. What actually happens in such cases is implementation dependent. However, it is rarely what a beginning programmer intends.

2.8.3 Conversion of Types in Mixed Expressions

Since C provides for integer and floating-point data types of different sizes, the language must also specify what happens when you perform arithmetic operations on different data types. For example, if **x** is a variable of type **int**, and **y** is of type **double**, what is the type of **x + y**? C provides an answer to this and similar questions through a set of rules on what are called *mixed expressions*.

The first rule is that C always converts values which are of type **char** and **short int** to type **int** before performing any operation on them. Thus, if the variables **ch1** and **ch2** are both of type **char**, the expression **ch1 + ch2** is of type **int**.

The second rule is simple and obvious. Once the value of type **char** and **short int** have been converted to **int**s, operations on values of the same type produce results of that type. For example, the sum of two **int**s is an **int**.

Situations in which values of different types are operands can be considerably more complicated. The broad rule is that when any two values of differing types are combined arithmetically, C "promotes" the value of the "lower" type to that of the "higher" type, and then performs the required operation, producing a value of the "higher" type. The terms "lower" and "higher" in this context refer to the size of the type in terms of the largest values which can be stored in it. C follows these rules to determine promotion of values in mixed expressions:

- If one of the operands is a **long double**, convert the other to a **long double**.
- Otherwise, if one of the operands is a **double**, convert the other to a **double**.
- Otherwise, if one of the operands is a **float**, convert the other to a **float**.
- Otherwise, if one of the operands is a **long int**, convert the other to a **long int**.

To illustrate the effects of these rules, consider a situation where the following variables have been defined:

```
float f_value;
double d_value;
char c_value;
short int s_value;
long int l_value;
int i_value;
```

The following table gives some expressions involving these variables and some constants. The resulting type of each expression is given.

EXAMPLES OF MIXED EXPRESSIONS

Expression	Type
c_value * i_value	int
f_value - 7.3	double
d_value + c_value	double
c_value - s_value	int
s_value - l_value	long int
s_value +7	int
s_value - 7.0	double
7 + 7.0	double

The rules get a little more complicated when one of the values is an unsigned integer quantity and the other is a signed integer. This is discussed in the appendix.

2.8.4 Forcing Type Conversions Using Casts

C provides a mechanism called *casts* to force the conversion of one data type to another. The use of a cast overrides the standard rules for type conversions.

Consider a case where the ratio of two integers is being assigned to a **double** as in the following code fragment:

```
double ratio;
int x, y;
x = 5;
y = 2;
ratio = x / y;
```

In this example the expression **x/y** would be evaluated using integer division, resulting in a value of 2. This resulting integer value would then be converted to a **double** and assigned as the value of the variable **ratio**. We could override this normal behavior by using a cast as follows:

```
ratio = (double) x / y;
```

The use of the keyword **double** in parentheses is the cast. It forces the conversion of the value of **x** from an **int** to a **double**. Because the cast operation has higher precedence than division, this conversion is done first. The division then becomes an operation involving a **double** (the cast value of **x**) and an **int**. Following the standard rules for mixed arithmetic, the **int** would be converted to a **double** before the division is performed, producing a **double** as the result. The value of **ratio** will therefore include the remainder from the computation.

Note that the cast operator in the example above does not change the value stored in the variable **x**. Instead, it creates an intermediate result which is the value of **x** converted to a **double**. This intermediate value is then used in computing the quotient.

Any valid C data type can be used as a cast by enclosing it in parentheses to the left of the value to be cast in an expression. If, for example, we wanted to compute the ratio of two **double** variables using integer arithmetic, we could use the following code fragment:

```
double ratio, q, r;
q = 7.0;
r = 2.0;
ratio = (int) q / (int) r;
```

This code would first convert the values stored **q** and **r** into temporary integers 7 and 2. The division operator would then be done using integer arithmetic. The resulting integer value of 3 would be converted to the **double** 3.0 and assigned as the value of the variable **ratio**.

2.9 INVOKING FUNCTIONS IN C

Every C program is built from what are called *functions*. All C statements that are executed in a C program must belong to a function. (The parts of a C program that define the types of variable are not actually executed when the program is run. They just allow the compiler to know how much space in memory will be needed for each variable and provide the information to determine how the values in each variable are stored and operated upon.) A function can accept input values, called *arguments*, and can produce a single result, called the *returned value*.

One way to think of functions is to imagine that you have some task that needs to be accomplished, and that you have a diligent but not particularly bright assistant who is willing to do the task for you. For example, you might need a set of three numbers averaged. You may need this work done many times for different sets of three numbers. In this analogy, the instructions to the assistant about how to add and average three numbers could be thought of as the "function." The three numbers you want averaged at any point in time would correspond to the input arguments. Whenever you need an average, you pass the input arguments to your assistant. The assistant then executes the procedure you taught him, and returns the average to you.

When a C program is run, the computer begins execution by running the function called **main()**. *Thus, every valid C program must have a function called* **main()**. The function **main()** can in turn execute other functions, and these can execute still other functions, etc. Thus, extremely complicated paths of execution can be created from programs that consist of only a small number of functions.

There are many advantages to organizing computer programs into functions. First, it allows you to develop logically distinct pieces of a complicated algorithm in separate chunks of computer code. This "divide and conquer" approach to computer programming allows you to focus your attention on a small part of the problem without being distracted by how that part will fit into the program as a whole. More significantly, different programmers can work on the separate chunks, each coding different functions. This is crucial to the development of very large programs where there might be one hundred or more separate programmers working together.

Organizing programs in separate functions is also an easy way to change one part of a program without affecting the other parts. For example, you might write an initial function to draw a complicated, three-dimensional image on a screen. This initial version might use an algorithm which is easy to program but very inefficient. After you get the complete program working, you could go back and write a three- dimensional rendering function that was much more efficient, without touching any of the other functions in the program.

Functions also provide a way in which you can directly integrate other people's software into your own work. For example, you can often find functions written by other people that you can use directly in your own programs, thereby avoiding having to "reinvent the wheel" each time you write new software.

C provides a syntax for writing and invoking functions. We reserve the discussion of how to write your own C functions until Section 2.16, and consider in this section only how to use functions.

The functions that make up C programs can come from at least three different sources.

- *Functions you write*. The most obvious case are functions that you write as part of your program. We discuss in great detail how these functions are prepared.
- *The standard C library*. Another source of functions you may use in your own programs is the "standard C library." This is a collection of functions provided with all C compilers. It includes functions that handle input and output, a variety of mathematical functions, such as computing the sine or cosine of an angle, and functions that get information from the computer you are running on, such as the current date and time.
- *Additional software libraries*. These are collections of functions that are written by others and often sold to computer owners. For example, there are many specialized C libraries for matrix manipulation, solving nonlinear equations, doing sophisticated statistical analysis, and creating graphical displays of data.

Generally, both the standard C library and third-party libraries are already compiled for you, so you never need to see the source code for them. In fact, many providers of software libraries keep their source code confidential in order to protect it from unauthorized copying and modification.

All C functions must have names; the rules for function names are the same as for C variables. Functions are invoked in C programs with statements in the following form:

```
function_name(input1, input2, input3,...inputn);
```

where **n** is the number of inputs to the function. These inputs are the function's *arguments*. Any valid C expression can be used as an argument. The list of arguments must be enclosed in parentheses. These parentheses are formally an operator; they indicate a function invocation.

For example, the standard C library includes a function that puts output on the program user's terminal or display. This function is called **printf()**. As a notational convention, we will denote functions in the text by following the function name with a pair of parentheses **()** to distinguish functions from simple variables in C. In its simplest form, **printf()** can be used as follows:

```
printf("Hello, world\n");
```

In this example, the string constant **"Hello world\n"** is the sole argument to the function **printf()**. The work of getting the characters in the string onto the user's display is done in the function. The function `printf()` itself has been written by a professional programmer. When executed as part of a C program, this statement results in the text **Hello, world**, followed by a newline character being handed to the function `printf()`, which in turn deals with the problem of displaying it on the user's terminal or computer screen.

Some functions do not have any inputs. In this case you still need to include the parentheses when you invoke the function so that the C compiler knows that you are calling a function, not referring to a variable. For example, the standard C library includes a function called `rand()`, which returns a randomly selected integer value. We explore the implementation and uses of `rand()` in detail in Chapter 8. `rand()` could be used in a program as follows:

```
i = rand();
```

Functions in C do not have to return a value. However, if they do, it has to be of some defined C type.

Consider a second example in which the function `average_ints()` averages three integers and produces the result as a value of type **double**. Invoking this function as

```
double answer;
answer = average_ints(3, 6, 5);
```

is a correct use of the function. You could also use integer variables as arguments, as in

```
double answer;
int i,j;
i=4;
j=2;
answer = average_ints(i, j, 5);
```

There is no requirement that the arguments be simple constants or variables. For example, the following is a legal use of `average_ints()`:

```
double answer;
int i,j;
i=4;
j=2;
answer = average_ints(i+j+1, j*5, (i+j)/5);
```

Each of the expressions in the argument list is first evaluated before the function `average_ints()` is invoked. The reader can verify that the value of **answer** after the last statement is executed is 6.0.

2.10 HEADER FILES AND THE C PREPROCESSOR

 Standard libraries (and most C libraries you buy) typically come with what are called "header files." These files provide information to the C compiler about the inputs and results produced by each function in the library. Header files are usually accessed by using the **#include** directive. This is a directive to the C compiler, which in words, means "replace this line by the contents of the file." For example, whenever you use the standard C input and output library, you generally put the following directive at the beginning of your program:

```
#include <stdio.h>
```

There are a few important aspects of **#include** directives. First, they are not executable statements. They are really directives to something called the *C preprocessor*, which goes through your program before it is compiled, makes the changes demanded by the preprocessor directives in your program, and hands the resulting, modified program to the C compiler. All program lines that begin with the character **#** are interpreted as preprocessor directives.

Second, the **#include** directive does not end with a semicolon. This is again because it is not truly a C language statement; it is a preprocessor directive.

Third, the part of the **#include** directive enclosed between the **<** and the **>** is the name of a file. The use of the **< >** symbols tells the C preprocessor to "look in the standard place for the file." The "standard place" varies depending on the specifics of how your C compiler was installed. However, as long as the C compiler was installed correctly, it should be able to find the header file. By convention, header files are given names that end with the suffix **.h**. The file **stdio.h**, for example, contains the header information for the standard C input and output library. You can also use your own files as header files, in which case the file name would be enclosed in double quotation marks (**"**). For example, the preprocessor directive

```
#include "myfile.h"
```

would direct the preprocessor to insert the file **myfile.h** into the C program. The specifics of how files are named depend on the computer and operating system you are using.

#include directives can be used anywhere in a program. However, when you are using various function libraries, their header files must be **#include**'d in your program before you use any of the functions. It is customary to put all **#include** directives at the beginning of a program.

Another type of preprocessor statement we will often make use of is the **#define** directive. In its simplest form, **#define** directs the preprocessor to replace one string of text by another. An example is

```
#define PI 3.14159
```

After the preprocessor reads this line, every time the string **PI** appears in the program it is replaced by 3.14159. C programmers often use **#define** directives as a way of making their programs clearer. It is customary though not required that the names of **#define**d values be all uppercase letters. We follow this practice in this book.

Note that the **#define** preprocessor directive does *not* have any effect on characters which appear within quotation marks. For example, the preprocessor directive defining **PI** would not replace the letters **PI** in the statement

```
printf("The value of PI is 3.14159\n");
```

2.11 PROGRAMMING PROJECT: A FIRST COMPLETE C PROGRAM

We are now in a position to write our first complete program. The program uses the function **printf()** to display some text on the user's display. Following the hallowed tradition of C textbooks (beginning with the original edition of Kernighan and Ritchie[Kernighan, Brian W. and Ritchie, Dennis M. 78]), we will write a complete program that displays the text **"Hello, world"** on the user's screen.

The program is as follows:

```
#include <stdio.h>
main()
{
  printf("Hello, world\n");
}
```

Recall that execution of any C program begins with the execution of a function named **main()**. The body of the function is enclosed in "curly braces," the **{** and **}** symbols.   In this program, the only C statement is an invocation of the **printf ()** function, the part of the standard C input/output library that outputs information on the user's display.

2.12 FUNCTION PROTOTYPES

Because C functions can return a value and require that arguments be presented with the correct types and in the correct order, the language provides a compact notation for declaring each function used. The declaration is called a *function prototype*. It informs the C compiler about the arguments each function expects and the type of value it produces. For example, the prototype for the function **average_ints()** would be

```
double average_ints(int, int, int);
```

Put into words, this C declaration means that the function **average_ints()** produces a result of type **double**, and it takes as arguments three values of type **int**.

This statement must appear *before* the function **average_ints()** is actually used because the compiler must know how to interpret the function's invocation.

The special keyword **void** is used to indicate that a function doesn't return a value or that it doesn't have any arguments. For example, the function prototype

```
void no_result(double);
```

declares that **no_result()** does not return a value. Similarly, the function prototype

```
int no_arguments(void);
```

indicates that the function returns an integer value but does not have any arguments.

C does allow you to omit the argument list in the function prototypes. However, including the argument types makes the intended use of a function unambiguous. More important, it provides the information the C compiler needs to *convert* each argument to the correct type. If a prototype is omitted entirely, C compilers assume that the function returns a value of type **int**.

Consider again the example of the function **average_ints()**. Suppose that the function is used in the following program fragment:

```
double average_ints(int, int, int);
double answer, d;
int i,j;
i=4;
j=2;
d = 9.7;
answer = average_ints(i, j, d);
```

In this case the value of **d** will be converted to an integer before the argument values are passed to the function **average_ints()**. Thus, the function will return the **double** value 5.0, the average of 4, 2, and 9. If, however, you omit the argument list in the function prototype, the value of 9.7 would *not* have been converted to an **int**, producing an incorrect result. The exact nature of this incorrect result varies with C implementations, but the result is rarely what the beginning programmer expects. Omitting the prototype altogether compounds the problem, often producing still stranger errors. In this case the compiler would assume that **average_ints()** returns an **int** rather than a **double**.

The header files for various function libraries generally contain a function prototype for each function in the library. Whenever you use an **#include** directive that includes a header file, the prototypes for the functions in the library are read automatically. This saves you the effort of writing function prototypes for any library functions used. However, you must write prototypes for your own functions.

Given the protection that function prototypes provide, we always use them in our programs. We urge the reader to follow this practice.

2.13 PASSING ARGUMENTS TO FUNCTIONS: CALL BY VALUE

The designers of C provided a straightforward method through which the values of arguments are passed to the function being invoked. The method is referred to as *call by value*. "Call by value" means that before any function is executed, copies of all its arguments are made. The function then works with the copies rather than with the original values. While call by value may at first seem a bit peculiar, it has some distinct advantages. For example, since the function is always working with a copy of the arguments, the code in the function can change values in the copies without affecting the values of the original arguments. This provides users of other people's functions with at least some level of protection. When they include a variable in an argument list, they know that its value will remain unchanged.

To summarize, when a function is invoked, the following occurs: [2]

- A copy of the value of each argument is made.
- In the copy of the arguments, each value is converted to the type specified in the function prototype.
- The modified copies of the arguments are provided to the function.
- The function is then executed.
- Control of the execution of the program returns to the location of the function invocation. If the function returns a result, this returned value replaces the function invocation.

For example, if the function **sqrt()** computes the square root of a **double**, then the following C code should result in the variable **answer** having a value of 3.0.

```
double sqrt(double);
double average_ints(int, int, int);
double answer;
int i,j;
i=11;
j=13;

answer = sqrt (average_ints(i, j, 3 ));
```

A second observation is that there is nothing in the foregoing rules for function invocation that prohibit a function from invoking itself. This is called *recursion*. We use this idea later in the book.

One significant problem with relying entirely on call by value for passing arguments is that there are some situations where we really do want a function to change the value of an argument. Since a function only gets a copy, it would seem that there

---

[2]It would be more correct to state that function invocations *behave* as though the set of listed steps were done. How the steps are actually accomplished depends on the compiler implementation.

is no way for it to change the value of the original argument. If no such mechanism existed, reliance on call by value would be a serious deficiency.

If we wanted to change only a single argument, we could simply use the returned value, and require the function's user to assign the returned value to the argument. For example, if we want the function **sqrt()** to change the value of some variable to its square root, we can use the following:

```
double sqrt(double);     /* prototype of sqrt() */
double answer;           /* declaration of answer */
answer = sqrt (answer); /* assigns square root of answer
                            as new value of answer */
```

However, the rules for function invocation allow a function to return only a single value. What do we do when we want a function to change the values of more than one argument? For example, we might want to have a function that reads the values of three integers typed by the user, perhaps as input to our function **average_ints()**. How could such a function ever change the values of its arguments when it only has access to copies rather than the original values? Or, we might want to use a function that took some value, and computed its square root, its square, its cube root, and its cubed value. Since C allows only a single returned value, we need some way to provide the various computed values in variables that the calling function could later access.

As one would expect, C provides an escape from this apparent dilemma. Rather than passing the value of an argument, you can pass what is called a *pointer* to the variable. In words, you can think of the pointer as "the place in the computer's memory where the value is stored." Once a function knows the address where the value is stored, it can then use the address to change the original value!

This mechanism does not require any changes in the rules for calling by value. As long as the function receives a copy of the memory address where a variable is stored, it can use that address to change the variable's value.

An example will help make this subtle, yet important mechanism clearer. Consider a function **interchange()** that is supposed to take two variables as arguments, and exchange their values. If we were to develop **interchange()** so that its arguments were the integers **i** and **j**, there is no possible C code that could exchange their values. The function **interchange()** would receive only copies of **i** and **j**, and no matter what it did with these copies, it could not affect the values of the original variables. However, if **interchange()** knows the *addresses* of **i** and **j**, it can alter their values.

Doing this in C requires three new ideas. The first is the "address of" operator, denoted by an ampersand (**&**). This is an example of a "prefix" operator—you use it in front of a variable name, as in the following statement:

```
interchange( &i, &j);   /* invokes function with two
                            addresses as arguments */
```

This makes the arguments to the function **interchange()** *pointers* to **i** and **j** rather than the values of **i** and **j**.

2/ The second thing you need to do is to establish that the function **interchange()** has pointers to **int**s as its arguments rather than **int**s themselves. You do this by using an asterisk (*****) in front of the defined C type as a unary operator. For example,

```
int *py; /*Defines py to be a pointer to an int*/
```

declares that the variable **py** is a pointer to an **int**. In a function prototype, you again use the asterisk notation to describe the arguments, as in the example

```
void interchange(int *, int *); /* prototype with two
                                   pointers as arguments */
```

This declares that the function **interchange()** has as its arguments two pointers to **int**s. It also declares that **interchange()** does not return a value.

3/ The third piece of C we need to implement the idea of using addresses is a mechanism for retrieving and changing the value of something given its address. In the example above, the function **interchange()** needs to know how to access and change the values pointed to by the address of **i** and the address of **j**. This is done in C by using the asterisk notation. In an expression, the notation ***py** means "the value pointed to by the pointer **py**." For example, execution of the statements

```
int i;    /* i is an int */
int *py; /* py points to an int */
py = &i; /* py is assigned the address of i */
*py = 4; /* the integer pointed to by py
            is assigned a value of 4 */
```

results in **i** having a value of 4.

Used in this context, the asterisk and the ampersand are inverse operators. Thus, the code

```
double a, b;
a = * (&b);
```

is exactly the same as

```
double a, b;
a = b;
```

It is somewhat unfortunate that the ***** symbol has multiple meanings (including arithmetic multiplication) in C. It results from the fact that there are a limited number of characters other than letters and numbers common to all computer keyboards, and C has more operators than there are universally available symbols. For example, the code

```
double *a, *b;   /* a and b are pointers to doubles */
double c, d, e;


a = &d;          /* a points to d */
b = &e;          /* b points to e */

d = 7.5;         /* what a points to is set to 7.5  */
e = 11.3;        /* what b points to is set to 11.3 */

c = (*a) * (*b); /* c is the product of what
                       a and b point to */
```

is extremely awkward but makes perfect sense to the C compiler. It means that c is assigned the product of what is pointed to by a and b. Thus, the value of c would be be 84.75.

As operators, the asterisk (meaning "what is pointed to") and the ampersand (meaning "address of") have equal precedence, with evaluation order from right to left. This means that the parentheses in the example

```
double a, b;
a = * (&b);
```

are superfluous.

Also, the "what is pointed to" and "address of" operators have higher precedence than any of the arithmetic operations division, multiplication, modulo division, addition, and subtraction. Thus, in the line of code

```
c = (*a) * (*b);
```

the parentheses are again not needed, although they will often be included for ease of interpretation.

2.14 OUTPUT WITH printf()

We have already introduced the standard library function printf(). However, this function is far more general than our simple "Hello, world" example illustrates. In fact, the function printf() can be used to display all the standard C types.

The general form of printf() is used as follows:

```
printf("control string", value1, value2, ..., valueN);
```

where the **"control string"** includes special markers for the various C data types to be output, and **value1** through **valueN** are the C expressions whose values are to be displayed. For example, the statement

```
printf("%lf", a);
```

would output the value of the **double** variable named **a**. The notation **%lf** in the control string is used to denote the output of a **double**. Similarly, if **i**, **j**, and **k** are all variables of type **int**, the statement

```
printf("%d   %d   %d", i,j,k);
```

outputs the values of **i**, **j**, and **k**. Here, the special marker **%d** denotes output of an **int**.

In the control string, all the characters other than the special markers are output. That is why the statement

```
printf("Hello, world\n");
```

produced the text **"Hello, world"** followed by the special newline character. This feature is used heavily in most C programs. For example, if the **float** variable **outval** is to be displayed, you might use the statement example

```
printf("The value of the output is %f\n", outval);
```

Here, the marker **%f** is used for the display of a **float**.

The **printf()** function always displays its output starting at the current location of the terminal cursor. For example, the series of statements

```
printf("Hello, w");
printf("orl");
printf("d\n");
```

produce exactly the same result as the original statement

```
printf("Hello, world\n");
```

The following are the most useful of the special markers in **printf()** control strings:

- **d** or **%i**— for integer data.
- **%s**— for character strings.
- **%f**— for floating-point numbers not to be displayed in scientific notation.
- **%e** or **%E**— for floating-point numbers to be displayed in scientific notation.
- **%g** or **%G**— a general form for floating-point numbers. This converts to either **%f** or **%e** format as needed.
- **%c**— for single characters.

All the special markers begin with the percent sign (%) and end with one of the conversion types. In between the percent sign and the conversion type, you may specify the following modifiers:

- An integer specifying the minimum number of characters or digits you want the output to be displayed in. The portion of the output corresponding to this special marker will be at least the specified number of characters wide.
- A minus sign (-), indicating that you want the result to be left justified.
- A plus sign (+), indicating that you always want the sign of the value displayed even when the number is positive.
- The letter **h** for short types (as in **%hd**) for output of **short int**s or the letter **l** for long types, as in **%ld** for **long int**s or **%lf** for **double**s. (The notation **%lf** is an older form for the C type **double**. It stands for **long float**.)
- An integer, followed by a period, followed by another integer, as in the example **%10.5f**. This form is used only for floating-point numbers. The first of the two integers indicates the minimum field width to be output, and the second number indicates the precision of the output (the number of digits after the decimal point). The default precision for both **%f** and **%e** specifications is 6.

You should remember that field widths must generally be large enough to include the sign of a number. Also, when output is formated in scientific notation, there must be sufficient room for the sign of the fraction part, the sign of the exponent, the letter **e**, the fraction part, and the exponent.

If you really want to produce a percent sign in your output, you need to use two of them together in the control string. For example, the statement

```
printf("I'm with you 100%%\n");
```

would produce the output

```
I'm with you 100%
```

The following program provides some examples of various **printf()** statements.

```
/* Example program using printf() */

#include <stdio.h>

main()
{
  double a, b,c;
  int i,j;

  i = 5;
  j = 7;
```

```
a = 43.8;
b = 12.0;
c = -7.9452e-25;

printf("%s, %s\n", "Hello", "world");
printf("The value of i+j is %+d\n", i+j);
printf("%12.6lf %+10.5lf\n", a, b);
printf("%-12s %12s\n", "Hello", "world");
printf("c=%15.6g\n", c);
}
```

This complete C program produces the following output:

```
Hello, world
The value of i+j is +12
   43.800000   +12.00000
Hello                world
c=      -7.9452e-25
```

It is the responsibility of the programmer to make sure that the types of the arguments to **printf()** match the special codes in the control string. Mistakes of this type can produce extremely odd output from what is otherwise an entirely correct C program.

While we have used the function **printf()** as though it did not return a value, it actually does have a return value. In particular, **printf()** returns an **int** equal to the number of characters actually output to the display. It is common practice to ignore this returned value, and many C implementations that predate the ANSI standard do not return the now-required value.

2.15 INPUT WITH scanf()

The standard C library also includes a function that reads in values. This function is called **scanf()**. It uses the same general control string format, as does **printf()**. However, unlike **printf()**, **scanf()** must be able to change the actual values of its arguments. This means that it must receive pointers to the variables to be changed rather than the values of those variables. Suppose, for example, that we had defined the following variables:

```
int ival;
long int lval;
short int sval;
float fval;
double dval;
```

All of the following are valid **scanf()** statements.

```
scanf("%d", &ival);
scanf("%sd %ld", &sval, &lval);
scanf("%lf %f", &dval, &fval);
```

One of the most common mistakes of beginning C programmers is to forget that **scanf()** takes pointers as its arguments. For example, the statement

```
scanf("%d", ival);   /* incorrect use of scanf */
```

is incorrect, and will produce unpredictable, but certainly wrong, results.

Most of the elements in the control string for **scanf()** are identical to those for **printf()**. However, there are some differences that are important.

- Since **scanf()** is reading values rather than writing them, any blanks or tabs in the control string are ignored.
- Again, because **scanf()** is reading rather than writing information, the modifiers + and – are not used.
- There is no need to specify the precision of floating-point representation. However, the maximum field width can be specified as an integer. For example, the control string **"%5d"** would be used to limit the integer to the next five characters input.
- There is another modifier to the standard set of conversion specifications. The ＊ is used to skip input fields. For example, the statement

```
scanf("%d %*d %lf", &ival, &dval);
```

    would be used to read an integer into **ival**, read another integer but skip assigning its value to anything, and read a floating-point number into **dval**. This mechanism is often used to skip over fields in data files.

- Any character in the control string other than a blank, tab, or part of a valid field specification must match the next non-white-space character being read. If it does not match, **scanf()** returns without reading further values.

As with **printf()**, the function **scanf()** also returns an **int** value. Specifically, it returns the number of fields that were successfully read. It is often important to check this value to determine whether **scanf()** failed in some way. One of the most common reasons why **scanf()** might return an integer other than the number of values you want to read is that it encountered the *end of file*.

When **scanf()** reaches the end of a file, it returns a specially defined value called **EOF**. This value is defined by a preprocessor directive in the header file **stdio.h**, and it can be used in your program just like a constant.

While **scanf()** is designed primarily to read values typed from the user's keyboard, most computer systems allow one to direct input from data files into programs as though it were typed. Thus, one of the most common reasons for **scanf()** to return a value other than the number of items you intended to read is that the end of an input file was reached. It also can occur on some computer systems when reading information from the user's keyboard if the user types a special symbol (often the letter D typed with the Control key held down).

Because **scanf()** sometimes returns a value other than the number of items, it is a good idea to check the returned value whenever you use **scanf()**. An example of this is provided in Section 2.18.

2.16 WRITING NEW FUNCTIONS: SCOPE OF VARIABLES

Up to this point, we have described how to *use functions*, but we have not made it clear how to *code* them. This turns out to be reasonably straightforward in C. Every function begins with a statement that looks very much like a function prototype. However, while a function prototype just tells the compiler what arguments the function takes and what type of value it returns, the function definition defines names for the arguments. In addition, the function definition is always followed by the body of the function–the series of variable definitions and statements that do the work of the function. Just as in our example program that displayed **"Hello, world"** in a function called **main()**, the body of every function is enclosed in curly braces (**{** and **}**).

The following C code implements the function **average_ints()**, which averages three values of type **int** and returns their average as a **double**.

```
/* function to average 3 integers */
double average_ints(int i, int j, int k)
{
    double average;
    average = (i + j + k) / 3.0;
    return (average);
}
```

A few key ideas are illustrated in this example. Note that the first line of the function defines the type of the value the function returns, in this case, a **double**. Like a function prototype, it also defines the types of the arguments. However, in this case, the arguments are given variable names. These names can then be used in the body of the function. Basically, the names of the arguments provide a way to reference the arguments' values in the function. If you think about what happens when the function **average_ints()** is invoked, the copies of the arguments can be thought of as being assigned to the variables **i**, **j**, and **k**.

One of the key concepts in using functions is the idea of the *scope* of a variable. Stated loosely, the scope of a variable is the set of C statements in the program in which the variable is defined. Consider, for example, the variables **i**, **j**, and **k** in the example above. Are the values of these three variables meaningful in parts of a C program outside the function **average_ints()**? What about the variable **average**, which is defined in the body of the function? Could this variable be used in other parts of a C program that included the function **average_ints()**?

In the example above, variables such as **i** and **average** are *local* in scope. Variables have local scope when their definitions are only in effect inside the function in which they are defined. This type of variable is called *internal* because the variable's definition is inside a function. There may be other functions in the same program that have internal variables named **i** or **average**. These variables are entirely distinct from the ones with the same name that are internal to the function **average_ints()**.

At first, the idea of having two variables with identical names as entirely distinct entities may seem odd. However, it is in fact an extraordinarily valuable aspect of the C language. It allows us to write functions separately without worrying whether the names of local variables in the different functions conflict with each other. This is extremely important in large programs, where teams of hundreds of programmers may produce millions of lines of code. Imagine the difficulties in developing such large programs if each programmer had to worry about choosing local variable names that were different from those used by all the others!

A second feature of the function **average_ints()** is the use of the **return** statement. The **return** statement allows you to pass the result of a function back to the calling function. In the example function **average_ints()**, the **double average** is returned to any function which invokes **average_ints()**. You may return any valid C expression, so that the function could also have been written as

```
/* another version of average_ints() */
double average_ints(int i, int j, int k)
{
   return ( (i + j + k) / 3.0);
}
```

The return statement automatically converts the expression to the data type that the function is declared to return. Also, the parentheses around the returned value are optional, so that the example above could also be written as

```
/* yet another version of average_ints() */
double average_ints(int i, int j, int k)
{
   return  (i + j + k) / 3.0;
}
```

As another example, let us consider the function **interchange()**, which takes two arguments which are pointers to two integer values to be interchanged. This function does not return anything. The code for **interchange()** is as follows:

```
/* function to interchange two integers */
void interchange(int *i, int *j)
{
```

```
    int temp;    /* define temporary variable */
    temp = *i;
    *i = *j;
    *j = temp;
}
```

Here, the arguments are two pointers to `int`s. Another integer variable, named `temp`, is used during the exchange of values as a temporary place to hold the value pointed to by the argument `i`. The value pointed to by `i` is then replaced by the value pointed to by `j`. Finally, the value pointed to by `j` is replaced by the value `temp`. The function does not have a `return` statement since it is defined as type `void`. The execution of `interchange()` ends when its last statement is executed.

While variables defined within functions are local in scope, C also allows you to define variables that are *global*. Any variable defined outside all functions is called *external*. Such variables are global in scope. The name of an external variable has meaning in all the functions after the variable has been defined. Consider, for example, the following complete C program:

```
    int i,j,k;    /* i, j, and k are external variables */
    double new_average_ints(void); /*no arguments */

    main()
    {
      double result;

      i = 7;
      j = 5;
      k = 10;
      result = new_average_ints(i,j,k);
      printf("The average is %lf\n", result);
    }


    /* function to average i, j  and k */
    double new_average_ints(void)
    {
      return ( (i+j+k)/3.0);
    }
```

Here, the variables `i`, `j`, and `k` are global in scope because they are defined externally to any function. Thus, their values have meaning inside all the functions after their definition in the source code. Note that the new function `new_average_ints()` is far less general than the earlier version. It can only average three particular global variables, while the earlier version can average any three integers passed to it as arguments. For this reason, functions such as `new_average_ints()` are not widely used.

It is reasonable to ask what would happen if a function tried to define a local variable with the same name as some global variable. The answer in C is that the "most recent" definition is the one in force. Thus, if the variable i were defined externally (and was therefore global in scope) and another variable with the same name was defined within some function, the local variable would be the one referenced by i inside the function. Outside the function, the global variable i would be used by statements referencing i.

Another interesting property of local variables is that by default, the space in memory where their values are stored is allocated only when the function they are defined in is executed. In fact, every time some function is invoked, memory is allocated for the arguments and the local variables in the function. This space is then deallocated when the function finishes. This type of storage is called *automatic*.

Aside from managing memory efficiently, the fact that C variables are by default allocated and deallocated automatically each time a function is invoked makes it possible for C functions to call themselves. Each time any function calls itself, a complete, new set of the local variables defined in that function is created, thus avoiding any conflict with the variables created in earlier invocations of the function. The idea of functions calling themselves is a powerful concept referred to as *recursion*. We will have a great deal to say about it in later chapters.

2.17 BLOCKS AND if...else if STATEMENTS

It is quite common for algorithms to require that different things be done, depending on the values of inputs or other circumstances. C allows this through the use of *conditional* statements. In the simplest form, a conditional statement takes the form, "If something is true, do the following."

In C, this would be written as

```
if (expression)
    statement;
```

where "expression" is something which, when evaluated, is either true or false. The "statement" is executed only when the expression is in fact true. In many situations you want to do several things if the expression is true. In this case, you group the statements you want to do into a *block* by enclosing them in curly braces, as in the following:

```
if (expression)
  {
    statement_1;
    statement_2;
         .
         .
         .
    statement_n;
  }
```

The statements inside a block can be as complicated as you wish. They may include function invocations, other **if** statements, assignments, and any other valid C statements.

C provides a range of operators for constructing expressions that evaluate to either true or false. This includes the following forms:

- !a — evaluates to true if **a** is false, and evaluates to false if **a** is true.
- a == b — evaluates to true if expression **a** equals expression **b**, and to false otherwise.
- a != b — evaluates to true if expression **a** does not equal expression **b**, and to false otherwise.
- a > b — evaluates to true if expression **a** is greater than expression **b**, and to false otherwise.
- a < b — evaluates to true if expression **a** is less than expression **b**, and to false otherwise.
- a >= b — evaluates to true if expression **a** is greater than or equal to expression **b**, and to false otherwise.
- a <= b — evaluates to true if expression **a** is less than or equal to expression **b**, and to false otherwise.

The negation operator (!) has higher precedence than all the arithmetic operators. The four inequality operators (<, >, >=, <=) all have equal precedence. They have lower precedence than all the arithmetic operators, and have higher precedence than the equality (==) and inequality (!=) operators.

Logical expressions in C evaluate to the integer 1 if they are true and 0 if they are false. Any integer value other than zero is treated in C as true.

As an example, consider a function we will call **maxfloat()**, which takes two **float**s as arguments and returns the larger of the two. The following code implements this function.

```
/* function to return the max of two floats */
float maxfloat(float g, float h)
{
  if(g > h)
    return g;
  return h;
}
```

This function tests if the value of **g** exceeds that of **h**. If so, the statement **return g** is executed, returning the value of **g** and ending the function's execution. If the expression **g > h** is not true, then the statement **return g** is not executed, and the next statement, **return h**, is executed.

Conditional statements may also provide for what to do if the expression tested is false. This form is written in C as

```
if (expression)
   statement_1;
```

```
else
    statement_2;
```

where **statement_1** is executed if the **expression** is true, and **statement_2** is executed otherwise. This could be used to write an equivalent but arguably somewhat clearer version of the function **maxfloat()** as follows:

```
/* equivalent function to return max of two floats */
float maxfloat(float g, float h)
{
  if(g > h)
    return g;
  else
    return h;
}
```

More complicated logical statements may require many tests, with different actions depending on the outcome of the various tests. C allows this through statements of the form

```
if (expression_1)
    statement_1;
else if (expression_2)
    statement_2;
else if (expression_3)
    statement_3;
         .
         .
         .
else if(expression_n)
    statement_n;
else
    statement_k;
```

In executing statements **if...else if...else** statements, C first evaluates **expression_1**. If it is true, **statement_1** is executed and the remainder of the **if... else if... else** statement is skipped. If **expression_1** is not true, **expression_2** is evaluated. If it is true, **statement_2** is executed and the remainder of the **if... else if... else** statement is skipped. This process continues until the **else** clause of the statement is reached. When this occurs, **statement_k** is executed. The inclusion of an **else** clause is optional. If there is none, and none of the expressions are true, then none of the statements are executed.

For example, the function **print_range()** below prints out different messages depending on whether its argument is negative, between 0 and 1000, between 1000 and 2000, or greater than 2000.

```
/*  function to print ranges */
void print_range(double d)
{
  if(d < 0.0)
    printf("The value is negative\n");
  else if (d <= 1000.0)
    printf("The value is between 0 and 1000\n");
  else if (d <= 2000.0)
    printf("The value is between 1000 and 2000\n");
  else
    printf("The value is greater than 2000\n");
}
```

As with any other place in C where a single statement is used, it is permissible to replace one statement in an **if...else if...else** statement with a block of statements enclosed in curly braces.

C also has what are called *Boolean* operators. The two operators provided are logical AND and logical OR. These are expressed as follows:

- a **&&** b evaluates to true if *both* a and b are true.
- a **| |** b evaluates to true if *either* a or b are true.

The logical AND operator (**&&**) has higher precedence than the logical OR (**| |**), and both have lower precedence than the logical comparison operators. For example, the expression

```
a<b | |  a==5 && b<12
```

would be evaluated as though the following parentheses were added:

```
((a<b)  | |  ((a==5) && (b<12))
```

Another property of the logical AND and OR operators is that the expressions being compared are evaluated from left to right, and once enough information is available to decide whether the entire expression is true or false, evaluation stops. In the example above, if the expression a==5 is false, the expression b < 12 is never evaluated because the entire expression a==5 && b<12 must be false if a==5 is false. Similarly, if the first expression in a logical OR operation is true, the second expression is never evaluated because the entire OR expression is true regardless of the value of the second operand. This is sometimes helpful, as in the expression

```
b != 0 && a/b > 20
```

where if the subexpression b != 0 is false, the subexpression a/b > 20 is never evaluated. This avoids the error of dividing the value a by 0.

It is possible to nest **if** statements, as in the example

```
if (b > 20)
  if(a == b)
    printf("b > 20 and a equals b\n");
  else
    printf("b > 20 and a does not equal b\n");
```

An interesting question is whether the **else** clause in the example above belongs to the first or second **if** statement. The text in the **printf()** control string as well as the indentation used in the example above serve to highlight the general rule in C that *unless otherwise indicated by the use of curly braces, an* **else** *clause belongs to the innermost* **if** *statement that does not yet have an associated* **else** *clause*. In this case, the test **b >20** is made first, and if it is true, the **if...else** statement is executed. Contrast this with the following example:

```
if (b > 20) {
  if(a == b)
    printf("b > 20 and a equals b\n");
  }
else
  printf("b <= 20\n");
```

In this case, the curly braces denote that the **else** clause belongs to the *first* **if** statement.

2.18 LOOPS

Many computer algorithms require that operations be repeated many times. For example, even simple procedures such as producing payroll checks require that the same set of operations be repeated for each employee. As with all other programming languages, C provides a syntax for describing repetition.

The simplest form of iteration is the **while** statement. This form is as follows:

```
while (expression)
    statement;
```

Put into words, this means, "while **expression** is true, execute the **statement**." If the **expression** is always true, then the **while** statement will loop forever, meaning that the program will never terminate. If the **expression** is never true, then the **statement** will never be executed.

For example, the following function **sum_squares()** sums the squares of positive integers between zero and the value of its single integer argument **n**, returning the sum.

```
/* function to sum squares between 1 and n */
int sum_squares(int n)
{
  int total;
  total = 0;
  while (n >0) {
    total = total + n*n;
    n = n-1;
  }
  return(total);
}
```

The function **sum_squares()** illustrates several points. Note first that the statement in the **while** loop can be replaced by a block of statements enclosed in curly braces. Second, if the value of the argument **n** is zero or negative, the **while** loop will never be executed. In this case the function will return the value zero. Third, the function **sum_squares()** changes the value of its argument **n**. This change in the argument has no effect on the value of the variable used in the invoking function because the function works entirely with a *copy* of the value of its argument, not the argument itself. Consider the **main()** function that invokes **sum_squares()** in the following example:

```
/* program to use the function sum_squares()*/

#include <stdio.h>
int sum_squares(int);

main()
{
  int i,j;
  while(scanf("%d", &i) != EOF) {
      j = sum_squares(i);
      printf("Values of i and j are %d and %d\n", i, j);
    }
}
```

When this function is executed, the value of the variable i which is passed to the function **sum_squares()** is not changed when **sum_squares()** is executed. Rather, the copy of the variable is passed to **sum_squares()** and it is this copy that is changed when the **sum_squares()** executes.

The sample **main()** function above also illustrates how the value returned by **scanf()** can be used as part of the test expression of a **while** loop. The program reads in a value for the variable i using **scanf()**. The function **scanf()** returns an integer, which is then compared with the special value **EOF**. If **scanf()** returns the value **EOF**, then the **while** loop finishes executing and the program terminates. If any value other than **EOF** is returned by **scanf()**, the program computes and outputs the sum of the squared integers. Thus, the program allows the user to test as many integers as desired. If the integers come from a file, then the program will terminate whenever the file is completely processed. Alternatively, if the user is entering numbers from the keyboard, then the program will end whenever the special "end of file" character (usually the letter D pressed with the Control key held down) is entered.

A second form of iteration that we will use frequently is the **for** loop. The general form of this type of loop is

```
for(expression_1; expression_2; expression_3)
   statement;
```

The best way to explain the **for** loop is to note that it is entirely equivalent to the following statements:

```
expression_1;
while(expression_2) {
   statement;
   expression_3;
}
```

The **for** statement might be translated into words as "evaluate **expression_1**, then execute the **statement** while **expression_2** is true, evaluating **expression_3** each time after you execute the **statement**." For example, a **for** loop might be used to rewrite the function **sum_squares()** as

```
/* revised function to sum squares between 1 and n */
int sum_squares(int n)
{
   int total;
   for(total=0; n>0; n=n-1)
      total = total + n*n;
   return(total);
}
```

The first expression in a **for** loop is often an assignment statement that initializes some value. The second expression is a logical test to determine whether to continue looping. The third expression is often another assignment statement that modifies some value used in the logical expression.

It is permissible to omit any of the three expressions by using a "null" statement, which in C is simply a semicolon. For example, we could rewrite the function **sum_squares()** as

```
/* one more function to sum squares between 1 and n */
int sum_squares(int n)
{
```

```
      int total;
      total = 0;
      for( ; n>0; n=n-1)
        total = total + n*n;
      return(total);
    }
```

In some cases, we may not need any statement after the expressions used in a **for** loop. It is permissible to use the null statement here as well.

You are also allowed to have any of the expressions in a **for** loop be multiple statements separated by commas. For example, yet another, equivalent way to write the function **sum_squares()** is as

```
    /* one more function to sum squares between 1 and n */
    int sum_squares(int n)
    {
      int total;
      for(total=0; n>0; total=total+n*n,   n=n-1)
        ;
      return(total);
    }
```

Note that the comma is formally an operator in C because an expression can itself consist of a series of expressions separated by commas. An expression including the comma operator is evaluated from left to right, so that the rightmost expression of a sequence separated by commas is the value of the entire expression. The comma operator has lower priority than that of any other C operator.

Indiscriminate use of the comma operator in a **for** loop can obscure the meaning of a program. As a matter of style, we urge students to avoid this usage entirely, making the expressions in **for** loops as simple and as clear as possible.

2.19 INCREMENT AND DECREMENT OPERATORS

Statements such as

```
    j = j+1;
```

appear so often in C programs that special operators are defined for them. C provides an operator denoted by **++** for incrementing by one and an operator denoted by **--** for decrementing by one. Thus, the statement above could be written as

```
    j++;
```

The increment and decrement operators are particularly useful for writing compact `for` statements. For example, the `--` operator could be used to rewrite the function that computes the sum of squares as follows:

```
/* revised function to sum squares between 1 and n */
int sum_squares(int n)
{
  int total;
  for(total=0; n>0; n--)
    total = total + n*n;
  return(total);
}
```

The `++` and `--` operators actually have two different meanings depending on whether they appear before or after the variable they are operating on. Consider first the *postfix* operator, where the `++` notation appears after the variable, as in

```
int i,j;
j = 7;
i = j++;   /* postfix increment operator */
```

This code fragment would result in `i` having the value 7 and `j` having the value 8. The right-hand side is evaluated *before* `j` is incremented and assigned to `i`. Only after this evaluation is the value of `j` incremented. Contrast this with the *prefix* incrementation operator, as in the code fragment

```
int i,j;
j = 7;
i = ++j;   /* prefix increment operator */
```

Here, `j` is incremented *before* the right-hand side of the assignment statement is evaluated. Thus, `i` and `j` would both have the value 8 after this code fragment is executed.

The decrement operator also has both a prefix and a postfix form. These behave in exactly the same way as the increment operator.

2.20 PROGRAMMING PROJECT: IS AN INTEGER PRIME?

Prime numbers are positive integers that are evenly divisible only by themselves and 1. For example, the numbers 2, 3, 5, and 7 are prime, but the number 9 is not because it is evenly divisible by 3. Tests for primality have fascinated both amateur and professional mathematicians for centuries. The ability to know whether a particular integer is prime can also have practical significance. For example, the generation of very large prime numbers with 100–200 digits is central to what is called the RSA data encryption method devised by Rivest, Shamir, and Adelman [Rivest, R. 78].

In this section we develop a simple algorithm to test whether or not an integer is prime. This algorithm works quite well for small or moderate-size integers such as those that can be represented in an **int** in C. However, the reader should be warned that the algorithm is not fast enough for dealing with the very large prime numbers required in RSA encryption.

The algorithm is based on the following observations:

- The only even integer which is prime is 2.
- If a number is not prime, then at least one of its factors must be less than or equal to its square root. For example, 10 is not prime because it has the pair 5 and 2 as factors. Since 5 is greater than $\sqrt{10}$, the other factor, 2, must be less than $\sqrt{10}$.

The program we develop below has a **main()** function that prompts the user to input an integer, reads the integer to be tested, invokes another function called **prime_test()** to check whether or not the integer is prime, and outputs an appropriate message. The function **prime_test()** has as its sole argument the number to be tested and returns an integer which is not zero (and therefore treated as true in C) if the argument is prime or returns zero (which C treats as false) otherwise.

We begin by presenting the code for the **main()** function. This code is as follows:

```
/* the main program reads and tests values */

#include <stdio.h>
#include <math.h>
#define TRUE 1
#define FALSE 0

int prime_test(int); /* function prototype */

main()
{
  int test_value;

/* prompt user and read in value to be tested */
  printf("Enter value to be tested:");
  scanf("%d", &test_value);

/* check if prime and output appropriate message */
  if(prime_test(test_value))
    printf("%d is prime.\n", test_value);
  else
    printf("%d is not prime.\n", test_value);
}
```

Four C preprocessor directives begin the program. The first two of these directives **#include**s the header files for the standard input/output and mathematics libraries.

The header file **math.h** is needed because we will later use the function **sqrt()**, which has a single **double** value as its argument and returns a **double** value which is the square root of the argument. The two other preprocessor directives **#define** two constants as values, which C treats as true and false, respectively. The preprocessor statements are followed by the function prototype for **prime_test()**. We present the code for this function later.

The body of **main()** uses **printf()** to output a prompt to the user and then uses **scanf()** to read in an integer value. Note that the second argument to **scanf()** is an address, as required. These statements are followed by an **if...else** statement which relies on the value returned by the function **prime_test()**. If **prime_test()** returns a value which is **TRUE**, then the number to be tested is prime; otherwise, the number is not prime.

The more difficult part of the complete program is the C code for the function **prime_test()**. This can be implemented in many ways. We chose the following algorithm:

- Step 1. If the number is even and not equal to 2, then it cannot be prime.
- Step 2. Otherwise, test whether any of the odd integers from 3 to the square root of the number divide evenly into the number. If any of these integers are factors, then the number being tested is not prime.

The following C code implements this algorithm.

```
/* function to test if integer>1 is prime */

int prime_test(int n)

{
  int m,p;
  int prime = TRUE;

/* check if n is odd and not 2 */

  if(n%2 == 0 && n!= 2)
    prime = FALSE;
  else {
    m = 3;
    p = sqrt(n);

/* loop through possible divisors */

    while (m<= p && prime)
      if (n%m == 0)
        prime = FALSE;
      else
        m = m+2;
  }
```

```
        return(prime);
}
```

The coding of this function makes use of the fact that for two integers $m < n$, if m is a factor of n, then the remainder of n divided by m is zero. This is used in the C implementation above in the expression

```
    n%2 == 0
```

to check if **n** is even and in the expression

```
    n%m == 0
```

to check if **m** is a divisor of **n**.

The C implementation exploits the property of the ANSI C standard for conversion of the arguments of functions. The statement

```
    p = sqrt(n);
```

works correctly even though its argument **n** is an **int** rather than a **double**. This is because the header file **math.h** contains the function prototype for the **sqrt()** function, allowing the C compiler to convert automatically the argument of **sqrt()** to the correct, **double** type.

It is also worth noting that the value **p** will be the integer equal to or less than the square root of **n** since the **double** returned from the **sqrt()** function will automatically be truncated when it is assigned to the **int p**. This follows the rules given in Section 2.8.2 for conversion between data types in assignment statements.

Note also that the **while** loop checks whether any of the odd integers is a divisor of **n**. This loop is terminated as soon as a factor of **n** is found or when the value of **m** exceeds the value of **p**. This avoids wasted computation since once a divisor is found, the number is known not to be prime whether or not there are other divisors.

2.21 PROGRAMMING PROJECT: GREATEST COMMON DIVISORS

In order to make concrete much of the general material presented in this chapter, we consider some elementary algorithms for determining the greatest common divisor (GCD) of two positive integers. The greatest common divisor is the largest integer which can be divided evenly into both integers.

We will implement *Euclid's algorithm*, which is based on the following observation:

> Given two nonnegative integers m and n, where $n > m$, then the greatest common divisor of m and n is also the greatest common divisor of $n\%m$ and m.

For example, the greatest common divisor of 55 and 1035 is the same as the GCD of 1035%55, which equals 45, and 55. We can apply this fact over and over again, successively reducing the values for which we are seeking the GCD. Eventually, the smaller of the two values will be zero, leaving the larger of the two values as the GCD.

If we apply the rule again to the integers 45 and 55, we find their GCD is the same as the greatest divisor of 55%45, or 10, and 45. Applying the rule once more we get the greatest common divisor of 5 and 10. Applying the rule once again we find that the greatest common divisor of 5 and 10 is the same as the GCD of 0 and 5. Since the smaller number is now zero, the GCD of 55 and 1035, the two original numbers, is 5.

Implemented as a C function, Euclid's algorithm is as follows:

```
/* Euclid's algorithm for finding the GCD of
        two integers. Assumes n>m */
int gcd(int m, int n)
{
  int t;

  while (m>0) {
    t = n%m;
    n = m;
    m = t;
  }
  return n;
}
```

This implementation is fairly straightfoward. The repeated process of applying the algorithm to reduce the value of **m** is handled inside a **while** loop. The loop continues until the expression **m > 0** is no longer true, and the remaining value **n** is returned.

We also need a **main()** function to create a complete C program. Our version of **main()** will use **printf()** to prompt the user for the two integers whose GCD we are seeking, invoke **scanf()** to read in these two values, and use **printf()** to output the two values and their GCD. An implementation that does this follows.

```
/* program to find greatest common divisor */

#include <stdio.h>

int gcd(int, int); /* prototype for gcd() function */

main()
{
  int n,m;
  printf("Enter two integers\n");
  scanf("%d %d",&m, &n);
  printf("GCD of %d and %d is %d\n",m, n, gcd(m,n));
}
```

A more sophisticated implementation of **main()** would check the values of the inputs to ensure that the second is greater than the first and that both values are positive. One of the exercises given at the end of the chapter explores this.

2.21.1 Recursive Implementation of Euclid's Algorithm

There is another way to implement Euclid's algorithm which takes advantage of the idea of recursion. In the recursive implementation, we directly exploit the observation that the GCD of m and n equals the GCD of $n\%m$ and m. The recursive version is given below.

```
/* Euclid's algorithm for finding the GCD of
        two integers--recursive version */
int recursive_gcd(int m, int n)

{
  if (m == 0)
    return(n);
  else
    return recursive_gcd(n%m ,m);
}
```

This new function, called **recursive_gcd()**, simply does one of two things. If the value of the argument **m** is zero, it returns the value of **n**, its other argument. If the value of **n** is not zero, it returns the result found by calling the function **recursive_gcd()** again with the arguments **n%m** and **m**. To see how this works, consider again the example of taking the GCD of 1035 and 55. The steps that the recursive version would execute are summarized as follows:

1. Invoke **recursive_gcd()** with the arguments 55 and 1035.
2. Since the argument **m** is not equal to zero, the statement
   return recursive_gcd(1035%55, 55);
   is executed. In order for the function to return this value, the function
   recursive_gcd (45,55) is invoked.
3. Since the argument **m** is not equal to zero, the statement
   return recursive_gcd(55%45, 45);
   is executed. In order for the function to return this value, the function
   recursive_gcd (10, 45) is invoked.
4. Since the argument **m** is not equal to zero, the statement
   return recursive_gcd(45%10, 10);
   is executed. In order for the function to return this value, the function
   recursive_gcd (5, 10) is invoked.
5. Since the argument **m** is not equal to zero, the statement
   return recursive_gcd(10%5, 5);

is executed. In order for the function to return this value, the function `recursive_gcd (0, 5)` is invoked.

6. At last, the value of **m** passed to `recursive_gcd()` is zero, so the value 5 is returned to the statement
`return recursive_gcd (5, 10);`

7. The value 5 is returned to the statement
`return recursive_gcd (10, 45);`

8. The value 5 is returned to the statement
`return recursive_gcd (45, 55);`

9. The value 5 is returned to the statement
`return recursive_gcd (55, 1035);`

10. Finally, the value 5 is returned to the original invocation of `recursive_gcd()`.

This sequence of function invocations and returns is depicted in Figure 2.1. The numbers in circles in this figure correspond to the numbered steps listed above.

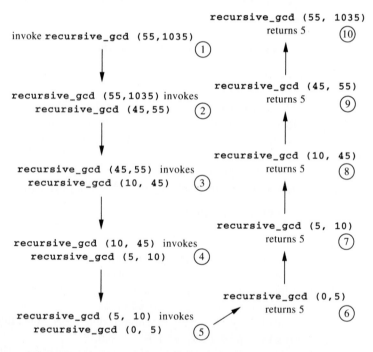

Figure 2.1 Sequence of invocations and returns in `recursive_gcd(55,1035)`.

All of this may seem to be a lot of work compared to the first version of Euclid's algorithm. Indeed, the recursive version does require greater computation time than the original, iterative version. However, we shall see situations later in this book where recursive versions of algorithms are clear and simple, while equivalent iterative versions would be extremely difficult to code.

2.22 SUMMARY OF CHAPTER 2

In this chapter we presented some essential components of the C programming language. Each C program consists of a series of statements to be executed in sequence. All C statements end with a semicolon.

C variables have names that begin with a character. These variables have values that can be modified during a program's execution. Variables can be one of the following types: **char**, **int**, **float**, **double**. C allows integers to be defined as **short** or **long** as well as **unsigned**. The type **long double** can also be defined but is rarely different from the type **double** in most C implementations.

C also allows for integer, floating-point, character, and string constants to be used in programs.

The equals sign (**=**) is used in C to denote an assignment. The right-hand side of an assignment statement can be any expression that produces a value, which is then assigned to the variable on the left-hand side of the assignment. The arithmetic operations addition (**+**), subtraction (**-**), multiplication (*****), division (**/**), and modulus (**%**) are provided.

C programs generally are written as a series of functions. All C programs must have a function named **main()**, which is invoked when execution of the program begins. Functions are invoked within a C program by referencing the function's name and passing it a set of arguments enclosed in parentheses. When a function is invoked, the arguments are copied; all operations on the arguments in a function are done on the copied values. This is termed *call by value*. C functions can return a single value to the function that called them by using the **return** statement.

C functions are described through a function prototype. This gives the type of value returned by a function and the types of each of its arguments.

In order for C functions to change the values of the arguments in the invoking function, C provides an operator to take the address of any variable. This is denoted with an ampersand (**&**). Within a function, arguments which are addresses of variables are defined as *pointers*. For example, if a variable **q** is declared as

```
int * q;
```

it is a pointer to a value of type **int**.

Header files in C provide various prototypes for function libraries. These files are customarily given names that end with the suffix **.h**. You incorporate them into your own C programs through the **#include** preprocessor directive. The C preprocessor also provides the **#define** directive that causes one text string to replace another. This is often used to give meaningful names to constants so that a program is easier to read.

The C library functions **printf()** and **scanf()** are used for output and input, respectively. Their function prototypes are given in the header file **stdio.h**. Both **printf()** and **scanf()** have a control string as their first argument. This string establishes the number and type of values to be output or input. The function **scanf()** must be called with pointers as its other arguments because it changes the values of these arguments, replacing them with values read in from the user's keyboard.

Functions you write yourself begin with the type returned by the function, the name of the function, and a list of definitions of the types and names of the function's arguments. This is followed by a series of variable definitions and statements enclosed in curly braces. Functions that do not return values are declared as being of type **void**. If a function has no arguments, the argument list should be declared with the keyword **void** enclosed in parentheses.

Variables used in functions can be either external or internal. Internal variables are defined within the body of a function. They are *local* in scope, meaning that their names only have meaning inside the function in which they are defined. Variables defined outside the body of any function are external and are *global* in scope.

C provides the **if...else if...else** statement for executing different statements depending on the truth of some expression. Expressions can include comparisons such as less than (**<**), greater than (**>**), equal to (**==**), not equal to (**!=**), less than or equal to (**<=**), and greater than or equal to (**>=**). The logical operators negation(**!**), AND (**&&**) and OR (**||**) are also provided. If you need to execute a group of statements in a clause of an **if...else if...else** statement, they must be enclosed in a pair of curly braces.

Statements (or groups of statements enclosed in curly braces) can be repeated in loops. The two types of loops presented are the **while** and the **for** loop. The **while** loop executes a group of statements until the test expression is false. The **for** loop provides an initialization, a test for whether to continue executing the loop, and an expression to be evaluated each time the loop is executed.

The following table summarizes the various operators introduced in this chapter. The operators are listed in their order of precedence; those nearer the top of the table are of higher precedence than those lower in the table. Operators on the same line of the table have equal precedence. The table also states whether the operators associate from right to left or from left to right.

OPERATORS IN DECREASING PRECEDENCE

Operator	Association	Type
( )	left to right	function invocation
! + - ++ -- * & (*cast type*)	right to left	unary operators
* / %	left to right	arithmetic operators
+ -	left to right	arithmetic operators
< <= > >=	left to right	logical comparison
== !=	left to right	logical comparison
&&	left to right	logical AND
||	left to right	logical OR
= += -= *= /= %=	right to left	assignment
,	left to right	expression separator

We will expand this table as we introduce other operators in later chapters.

2.23 EXERCISES

2-1. Suppose that you had three `int`s named **x**, **y**, and **z** declared in `main()`.

    (a) Write a function in C named `rotate()` which takes pointers to three integer arguments **x**, **y**, and **z**. This function should manipulate those pointers so that the original value of **x** ends up with the value **z** had, the original value of **y** ends up with the value **x** had, and the original value of **z** ends up with the value **y** had. The function should not return a value.

    (b) Write the function prototype for `rotate()`.

    (c) Show the line of code you would use to invoke `rotate()` on the variables **v1**, **v2**, and **v3** after the following C code:

```
int v1 = 5;
int v2 = 7;
int v3 = 9;
```

2-2. The following program is supposed to read two positive integers a and i, compute a^{-i} (which is equal to $1/a^{i}$), and output the result. Find at least five errors and give the corrected code.

```
main()
{
  int a,i;
  scanf("%d%d", a, i);
  for(j=1; j=i; j=j+1)
    total = 1/a*total;
  printf("The answer is %d\n", total);
}
```

2-3. Explain in words why the following C statement is incorrect when **x** equals zero.

```
if((z-x)/x*x < 2.0  &&  (x != 0.0))
      printf("Hello\n");
```

Rewrite the statement so that it will work correctly.

2-4. The following C program is supposed to tell a user whether he or she has guessed the correct value of an integer between 0 and 10. It has some errors in it. Find all the errors and give the appropriate corrections that will make the program work properly.

```
main()
{
  int x, y, answer;
  x = 0;
  y = 10;
  answer = 3;
  printf("Guess an integer between %f and %f\n", answer);
  scanf("%d", z);
  if (z<x || z>y)
```

```
      printf("Error...out of range\n");
  if (z = answer);
      printf("Correct...the number is %f\n", answer);
  else
      printf("Sorry...better luck next time\n");
  }
```

2-5. The following program contains one or more errors. Find them and provide the needed corrections. (The output expected from the program when it is working correctly is given below.)

```
main()
{
  int a, b, c;

  a = 0;
  b = 25;
  printf ("Enter an integer between %d and %lf: ", a, b);
  scanf ("%lf", c) ;

  if (a <= c <= b)
    printf ("\nGreat! %d is in the interval!\n",&c) ;
  else
    printf ("\n%d is out of range.\n", c) ;
}
```

Expected Output: If 25 is entered:

```
Enter an integer number between 0 and 25: 25

Great! 25 is in the correct interval!
```

If 27 is entered:

```
Enter an integer number between 0 and 25: 27

27 is out of range.
```

2-6. Write a C program that takes the sale price of an item and the cash tendered by the customer and outputs the cash to be returned such that the number of coins is a minimum. For example, if the sale price of an item is $5.32 and the cash tendered by the customer is $10, then the cash to be returned is $4.68, where the 68 cents can only be returned in the form of two quarters, one dime, one nickel, and three pennies.

2-7. The following program contains one or more errors. Find them and provide the needed corrections. (The output expected from the program when it is working correctly is given below.)

```
main()
{
  int i ;
  int y ;

  i = 0 ;
  while ( i < 10 )
    {
      y = 1.0 / (i * i)
      printf ("y = %d\n", y) ;
    }
}
```

Expected Output:

```
y = 1.000000
y = 0.250000
y = 0.111111
y = 0.062500
y = 0.040000
y = 0.027778
y = 0.020408
y = 0.015625
y = 0.012346
y = 0.010000
```

2-8. You have been hired by a mining company to develop a computer program to evaluate the ease with which a deposit of titanium can be exploited. The deposits are known to be cone shaped, with the base of the cone at surface level and the tip a certain distance underground. To be commercially viable, a deposit should have a volume of at least 200,000 cubic meters. In addition, because of the mining equipment available, any deposit with a depth of less than 20 meters or more than 250 meters cannot be mined. Moreover, the area of the base of the cone should be at least 10,000 square meters. A team of geologists has identified several deposits and has measured the height of the cone and the diameter of the base for each of them.

Write a program that accepts as inputs the diameter and depth of the cone, and then evaluates the feasibility of exploiting the ore deposit. Your program should display the following messages depending on the inputs:

```
Deposit is not viable because volume is XXXXXX
Deposit is not viable because of wrong depth
Deposit is not viable because base has insufficient area
Deposit is viable with volume of XXXXXX cubic meters
```

Remember that the volume of a cone is $\pi r^2 h/3$, where r is the radius of the base of the cone and h is its height.

2-9. A common requirement in all engineering fields is the calculation of material quantities. Most designs are built up from a set of components of different shapes and materials. These component descriptions are collected into lists according to material type. The description contains information about the shape of the component and unique dimensions to ascertain its volume.

Suppose that the component file has the following structure:

```
15
100 <length of side>
105 <Outside radius> <inside radius>
101 <radius of base> <height>
102 <radius of base> <height>
103 <radius>
101 <radius of base> <height>
104 <semiaxis1> <semiaxis2> <semiaxis3>
105 <distance to center line of torus body>
                <torus body radius>

        .
        .
        .
```

The first entry in the file to be read by your program is an integer. This is the number of components to be processed. The subsequent lines contain the following information. The initial integer number indicates the shape of each component. The remaining numerical entries correspond to the parameters from which the volume of each component can be evaluated.

The integer numbers used to identify the components are specified below.

- 100– Box (a cube).
- 101– Cylinder.
- 102– Cone.
- 103– Sphere.
- 104– Ellipsoid.
- 105– Torus.

The equations to calculate the volume of these geometric shapes are:

Part Type	Formula for Volume	Definitions
cube	$V = a^3$	a is the length of a side of the cube
cylinder	$V = \pi r^2 h$	r is the radius of the base
		h is the height of the cylinder
cone	$V = \dfrac{\pi r^2 h}{3}$	r is the radius of the base
		h is the height of the cone
sphere	$V = \frac{4}{3}\pi r^3$	r is the radius of the sphere
ellipsoid	$V = \frac{4}{3}\pi abc$	a, b and c are the lengths of the semiaxes
torus	$V = 2\pi^2 Rr$	R is the distance to the center of the torus body
		r is the torus body radius

The problem is one of selection and action. Here is an approach that could be used.

(a) Initially, determine how many components need to be processed.

(b) For this number of components do the following:

- Read in the type of the component.
- Select which component this is.
- Read in the required volumetric parameters for the component selected.
- Issue a call to a separate function which calculates the volume and returns this value.
- Update the total volume of the objects processed so far.

(c) Finally, output the total volume of the components listed.

Test your program by entering some component data from the keyboard.

2-10. You have recently been hired by a software firm to develop a small program for the American Airport Authority (AAA). Apparently, to save money during a period of federal budget cuts, the AAA bought imported weather-sensing equipment. This equipment will be used to obtain the air temperature and relative humidity at ground level to see when deicing equipment is required for the airplanes.

The imported equipment is capable of giving temperatures only in degrees Celsius. Your program should read in values for the temperature and relative humidity, then it should convert the temperature value from Celsius to Fahrenheit.

After the temperature has been converted, your program should check to see whether or not deicing is needed. The AAA has decided that deicing should be done prior to takeoff whenever *two consecutive* readings are taken where both the temperature falls below 35 degrees Fahrenheit and the relative humidity is above 0.9.

Your program should output the temperature in Celsius and in Fahrenheit, the relative humidity, and an appropriate message stating whether or not deicing is needed, as shown in the following example:

```
Temp. (C)   Temp.(F)   Rel. Humidity   De-Icing
---------   --------   -------------   --------
     3.46      38.23       0.763       No De-icing Needed
    -2.34      27.79       0.924       No De-icing Needed
    -3.57      25.57       0.936       De-icing is Needed
```

The input to your program begins with an integer value which is the number of pairs of temperatures (in degrees Celsius) and relative humidity you will need to process. The remaining inputs are the values to be processed. Develop and test your program on the following input data:

```
10
  0.0 0.99
  0.0 0.92
  2.0 0.83
  3.1 0.95
  0.1 0.87
  2.5 0.97
 -2.0 0.95
 -1.0 0.98
  1.5 0.91
 10.0 0.93
```

2-11. The factorial value of any nonnegative integer *n* is defined as 1 if *n* is zero, and as the product of 1, 2, ..., *n* otherwise. Write both a recursive and iterative implementation of a function that computes *n* factorial. Write a `main()` function that accepts as input an integer and prints the value of that integer factorial.

2-12. Take the function `sum_squares()` and modify it so that it adds the squared integers from zero to the value of its argument even if the argument is negative. Compile and test the function you have written by preparing a `main()` function that calls it.

2-13. Suppose that you have a function named `func()` that is defined as follows:

```
int func(int i, int j)
{
    int w=0, v=0;
    while(++i<10){
        w=2*i+j++;
        v=j+2*i++;
        printf("%d\t%d\n", w, v);
    }
    return(w+i*j++);
}
```

What would the output of the following function call be? What would the value of the integer `result` be after the assignment statement?

```
result=func(0,3);
```

2-14. The following function is supposed to compute the value of the series

1+ 1/2 + 1/3 + 1/4 + 1/5 + ...

until the change in the sum is less than some small positive value. Find six errors in the function. Suggest changes that would make the program work correctly.

```
sum_up(double epsilon)
{
    int i, sum;
    double oldvalue;
    sum = 0.0;
    oldvalue = epsilon + 1;
    for(i=0; sum-oldvalue > epsilon; i++) {
        oldvalue = sum;
        sum += 1/i;
    }
}
```

2-15. The following function returns TRUE if its integer argument is prime, FALSE otherwise. Assume that the function is always called with a positive argument.

```
#define TRUE 1
#define FALSE 0
int prime_test(int n)
{
  int i;
  for(i=n-1; i>2; i--)
    if (n%i == 0)
      return(FALSE);
  return(TRUE);
}
```

Suggest at least two improvements on this algorithm. You do not have to write C code. Just describe the improvements you would make.

2-16. It is conjectured that every even integer greater than 2 can be written as the sum of two prime numbers. Write a C function which has as its sole argument an **int** containing a positive, even integer greater than 2 and which returns one of the two prime numbers which, when added, equals the value of the argument. You may use the function **prime_test()** described in Section 2.20. Also code a **main()** function which prompts the user for an integer, reads the value typed by the user, and outputs the two integers which sum to the value input by the user. Run your complete program to compute the primes which sum to 48, 62, and 128.

2-17. Try simulating on paper both the iterative and the recursive versions of the routine that computes the greatest common divisor for the integers 385 and 7245. What is the resulting greatest common divisor? How many times does the **while** loop get executed in the iterative version? How many times does the function **recursive_gcd()** get invoked in the recursive version?

2-18. Two integers are *relatively prime* if their greatest common divisor is 1. Write, compile and test a complete C program that reads two integers typed by the user and prints a message that gives the values of the integers and states whether or not they are relatively prime.

2-19. Rewrite the **main()** function in Section 2.21 so that the integers input by the user are checked to ensure that they are both positive and that the second integer is larger than the first. Compile and test the complete program.

2-20. The Fibonacci numbers are defined as series of nonnegative integers produced by the following rule:

$$F(0) = 0$$
$$F(1) = 1$$
$$F(n) = F(n-1) + F(n-2) \text{ if } n > 1$$

Thus, the first few Fibonacci numbers are

0, 1, 1, 2, 3, 5, 8, 13 ...

Write a C program that consists of a `main()` function that reads in an integer, calls another function to return $F(n)$, and then outputs the value. Try writing the function that computes $F(n)$ both recursively and iteratively.

2-21. Consider the following C program.

```c
#include <stdio.h>
int func(int);

main()
{
  printf("%d", func(6));
}

int func(int k)
{
 if(k==0)
        return(1);
 else
        return(k*func(k/2));
}
```

(a) How many times is `func()` called in this program?

(b) What values does each invocation of `func()` return?

(c) What value is printed by the `printf()` statement in `main()`?

CHAPTER

3

NUMERICAL ANALYSIS

3.1 INTRODUCTION

It is quite common for scientists and engineers to formulate *mathematical models* of the systems they study and design. These mathematical models usually describe complicated phenomena by one or more equations. Unfortunately, many of these systems of equations cannot be solved mathematically. Instead, people who study such systems rely on computers to develop approximate solutions. The algorithms used for this purpose are generally grouped under the term *numerical analysis*.

For example, the paths of celestial bodies moving in space can be theoretically described by the straightforward application of Newton's laws of gravitation. Given the masses of all the bodies that exert any significant force on an object and the objects' current velocities, the movement of each body in space is described by two equations. First, the net force exerted on the body is the sum of the gravitational forces that all the other bodies exert. Each pair of bodies are attracted by a force that is proportional to the product of their masses and inversely proportional to the square of the distance between them. Second, the movement of each body is described by the equation $F = ma$, where F is the net gravitational force acting on each body, m is mass of the body, and a is the body's acceleration.

It would seem that such a simple system of equations would be straightforward to solve. In fact, when there are more than two bodies involved, solution of the equations of motion is extremely complex. Scientists rely on computational methods to solve these equations in numerical rather than symbolic form.

Another motivation for the development and application of algorithms for numerical analysis is that some equations are demonstrably unsolvable. Consider, for example, the so-called "bell-shaped curve" (or more properly, the normal or Gaussian distribution) that is often used to characterize the distribution of students' performance on a test or an attribute such as intelligence or physical strength. Suppose that one is interested in the area underneath the normal curve shown in Figure 3.1 between two points on the x axis. Even though the equation describing this distribution is relatively simple, it can be shown that there exists no closed-form solution for the area under this curve. Numerical algorithms are needed to solve such problems.

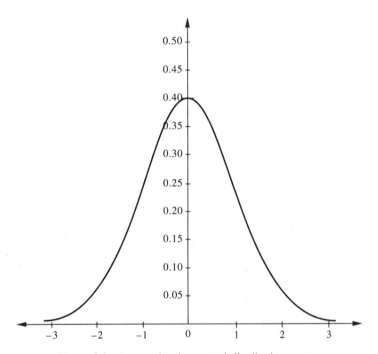

Figure 3.1   Area under the normal distribution curve.

In this chapter we introduce some of the algorithms used in numerical analysis. We try to give the reader a sense about both the value of such methods and the potential hazards of their indiscriminate use. In particular, many standard programs exist for solving numerical problems, and it is often important for the user to understand both the strengths and weaknesses of the procedures these programs use. As we shall discuss further, many numerical analysis methods can give results that are seriously in error, and the causes of the errors may be difficult to detect.

Our study of numerical methods will consider the following topics:

- Representation of floating-point numbers, and the sources of error when various arithmetic operations are performed.
- Solving for the roots of an equation.
- Numerical integration.
- Solution of simple, ordinary differential equations.

3.2 FLOATING-POINT REPRESENTATION

In Chapter 2 we introduced the concept of floating-point variables. In C, floating-point numbers are implemented using the types **float**, **double**, and **long double**. We stated that a number in floating-point representation has a sign, a fraction part, and an exponent. The three floating-point types can differ in the range of exponents they can represent and the number of significant digits in their fraction part.

In this section we explore some of the consequences of using floating-point representation. The major issues covered in this section are applicable to all computers. However, the details of floating-point representation do vary, and some of the specific examples in this section may not apply to all computers.

3.2.1 Typical Implementation

Consider a typical case in which a variable of type **float** is stored in 32 bits (binary zeros and ones). For the purposes of this chapter, we assume that the 32 bits are used as follows:

- The first bit is used to represent the sign of the number, with a zero indicating a positive value and a one indicating a negative value.
- The next eight bits are used to represent the base 2 exponent. The exponent of any floating-point number is the value of these eight bits (in base 2) minus a fixed number called the *bias*. In our examples we will use a bias of 127. This would often be referred to as *excess* 127 representation.
- The remaining 23 bits are the fraction part. This value is represented in the base 2 equivalent of decimal notation, with the first binary digit representing units of 1, the second representing units of 1/2, the third representing units of 1/4, ..., and the last digit representing units of 2^{-22}.

The format above is typical for floating-point numbers. However, the actual size of a **float** as well as the number of digits used for the fraction part and exponent vary across computers. The representations for variables of type **double** and **long double** use a similar format but generally use more than 32 bits. (The name **double** comes from the fact that on many computers a **double** occupies 64 bits while a **float** occupies 32.) This allows **double**s to have greater precision, and in some cases, exponents that are greater in magnitude.

The following are examples of floating-point values in this representation.

```
3   = 0 10000000 11000000000000000000000 = 3/2 × 2¹

-.5 = 1 01111110 10000000000000000000000 =  -1 × 2⁻¹

1/8 = 0 01111100 10000000000000000000000 =   1 × 2⁻³
```

One characteristic of the representation chosen is that there is more than a single way to represent any given value. In particular, as long as the last digit of the fraction part is zero, one can shift the fraction part right one digit (multiplying it by 1/2) and increase the exponent by one (multiplying the entire number by 2) without changing the value.

For example, the following are all equivalent representations of the number 1/16:

```
1/16 = 0 01111110 00010000000000000000000 = 1/8 × 2⁻¹
       0 01111101 00100000000000000000000 = 1/4 × 2⁻²
       0 01111100 01000000000000000000000 = 1/2 × 2⁻³
       0 01111011 10000000000000000000000 =   1 × 2⁻⁴
```

We follow the convention that the fraction part of any floating-point number is as "left-shifted" as possible. In this left-shifted form, the first digit of the fraction part, corresponding to the "ones" place, is always one. In the example showing four equivalent representations of 1/16, the last of them would be used. This normalizes the fractional part to be between 1 and 2. Since in this form the first digit of the fraction part is always known, many computer architectures do not even store the first digit of the fraction part, relying on the fact that it is always one. This gives an extra bit of precision in the fraction part. In this form, the representation of 1/16 would be

```
1/16 = 0 01111011 00000000000000000000000
```

The representation described above, including the assumption that the first binary digit of the fractional part is one and that it therefore need not be represented explicitly, corresponds to the IEEE (Institute of Electrical and Electronics Engineers) 754 standard [Institute of Electrical and Electronics Engineers 85] for 32-bit floating-point numbers. This is often called *single precision*, and in many C implementations corresponds to the **float** data type. This IEEE standard is used widely (though not universally). Similarly, the same standard specifies that 64-bit floating-point numbers use a sign bit, 11 bits for the exponent (in excess 1023 representation), and the remaining 52 bits for the fractional part, with the first place of the fractional part not represented and always assumed to be one. This is often called *double precision*, and corresponds in many C implementations to the **double** type.

The rules for representing floating-point numbers also leave some ambiguity about how to represent the value 0.0. The standard convention is that a floating-point value with all the binary digits set to zero represents the value floating point 0.0.

3.2.2 Overflow and Underflow

In Chapter 2 we stated that there is a largest and smallest value that can be represented by any floating-point number. Using the hypothetical representation of a **float** described above, the largest number would correspond to all bits except the sign set to one. This would be a decimal value that is very close to 2^{128}. The same limitation applies to the absolute value of negative numbers.

An attempt to compute a **float** larger than the greatest representable value produces what is called an *overflow*. What happens in this case is entirely machine dependent. It is generally up to the programmer to detect cases where overflow is likely to occur and take appropriate actions such as warning the user of the program that the results are likely to be highly suspect. In some cases the computer hardware sets a special indicator when a floating-point overflow occurs. The programmer can test when this indicator is set and take appropriate action in the program.

A related possible condition is called *underflow*. This occurs when computations yield values that are too close to zero to be represented. Using our hypothetical floating-point representation, any value closer to zero than 2^{-127} in absolute magnitude is not representable. The C language definition treats the action taken in case of underflow as machine dependent. However, many computers produce a zero as the result of a floating-point computation that underflows.

3.2.3 Limitations on Precision

The fact that the fraction part of a floating-point number has a finite number of bits means that most values cannot be represented exactly. For example, the value 1/3 is not representable exactly in a finite number of decimal digits or in floating-point form. In our example, any quantity with more than 2^{24} binary digits is not exactly representable as a **float**. A similar limit will exist for the other floating-point types.

What is somewhat more subtle is that even if two numbers are both exactly representable as floating-point values, their sum may not be. This can be seen using our hypothetical **float** representation. The values 5 and $(1/2)^{-24}$ can both be represented exactly in our floating-point form. However, their sum cannot be represented. In fact, their sum has the same representation as the number 5! This illustrates the more general problem that if two floating-point numbers to be added differ in magnitude by an amount that is larger than the precision of the floating-point representation for that type of value, then the smaller of them is in effect treated as a zero.

The largest number which can be added to the floating-point representation value for 1.0 without changing the value to something other than 1.0 is called the *machine accuracy*. Almost any arithmetic operation on floating-point values can introduce fractional errors of at least the machine accuracy. This is often called *roundoff error.*

Roundoff errors can be considerably greater than the machine accuracy. The most serious roundoff errors are often introduced when quantities of very different magnitudes are subtracted. Knuth[Knuth, Donald E. 73b] gives the example of a hypothetical computer that works in eight digit decimal notation (rather than binary).

The computation

```
(11111113 - 11111111) + 7.511111
```

on such a computer produces the value 9.5111111, while the mathematically equivalent computation

```
11111113 +   ( 7.511111 - 11111111)
```

produces the result 10.000000.

One of the important consequences of the roundoff error introduced by floating-point arithmetic is that you almost never want to test two computed floating-point values for equality. For example, on many computers the following program will produce a loop that never terminates:

```
/* test for inequality in floating-point arithmetic */

#include <stdio.h>

main()

{
  float a, c;
  c = 0.0;
  a = 0.0;

  while( a !=  10.0) {    /* loops forever */
    c = c+a;
    a = a + .2;
  }
  printf("Value of c = %f\n", c);
}
```

The intent of the programmer was to sum the values between 0 and 10 in increments of .2. However, since the value .2 cannot be represented exactly in a finite number of bits, roundoff errors in incrementing the variable **a** will accumulate, and **a** may never be exactly 10.0. Thus, the inequality test in the **while** loop will never be false, and the program will loop forever.

The appropriate way to code this program is to have the loop continue while **a < 10.00**. More generally, loops that must terminate on some condition that involves comparisons of floating-point numbers should check if the floating-point values are *nearly* identical, that is, whether they are within some reasonably small value of each other. This "reasonably small value" must be chosen to be small enough so that the condition is not incorrectly met and large enough to be meaningful when compared to the machine accuracy.

All of the discussion of floating-point arithmetic above should serve as a warning to anyone intending to do serious numerical analysis on a computer. The issues are not merely ones of technical interest. Failure to account for the fact that floating-point arithmetic always introduces errors can produce results that are completely misleading. The reader should approach any use of floating-point arithmetic with some caution.

3.2.4 Header file float.h

The ANSI C standard specifies that a header file named **float.h** must be provided in every implementation. This file defines constants which reflect the characteristics of that machine's floating-point arithmetic. Entries in this file include items such as the largest and smallest representable **float** and **double** and the number of significant digits in the floating-point types.

The most widely used values defined in **float.h** are given in the following table.

SOME ITEMS IN FLOAT.H

Name	Meaning
FLT_DIG	number of decimal digits of precision for **float**
DBL_DIG	number of decimal digits of precision for **double**
FLT_EPSILON	machine precision for **float**
DBL_EPSILON	machine precision for **double**
FLT_MAX	maximum **float**
DBL_MAX	maximum **double**
FLT_MIN	minimum positive **float** (other than zero)
DBL_MIN	minimum positive **double** (other than zero)

The ANSI C standard also gives minimum and maximum allowed values for all of the constants above. These values are given in the following table.

REQUIRED VALUES IN FLOAT.H

Name	Requirement
FLT_DIG	6 or greater
DBL_DIG	10 or greater
FLT_EPSILON	10^{-5} or smaller
DBL_EPSILON	10^{-9} or smaller
FLT_MAX	10^{37} or greater
DBL_MAX	10^{37} or greater
FLT_MIN	10^{-37} or smaller
DBL_MIN	10^{-37} or smaller

The values in `float.h` can be used to test for possible overflow before it occurs. For example, we might want to read floating-point values known to be positive into a **double** and test the magnitude of the **double** before assigning it to a **float**. The following fragment illustrates this:

```
/* fragment using values in float.h */

#include <stdio.h>
#include <float.h>

double temp;
float value;

scanf("%lf", &temp);
if(temp > FLT_MAX || temp < FLT_MIN)
  printf("Unable to assign value to float \n");
else
  value=temp;
```

The reader is referred to [American National Standards Institute 88] for further details on the contents of the header file `float.h`.

3.3 THE STANDARD C MATHEMATICAL FUNCTION LIBRARY

In Chapter 2 we introduced the standard C input and output library and noted that almost all C programs use the preprocessor directive

```
#include <stdio.h>
```

which includes the standard header file for this library in the program. C also provides other libraries for the programmer, including one that provides a set of mathematical functions that are commonly used by engineers and scientists. These functions are carefully constructed by professional programmers to be as accurate and efficient as possible. C programs that use these functions should have the preprocessor directive

```
#include <math.h>
```

in the code.

The reader should be aware that unlike the standard C library, the C mathematical functions are usually not automatically linked into a compiled program. The programmer must generally tell the compiler which libraries of functions (other than the standard set) he or she is using. There is no C language standard for how this is done, but in most C compilers the command that invokes the compiler has an option of the form

-l (the **l** is a lowercase letter 'el'). This option is followed by an abbreviation for the particular library. For the mathematical function library, the usual command line option is the form **-lm**.

The ANSI standard for the the C language specifies that the functions listed in the following table should be available in the mathematical library. The table lists only a subset of the mathematical functions provided in C. (The complete list is given in the appendix.) All of these functions return a value of type **double**. The returned value is generally the result of evaluating a mathematical function. For example, the C function **cos(x)** returns a **double** which is the cosine of its argument **x**.

MATH FUNCTION LIBRARY

Function	Arguments	Value Returned by Function
acos()	double x	arc cosine
asin()	double x	arc sine
atan()	double x	arc tangent
atan2()	double y, double x	arc tangent of y/x
ceil()	double x	smallest **double** >= **x** that can be represented as an **int**
cos()	double x	cosine
cosh()	double x	hyperbolic cosine
exp()	double x	exponential function
fabs()	double x	absolute value
floor()	double x	largest **double** <= **x** that can be represented as an **int**
ldexp()	double x, int n	computes $x*2^n$
log()	double x	natural logarithm
log10()	double x	logarithm base 10
pow()	double x, double y	x^y
sin()	double x	sine
sinh()	double x	hyperbolic sine
sqrt()	double x	square root
tan()	double x	tangent
tanh()	double x	hyperbolic tangent

All of the trigonometric functions in the C math library use radians to measure angles. Similarly, the arc cosine, arc sine, and arc tangent functions all return angles measured in radians. The arc cosine returns a value between 0 and π. The arc sine and arc tangent functions both return values between $-\pi/2$ and $\pi/2$.

The function **atan2()** uses the signs of its two arguments to determine the quadrant for the arc tangent of **y/x**. It returns a value in radians between $-\pi$ and π.

The math library functions can generate two types of errors. For example, the arc sine and arc cosine functions cannot be evaluated meaningfully when their arguments are greater than 1 or less than -1. Cases such as this where the arguments to a function are inappropriate are said to produce a *domain* error. The other possible error type is where the value to be returned is too large in absolute value to be represented in a **double**. This is called a *range* error.

Errors from library routines are signaled in C through a special variable named **errno**.[1] This **int** is an external, global value which is defined in the header file **errno.h**. Library routines set the value of **errno** to one of a list of predefined error codes whenever an error is found. Each error code is some positive value.

For example, the following fragment of C code uses the error detection capability to determine whether the result of computing x^y produced an overflow error.

```
/* fragment of code showing detection of errors
        in math library functions */

#include <stdio.h>
#include <math.h>
#include <errno.h>

double x,y,z;

errno = 0;   /* set value of errno */

x = 5.0;      /* set values of x and y */
y = 100.0;

z= pow(x,y);   /* compute x to the y power */

if(errno != 0)   /* check if error found */
   printf("Error in computing %lf to the %lf\n",
               x, y);
```

In this code fragment, the three **#include** statements include the standard header file, the math library header file, and the error header file. The math library function **pow()** for computing x^y is invoked and the value of the variable **errno** is checked to determine if an error was encountered. The reader should be aware that the value of **errno** is not automatically reset to zero when a library routine is called. It is up to the programmer to reset **errno**.

In order to make a determination of the source of an error easier, the header file **errno.h** has a series of **#define** statements that give names to various integer values. The two names **EDOM** and **ERANGE** correspond to domain and range errors.

---

[1]Technically, the value **errno** may not actually be a C variable. It may be the result of a **#define** preprocessor directive which expands into an integer value which can be used on the left-hand side of an assignment statement.

Thus, the fragment above could be rewritten to be clearer about the nature of the error encountered as follows:

```
/* fragment of code showing detection of errors
      in math library functions */

#include <stdio.h>
#include <math.h>
#include <errno.h>

double x,y,z;

errno = 0;   /* set value of errno */

x = 5.0;      /* set values of x and y */

y = 100.0;

z= pow(x,y);   /* compute x to the y power */

if(errno == EDOM)   /* check  for domain error */
   printf("Domain error in computing %lf to the %lf\n",
                x,  y);

else if(errno == ERANGE) /* check for range error */
   printf("Range error in computing %lf to the %lf\n",
                x,  y);
```

3.4 POINTERS TO FUNCTIONS

All of the algorithms we present in this section have as one of their arguments a function. C provides a mechanism for using functions as arguments. The central idea behind this concept is that a *pointer to a function* is a valid variable type.

At first, the idea of passing a function as an argument may seem strange. However, imagine that we wanted to code a C function that computed a sum of terms, where each term was the value of a function evaluated at a different point. If we had to compute many such sums, it would be handy to have a single function that summed *any* set of terms. We could then pass the function that computes the specific terms of any series to the more general summation function as an argument.

For example, suppose that we wanted to compute the values of the following three series:

$$x^{.1} + x^{1.1} + x^{2.1} + x^{3.1} + \cdots + x^{14.1}$$
$$x^{1.5} + x^{2.5} + x^{3.5} + \cdots + x^{12.5}$$
$$x^{5.25} + x^{6.25} + x^{7.25} + \cdots + x^{9.25}$$

One could code a function for each of these summations, but this would require a new function for every new series encountered. A better alternative would be to code a general-purpose program that computed the value of any series of the form

$$\sum_{i=a}^{b} f(x, i)$$

Once such a function was written, you could write a small function for each $f(x, i)$ and pass this new function to the more general procedure as an argument. In the three series given above, the terms have the forms $x^{i+0.1}$, $x^{i+0.5}$, and $x^{i+0.25}$, respectively.

Several examples will serve to demonstrate how pointers to functions are declared as arguments. Consider, for example, an argument **f** which is a function that has a **double** and an **int** as arguments and returns a **double**. This function might evaluate a single term in a series such as $x^{i+0.1}$. It would have two arguments: the values of x (in a **double**) and i (in an **int**). If this function is an argument to some other function, it would be declared in that other function's prototype as follows:

```
double (*f) (double, int)
```

Note the use of the parentheses in (***f**) ( ). This is because the declaration

```
double *f(double, int)
```

declares **f**() to be a function that returns a *pointer to a* **double** rather than a pointer to a function that returns a **double**. The parentheses denoting a function have higher precedence than the *****. The use of the first pair of the parentheses in (***f**) ( ) overrides the normal order of precedence.

With this in mind, we can write our general-purpose routine that sums a series of terms as follows:

```
/* general-purpose summation routine */

double summation(
     double x,                        /* value of x */
     double (*f)(double, int),  /* function for individual
                                                        terms */
     int a,                             /* initial index for sum */
     int b)                             /* final index for sum */
{
  double sum;

  for(sum = 0.0; a <= b; a=a+1)
    sum = sum + f(x, a);
  return(sum);
}
```

In this function, the argument **f** is used just as any other function. Any C variable which is a pointer to a function can be used to invoke the function it points to. In fact, the name of a function can be thought of as a pointer to that function. When we want to invoke that function, we follow the name by an argument list in parentheses.

The function prototype for **summation()** would be as follows:

```
double summation(double,double (*)(double,int),int,int);
```

We would use the function **summation()** as follows:

```
\* example of program using summation */

#include <stdio.h> /* I/O header file */
#include <math.h>  /* math header file */
double summation(double,double (*)(double,int),int,int);
double f1(double,int), f2(double,int), f3(double,int);

main()
{
  double total,x;

  printf("Enter value of x for series:");
  scanf("%lf", &x);

  total = summation(x, f1, 0, 14);
  printf("First series sum is %lf\n", total);

  total = summation(x, f2, 1, 12);
  printf("Second series sum is %lf\n", total);

  total = summation(x, f3, 5, 9);
  printf("Third series sum is %lf\n", total);

}


/* terms for first series */

double f1(double x, int i)
{
  return( pow(x, i+.1));
}


/* terms for second series */

double f2(double x, int i)
{
```

```
    return( pow(x, i+.5));
}


/* terms for third series */

double f3(double x, int i)
{
    return( pow(x, i+.25));
}
```

This example uses the standard C mathematical library function **pow()**. This function has two **double**s as its arguments. **pow(x,y)** computes x^y.

The ability to pass pointers to functions makes it possible to code general-purpose libraries of functions that solve a range of problems. This avoids the need to recode complicated procedures to customize them to work with different functions. We will see the usefulness of this in the following sections.

3.5 ROOT FINDING

One common problem encountered in many forms of mathematical analysis is finding the roots of some equation. For example, consider the equation

$$x^4 - 8x^3 + 22x^2 - 24x + 9 = 0$$

The values of x which satisfy this equation are called its *roots*. This equation can have as many as four real roots. While some equations (such as this one) can be solved analytically, many important ones can only be solved using numerical methods.

Root-finding problems arise in many contexts. For example, in predicting how many people might use a particular highway, transportation analysts often assume that there is both a demand for travel and an ability of the highway facility to supply transportation services.

The demand for travel depends on the average travel time. This demand might be represented by the function $V = D(t)$, where t is the travel time on the facility and V is the number of users. As the time required to travel on the highway increases, the demand for it decreases.

The travel time on the facility in turn depends on the demand for its use. As more people try to use the highway, congestion builds up, increasing the travel time. This relationship can be represented by the function $t = S(V)$.

The problem of finding the travel time and volume of users on the highway can be reduced to a root-finding problem by noting that the demand relationship can usually be inverted, expressing time as a function of volume. We denote this as $t = D^{-1}(V)$.[2]

---

[2] The notation $D^{-1}(V)$ should not be confused with $1/D(V)$. It represents the transformation of the function from V as a function of t to an equivalent form where t is a function of V.

The value of V which satisfies both the inverse of the demand function and $S(V)$ is the root of the equation

$$D^{-1}(V) - S(V) = 0$$

Figure 3.2a and b illustrate the two functions and their difference. The root of $D^{-1}(V) - S(V)$ is also shown.

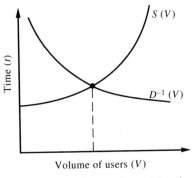

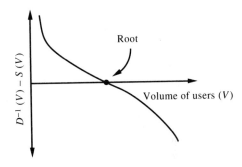

(a) Supply and inverse demand functions

(b) Difference between inverse demand and supply function

Figure 3.2

This example is a specific case of the more general problem of solving for a point where two functions intersect. If $f_1(x)$ and $f_2(x)$ are two functions, then the root of $f_1(x) - f_2(x)$ will be a value of x at which the functions intersect.

Some of the most useful root-finding methods are described in this section. We restrict our attention to solving for real roots rather than complex roots. Also, while all of the methods we discuss generalize to multivariate functions, our presentation is limited to single-variable equations.

Root-finding methods all share some common characteristics. In particular, the methods we will examine share the following:

1. They all require either a known interval $[x_1, x_2]$ in which a root is to be searched for or some initial starting value of x_0 from which a search is to begin.
2. None of the methods are guaranteed to find *all* the real roots of an equation. Instead, they find at most one root.
3. If they succeed in finding a root, they do so only approximately. The approximate nature of the solution is only in part because they rely on floating-point arithmetic. Another reason is that the methods are intrinsically iterative, converging upon a solution step by step. Even on a computer with infinite precision, the methods would not reach the true root in a finite number of steps.

Despite these limitations, numerical root-finding methods are often the only feasible means of solving many real-world problems.

3.5.1 Finding an Interval Containing a Root

Many of the algorithms that find a root of an equation require as one of their arguments an interval that contains a root. A simple algorithm for finding an interval that contains a root of a function $f(x)$ exploits the fact that any interval $[x_1, x_2]$ where

$$f(x_1) \cdot f(x_2) \leq 0$$

must contain at least one root. In fact, such an interval must contain an odd number of roots. To find such an interval, we take a broad range of x, divide it into subranges, and search for an interval that satisfies the condition above. A C function named `find_interval()` that does this search requires the following arguments:

f — a pointer to the function for which an interval containing a root is to be found.

xstart and **xend** — the starting and ending values of x defining the interval over which a search for an interval containing a root is to be done.

stepsize — the size of the intervals to be tested.

xleft and **xright** — pointers to variables of type **double** that point to the beginning and end of an interval containing a root.

The values **xleft** and **xright** must be pointers because `find_interval()` must be able to change the values of the interval in the function that calls it. If the arguments **xleft** and **xright** were simply **doubles**, then `find_interval()` would only be able to change copies of these arguments.

The function `find_interval()` returns an integer which is set to 1 if an interval that contains a root was found, and zero otherwise. The values 1 and 0 are chosen because they can be used as indicators in a logical expression. (Recall that logical expressions in C evaluate to 0 if they are false and to 1 if they are true.)

The implementation of `find_interval()` is as follows:

```
/* function to find an interval containing a root */

#define TRUE 1
#define FALSE 0

int find_interval(
   double (*f)(double),    /* function */
   double xstart,          /* start of search */
   double xend,            /* end of search */
   double stepsize,        /* interval of search */
   double  *xleft,         /* pointer to  left
                              of found interval */
   double *xright)         /* pointer to right
                              of found interval */
```

```
{
    int found_root = TRUE; /* initialize indicator */

    /* initialize interval */
    *xleft = xstart;
    *xright = *xleft + stepsize;

    /* search interval */
    while (*xleft < xend && f(*xleft) * f(*xright)>0.0) {
        *xleft = *xright;
        *xright += stepsize;
        if(*xright > xend)  *xright = xend;
    }

    /* check if root found */
    if(f(*xleft) * f(*xright)> 0.0)
        found_root = FALSE;

    return(found_root);
}
```

This implementation of **find_interval()** assumes that the value of **stepsize** is less than or equal to **xend-xstart**. It is coded to avoid attempting to evaluate the function **f()** outside the range of the initial interval. This is to avoid the possibility that the function is not defined for values of x smaller than **xstart** or larger than **xend**.

A typical use of **find_interval()** to find an interval between -10 and 10 in which the function

$$f(x) = x^3 - 4x^2 - 4x + 15$$

contains a root would be as follows:

```
/* program that uses find_interval() */

#include <stdio.h>
main()
{
    double polycubic(double);
    int find_interval(double (*f)(double), double, double,
                        double, double *, double *);
    double x1, x2;

    if(find_interval(polycubic, -10.0, 10.0,
                    0.1, &x1, &x2))
        printf("Interval is %lf to %lf\n", x1, x2);
    else
        printf("No interval was found\n");
}
```

```
/* function whose root to find */
double polycubic(double x)
{
   return(x*x*x - 4*x*x - 4*x + 15);
}
```

Note that the algorithm above finds only the first interval containing the root and may fail to find an interval if an even number of roots are sufficiently close to one another. The first shortcoming can be alleviated by applying the function `find_interval()` again after a first interval is found, searching from the end of the first interval. The second shortcoming is intrinsic to the algorithm and cannot be eliminated entirely. Plotting the function and knowing its mathematical properties can often provide clues to intervals where roots must lie.

3.5.2 Bisection Method

Assuming that an interval containing a root has been found, the most straightforward approach to root finding is called *bisection*. This method searches over a given interval known to contain at least one root and successively halves that interval, restricting the search to the half known to contain the root. This successive halving converges to a very small interval in which a root must lie. The algorithm terminates when the interval is "small enough" by some criterion. What constitutes an interval which is small enough should be controlled by the user of the algorithm. However, it makes no sense to attempt to use bisection to obtain an interval which, as a fraction of the initial interval, is smaller than the machine accuracy.

Bisection is a classic example of a computational strategy often referred to as *divide and conquer*. The initial interval $[a, b]$ is successively halved, implying that at the nth iteration the size of the interval is $(b - a)/2^n$. Such algorithms converge very quickly to intervals that are small. If the floating-point representation of a **double** has d significant digits in binary form, then bisection will never require more than d iterations to converge to an interval that, as a fraction of $(b - a)$, is as small as the machine accuracy.

Bisection can be implemented either recursively or iteratively. The iterative implementation is as follows:

```
/* bisection method */
#include <math.h>
double bisect(
   double (*f)(double), /* function */
   double x1, /* start of interval */
   double x2, /* end of interval */
   double epsilon) /* convergence tolerance */
{
   double y;
   for(y=(x1+x2)/2.0; fabs(x1-y)>epsilon; y=(x1+x2)/2.0)
```

```
      if(f(x1)*f(y)<= 0.0)
          x2 = y; /* use left subinterval */
      else
          x1 = y; /* use right subinterval */
   return(y);
}
```

The function **fabs()** is a standard C mathematical library function. It takes a single argument of type **double** and returns a **double** which is the absolute value of the original argument. The prototype for **fabs()** is part of the header file **math.h**.

The recursive implementation of bisection is as follows:

```
/* recursive version of bisection */
#include <math.h>

double rbisect(
   double (*f)(double), /* function */
   double x1,          /* start of interval */
   double x2,          /* end of interval */
   double epsilon)     /* tolerance */
{
   double y;

   y = (x1+x2)/2.0;
   if( fabs(x1-y) > epsilon) /* check for convergence */
      if(f(x1)*f(y) <=0)
         y = rbisect(f,x1,y,epsilon);/* use left side */
      else
         y = rbisect(f,y,x2,epsilon);/* use right side */
   return(y);
}
```

In actual practice, the iterative version would be used because it is somewhat more efficient and probably clearer to most users.

3.5.3 Secant Method

The *secant method* uses an entirely different approach to root finding than the bisection method. The algorithm works by fitting a straight line between the points $(x_1, f(x_1))$ and $(x_2, f(x_2))$. It then finds x^*, the root of the straight line. If the result is sufficiently close to x_2, it returns that value as the root of the original equation. If not, it resets the value of x_1 to x_2 and x_2 to x^*, and tries the method again. This proceeds until a solution close to x_2 is found or some number of attempts to find a solution have failed.

Figure 3.3 shows a typical sequence of steps of the secant method. The points (x_1, y_1) and (x_2, y_2) are the starting points for the algorithm. The line drawn between these two points is the secant, and the point $(x_3, 0)$ is where the secant intersects the x

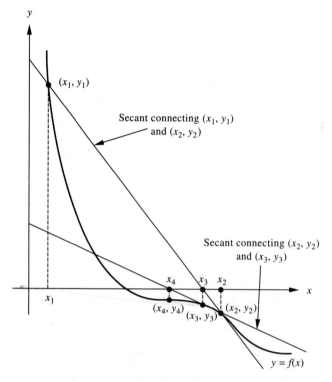

Figure 3.3 Secant method.

axis. The next step in the algorithm would use the line between (x_2, y_2) and (x_3, y_3) to define the next secant, producing the value x_4 as the next estimate of the root. The algorithm proceeds in this fashion until either the convergence criterion is satisfied or some upper limit on the number of iterations is reached.

Implemented in C, the algorithm is as follows:

```c
/* implementation of the secant method */
#include <math.h>
#define TRUE 1
#define FALSE 0


double secant(
  double (*f)(double),    /* function to find root of */
  double x1,              /* start of interval */
  double x2,              /* end of interval */
  double epsilon,         /* tolerance */
  int max_tries,          /* maximum number of tries */
  int *found_flag)        /* pointer to flag indicating
                                            success */
  {
```

```
int count = 0;          /* counter of loops */
double root = x1;       /* root value */
*found_flag = TRUE;     /* initialize flag to success */

while(fabs(x2-x1)>epsilon && count<max_tries) {
  root = x1 - f(x1)*(x2-x1)/(f(x2)-f(x1));
  x1=x2;
  x2 = root;
  count = count + 1;
}

if(fabs(x2-x1) > epsilon)/* check for convergence */
  *found_flag = FALSE;

return(root);           /* return root */

}
```

In this implementation, the value **found_flag** is a pointer to an integer which is set to **TRUE** (defined as 1) if the algorithm succeeds in finding a root and **FALSE** (defined as 0) if the maximum number of tries is reached without finding a root.

There are a number of shortcomings of the secant method. First, any iteration of the algorithm can result in a value that lies outside the initial interval. This is not true for the bisection method. In addition, there is no way for the algorithm to detect that it will fail to find a root. The implementation above uses a counter for the maximum number of allowed iterations to prevent the function from looping forever. This, however, is an entirely *ad hoc* way of dealing with the algorithm's shortcomings. Finally, the algorithm may encounter significant problems with overflow when the magnitude of **f(x2) – f(x1)** gets very small. This is because the solution for the root of the secant requires division of **f(x1) * (x2 -x1)** by **f(x2) - f(x1)**.

For all these reasons, the secant method is not widely used in practice.

3.5.4 Newton's Method

Unlike bisection and the secant method, Newton's method does not require an initial interval. Instead, it begins the search for a root with some initial guess. It then fits a tangent to $f(x)$ through the guess and finds the root of the tangent. This then becomes the next guess. This process continues until the difference between the guess and the root of the tangent line is small.

Newton's method uses the derivative of $f(x)$ to find the slope of the tangent line. Thus, it requires two functions as inputs: the original function $f(x)$ and the derivative of $f(x)$, which we will denote as $f'(x)$. Each iteration of Newton's method is simply

$$x_{n+1} = x_n - \frac{f(x_n)}{f'(x_n)}$$

Figure 3.4 illustrates two steps in Newton's method. The value x_0 is the initial value for x. The line tangent to $f(x)$ through the point (x_0, y_0) is used to find the value x_1 where the tangent crosses the x axis. This value is then used to fit the tangent to $f(x)$ through the point (x_1, y_1) to find the point x_2. The algorithm continues in this fashion until it converges to the root of $f(x)$.

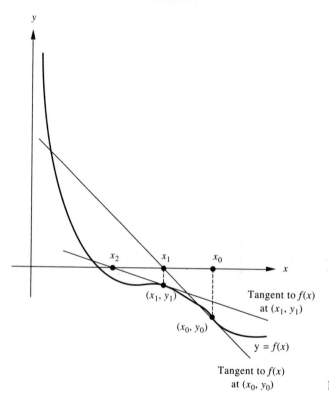

Figure 3.4 Newton's method.

A careful implementation of Newton's method must deal with the possibility that $f'(x_n)$ will be so small that the ratio $f(x_n)/f'(x_n)$ will result in a floating-point overflow. When this occurs, execution should not continue; it should terminate and signal that an error has occurred. In the following C function, the argument **dmin** is the minimum value of $f'(x)$ that will be allowed and the pointer argument **error** is used to change an error indicator in the calling function. The C implementation is as follows:

```
/* implementation of Newton's method */

#include <math.h>
#define TRUE 1
#define FALSE 0

double newton(
   double (*f)(double),        /* function */
```

```
  double (*fprime)(double),/* derivative of f */
  double dmin,              /* minimum allowed value of
                                                    fprime */
  double x0,          /* initial guess of solution */
  double epsilon,     /* convergence tolerance */
  int *error)         /* pointer to error indicator */
{
  double deltax;
  deltax = 2.0 * epsilon; /*initialize deltax>epsilon */
  *error = FALSE;         /* initialize error indicator */

  while( !(*error) && fabs(deltax) > epsilon)
    if(fabs(fprime(x0)) >dmin)   {
      deltax = f(x0)/fprime(x0);
      x0 = x0 - deltax;
    }
    else
      *error = TRUE;

  return(x0);
}
```

The function **newton()** above has pointers to functions as its first two arguments. They are used for the functions $f(x)$ and $f'(x)$. The remaining arguments are the minimum allowed derivative value, the starting value x_o, and the convergence tolerance and a pointer to an error indicator. A typical use of **newton()** would be as follows:

```
/* program that uses Newton's method  */
#include <stdio.h>

double polycubic(double);
double  dpolycubic(double);
double newton (double (*)(double), double (*)(double),
               double, double, double, int * );

main()
{
  double root;
  int flag;

  root = newton(polycubic,dpolycubic,10e-30,-1.9,
                0.00001,&flag);
  if(flag)
       printf("Error found in Newton's method\n");
  else
       printf("Value of root is %lf\n", root);
}
```

```
/* function f(x) */
double polycubic(double x)
{
   return(x*x*x - 4*x*x - 4*x + 15);
}

/* derivative of f(x) */
double dpolycubic(double x)
{
   return(3*x*x - 8*x - 4);
}
```

For many problems, Newton's method converges to a root quite quickly. When the method fails to find a root it is often because $f'(x)$ is too small. In such cases it is often possible to select a different initial starting value for which the method will converge to a solution. Newton's method also has the advantage of not requiring an interval containing a root as an input.

3.5.5 Problems In Applying Root Finding Methods

In applying root-finding methods, it is not unusual to encounter a variety of problems reaching convergence on a true root. These difficulties arise from many sources, including the problems of overflow, underflow, and loss of precision in floating-point operations. Such problems are often eliminated simply by selecting a different starting value of x or a different starting interval. However, there are other potential pitfalls in root finding the reader should be aware of.

One problem with the secant and Newton's method as we have presented them is the possibility of *false convergence*. The measure of convergence we have used to test whether the algorithms have reached a root examines the change in the x value between successive iterations. It is possible for this change to be very small even though the value of x is far from a root of the function. Figure 3.5 illustrates how this might occur graphically in the secant method. The points on the x axis labeled x_{i-1} and x_i are the starting values for the secant algorithm. When these two points are used in an iteration of the secant method, they produce the point labeled x_{i+1} as the next estimate of the root. The difference between the endpoint of the initial interval, x_i, and the next estimate of the root, x_{i+1}, is very small in this figure, so the algorithm as coded could terminate. However, when the function $f(x)$ is evaluated, it is clear that neither x_i nor x_{i+1} is even close to a root of the equation.

The solution to this potential problem is that after root-finding algorithms converge in the sense of producing very small changes in the value of x between successive iterations, you should conduct a second check to determine whether the value returned by the algorithm is in fact a root. This check is straightforward; you evaluate $f(x)$ at the value returned and see if by some measure, $f(x)$ is "close to" zero. The exact test as to what constitutes a value of $f(x)$ close to zero depends on the problem at hand.

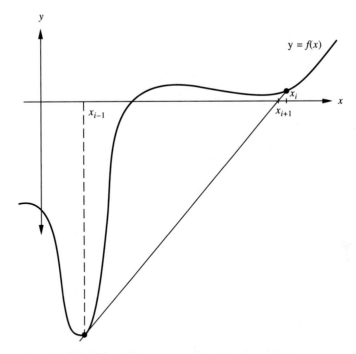

Figure 3.5 False convergence in secant method.

A second potential problem is called *cycling.* This occurs when a series of iterations results in a pattern of values of x which repeats itself. Consider as an example the function

$$f(x) = \frac{1}{1 + e^x} - \frac{1}{2}$$

shown in Figure 3.6.

One way Newton's method can cycle when finding the root of this function is for it to oscillate between two values of x on either side of the y axis. For the function shown in Figure 3.6, this type of oscillation will occur for two particular starting values of x_0. The specific values that produce this oscillation are those for which the change in x in one iteration of Newton's method generates a value x_1 exactly equal to $-x_0$. The symmetry of the function around the y axis will guarantee that if x_1 is $-x_0$, then the next value, x_2, will be exactly equal to x_0, producing a complete cycle.

Figure 3.7 shows graphically how Newton's method can cycle. If the point on the x axis labeled x_n is a trial point, then the next iteration of Newton's method will fit a tangent to the function through the point $(x_n, f(x_n))$, producing the point labeled x_{n+1} as the next estimate of the root. The tangent to the function through the point $(x_{n+1}, f(x_{n+1}))$ in turn produces the next estimate of the root as x_n, completing the cycle.

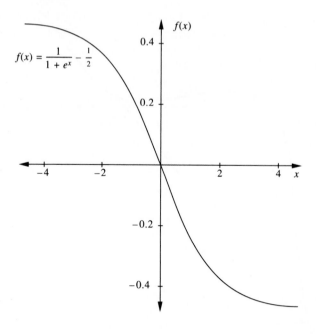

$$f(x) = \frac{1}{1 + e^x} - \frac{1}{2}$$

Figure 3.6 Example function for cycling.

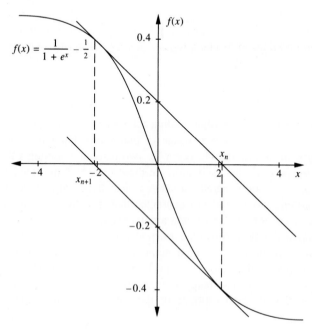

$$f(x) = \frac{1}{1 + e^x} - \frac{1}{2}$$

Figure 3.7 Cycling in Newton's method.

We can find the points that produce cycling of Newton's method for a symmetric function such as shown in Figure 3.6 by noting that each iteration of Newton's method is found with the equation

$$x_{n+1} = x_n - \frac{f(x_n)}{f'(x_n)}$$

A value of x such that

$$x_n = -x_{n+1}$$

will satisfy the equation

$$-x_n = x_n - \frac{f(x_n)}{f'(x_n)}$$

or, letting $x = x_n$,

$$2x - \frac{f(x)}{f'(x)} = 0$$

For the equation depicted in Figure 3.6, the reader can verify that x must satisfy

$$2x - \frac{\dfrac{1}{1+e^x} - \dfrac{1}{2}}{\dfrac{-e^x}{(1+e^x)^2}}$$

While there is no analytic solution for the root of this equation, the values of x which solves the foregoing equation are approximately ± 2.177319.

Because of roundoff errors, actual cases of cycling generally take the form of very slow convergence of Newton's method. This can often be alleviated by selecting a different starting value for the algorithm.

3.6 PROGRAMMING PROJECT: ACCELERATION OF A TRAIN

As an example of an application of root-finding methods, we consider a rail rapid transit train which is operating under automatic control. The train is assumed to have a speed governor which limits it to a top speed of 85 kilometers per hour. We will use the bisection method to determine to the closest second how long after the train leaves the station it will attain its top speed.

The train leaves a station at time $t = 0$ seconds and is assumed to accelerate to some maximum velocity. The velocity of the train, $v(t)$, is assumed to be given by the following equation:

$$v(t) = 29.4 + .795t + \frac{1}{(1 - 1.034e^{0.0061667t})}$$

Figure 3.8 depicts the velocity profile determined by the equation above. The x axis is in seconds and the y axis is in kilometers per hour. It is apparent from the figure that the speed limit of 85 kilometers per hour will be attained before 100 seconds has elapsed.

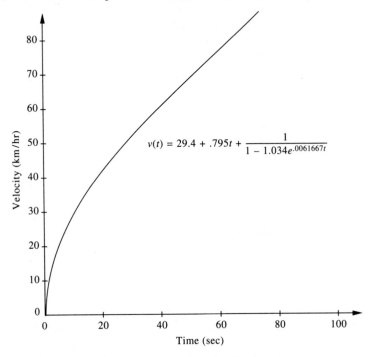

$$v(t) = 29.4 + .795t + \frac{1}{1 - 1.034e^{.0061667t}}$$

Figure 3.8 Velocity of train vs. time in seconds.

The program that solves this problem begins with the following preprocessor directives and function prototypes:

```
#include <stdio.h>
#include <math.h>


/* function prototypes */
double velocity(double), func(double);
double bisect(double (*)(double), double,
              double, double);

#define TOLERANCE .00001 /* tolerance for convergence */
#define CLOSE   .001      /* check if root found */
```

The symbols **TOLERANCE** and **CLOSE** are defined for use later in the program. **TOLERANCE** is the tolerance value used in the bisection method to determine whether the change in the estimate of the root is small between iterations. The value **CLOSE** will be used to test whether the value returned by **bisect()** is "close enough" to zero to be acceptable as a root.

The function **velocity()** is a C version of the function describing the velocity of the train over time. The function **func()** is a C implementation of $85 - v(t)$. The computation of the train's velocity could be integrated into the implementation of **func()** to reduce both the amount of code and the computational time. We leave them separate here for clarity.

The function **bisect()** is the root-finding function given in Section 3.5.2. This code is not reproduced here. We assume that the code for the function **bisect()** is in the same source code file as our code below.

The remainder of the program is the code for the functions **main()**, **velocity()**, and **func()**.

```
/* main function for train acceleration problem */

main()
{
  double root;

  root = bisect(func,  0.0, 100.0, TOLERANCE);

  if(fabs(func(root)) < CLOSE)
    printf("Max speed reached in %7.01f secs.\n",
            floor(root+.5));
  else

    printf("Value %1f not close to root.\n", root);
}

/* compute velocity as function of time */

double velocity(double t)
{

  return(29.4+.795*t+1.0/(1.0-1.034*exp(.0061667*t)));
}

/* function computes 85 minus  velocity of train  */

double func(double t)
{
  return(85.0-velocity(t));
}
```

Note that after we invoke **bisect()** from **main()** we check whether the value **root** returned is in fact within **CLOSE** of a true root. This is to avoid the possibility of false convergence in the root-finding method.

We also use the math library function **floor()** to round off the value of **root** to the nearest integer. The expression **floor(root+.5)** adds one half to **root** and then finds the largest **double** which is less than **root+.5** and is representable as an integer. This has the effect of rounding **root** to the nearest integer.

The result output by this program is that, to the nearest second, the maximum speed is reached in 72 seconds. The bisection method finds a true root (or more accurately, a value close enough to the true root) for this case.

3.7 NUMERICAL INTEGRATION

A second type of commonly encountered mathematical problem is solving for the value of some definite integral. In most calculus courses, students are taught a range of analytic methods for solving integrals. However, there are many integrals which are inherently unsolvable. In the introduction to this chapter, we discussed the fact that the integral of the normal (or Gaussian) distribution has no closed-form, analytic solution. Stated somewhat more formally, the value of the integral

$$\int_a^b \frac{1}{\sqrt{2\pi}} e^{-x^2/2} \, dx$$

has no closed-form solution. Numerical methods are used to evaluate this integral for specific values of a and b.

3.7.1 Rectangular Rule

The simplest numerical integration technique is called the *rectangular* method. The x axis is divided into n equal segments in the interval $[a, b]$, creating a series of panels as shown in Figure 3.9a. The area under the function $f(x)$ is approximated by the sum of the areas of the rectangles, the heights of which are either the left sides or the right sides of the panels. Figure 3.9b and c depict the areas for the left- and right-side rules, respectively. Clearly, the use of the two different sides will produce different approximations for the integrals.

The rectangular method is rarely used in practice because alternative approaches that are considerably more accurate involve only a little more complexity. For this reason, we will not show the implementation of the rectangular method in C.

3.7.2 Trapezoidal Rule

One way to improve on the rectangular method for solving integrals numerically is to divide the x axis into n equal intervals and to approximate the area under the function as the sum of the areas of trapezoids. Not surprisingly, this technique is called the

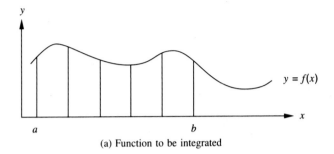

(a) Function to be integrated

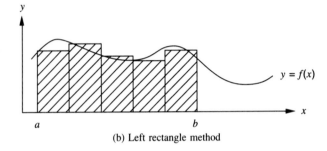

(b) Left rectangle method

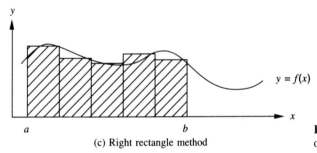

(c) Right rectangle method

Figure 3.9 Graphical interpretation of the rectangle method.

trapezoidal method. The trapezoidal method requires almost the same computation as the rectangular method and for a fixed number of subdivisions of the x axis yields more accurate approximations. Figure 3.10 depicts the approximate areas computed with this method.

The reader can verify that the trapezoidal method is equivalent to averaging the results from two versions of the rectangular method, one using the right side of each panel to determine the height of the rectangle and the other using the left side. However, computing the trapezoidal approximation this way is extremely inefficient because it

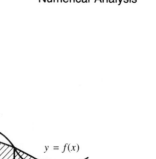

Figure 3.10 Graphical interpretation of the trapezoidal method.

requires many more calls to evaluate the function $f(x)$ than is needed. A more efficient implementation of the trapezoidal rule in C is as follows:

```
/* implementaton of trapezoidal method */
double trapezoidal(
   double (*f)(double),   /* function to be integrated */
   double a,              /* starting x */
   double b,              /* ending x   */
   int n)                 /* number of panels */
{
   double answer, h;      /* result and panel width */
   int i;                 /* counter for intervals */

   answer = f(a)/2;
   h = (b-a)/n;

   /* sum panel areas */
   for(i=1; i<=n; i++)
     answer = answer + f(a+i*h);

   answer = answer - f(b)/2;
   return(h*answer);
}
```

The function prototype for **trapezoidal()** is

```
double trapezoidal(double (*)(double),
                   double, double, int);
```

In implementing the trapezoidal rule, the two endpoints a and b must be handled separately because they are used for computing the area under only one interval, while the other points $f(x+h)$, $f(x+2h)$, ..., $f(x+(n-1)h)$ are each used in approximating the area under two intervals. The function `trapezoidal()` deals with the endpoints by initializing `answer` to `f(a)/2` and subtracting `f(b)/2` from `answer` before it is multiplied by `h`.

3.7.3 Simpson's Rule

A considerable improvement over the trapezoidal rule can be achieved by approximating the function within each of the n intervals by some polynomial. When second-order polynomials are used, the resulting algorithm is called *Simpson's rule*.

If we define h as the width of each of the subdivisions on the x axis and apply Simpson's rule, then the area under the curve in the interval $(x, x + h)$ is approximated by

$$\frac{h}{6}\left[f(x) + 4f\left(x + \frac{h}{2}\right) + f(x + h)\right]$$

This mathematical result is used in the implementation of Simpson's rule given below.

```
/* implementation of Simpson's rule */
double simpson(
  double (*f)(double),   /* function to be integrated */
  double a,              /* starting x */
  double b,              /* ending x   */
  int n)                 /* number of panels */
{
  double answer, h;      /* result and panel width */
  double x;
  int i;

  answer = f(a);
  h = (b-a)/n;

/* sum panel areas */
  for(i=1; i<=n; i++) {
    x = a+i*h;
    answer = answer + 4*f(x-h/2) + 2*f(x);
  }
  answer = answer - f(b);
  return(h*answer/6);
}
```

It is possible to derive approximations that involve higher-order polynomials. However, unless the function $f(x)$ is particularly burdensome to compute, it is often simpler to increase the number of intervals rather than implement more complicated approximations.

3.7.4 Adaptive Integration

The methods described above all require the user to select a value for the number of intervals, n. This shortcoming can be alleviated by starting with a small number of intervals and successively doubling that number until the change in the approximated integral is small by some measure. This method relies on the hypothesis that the error in the integral approximation decreases as n increases. While this is not always true, it is a reasonable working hypothesis for most functions.

Below is a simple (but not particularly efficient) implementation of this procedure for Simpson's rule.

```
#include <math.h>
double new_simpson(
   double (*f)(double),    /* function to be integrated */
   double a,               /* starting x */
   double b,               /* ending x   */
   int n0,                 /* number of panels */
   double tolerance)       /* measure of convergence */

{
   double check= tolerance +1.0;
   double lowval, val;

   lowval = simpson(f, a, b, n0);
   while(check  > tolerance) {
      n0 = 2 * n0;
      val = simpson(f, a, b, n0);
      check = fabs((val-lowval)/val);
      lowval = val;
   }
   return(val);
}
```

A more serious shortcoming of the integration methods we have described is that they use the same interval width over the entire integral. A better procedure would be to use a wide interval on portions of the function that are nearly linear (when the trapezoidal rule is being used) or nearly quadratic (when Simpson's rule is being used), and smaller intervals for portions of the function that are more complicated. A technique which can do that is called *adaptive* because its adapts the interval width to the shape of the function. Adaptive methods offer the potential for reducing computation costs and increasing the accuracy of numerical methods. In this subsection we explore only the simplest forms of adaptation.

Our adaptive integration method begins with a small number of intervals. Define n_0 to be that initial number. It then uses a nonadaptive integration method to integrate the function with both n_0 intervals and $2n_0$ intervals. If the difference between the results of these two approximations is small, the algorithm returns the result using $2n_0$ intervals. If, however, the difference exceeds some tolerance, then the initial interval (a, b) is divided into two intervals of equal size. The adaptive method is then applied on both halves, and the results are added together.

This procedure is intrinsically recursive. Each half interval may be divided further depending on whether such subdivision is needed. Below is an implementation of this method that uses the function **simpson()**.

```
#include <math.h>
double adapt(
    double (*f)(double),    /* function to be integrated */
    double a,               /* starting x */
    double b,               /* ending x   */
    int n,                  /* number of panels */
    double tolerance)       /* measure of convergence */


{
    double val, check;
    val = simpson(f,a,b,2*n);

    check = fabs((simpson(f,a,b,n)-val)/val);
    if(check  > tolerance)
      val = adapt(f,a,(a+b)/2.0,n,tolerance) +
              adapt(f,(a+b)/2.0,b, n,tolerance);
    return(val);
}
```

3.7.5 Other Methods

All of the algorithms for numerical integration presented in this section are what are usually called *classical methods*. They rely on dividing the x axis in some regular way. There are other numerical integration algorithms called *quadrature methods*, that are beyond the scope of this book. The reader is referred to Press et al. [Press, William H. 88] for a detailed discussion of these widely used techniques. Another method, called *Monte Carlo integration*, is described in Chapter 8.

3.8 PROGRAMMING PROJECT: THE FRESNEL SINE INTEGRAL

A slightly modified form of the Fresnel sine integral is the function

$$f(x) = \int_{x=a}^{b} sin\left(\frac{\pi}{2}x^2\right) dx + 1$$

One way to view this function is as the area below the curve shown in Figure 3.11. This function cannot be integrated symbolically, so solution of its value for some particular interval $[a, b]$ requires numerical methods. In this section we explore how accurate various alternative approaches are in solving this integral for various intervals.

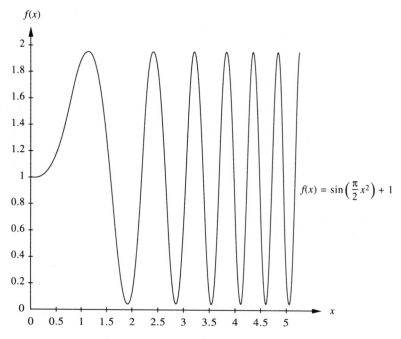

Figure 3.11   Fresnel sine integral as area under curve.

The Fresnel sine function is interesting because its curvature varies enormously for different intervals. In the interval $[0, 1]$, it is relatively flat, while in later intervals it is highly curved. This should result in simple integration methods working quite well for low values of a and b and working poorly for higher values.

In order to test the various integration methods introduced above, we will compute the integral of the Fresnel sine function for different intervals in different ways, using as a reference the value computed using Simpson's method with an extremely large number of intervals. In this case, we will use the integral computed with 10,000 intervals as the reference value. This will be compared with using the trapezoidal and Simpson's method with 10 intervals and using adaptive integration with 10 initial intervals and a tolerance of .0001 to determine whether to further subdivide an interval.

The program that performs this comparison is given below.

```c
#include <stdio.h>
#include <math.h>

/* #define directives */

#define TOL .0001
#define PI 3.14159

/* function prototypes for Fresnel
   and integration functions */

double fresnel(double);
double trapezoidal(double(*)(double),double,double,int);

double simpson( double(*)(double), double, double, int);
double adapt(double(*)(double), double,
             double, int, double);

/* main function */

main()
{
  double low;

/* output the labels */
  printf(" a    b  Trapezoidal   Simpson's      Adap");
  printf("tive     Reference\n");
  printf("--- --- ------------ ------------ ------");
  printf("------ ------------\n");

/* loop through unit intervals from 0 to 20 */
  for(low=0.0; low<20.0; low++)
    printf("%3.01f %3.01f %12.6g %12.6g %12.6g %12.6g\n",
           low, low+1.0,
           trapezoidal(fresnel, low, low+1, 10),
           simpson(fresnel, low, low+1, 10),
           adapt(fresnel, low, low+1, 10, TOL),
           simpson(fresnel, low, low+1, 10000));

}

/* compute function to be integrated */

double fresnel(double x)
{
  return(sin(PI/2.0*x*x)+1.0);
}
```

```
/* code for functions trapezoidal(), simpson(),
      and adapt() are omitted here */
```

The code begins with two **#include** directives for the standard and math header files. Function prototypes for the slightly modified Fresnel function and the three integration functions developed earlier are then given. This is followed by the **main()** function, which outputs the labels for a table using **printf()** statements and then loops through intervals of unit length from 0 through 20. Four different numerical approximations are computed for each interval; the results of these approximations are output using a **printf()** statement. The function **fresnel()** is used to evaluate the integrand.

Note that the control string in the **printf()** statements establish both field widths and the number of decimal places for the results. This is done to keep the output table organized. For example, the portion of the control string **%3.01f %3.01f** defines two fields each three characters wide. Each of these two fields is encoded to have no values after the decimal point. This has the effect of producing a truncated integer in the output. The other fields use **%12.6g** as their corresponding control strings. This implies fields that are twelve characters wide with six digits after the decimal point. The **g** field specification will ensure that **printf()** uses either **lf** or **e** format depending on the magnitude of the value being output. Note that the C code for the functions **trapezoidal()**, **simpson()**, and **adapt()** have not been repeated here.

The resulting output of this program is given below.

a	b	Trap.	Simpson's	Adaptive	Reference
0	1	1.43826	1.43826	1.43826	1.43826
1	2	0.910423	0.905149	0.905156	0.905157
2	3	1.14764	1.1529	1.1529	1.1529
3	4	0.934949	0.924135	0.9242	0.924204
4	5	1.06794	1.07874	1.07868	1.07867
5	6	0.96447	0.947518	0.947771	0.947771
6	7	1.03606	1.05299	1.05274	1.05274
7	8	0.98401	0.959849	0.96051	0.960512
8	9	1.01618	1.0403	1.03965	1.03964
9	10	1.00006	0.966832	0.968312	0.968313
10	11	1.00007	1.03321	1.03175	1.03175
11	12	1.01618	0.970491	0.973554	0.973555
12	13	0.984014	1.02949	1.02647	1.02647
13	14	1.03606	0.971057	0.977315	0.977315
14	15	0.964484	1.02879	1.0227	1.0227
15	16	1.06793	0.966563	0.980141	0.980142
16	17	0.934986	1.03248	1.01987	1.01987
17	18	1.1476	0.945541	0.982342	0.982344
18	19	0.91056	1.03509	1.01767	1.01766
19	20	1.43787	0.854051	0.984108	0.984107

As expected, the trapezoidal method works well when **a** and **b** are small but produces large errors for unit intervals with higher values of **a** and **b**. The adaptive method is accurate to at least five significant digits for all the intervals tested. Simpson's method works better than the trapezoidal method but also begins to fail for the later intervals tested.

3.9 ORDINARY DIFFERENTIAL EQUATIONS

Note to Reader: The reader of this section is assumed to be familiar with differential calculus. The section can be skipped without loss of continuity.

A vast range of problems in science and engineering are characterized by *differential equations*, where the rate of change of some quantity is a function of the values of other variables, potentially including other rates of change. It is quite common for these differential equations to be mathematically unsolvable, requiring that numerical methods be applied.

We restrict our presentation here to the solution of first-order ordinary differential equations. These are of the form

$$\frac{dy}{dx} = g(x, y)$$

or, defining $y' = dy/dx$,

$$y' = g(x, y)$$

Restricting attention to only first-order differential equations is not as limiting as it first may seem. It is quite simple to convert an mth-order differential equation into a system of m first-order equations. Thus, with minor extensions all the methods we explore below allow for solution of ordinary differential equations of arbitrary order.

The simplest way to transform an mth-order equation to a system of first-order equations is to define a new variable for each of the derivatives of y up to order $(m - 1)$. Suppose that the original differential equation is of the form

$$y''' = g(x, y, y', y'')$$

Then we can define

$$y_0 = y$$

$$y_1 = y'$$

$$y_2 = y''$$

The original third-order differential equation can now be written as

$$y_2' = g(x, y_0, y_1, y_2)$$

$$y_1' = y_2$$

$$y_0' = y_1$$

In order to keep the notation and examples simple, we focus mostly on single equations in this chapter. However, as illustrated in Section 3.10, the methods we present easily generalize to systems of first-order differential equations.

The solution of any differential equation is not unique unless there is a set of constraints. We consider here only initial value problems, where the constraints are the values of $y_0, y_1, \ldots, y_n$ at some initial value of the independent variable x. We will define the initial values of x and y to be x_0 and y_0, respectively. Solution of systems of ordinary differential equations with other boundary conditions is considerably more complicated. The reader is referred to Press et al. [Press, William H. 88].

The numerical algorithms described in this section do not really "solve" differential equations in the mathematical sense. Rather, they compute a series of points that are numerically close to the solution. The function $y = f(x)$ that satisfies the differential equation remains unknown. For most applications, knowing a sufficient number of points on the function $y = f(x)$ is adequate.

3.9.1 Euler's Method

The simplest numerical algorithm for solving differential equations is called *Euler's method*. This method is by far the most straightforward, but unfortunately is inaccurate. For this reason it is rarely used in practice. We present it here because it serves as the basis for more accurate algorithms.

Euler's algorithm can be summarized as follows:

- **Step 1.** Define the following variables:
    x = x_0, the initial value of x
    y = y_0, the initial value of y
    xlast, the largest value of x for which a solution is desired
    h, an increment of x
- **Step 2.** Output **x** and **y**.
- **Step 3.** Set **x = x + h**.
- **Step 4.** Compute **y = y + h*g(x,y)**.
- **Step 5.** If **x > xlast**, terminate. Otherwise, go to step 2.

The following C function implements Euler's method. Its arguments are:

   x0 and **y0** — initial values for x and y.
   g — a pointer to the function $g(x, y)$ used to compute the derivative.
   h — a step size.

xlast — the largest value of x for which points along the equation are to be computed.

```
/* this function implements Euler's method */

#include <stdio.h>

void euler(
   double x0,        /* Initial x */
   double y0,        /* Initial y */
   double (*g)(double,double),
            /*pointer to derivative function */
   double h,         /* increment */
   double xlast)     /* largest x */

{

   printf("         x                f(x)\n");
   for ( ; x0 <= xlast; x0 = x0+h) {
     printf("%15.6g  %15.6g\n", x0, y0 );
     y0 = y0 + h * g(x0, y0);
   }
}
```

The implementation of Euler's method above takes advantage of the fact that C passes arguments by value. This makes it possible for the function to use the arguments **x0** and **y0** without affecting the values of the variables used in the function's invocation.

Using the function **euler()** in a program requires coding the function $g(x, y)$. For example, if the differential equation to be solved is

$$y' = -\frac{y-4}{x}, \qquad y(1) = 0$$

then the C function for the differential equation would be

```
double func(double x, double y)
{
   return( -(y-4)/ x );
}
```

With the code above, the function **euler()** could be used to find the path of the solution for x going from 1 to 4 in steps of .1 as follows:

```
/* function prototypes */

void euler(double, double, double (*)(double, double),
                double, double);
```

```
double func(double, double);

/* invocation of Euler's method */

euler(1.0, 0.0, func, .1, 4.0);
```

3.9.2 Sources of Error in Euler's Method

Euler's algorithm uses $g(x, y)$ repeatedly to compute the derivative of y with respect to x, and then applies that derivative to take a step along the x axis. This is shown graphically in Figure 3.12. In that figure, the solid line represents the true solution to the differential equation, while the line connecting the boxes shows the path computed by Euler's algorithm.

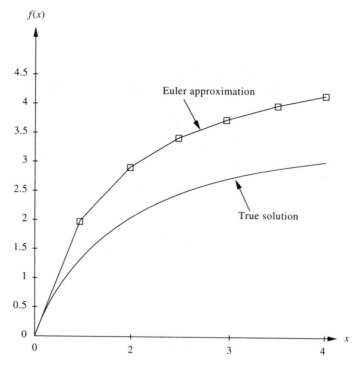

Figure 3.12 Graphical interpretation of Euler's method.

The first step in Euler's method moves along the tangent to the true solution of the differential equation by **h** along the x axis and **h*g(x,y)** on the y axis. This produces a point $(x_0 + h, y_0 + hg(x_0, y_0))$. This point differs from the true solution by some amount Δy_1, the "local" error. This error can be shown to be of order h^2, where h is assumed to be small. We use the notation $O(h^2)$ to denote that the error is of order h^2.

In the second and subsequent steps, the local error is only one source of error. The second source is the fact that the derivative is being computed at a point which is different from the true solution to the differential equation. The size of this second error depends crucially on how close the computed derivative is to the true derivative, which in turn depends on the peculiarities of the specific differential equation being solved. Some differential equations are unstable in the sense that small deviations from the true solution result in very large differences in the derivative. The use of Euler's method on these equations can produce huge errors after a relatively small number of steps.

Consider, for example, the unstable differential equation

$$y' = 6y - 8e^{-2x}, \qquad y(0) = 1$$

The analytic solution to this differential equation is

$$y = e^{-2x}$$

However, the function

$$y' = e^{-2x} + ce^{6x}$$

is a general solution applicable to other initial conditions. As local errors in Euler's method accumulate, the second term of the general solution contributes significantly to subsequent steps of Euler's method, changing the derivative in each step away from the true value. These errors accumulate over the steps, leading to entirely erroneous results. Even with very small step sizes, Euler's method will diverge from the true solution quite quickly.

3.9.3 Runge-Kutta Methods

Because of the relatively large local error and the shortcomings of Euler's method for differential equations that are unstable (or nearly so), the method is rarely used in practice. However, the basic idea of Euler's method can be adapted to produce a far more robust and useful algorithm. These adaptations are grouped together in a class of algorithms called *Runge-Kutta methods*.

Runge-Kutta methods are based on the observation that each step of Euler's method relies entirely on the derivative evaluated at a single point. If one could compute a better estimate of the derivative, it would be possible to improve on each Euler method step. Runge-Kutta methods do this by evaluating the derivative at more than one point for each step and combining the various computed derivatives to obtain a better approximation of the solution. The goal is to reduce the local error at each step to something considerably smaller than $O(h^2)$.

The simplest variant of Runge-Kutta methods uses the same derivative as used in Euler's method and a derivative computed at the point $x + h/2$, the midpoint of the interval spanned by a single Euler method step. The algorithm for this is as follows:

- **Step 1.** Define the following variables:

  $x = x_0$, the initial value of x

  $y = y_0$, the initial value of y

  xlast, the largest value of x for which a solution is desired

  h, an increment of x

  temp, a temporary variable

- **Step 2.** Output **x** and **y**.

- **Step 3.** Compute **temp = h*g(x,y)**.

- **Step 4.** Compute **y = y + h*g(x + h/2, y+temp/2)**.

- **Step 5.** Set **x = x + h**.

- **Step 6.** If **x > xlast**, terminate. Otherwise, go to step 2.

In this algorithm, the derivative at the midpoint between x and $x + h$ is used to compute the direction for the next step. This reduces the local error per step from $O(h^2)$ in Euler's method to $O(h^3)$. This is called the *second-order* Runge-Kutta method. (Euler's method can be viewed as the first-order Runge-Kutta method.)

Higher-order Runge-Kutta methods involve more complicated combinations of intermediate derivatives. By appropriately combining additional estimates of the derivative, we can reduce the order of the error term to still higher powers of h. Solutions for the appropriate weights for the various terms are beyond the scope of this book.[3] Instead, we state the results for one of the most widely used Runge-Kutta variants, the fourth-order method. This is given in the following algorithm.

- **Step 1.** Define the following variables:

  $x = x_0$, the initial value of x

  $y = y_0$, the initial value of y

  xlast, the largest value of x for which a solution is desired

  h, an increment of x

  ta, tb, tc, and **td**, temporary variables

- **Step 2.** Output **x** and **y**.

- **Step 3.** Compute:

  ```
  ta =  h*g(x, y)
  tb =  h*g(x+h/2, y+ta/2)
  tc =  h*g(x+h/2,y+tb/2)
  td =  h*g(x+h, y+tc)
  ```

- **Step 4.** Compute **y = y + ta/6 + tb/3 + tc/3 + td/6**.

- **Step 5.** Set **x = x + h**.

- **Step 6.** If **x > xlast**, terminate. Otherwise, go to step 2.

---

[3]Readers are referred to Abramowitz and Stegun [Abramowitz, Milton 64].

An implementation of this algorithm in C is as follows:

```
/* fourth-order Runge-Kutta method */
void runge_kutta(
  double x0,      /* Initial x */
  double y0,      /* Initial y */
  /*pointer to derivative function */
  double (*g)(double,double),
  double h,       /* increment */
  double xlast)   /* largest x */
{

  double ta, tb, tc, td;
  printf("        x                f(x)\n");
  for ( ; x0 <= xlast; x0 = x0+h) {
    printf("%15.6g %15.6g\n", x0, y0 );
    ta =  h * g(x0, y0);
    tb =  h * g(x0+h/2.0, y0+ta/2.0);
    tc =  h * g(x0+h/2.0,y0+tb/2.0);
    td =  h * g(x0+h, y0+tc);
    y0 = y0 + (ta +2.0* tb +2.0*tc + td)/6.0;

  }
}
```

The differences between the accuracy of a fourth-order Runge-Kutta method and Euler's algorithm can be seen by comparing them on a simple problem with a large step size. Consider the following differential equation:

$$y' = -\frac{y-4}{x}, \qquad y(1) = 0$$

The true solution to this equation is

$$y = 4 - \frac{4}{x}$$

If we use Euler's method to solve this equation in the interval $1 \le x \le 4$ using a step size of .1, we find the errors depicted in Figure 3.13. This figure plots the difference between the function computed by Euler's method and the true function. If we apply the Runge-Kutta method to this same problem with an identical step size, the absolute value of the errors are always less than 1.2×10^{-16}. Thus, even with a relatively large step size, the Runge-Kutta method produces very accurate results on this problem, while the errors in Euler's method are significant.

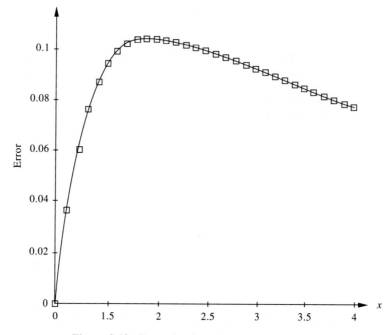

Figure 3.13   Example of errors in Euler's method.

3.10 PROGRAMMING PROJECT: MOTION OF A PENDULUM

We now consider the application of the Runge-Kutta method to solving for the motion of a pendulum. The pendulum consists of a mass at the end of a rigid rod of length l that is attached to a frictionless pivot as shown in Figure 3.14. We assume for simplicity that the weight of the rod is negligible compared to the mass.

Figure 3.14 shows the geometry of the pendulum's motion. We call s the *arc length* as measured along the circle of radius l centered at the pivot. The value $s = 0$ corresponds to the position of the pendulum at rest. If moved away from the rest position, the mass will move along the circle, changing the value of s. We denote that path of the mass over time by the function $s(t)$.

From the geometry shown in Figure 3.14, we can show that $s = l\theta$. If we use a rectangular coordinate system centered at the pivot of the pendulum, we can also show that

$$x(t) = l \sin\theta(t) = l \sin\frac{s(t)}{l}$$

$$y(t) = -l \cos\theta(t) = -l \cos\frac{s(t)}{l}$$

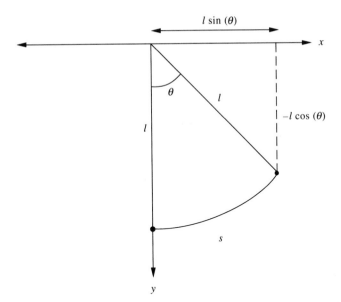

Figure 3.14 Geometry of a simple pendulum.

We assume that the pendulum starts from an initial position $s(0) = s_0$. By applying Newton's law of gravitation and the equation that force equals mass times acceleration, it can be shown that the movement of the pendulum is governed by the differential equation

$$\frac{d^2 s}{dt^2} = -g \sin \frac{s(t)}{l}$$

where g denotes the gravitational constant (9.8 meter/sec^2). Once we solve for $s(t)$, the movement of the pendulum in the (x, y) coordinate system can be computed from the geometric relationships above.

It is common in introductory physics texts to make the assumption that movements of the pendulum are small, and that therefore the value of $\sin \theta$ can be approximated by θ. This makes analytic solution of the differential equation easier. Our approach in this section will be to keep the correct differential equation and solve for the path of the pendulum over time numerically using the Runge-Kutta algorithm.

Since the differential equation has a second derivative term, we will solve it as a system of two first-order differential equations by introducing the function $z(t)$ defined as the derivative of $s(t)$ with respect to t. Using this intermediate function, the movement of the pendulum can be described by a system of two first-order differential equations given as follows:

$$\frac{dz(t)}{dt} = -g \sin \frac{s(t)}{l}$$

$$\frac{ds(t)}{dt} = z(t)$$

The following C program adapts the fourth-order Runge-Kutta function developed in Section 3.9.3 to solve this system of two first-order differential equations. Each step of the algorithm will require keeping track of two dependent variables, s and z. As with the single-variable case, we will update the variables in four substeps. The program will output the values of $s(t)$, $x(t)$, and $y(t)$. The C code is as follows.

```c
/* program to solve for movement of a pendulum */

#include <stdio.h>
#include <math.h>
#define GRAVITY -9.8   /* gravitational constant */

main()
{
  double h;         /* time increments for computation */
  double s0;        /* initial  pendulum position */
  double tlast;     /* time limit for computation */
  double length;    /* length of pendulum */
  double s,z,t;              /* values of s,z and t */
  double sa, sb, sc, sd; /* intermediate values of s */
  double za, zb, zc, zd; /* intermediate values of z */

/* prompt for and read input values */
  printf("Enter initial value of s:");
  scanf("%lf", &s0);
  printf("Enter last value of t:");
  scanf("%lf", &tlast);
  printf("Enter value of time increments:");
  scanf("%lf", &h);
  printf("Enter length of pendulum:");
  scanf("%lf", &length);

/* print labels */
  printf("     t         s(t)         x(t)        y(t)\n");

/* initialize values */
  s = s0;
  z = 0;

/* perform runge-kutta iterations */
  for (t=0 ; t <= tlast; t = t+h) {

  /* output the values of key variables */
    printf("%12.6g  %12.6g %12.6g %12.6g\n", t, s,
      length*sin(s/length), -length*cos(s/length));
  /* update z and s */
```

```
            za = h * GRAVITY * sin(s/length);
            sa = h * z;
            zb = h * GRAVITY * sin((s+sa/2)/length);
            sb = h * (z+za/2);
            zc = h *GRAVITY * sin((s+sb/2)/length);
            sc = h * (z + zb/2);
            zd = h * GRAVITY * sin((s+sc)/length);
            sd = h * (z + zc);
            z = z + za/6 + zb/3 + zc/3 + zd/6;
            s = s + sa/6 + sb/3 + sc/3 + sd/6;
        }
    }
```

3.11 SUMMARY OF CHAPTER 3

In this chapter we introduced the key ideas in using computers to solve numerical problems. The methods are applicable to a broad range of problems encountered in science, engineering, management, and the quantitative social sciences.

The representation of floating-point values in a modern, digital computer was described. While different computers may use different representations, all computers separate a floating-point number into a sign indicator, a fraction part, and an exponent. The range of values which can be represented and the precision of any floating-point number varies across machine types.

Despite this variation, all computers that use floating-point numbers share the characteristic that not all numerical values can be represented exactly. As a consequence, all arithmetic operations involving floating-point numbers must be viewed as introducing at least some small error. Measured as a fraction of the result of a floating-point computation, this error is at least as large as the *machine precision*, the largest number which when added to 1.0 does not change the value 1.0.

Floating-point errors can accumulate as the results from one floating-point operation are used in subsequent operations, resulting in numerical answers that can be considerably in error. Programmers must be aware of the potential for floating-point errors, and must design their algorithms to minimize the effects of such errors.

In the chapter we described some of the methods used for finding a root of an equation. Writing this type of algorithm in general form required the ability to pass functions as arguments to other functions. This is accomplished in C by passing a *pointer to a function* as an argument.

The particular root-finding methods described are *bisection*, the *secant method*, and *Newton's method*. Bisection and the secant method require an interval known to contain a root as an input, while Newton's method requires only an initial guess of the root. Neither method offers any guarantee that all roots of the function will be found.

Methods for numerical integration were then introduced. The approaches developed included the rectangular, trapezoidal, and Simpson's rules. Techniques that allow the level of detail to vary automatically depending on characteristics of the function to be integrated were demonstrated. These methods are generally termed *adaptive* algorithms.

In the final section we introduced algorithms to solve ordinary first-order differential equations. The simplest technique, Euler's method, has poor numerical properties. Small local errors can produce very large errors later in the algorithm's execution. A more sophisticated class of algorithms, called Runge-Kutta methods, provides much greater accuracy at the cost of additional computational effort. One of the most widely used Runge-Kutta methods, the fourth-order approximation, was shown.

3.12 EXERCISES

3-1. Imagine a computer in which floating-point numbers are represented in eight binary digits as follows:

- The first digit represents the size. A 0 implies a positive value, a 1 implies a negative value.
- The next three digits are the base 2 exponent represented in "excess 4" form, that is, the true exponent is four less than the represented value.
- The remaining four digits are the fraction part in base 2, with an implied decimal point in front of the fraction part.

Answer the following:

(a) What base 10 number does the floating-point value `01001000` represent?

(b) What are the largest and smallest representable values?

(c) What is the smallest positive value that is representable?

(d) How would you represent the value $-\frac{9}{16}$?

3-2. The following function is supposed to compute the value of the infinite series

$$1 + \frac{1}{2} + \frac{1}{3} + \frac{1}{4} + \frac{1}{5} + \cdots$$

until the percentage change in the sum is less than some small value. Find six errors in the function. Suggest changes that would make the program work correctly.

```
sum_up(epsilon)
    double epsilon;
{
 int i, sum;
 double  oldvalue;
 sum = 0.0;
 oldvalue = epsilon + 1;
 for(i=0; sum-oldvalue > epsilon; i++) {
     oldvalue = sum;
     sum += 1/i;
 }
}
```

3-3. The value of e^x can be approximated by the following series:

$$e^x = 1 + x + \frac{x^2}{2!} + \frac{x^3}{3!} + \cdots + \frac{x^n}{n!} + R_n(x)$$

where $R_n(x)$ is a remainder term that can be shown to be bounded as follows:

$$\left| R_n(x) \right| \le 3^x \frac{x^{n+1}}{(n+1)!}$$

Create a function that computes and returns a **double** containing the approximate value of e^x. The function should have as its arguments the value of x and a tolerance value, **tol**, defined such that e^x is computed with error no larger in absolute value than **tol**. Both arguments should be **double** values. Write a **main()** function that invokes your new function for values of x equal to .1, .5, 1.0, 3, and 7 and outputs the resulting approximation to e^x. Your function should use a value of **tol** equal to .000001. You should also output the value computed by the math library function **exp()** for the same values of x.

3-4. Given the coefficients of a second-degree polynomial, we can calculate that polynomial's roots by using the quadratic equations, which say that the roots of the function $ax^2 + bx + c$ are

$$x = \frac{-b \pm \sqrt{b^2 - 4ac}}{2a} = \frac{2c}{-b \pm \sqrt{b^2 - 4ac}}$$

(a) Write two C functions, each of which will implement one of these two formulas.
(b) Which of these two formulas is more accurate?

3-5. A function is *even* if for every value x, $f(x) = f(-x)$, and odd if $f(x) = -f(-x)$. While numerical tests cannot prove that a function is odd or even, they can be used to disprove it. Develop and implement a function in C that will test whether a function is odd, even, or neither. The function should work by selecting points along the x axis in some interval and checking whether the values of $f(x)$ and $f(-x)$ meet the criteria for odd or even functions. Because of potential numerical roundoffs, you should consider two values equal if they are within some user-specified tolerance of each other. The function you create should have as arguments a pointer to the function being tested, the beginning and ending points of the interval being tested, the number of points to test, and the tolerance value. Use your function as part of a complete program to test check whether three different functions you invent are odd, even, or neither.

3-6. The method of *Lagrangian polynomials* is a general procedure for finding an nth order polynomial passing through $n+1$ points. For the case of four points $(a, f_a), (b, f_b), (c, f_c)$, and (d, f_d) the Lagrangian polynomial is

$$P(x) = \frac{(x-b)(x-c)(x-d)}{(a-b)(a-c)(a-d)} f_a + \frac{(x-a)(x-c)(x-d)}{(b-a)(b-c)(b-d)} f_b$$

$$+ \frac{(x-a)(x-b)(x-d)}{(c-a)(c-b)(c-d)} f_c + \frac{(x-a)(x-b)(x-c)}{(d-a)(d-b)(d-c)} f_d$$

Do the following:

(a) Show that this polynomial passes through all four points $(a, f_a), (b, f_b), (c, f_c),$ and (d, f_d).

(b) Write a C function that has as its arguments the eight values $a, b, c, d, f_a, f_b, f_c, f_d,$ and pointers to four variables where the coefficients for the third-order polynomial computed by the Langrangian method are to be placed.

(c) Write a C function that has the four coefficients of the third-order Lagrangian polynomial equation and some value x as arguments and returns the value of the Lagrangian polynomial $P(x)$.

(d) Write a `main()` function which reads the eight values from the user and invokes the function that finds the coefficients of the Lagrangian polynomial, prompts for a value of x, and uses the Lagrangian polynomial to compute the value $P(x)$. Your `main()` function should output both the coefficients and the computed value of $P(x)$.

3-7. Numerical methods can be used to compute the derivatives of a function. To compute the first derivative of $f(x)$ at some point x, we can use some small increment h and find

$$\frac{f(x + h) - f(x)}{h}$$

as an approximation to the derivative. Another possible formula is

$$\frac{f(x + h) - f(x - h)}{2h}$$

Yet a third possible formula relies on three points, $x + 2h$, $x + h$, and x and fits a quadratic equation through them. This approach yields the approximation

$$\frac{-f(x + 2h) + 4f(x + h) - 3f(x)}{2h}$$

Write C functions that implement each of these methods. These functions should have a pointer to f and the value of h as arguments and should return the approximate derivative. Then write a `main()` program which uses these three functions to compute the value of the derivative of e^x for values of x between .1 and 1.0 in intervals of .05. Since the derivative of e^x is just e^x, you can compute the error in each of the approximations using the math library function `exp()`. Try your program with values of h of .001, .00001, and .0000001.

3-8. Suppose you needed to write a function that computes the square root of some value k. You decide to set up an equation of the form

$$x^2 - k = 0$$

The root of this equation is the square root of k.

(a) Write the general form of Newton's method for this equation in which the new estimate of the root is a function of the current estimate.

(b) If the initial guess of the root of this equation is $x = k/2$, what is the estimate after a single step of Newton's method?

(c) Code the algorithm in C and write a `main()` function to test it.

3-9. Consider two cities that are served by both truck and rail modes of transportation for hauling freight. Define the variables V_R and V_T as the rail and truck tonnage shipped per day. Assume that the total tonnage per day is 1000 and that the share of the freight moving by rail is approximated by a demand equation as follows:

$$\frac{V_R}{V_R + V_T} = \frac{1}{1 + e^{-0.5 + 0.02(t_R - t_T)}}$$

where t_R and t_T are the travel times per trip for rail and truck, respectively. Assume further that because of congestion, the travel times for the two modes increase as the volume of traffic moving on those modes increases. As an approximation, we will use the following two equations to describe this congestion:

$$t_R = 100 + .066V_R$$

$$t_T = 25 + .081V_T$$

Noting that $V_T = 1000 - V_R$, rearrange the equations above into a single equation of the form $f(V_R) = 0$. Write a program that uses the bisection algorithm shown in Section 3.5.2 to solve for V_R and outputs all the unknowns in the problem. Your program should output the daily tonnage and travel times for both rail and truck.

3-10. Suppose that we have three points $a < b < c$ where the interval $[a, c]$ is known to contain a local minimum of a function $f(x)$ and where $f(b)$ is less than both $f(a)$ and $f(c)$. One way to find the minimum is to select any point x between b and c. If $f(b) < f(x)$, then we know that the minimum is in the interval $[a, x]$. In this case we can use the points a, b, and x just as we used a, b, and c. If $f(b) > f(x)$, then we know the minimum is in the interval $[b, c]$. In this case we can use the points b, x, and c just as we used a, b, and c. In both cases we have narrowed the interval down. By using this approach repeatedly we can narrow the interval until it is "small enough" that we can declare it converged on the minimum. Write a C function that implements this algorithm. It should have a pointer to $f(x)$, a, b, c and the tolerance value as arguments, and should return the midpoint of the interval when it is narrowed down to a size smaller than the tolerance. Then write a **main()** function that uses your method to find a local minimum of some function you invent.

3-11. The *regula falsi* method for finding the root of a function begins with an interval known to contain a root. Call the endpoints of this interval $(x_0, f(x_0))$ and $(x_1, f(x_1))$. The method works by fitting a straight line between the two current endpoints and finding the point x_2 where that line intersects the x axis. The point $(x_2, f(x_2))$ becomes one of the endpoints of the next interval. The other endpoint is whichever of $(x_0, f(x_0))$ and $(x_1, f(x_1))$ ensures that the new interval still contains a root of the function. This procedure continues until the interval is very small. Given this description, do the following:

(a) Write the equation for the line between $(x_0, f(x_0))$ and $(x_1, f(x_1))$ and solve it for the value of x_2 where the line crosses the x axis.

(b) Write a C function that implements the regula-falsi method. This function should have as its arguments a pointer to the function f, the values of x_0 and x_1 defining the initial interval, and a tolerance value that defines when the interval is "small enough" to declare the method to have converged on a root.

(c) Write a C function which returns the value computed by $f(x) = 2x^4 - 20x^3 + 62x^2 + 624x + 740$ for any argument x.

(d) Write a **main()** function that uses the functions you have implemented above to solve for a root of f.

3-12. *Muller's method* is a generalization of the secant method for root finding. Instead of using a straight line between two points to approximate some function, this method uses a quadratic function fit through three points.

Muller's method begins by using three values of the independent variable, which we will call x_0, x_1, and x_2. Order the values so that $x_2 < x_0 < x_1$. A second-degree polynomial $ax^2 + bx + c$ is then fit through the three points $(x_0, f(x_0))$, $(x_1, f(x_1))$, and $(x_2, f(x_2))$. The coefficients of a, b, and c can be computed most easily if we define $d_1 = x_1 - x_0$ and $d_2 = x_0 - x_2$. We also define $r = d_2/d_1$. In this case it can be shown that

$$a = \frac{r\, f(x_1) - f(x_0)(1 + r) + f(x_2)}{r\, d_1^2\,(1 + r)}$$

$$b = \frac{f(x_1) - f(x_0) + a\, d_1^2}{d_1}$$

$$c = f(x_0)$$

After finding a, b, and c the quadratic formula is used to find the two roots. The root closest to x_0 is used in the next iteration. If this root is greater than x_0, then x_0, x_1, and the root become the three values for the next iteration. Otherwise, x_0, x_2, and the root are used for the next iteration. The iterative process proceeds until the value of the function at the approximate root is less than some tolerance. Implement Muller's method in C and write a `main()` program to test it on the function $\sin(x) - x/2$. Use 1.75, 2.0, and 2.25 as initial values of x.

3-13. It is sometimes possible to rewrite an equation $f(x) = 0$ in the form $x = g(x)$. Under certain conditions on $g(x)$, we can use the iterative formula $x_{n+1} = g(x_n)$ to find a root of $f(x)$. The method begins with an initial value x_0 and computes $x_1, x_2, x_3, \ldots$ by repeated application of $g(x)$ until the absolute value of $x_{n+1} - x_n$ is less than some threshold.

(a) Write a C function that implements this method. It should have a pointer to the function g, the initial value of x, and the tolerance value as arguments. The function should output the value of x_n computed at each iteration and should return the approximate root.

(b) Write the equation $f(x) = x^2 - 8x + 7 = 0$ in the form $x = g(x)$.

(c) Write a C function that returns the value $g(x)$ for the function g found in part b above.

(d) Write a `main()` function that uses the method described above to solve for a root of $f(x) = x^2 - 8x + 7 = 0$ using a starting value of $x = 0$.

(e) Try the method again using a starting value of $x = 10$. Explain what happens by graphing the function and the series of steps.

3-14. Find the values of x for the function $f(x) = x^2 + 12$ where Newton's method will cycle.

3-15. Take the C program `new_simpson()` in Section 3.7.4 and rewrite it so that it never invokes $f(x)$ more than once for the same value of x.

3-16. The normal, or Gaussian, function is characterized by its mean (or central tendency) μ and its standard deviation σ, which measures how spread out the function is. The equation for the normal distribution is

$$f(x) = \frac{1}{\sqrt{2\pi}\,\sigma} e^{-\frac{1}{2}\left(\frac{x-\mu}{\sigma}\right)^2}$$

Write a function that computes the integral of $f(x)$ from some value x_1 to another value $x_2 > x_1$. This function should return the value of the integral. Use the adaptive version of Simpson's rule given in Section 3.7.4. The values x_1, x_2, μ, σ and a tolerance level should be arguments to the function. Write a main function that reads a set of inputs for each of the arguments, invokes the integration function, and prints out the value.

3-17. Suppose that we have a function $f(x, y)$ of two variables x and y.
   (a) Write a C function that generalizes the rectangular integration method to compute the double integral

$$\int_{y=y_1}^{y_2} \int_{x=x_1}^{x_2} f(x, y) \, dx \, dy$$

   (b) Write a C function which computes the value of the function $f(x, y) = e^{x^2 + 2xy + y^2}$.
   (c) Write a **main()** function that uses the two functions above to compute the integral of $f(x, y)$ for values of x between zero and one and values of y between zero and 2.

3-18. The natural logarithm of a value x is defined by the integral

$$\int_1^x \frac{1}{t} \, dt$$

Write a program that uses Simpson's rule to compute the natural logarithm by approximating the integral above for values of $x = 2, 4, 8$ using 10, 50, 100, and 1000 intervals. Also output the difference between the values obtained when approximating the integral and the value of the natural logarithm as computed by the math library function **log()**. (Remember to include the header file **math.h** in your program.)

3-19. Figure 3.15 illustrates two masses, m_1 and m_2, suspended from a fixed beam by two springs with elasticity k_1 and k_2, respectively. It is convenient to measure the positions of the centers of gravity of the masses relative to their "at rest" position. Thus, y_1 and y_2

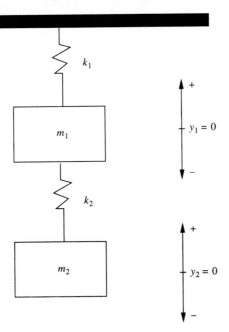

Figure 3.15 Two masses suspended on springs.

represent any displacements from the positions of masses m_1 and m_2 respectively when the entire system is at rest. We measure positive values of y in the up direction.

If one or both of the masses is moved in the vertical direction from its initial position and then released, the two masses will oscillate up and down. The positions of the masses are governed by Newton's law, $F = ma$. If t denotes time, the equations of motion are as follows:

$$m_1 \frac{d^2 y_1}{dt^2} = -k_1 y_1 - k_2(y_1 - y_2)$$

$$m_2 \frac{d^2 y_2}{dt^2} = -k_2(y_1 - y_2)$$

Write a C program that uses the fourth-order Runge-Kutta method to approximate the positions of the masses. The program will have to adapt the Runge-Kutta method to handle two second-order differential equations. (You may want to examine the example in Section 3.10.) Your program should read in values for m_1, m_2, k_1, k_2, and initial positions y_1 and y_2. It should then produce a table showing the displacements of the masses for 2 seconds at increments of .05 second.

3-20. One way to improve on Euler's method to solve the linear differential equation $y' = g(x, y)$ is to:

(a) Take a regular Euler's step $x_{n+1} = x_n + h$ along the x axis, using the unmodified Euler method to find a tentative value of y_{n+1} by computing $y_{n+1} = y_n + hg(x_{n+1}, y_n)$.

(b) Recompute the derivative at the tentative value of y_{n+1} as $g(x_{n+1}, y_{n+1})$.

(c) Use the average of the derivative estimates $g(x_{n+1}, y_n)$ and $g(x_{n+1}, y_{n+1})$ to compute the actual step. The formula to be used is

$$y_{n+1} = y_n + \frac{h[g(x_{n+1}, y_n) + g(x_{n+1}, y_{n+1})]}{2}$$

Write a C function that implements this modified Euler's method. Use it to solve the differential equation

$$y' = \frac{4 - y}{x}, \qquad y(1) = 0$$

for x going from 1 to 4 in steps of .1.

CHAPTER

4

LINEAR ALGEBRA

4.1 INTRODUCTION

In this chapter we explore numerical methods that make use of C's ability to represent arbitrary collections of elements of the same type as a single unit. These collections are called *arrays*.

One use of arrays we will explore extensively is their use in solving problems in *linear algebra*. These methods are important because of the wide range of real-world problems which can be approximated by linear systems of equations. In addition, nonlinear problems are often solved by methods which rely on the ability to solve linear approximations. For example, Newton's method for finding a root of an equation, described in Chapter 3, relies on successive linear approximations.

In order to develop functions that solve key problems in linear algebra, we will need a way to represent *vectors* and *matrices*, the key building blocks of linear systems. C (and virtually all other general-purpose programming languages) provides a straightforward way to represent such objects.

Arrays have uses that go well beyond their application in linear algebra. In this chapter we demonstrate their usefulness in diverse areas, including population forecasting, the analysis of transportation networks, and the simulation of one computer in a program executing on another computer.

We begin by introducing single-dimension arrays in C as a way to represent vectors. We demonstrate how functions that manipulate single-dimension arrays can be written, using simple operations such as the dot product of two vectors as examples. We also develop a complete population forecasting model as a programming project.

We then consider the more general case of representing matrices using two-dimensional arrays. This provides the needed background for developing more complicated algorithms, such as solving systems of linear equations and inverting a matrix.

The final two sections of the chapter are programming projects that show two very different uses of arrays. The first project solves what is called the *all-pairs shortest path problem*, in which a transportation or other network linking various points is analyzed to find the shortest way to get from every point to every other point. The second project develops a simulator for the simple robot introduced in Chapter 1.

4.2 REPRESENTING VECTORS IN C

4.2.1 What Are Arrays?

C

Suppose that we wanted to represent a group of data points corresponding to some measurements. For example, we might have a series of measurements on the level of carbon monoxide in the air for n different days, and we might want to take the average of the data. If there are n such values $x_0, x_1, \ldots, x_{n-1}$, we could define a separate variable for each measurement. If there were seven such measurements, we might have the definition

```
float x0, x1, x2, x3, x4, x5, x6;
```

The average could then be computed as

```
float average;
average = (x0+x1+x2+x3+x4+x5+x6)/7.0;
```

While this approach might work on data for just seven days, it would be unmanageable if we had data for thousands of measurements. In addition to having to define a huge number of separate variables, we would have to code a gigantic summation. Even worse, every time we added yet another observation, we would have to modify the code and recompile it. Clearly, a very different approach is needed.

The C language provides such a different approach by allowing the programmer to collect groups of variables of the same type into a single "object" called an *array*. For example, if we had 1000 observations, we could define a single array called **x** that had 1000 **float**s. This would be defined in the statement

```
float x[1000]; /* x is an array with 1000 entries */
```

The square brackets ([and]) indicate that **x** is an array, and the integer constant **1000** denotes that the array has 1000 entries. C allows definition of arrays of any standard type. There are no fixed limits on how many entries a single array may have, though some C implementations do enforce specific restrictions.

Once we have defined an array, we can reference any element of the array as **x[ex]**, where **ex** is an expression that evaluates to some integer data type. The expression is called the *subscript*. In C, the first entry in any array **x** is **x[0]**, and the elements in the array with **n** elements are referenced as **x[0]**, **x[1]**, **x[2]**, ..., **x[n-1]**. For example, we could read data into an array with the following statements:

```
/* read 1000 values into array x  */
float x[1000];
int i;
for(i=0; i<1000, i++)
  scanf("%f", &x[i]);
```

Note that the second argument to the function **scanf** in this example is **&x[i]**. This relies on the fact that the precedence of the subscript operator (denoted by the square brackets) is higher than that of the "address of" operator.

Similarly, the average of the 1000 values could be computed as

```
/* compute average of 1000 values in array */
float x[1000];
float average = 0.0;

for(i=0; i<1000; i++)
   average = average + x[i];
average = average/1000;
```

One way to view arrays is to visualize them as a block of adjacent memory locations. The beginning of the array (the zeroth element) is the first location in the block, the next location holds element one of the array, etc. Figure 4.1 depicts a section of a computer's memory and the elements of an array that has **n** values. Note that the figure shows array elements in sequential memory locations. Depending on the type of array (**char**, **int**, etc.), each array element may occupy more than one memory location. For example, on many computers, a **double** occupies eight bytes, so an array of 10 **double**'s would occupy 80 bytes in total.

4.2.2 Arrays, Pointers, and Address Arithmetic

Arrays and pointers are closely related in many ways. Perhaps the most important relationship is that *the name of an array is a synonym for the address of its zeroth element*. For example, the C fragment

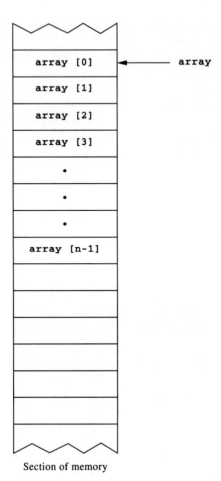

Section of memory

Figure 4.1 Arrays in memory.

```
int   values[1000];
int *pvalues;
pvalues = &values[0];
```

declares **values** to be an array of **int**s and **pvalues** to be a pointer to an **int**. The fragment then assigns **pvalues** the address of the zeroth element of **values**.

What is less obvious is that the assignment

```
pvalues = &values[0];
```

is entirely equivalent to the statement

```
pvalues = values;
```

This is because the name of an array is a synonym for its starting address. Thus, after an assignment such as

```
pvalues = values;
```

the statements

```
int i;
i = values[0];
```

and

```
int i;
i = *pvalues;
```

are entirely equivalent. Similarly, the statements

```
values[0] = 40;
```

and

```
*pvalues = 40;
```

are exactly equivalent.

The ability to use a pointer instead of referencing element zero of an array would be just a curiosity in C if there were no easy way to use pointers to select other elements of an array. However, C allows you to perform *arithmetic operations* on pointers that change the array element they point to. For example, if **pvalues** points to the beginning of the array **values**, then **pvalues + 2** points to **values[2]**. More generally, any integer expression can be added to a pointer. Similarly, the assignment statement

```
values[2] = 45;
```

is equivalent to the statement

```
*(pvalues+2) = 45;
```

In pointer arithmetic, C automatically increments or decrements the pointer by the proper amount for the type of variable the pointer is declared as pointing to. For example, if **pd** is declared as a pointer to a **double** and **j** is an integer, then **pd + j** points to the address that is **j** * *the number of storage locations needed for a double* beyond the address pointed to by **pd**.

Operations such as adding or subtracting a constant from a pointer are allowed in C. Multiplication, division, or modulo arithmetic on pointers are not allowed. It is legal to subtract one pointer from another. For example, you might have two pointers to elements in an array of **float**s, and the difference between those two pointers minus 1 would be the number of values in the array between the two pointers.

C does not allow you to add two pointers together. Operations on pointers to different data types are also not allowed. For example, subtracting a pointer to a **double** from a pointer to an **int** is illegal.

Pointers of the same type can also be compared. For example, if you had two pointers **p1** and **p2** that pointed to different elements in the same array, you might want to check which pointer was "deeper" into the array with the comparison **p1 < p2**.

While the relationship between pointers and array names in C is very strong, they are not entirely identical. In particular, while the name of an array is an address, its value cannot be changed. Thus, if **pd** is a pointer, the statement

```
pd = pd + 1; /* valid if pd is a pointer */
```

is entirely legal. However, if **values** is an array, the statement

```
values = values + 2; /* not valid if values is an array */
```

is not a legal C statement.

As an example of the uses of pointers, we rewrite the fragment of code that reads values into an array of **float**s. The original code,

```
/* read 1000 values into array x */
float x[1000];
int i;
for(i=0; i<1000; i++)
  scanf("%f", &x[i]);
```

could have been written as follows:

```
/* another way to read 1000 values into x */
float x[1000];
float *px;
for(px = x; px < x + 1000; px++)
  scanf("%f", px);
```

In this example, the pointer **px** is used instead of an array subscript. The condition **px < x+ 1000** uses pointer arithmetic and comparison of two pointer values. The statement **px++** increments **px**, moving it through the original array. Finally, since **px** is a pointer to a **float**, it can be used as an argument to **scanf()** instead of the awkward construction **&x[i]**.

4.2.3 Arrays as Arguments to Functions

C allows you to pass the name of an array as an argument to a function. *However, when an array name is passed as an argument, the value passed to the function is a copy of the address of the beginning of the array, not a complete copy of the entire array.* This is entirely consistent with the interpretation of an array name as a synonym for the address of the zeroth element in the array. Because the array is not copied when its name is used as an argument, the function that is passed the array name is free to interpret that argument either as an array name or a pointer to a value of the same type as the array.

For example, if we wanted to write a general-purpose function that averaged the elements in an array of **float**s, we might code it as follows:

```
/* function to average array of floats */
float average_floats(
   float a[],    /* array of elements to be averaged */
    int n)       /* number of elements to be averaged */
{
   float average = 0.0;
   int i;
   for(i=0; i<n; i++)
     average = average + a[i];
   return(average/n);
}
```

Note that in this example **a**, the argument to the function which is the array of values to be averaged, is declared as

```
float a[];
```

The reason there is no value between the brackets to denote the number of elements in **a** is that the value passed to the function is simply the starting address of the array. The function does not need to know how many elements are in the array because it does not allocate any storage in memory for the array. Only an address is passed to the function. The argument **n** is used to convey how many elements in the array are to be averaged.

This function might be invoked with the following program:

```
/* main function using average_floats() */
#include <stdio.h>
#define SIZE 1000
float average_floats(float[], int);

main()
{
```

```
    float x[SIZE];
    int i;
    for(i=0; i<SIZE; i++)
      scanf("%f", &x[i]);
    printf("Average is %f\n",average_floats(x, SIZE));
}
```

This program also illustrates a common use of the **#define** preprocessor directive. Defining **SIZE** to be the number of elements in the array makes it easy to change the program for different numbers of values to be averaged. Rather than changing the value in three different places, only the **#define** statement would have to be changed. The program also shows the prototype for an array argument in the declaration of **average_floats()**. The prototype

```
float average_floats(float *, int);
```

would be equivalent.

The function **average_floats()** could also be coded using a pointer to the beginning of the array as an argument and using pointer arithmetic to loop through the array entries. This would be implemented as follows:

```
/* using pointers to average array of floats */
float average_floats(
   float *pa, /* pointer to start of array */
   int n)     /* number of elements to be averaged */
{
  float average = 0.0;
  float *pf;

  for(pf = pa; pf-pa < n; pf++)
    average = average + *pf;
  return(average/n);
}
```

The close relationship between arrays and pointers can also be used to pass portions of large arrays to functions. For example, if you wanted to average elements 10 through 24 of a large array **x** that had 100 elements, you could invoke the function **average_floats()** as

```
float subaverage;
subaverage = average_float( x+10, 15);
```

Whether you use pointers or array notation is largely a matter of taste. For most linear algebra problems, array notation often expresses the intended purpose of a function more clearly than the same function written using pointers. However, as we shall see in Section 4.4, the use of subscript notation for arrays with multiple dimensions can be somewhat limiting compared to the use of pointers.

4.2.4 Initialization of Arrays

Arrays can be initialized in C as part of their definitions. For example, suppose we wanted to create an array that contained the passing grades on six different quizes. The following C statement both declares the array and initializes its values:

```
float grades[6] = {65, 55, 65, 70, 65, 65};
```

The initial values are enclosed in curly braces. If the array is defined as having more elements than the number of initial values, then the remaining elements are initialized to zero. Thus, the definition

```
float y[2000] = {0.0};
```

initializes all 2000 elements in the array **y** to zero.

You are also allowed to have the size of an array determined automatically by the number of initializing values. For example, the declaration

```
float grades[] = {65, 55, 65, 70, 65, 65};
```

would automatically define the array **grades** to have six elements.

4.2.5 Subscript Checking in C

The C language does not perform any checking when referencing an element of an array. It will therefore accept subscripts that reference places in memory beyond the bounds of the array. This will usually produce serious (and often hard to diagnose) errors. For example, the following is legal C code that will rarely do what any programmer actually intended:

```
double x[1000];
int i;
for(i=0; i<1001; i++)
  scanf("%lf", &x[i]);
```

The advantage of computer languages that, unlike C, check whether subscripted references to arrays are inside the array's defined boundaries is that such languages often detect a common type of programming error. However, array subscript checking adds a significant computational burden to using arrays, slowing down many computational procedures. In addition, there are some situations where a programmer has a good reason for subscripting outside the memory allocated for an array. The fact that C does not prevent the programmer from subscripting outside the boundaries of an array is entirely consistent with the C's philosophy of providing fast computation and allowing the programmer as much flexibility as possible.

4.3 REPRESENTING STRINGS IN C

Arrays of **char**s are used in C to store character strings. For example, the array **str** defined with the statement

```
char str[20];
```

can be used to store a character string of up to 20 characters. Arrays of this type are used for input and output of strings with **scanf()** and **printf()** using the **%s** format in the control string.

For example, the following fragment of code reads two strings of up to 20 characters and then outputs their values along with some commentary.

```
/* fragment using strings in scanf() and printf() */
char str1[20], str2[20];
scanf("%s %s", str1, str2);
printf("The two strings are %s and %s\n", str1, str2);
```

When used in **scanf()**, the **%s** format control will read consecutive characters that are not separated by white space as a single string. Thus, the input

```
Hello world
```

would be treated as two distinct input strings, while the input

```
Hello,world
```

would be treated as a single string.

By convention, the end of a character string in C is denoted by a special marker, called the *null character*, after the last real character in an array. The null character is represented by the special character constant **'\0'**. [1]

For example, the string representing the word **"example"** would be stored in an array of at least eight characters as shown in Figure 4.2. Each element of the array is a **char**. For example, the value of **str[4]** is the character **'p'**.

---

[1]The reader should not confuse the null character, as represented by the character constant **'\0'**, with the null pointer. The former occupies a single byte, while the latter occupies as many bytes as required by a pointer.

Figure 4.2 Example of using an array of char for a string.

Strings can be initialized in C just as any other array. For example, the variable definition

```
/* initialization of a string */
char str[] = {'e', 'x', 'a', 'm', 'p', 'l', 'e', '\0'};
```

would create an array of eight characters containing the string **"example"** . C also provides a more convenient form in which using double quotation marks (**" "**) enclosing the initial value. In this form, we would use the definition

```
/* simpler initialization of a string */
char str[] = "example";
```

Note that in the second form, the null character is not explicitly included. This is because the C compiler automatically appends the null character to string constants such as **"example"**.

The standard C library provides a library of functions for manipulating strings. The header file containing the prototype for these functions is **string.h**. In these functions character strings are passed and returned as pointers to the beginning of the array of characters (i.e. with type **char ***). For example, the library function **strcpy()** has two arguments, each of which is a pointer to a character array. It copies the contents of the array of **char** pointed to by the second argument to the similar array pointed to by the first argument. This copies an entire character string, up to and including the null character that terminates the string. **strcpy()** also returns the pointer to the first string. A typical use of **strcpy()** is shown in the following code fragment.

```
/* fragment showing copying of a character string */
#include <string.h>

char str1[]= "test string";
char str2[20];

strcpy(str2, str1);
```

The function call to **strcpy()** would copy the first 12 characters (the four in the word **test**, the blank space between the two words, the six in the word **string**, and the null character that C always appends to a string constant) from the array **str1** to the array **str2**. The remaining eight characters in the array **str2** would be unchanged.

The most commonly used of the string manipulation functions are as follows:

KEY PARTS OF THE STRING FUNCTION LIBRARY

Function	Arguments	Description of Key String Functions
strcpy()	char *s1, char *s2	copies **s2** to **s1**; returns **s1**
strncpy()	char *s1, char *s2, int n	copies at most **n** characters of **s2** to **s1**; returns **s1**
strcat()	char *s1, char *s2	concatenates **s2** to end of **s1**; returns **s1**
strncat()	char *s1, char *s2, int n	concatenates first **n** characters of **s2** to end of **s1**; returns **s1**
strcmp()	char *s1, char *s2	compares **s1** to **s2**; returns **int** < 0 if **s1** < **s2**, 0 if **s1**==**s2** or > 0 if **s1**>**s2**
strlen()	char s1	returns **int** equal to length of **s1** (not including '\0')

The following example illustrates how some of the string manipulation functions are used.

```
/*  test various functions in string library */

#include <stdio.h>
#include <string.h>

main()
{
  char string1[] = "elephant"; /* first test string */
  char string2[] = "bull ";    /* second test string */
  char s3[20], s4[20], s5[20];     /* empty strings */

/* test strlen()*/
  printf("Length of string 1 is %d\n", strlen(string1));

/* test string copy functions */
  strcpy(s3, string2);
  strncpy(s4, string2, 3);
  printf("Two copied strings are %s and %s\n", s3, s4);

/* test string concatenation functions */
  strcat(s3, string1);
  strncat(s4, string1, 3);
  printf("Two concatenated strings are %s and %s\n", s3,
    s4);
```

```
/* test string comparison */
  if(strcmp(s3, s4))
    printf("Strings are different\n");
  else
    printf("Strings are identical\n");
}
```

The simple program initializes two strings and uses the string length, copy, concatenation, and comparison functions. When compiled and executed, it produces the following output:

```
Length of string 1 is 8
Two copied strings are bull  and bul
Two concatenated strings are bull elephant and bulele
Strings are different
```

4.4 VECTOR OPERATIONS

We can use arrays as a convenient way of representing vectors. For example, if **v** is a vector with *n* entries, then the *length* of **v** (generally denoted as |**v**|) is the square root of the sum of squared entries in **v**. The following C function takes an array of **double**s representing the vector and the value of *n* as inputs, and returns the vector's length as a **double**. The code is as follows:

```
/* function to compute the length of a vector */

#include <math.h>
double length(double v[], int n)
{
  double total = 0.0;
  int i;
  for(i=0; i<n; i++)
    total += v[i]*v[i];
  return (sqrt(total));
}
```

The file **math.h** must be included because it contains the prototype for the C math library function **sqrt()** that computes square roots.

Another example is the computation of the *inner product* of two vectors. A graphical interpretation of the inner product is that it finds a scalar value which equals the product of the lengths of the vectors times the cosine of the angle between them. The inner product of two vectors **v** and **w** is usually denoted as **v · w**. In C, the following function computes the inner product of two vectors each with n entries. The vectors are each represented with an array of **double**s.

```
/* function to compute an inner product */

double inner_product(double v[], double w[],  int n)
{
  double total = 0.0;
  int i;
  for(i=0; i<n; i++)
    total += v[i]*w[i];
  return (total);
}
```

Yet another common problem is finding the *vector product* of two vectors. While the idea of vector products can be generalized to any number of dimensions, the most common case requires the vector product of three-dimensional quantities, with the dimensions representing the x, y, and z axes. The result of a vector product is itself a vector. If **v** and **w** are two vectors, then their vector product is typically denoted by **v** × **w**.

We need to pass as arguments the two vectors we want to multiply and a vector into which the function will place the result. No return value is needed.

The C function **vector_3_product()** given below has as its arguments **v** and **w**, the two vectors to multiply, and the vector **result** into which the product of **v** and **w** is placed. No return value is needed, so the function is declared as **void**.

```
/* compute vector product for three dimensions */

void vector_3_product(
  double v[], /* first vector */
  double w[], /* second vector */
  double result[]) /* computed product */
{
  result[0] = v[1]*w[2]  - v[2]*w[1];
  result[1] = v[2]*w[0]  - v[0]*w[2];
  result[2] = v[0]*w[1]  - v[1]*w[0];
}
```

A brief example can illustrate the potential value of even this small library of vector functions. Consider a box defined by three vectors **a**, **b**, and **c**, all of which begin at the same point as shown in Figure 4.3. The volume V contained in the "box" (which is technically a parallelepiped) can be shown to be given by the formula

$$V = |(\mathbf{a} \times \mathbf{b}) \cdot \mathbf{c}|$$

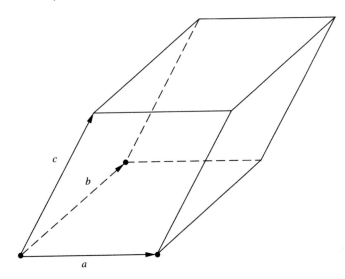

Figure 4.3 Volume defined by three vectors with a common origin.

If we had the three vectors **a**, **b**, and **c** originating at the point (0,0,0) and ending at (1.7,0,0), (0,2.3,0), and (1,2,3), respectively, then the following program could be used to find the volume of the box these vectors define.

```
/* main program to compute volume of parallelepiped */
#include <stdio.h>
#include <math.h>

double inner_product(double *, double *,  int);
double length(double *, int);
void vector_3_product(double *, double *, double *);

main()
{
  double a[] = {1.7, 0.0, 0.0}; /* vector a */
  double b[] = {0.0, 2.3, 0.0}; /* vector b */
  double c[] = {1.0, 2.0, 3.0}; /* vector c */
  double temp[3]; /* temporary vector for a x b */
  double volume;

  vector_3_product(a,b,temp);
  volume = fabs (inner_product(temp, c, 3) );
  printf("Volume is %lf\n", volume);
}
```

4.5 PROGRAMMING PROJECT: POPULATION FORECASTING

In this section we use arrays to build a computer simulation to forecast future growth of a country's population. We will use what is termed a *discrete step* simulation. In this type of model, we update the state of some known system in a series of steps, each corresponding to some fixed time interval.

In the case of population forecasting, the state of the system will be represented by the number of people in each of a set of age and sex categories. For example, the array **males** will hold the number of males in the population. Each entry in the array **males** will correspond to a range of ages. **males[0]** will hold the number of males between the ages of 0 and 9, **males[1]** will hold the number of males between ages 10 and 19, etc. We will define **males** to have 10 entries, with the last entry, **males[9]**, used to hold the number of males 90 years of age or older. The array named **females** will be defined similarly to hold the population of females by age group.

We will model population change in 10-year intervals. Over that period, the number of people of either sex in any given age group depends on four factors: mortality, births, aging, and net immigration.

The mortality process will be predicted using age- and gender-specific mortality rates. The arrays **male_mortality** and **female_mortality** will hold these mortality rates. For example, **male_mortality[i]** will contain the fraction of males in age category **i** that will die in a 10-year period.

The second process in population dynamics is the birth of infants. It is common to predict births using age-specific birth rates applied to the population of women. This is usually represented in "live births per woman." We shall define the array **birth_rate** to store these values, with the value **birth_rate[i]** holding the average number of live births in a 10-year period for women in age category **i**. For simplicity, we will assume that live births are divided equally between male and female babies.[2]

The aging of the population can be represented straightforwardly. In any time interval, the surviving population of both men and women in age interval i will become the population in age interval $i + 1$. The only exception to this is that men and women in the oldest age group (those 90 or older) stay in their respective age categories.

Finally, there may be some net outmigration or immigration that adds to, or subtracts from, the population in any age group. Net immigration is often the most difficult component of demographic change to predict. This is particularly true for smaller countries that may border regions of political upheaval, where large numbers of refugees may migrate across a border. For the sake of simplicity, we will assume that net in-migration is negligible in this example.

We can express each of these demographics processes in a C function. The first function, named **mortality()**, handles the deaths in the population. Its implementation

---

[2]The assumptions on birth rates are not exactly true. Slightly more than half of all babies born are males. This is generally compensated for by a higher male infant mortality rate. In addition, situations where the number of adult males is decreased, as in post-World War II Soviet Union, may reduce birth rates.

is as follows:

```
/* function to compute deaths */
void mortality(
  double pop[], /* population array */
  double rates[], /* mortality rate */
  int n) /* number of age categories */
{
  int i;
  for(i=0; i<n; i++)
    pop[i] *= (1.0-rates[i]);
}
```

This function has three arguments. The first is an array **pop** holding some population, and the second is the array **rates** that holds the mortality rates, and the third is an **int n**, the number of age categories. The function simply multiplies the population in each age category by one minus the mortality rate for that age category.

The computation of the number of births can be done using a function we have already written. This is because the number of children born is simply the inner product of a vector representing the population of females and the vector of birth rates. For completeness, we repeat the code of the function **inner_product()**:

```
/* function to compute an inner product */

double inner_product(
  double v[], /* first vector */
  double w[], /* second vector */
  int n) /* number of entries in vectors */
{
  double total = 0.0;
  int i;
  for(i=0; i<n; i++)
    total += v[i]*w[i];
  return (total);
}
```

This function would be called using the arrays **females** and **birth_rate** as the first two arguments, and the number of age categories as the third.

The third function, named **aging()**, represents the aging process. Its implementation is as follows:

```
/* function to age population */
void aging(
  double pop[],          /* population array */
  int n)                 /* number of age categories */
```

```
{
  int i;

  pop[n-1] += pop[n-2];
  for(i=n-2; i > 0; i--)
    pop[i] = pop[i-1];
  pop[0] = 0.0;
}
```

This function has two arguments. The first is an array **pop** holding some population, and the second is an **int n**, the number of age categories. The function first updates the oldest age category by adding the number in the next-to-last age group to the current cohort. It then updates all the other age categories. Finally, it sets the population in the youngest age category to zero.

We will also need functions to read in an array of values and to output an array. The functions **read_vector()** and **output_vector()** below serve this purpose.

```
/* function to read a vector */

void read_vector(
  double array[], /* the array */
  int n)          /* number of values in array */
{
  int i;
  for(i=0; i<n; i++)
    scanf("%lf", array+i);
}

/* function to output a vector */

void output_vector(
  double vec[],     /* vector to be output */
  int n)            /* number of entries in vector */
{
  int i;
  for(i=0; i<n; i++)
    printf("  %d   %10.0lf\n", i, vec[i]);
}
```

Note that the function **output_vector()** displays the subscript index as well as the corresponding value.

The last step is to combine these functions into a single program. Our program begins with the usual **#include** directives and has a series of declarations for the various constants, variables, and function prototypes. The **main()** program then reads in the number of time intervals to be simulated and makes calls to the different functions to perform the simulation. While the functions **mortality()** and **birth()** are coded to allow for the possibility that we might have different mortality and birth rates in each time period, we have coded the implementation of **main()** under the assumption these factors remain fixed over the interval being forecasted.

The C code implementing **main()** is given below.

```c
/*  population forecasting system
    using aging and mortality */

#include <stdio.h>
#define AGE_GROUPS  10

/* function prototypes */

void mortality(double[], double[], int);
double inner_product(double[], double[], int);
void aging(double[], int);
void read_vector(double[], int);
void output_vector(double[], int);

main()
{
/* various arrays used in program */
  double males[AGE_GROUPS], females[AGE_GROUPS];
  double male_mortality[AGE_GROUPS]
  double female_mortality[AGE_GROUPS];
  double birth_rate[AGE_GROUPS];

  int i, periods;
  double newborn;

/* read in number of periods and arrays */
  scanf("%d", &periods);
  read_vector(males, AGE_GROUPS);
  read_vector(females, AGE_GROUPS);
  read_vector(male_mortality, AGE_GROUPS);
  read_vector(female_mortality, AGE_GROUPS);
  read_vector(birth_rate, AGE_GROUPS);

/* loop through all periods */
  for(i=1; i<=periods; i++) {
  /* predict mortality */
    mortality(males, male_mortality, AGE_GROUPS);
    mortality(females, female_mortality, AGE_GROUPS);

   /* predict births */
    newborn = inner_product(birth_rate,
                              females, AGE_GROUPS);
```

```
/* predict aging */
  aging(males, AGE_GROUPS);
  aging(females, AGE_GROUPS);

/* update number of children in first age category */
  males[0] = newborn/2.0;
  females[0] = newborn/2.0;

/* output current populations */
  printf("\nPopulation of males for period %d\n", i);
  output_vector(males, AGE_GROUPS);
  printf("\nPopulation of females for period %d\n",i);
  output_vector(females, AGE_GROUPS);
}
}
```

To see how this model works, consider an entirely hypothetical population. The initial populations of males and females and the age-specific mortality rates are given by the following table. Note that this hypothetical population is relatively young. This is characteristic of many third-world agrarian countries where population growth is quite rapid and reductions in infant mortality have not yet been offset by decreases in birth rates.

HYPOTHETICAL POPULATION AND MORTALITY RATES

Age Range	Females	Males	Female Mortality	Male Mortality
0-9	2400	2400	.05	.05
10-19	2300	2300	.05	.05
20-29	1200	1200	.05	.05
30-39	1100	1100	.05	.05
40-49	1100	1000	.05	.07
50-59	800	600	.15	.20
60-69	400	200	.25	.30
70-79	200	100	.35	.40
80-89	170	70	.75	.80
90+	130	30	.75	.80
TOTAL	9800	9000	NA	NA

The model also requires the expected number of live births per woman, by age. We will assume values that are characteristic of still-growing populations as given in the following table:

HYPOTHETICAL BIRTH RATES

Age Range	Birth Rate
0-9	0.0
10-19	.3
20-29	1.2
30-39	1.0
40-49	.2
50-59	0.0
60-69	0.0
70-79	0.0
80-89	0.0
90+	0.0

We can use these assumptions as inputs to the simple demographic model to predict the population of males and females in the future. Figure 4.4 depicts how the

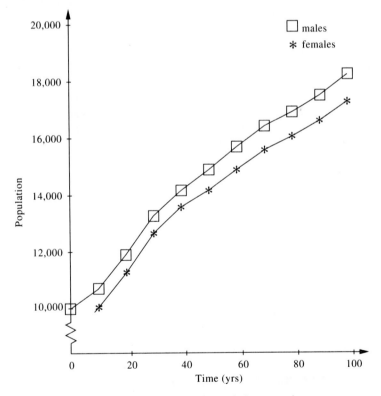

Figure 4.4 Evolution of population over time.

total number of males and females evolve over time. The growth of the population over time in this example is fueled by the combination of a relatively young population and the high birth rate.

4.6 REPRESENTING MATRICES IN C

4.6.1 Multidimensional Arrays

The basic idea of arrays in C generalizes to accommodate matrices reasonably straightforwardly. For example, a matrix of **double**s with three rows and two columns could be defined with the following C statement:

```
double mat[3][2];
```

The two array indices enclosed in square brackets denote the fact that the array is two-dimensional. Higher-order arrays can be defined simply by adding more subscripts.

The rules for referencing elements of a matrix in C are identical to those for single dimensional arrays. As with single-dimensional arrays, the subscripts begin with zero. Thus, the element in the first row and column of the array **mat** defined above would be **mat[0][0]**.

C stores the elements of multidimensional arrays in sequential memory locations. The rule in C is that the elements of a multidimensional array are stored in sequential memory locations with the *outer subscripts varying before the inner ones*. Thus in our example, the elements of **mat** would be stored in the following order:

```
mat[0][0], mat[0][1], mat[1][0], mat[1][1],
        mat[2][0], mat[2][1]
```

This is shown diagramatically in Figure 4.5. In this figure, the six elements of the array **mat** are arranged in sequential memory locations, with the outermost subscript varying first.

As with single-dimension arrays, it is possible to use pointers to address elements within a multidimensional array. For example,

```
mat[i][j]
```

is the same as

```
*(&mat[0][0] + 2*i + j)
```

In the form ***(&mat[0][0] + 2*i + j)**, the expression **&mat[0][0]** evaluates to a pointer to the address where the array **mat** begins. From this beginning address, we can

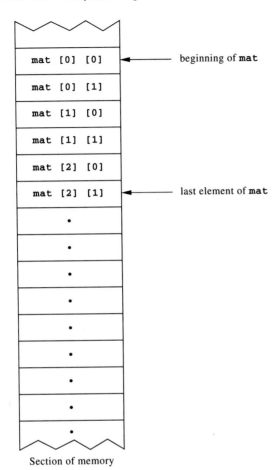

Figure 4.5 Two-dimensional array in memory.

Section of memory

find the number of array entries beyond the first that the element `mat[i][j]` lies. In this case, because `mat` has two columns, the entry `mat[i][j]` lies `2*i+j` elements beyond `mat[0][0]`. Finally, the indirection operator, `*`, outside the parentheses produces the value pointed to by `&mat[0][0]+2*i+j`

The use of a pointer to the starting address of an array (sometimes referred to as a *base address*) incremented by the number of elements beyond the start of the array (sometimes referred to as an *offset*) exploits the properties of pointer arithmetic. This approach works regardless of the type of the array because the rules for pointer arithmetic in C automatically take the storage requirements of the C data types into account. In the example above, the address computed in the pointer arithmetic expression

> `&mat[0][0]+2*i+j`

will automatically take into account the storage required by **doubles** in C.

More generally, if a two-dimensional array **m** is defined as having **ncol** columns, then the element **m[i][j]** can be equivalently written as ***(&m[0][0]+i*ncol+j)**. While the second form is considerably more awkward than the first, it is often used because of the way multidimensional arrays are passed as arguments to functions. This issue is explored in depth in the next subsection.

4.6.2 Multidimensional Arrays as Arguments to Functions

Multidimensional arrays are passed as arguments to functions in the same way as single-dimensional arrays. Thus, only the address to the beginning of the array is passed. One important difference, however, between single- and multidimensional arrays is that in order for a function to make use of a multidimensional array as an argument, *the function must know all but the innermost dimension of the array.*

For example, consider a function that simply adds up all the elements of **m**, an array of **double**s, and returns the sum as a **double**. The following code shows such a function.

```
/* function to sum values in a matrix with two columns */

double sum_vals(
   double m[][2],  /* the array */
   int nrows)      /* number of rows */
{
   int i,j;
   double sum = 0.0;
   for(i=0; i<nrows; i++)
     for(j=0; j<2; j++)
       sum += m[i][j];
   return(sum);
}
```

The reason that the function **sum_vals()** needs to know the number of columns in the array is that without such information it cannot compute how many elements beyond the beginning of the array the element **m[i][j]** lies. Put another way, the reference to **m[i][j]** is translated into ***(&m[0][0]+i*NCOLS+j)**, where **NCOLS** is number of columns in **m**. Unless **NCOLS** is known, the C compiler cannot compute the appropriate quantity to add to **m** to obtain the value in the ith row and jth column.

As coded above, the function **sum_vals()** is extremely limited in its usefulness. It works only on arrays that have two columns rather than on all arrays. For this reason, a more general-purpose function that adds the elements in an array would usually be coded using a pointer to the first element in the array along with the number of rows and columns in the array as its arguments. It would then use pointer arithmetic to compute the *offset* from the beginning of the array to access the array's elements. One possible implementation is as follows:

```
/* general function to sum the values in a matrix */

double sum_vals(
   double *m,   /* pointer to first element of array */
   int nrows,   /* number of rows */
   int ncols)   /* number of columns */
{
   int i,j;
   double sum = 0.0;
   for(i=0; i<nrows; i++)
     for(j=0; j<ncols; j++)
       sum += *(m + i*ncols + j);
   return(sum);
}
```

If the array **mat** has three rows and two columns, this function would be invoked as in the following code fragment:

```
double mat[3][2], sum;

sum = sum_val(&mat[0][0], 3, 2);
```

Note that the first argument is **&mat[0][0]**, which is the address of the first element of the array. This is technically different from the variable **mat**, which is pointer to a two-dimensional array.

To understand the distinction between a pointer to the first element of a two-dimensional array and a pointer to the array itself, one must understand how arrays are treated in C. The appropriate way to think about a two-dimensional array is as an *array of one-dimensional arrays*. Thus, if **mat** is a 3 by 2 array of **double**s, then **mat[0]** and **mat[1]** are both arrays of two **double**s. Thus the expression

```
*(mat[1] + 1)
```

is entirely equivalent to

```
mat[1][1]
```

The reason this is true is that **mat[1]** is itself an array, and its value is therefore the address of the beginning of that array. When we add **1** to **mat[1]**, we are doing pointer arithmetic. The dereferencing operator (*****) gives the value pointed to by **mat[1]+1**.

Because C treats objects such as **mat[1]** as arrays, the value of **mat** (without any brackets) is the address of **mat[0]**, and its type is a pointer to an array of arrays of **doubles**. The expression **mat+1** increments the pointer **mat** by one array (*not* one **double**), making it a pointer to row 1 of the array **mat**. Thus ***(mat+1)** points to element 0 in row 1, and the values ***(mat+1)[0]** and ***(mat+1)[1]** are legal references to **mat[1][0]** and **mat[1][1]**, respectively.

Some of these complicated relationships are shown in Figure 4.6, which depicts a section of memory where the six elements of the two-dimensional array **mat** are stored. The elements **mat[0]**, **mat[1]**, and **mat[2]** are themselves arrays and are therefore pointers to the place in memory where the arrays begin. Each of those arrays corresponds to a row of the complete array **mat**. In addition, the figure shows the value **mat** as itself an array consisting of **mat[0]**, **mat[1]**, and **mat[2]**. The value of **mat** is a pointer to **mat[0]**, the first element in that array of arrays.

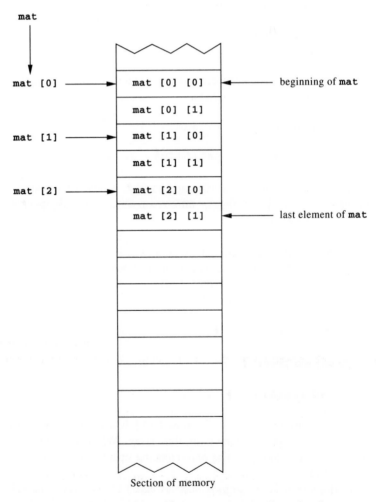

Figure 4.6 Relationships among parts of a two-dimensional array.

One of the consequences of the relationship between pointers and arrays is that there are many equivalent ways of accessing elements of two-dimensional arrays. Consider, for example, an array named `test` defined as

```
int test[10][20];
```

All of the following are equivalent ways of accessing `test[i][j]`:

```
*(test[i]+j)
(*(test+i))[j]
*((*(test+i))+j)
*(&test[0][0] + 20*i + j)
```

4.6.3 Initialization of Multidimensional Arrays

Multidimensional arrays can be initialized in a way that is similar to the method used for one-dimensional arrays. The most commonly used form relies on nested curly braces, as in the definition

```
int vals[3][2] = { {10, 20}, {20, 40}, {5, 10} };
```

You may also list the values without grouping them, as in the statement

```
int vals[3][2] = {10, 20, 20, 40, 5, 10};
```

You may also omit the size of the innermost dimension, so that the statement

```
int vals[][2] = { {10, 20}, {20, 40}, {5, 10}};
```

is legal. All dimensions other than the innermost must be given. The compiler will automatically compute the innermost dimension from the number of initial values provided.

As was the case with one-dimensional arrays, if the array contains more elements than there are initializers, then the remaining values are initialized to zero.

4.6.4 Using Macros with Arguments to Reference Array Elements

Using a base address and computing the offsets makes using multidimensional arrays in functions somewhat awkward. This shortcoming of C can be partly ameliorated by taking advantage of the C preprocessor's ability to have **#define** directives with arguments. This is an extended version of the **#define** directive that was first introduced in Section 2.10. **#define** directives that have arguments are sometimes called *macros*.

Consider, for example, a macro named **CUBE** created by the following **#define** directive:

```
#define CUBE(X)  ((X)*(X)*(X))
```

After the macro is defined, an occurrence of the text **CUBE** followed immediately by an argument in parentheses will be replaced by the preprocessor. This replacement is called *expanding* the macro. For example, suppose that the source code file has the statement

```
double a=5.0;
a = CUBE(a);
```

The C preprocessor would expand the macro **CUBE(a)**, changing the statement to

```
double a=5.0;
a = (a)*(a)*(a);
```

It might appear that enclosing the body of the macro and each of the parts of the macro expression in parentheses is unnecessary. However, suppose that the **#define** statement for **CUBE** been written as

```
#define CUBE(X) X*X*X
```

If we used the macro in the statement in the code fragment

```
double a=5.0;
a = CUBE(a+1.0);
```

the preprocessor would transform the assignment statement to

```
double a=5.0;
a = a+1.0 * a+1.0 * a+1.0;
```

which, given the rules for precedence of arithmetic operators, would result in a value of **a** equal to 16 rather than the cube of **a+1.0**, which equals 216.

Macros with arguments look like functions when used in a program. It is important to remember, however, that a macro is simply a rule for text substitution. The arguments of a macro do not have any variable types associated with them, and there is no way to enforce type restrictions in their use. In some situations, macros and functions that appear to do exactly the same thing can have entirely different effects. For example, consider a function named **cube** that returns the cube of an **int**.

```
/* function that returns cube of an int */
int cube(int x)
{
```

```
   return(x*x*x);
}
```

If we use this function in the fragment

```
int i=3;
int j;

j = cube(i++);
```

the result will be that **i** has the value 4 and **j** has the value 27. If we performed the seemingly same operation using the macro **CUBE**, as in

```
int i=3;
int j;

j = CUBE(i++);
```

the preprocessor would expand the macro **CUBE** so that the assignment statement would be

```
j=(i++)*(i++)*(i++);
```

This would result in **j** having the value 20 (**3*4*5**) and **i** having the value 6.

Because macros are fundamentally different from functions, we will always use capital letters for the names of macros. This is a common, though not universal, convention among C programmers.

One use for macros with arguments is as a means of avoiding the awkwardness associated with arrays that are arguments to functions. As an example, we can rewrite the function **sum_vals()** in Section 4.6.2, which sums all the values in a two-dimensional array, as follows:

```
/* function using macros to sum values in a matrix */

/* macro for m[i][j] */
#define M(I,J)  (*(m+(I)*ncols+(J)))

double sum_vals(
   double *m,   /* pointer to first element in array */
   int nrows,   /* number of rows */
   int ncols)   /* number of columns */
{
   int i,j;
   double sum = 0.0;
```

```
      for(i=0; i<nrows; i++)
        for(j=0; j<ncols; j++)
          sum += M(i,j);
    return(sum);
}

    #undef M
```

The macro **M** has two arguments, **I** and **J**, because references to the array **m** will require a row and column number. The parentheses around the body of the macro, **I** and **J**, avoid some of the problems arising from the fact that macros are only text substitutions, not functions.

The macro gets used in the statement

```
sum += M(i,j);
```

which the C preprocessor converts to

```
sum += (*(m+(i)*ncols+(j)));
```

Note that we introduce a new preprocessor directive, **#undef**. This has the effect of *undefining* a macro so that all statements after the appearance of the **#undef** will not have that macro substitution done. In this case the directive **#undef M** undefines the macro **M**. While this step is not essential, it is good programming practice to undefine a macro after the portion of the code that uses it. This limits the range of statements in your program where the macro is defined, avoiding mistakes if you use the same macro name for a different purpose later.

This new version of **sum_vals()** is used in exactly the same way as the earlier implementation. For example, if we had defined a two-dimensional array named **mat** with three rows, we could use this new version of **sum_vals()** with the statement

```
printf("Sum of values is %lf\n",
        sum_vals(&mat[0][0],3,2));
```

We will use macros for accessing elements of multidimensional arrays in the remainder of this chapter because they make code easier to follow.

4.7 BASIC MATRIX OPERATIONS

We can illustrate the use of multidimensional arrays in C by developing some general-purpose functions for matrix manipulation. For example, in linear algebra, the product of a matrix **A** that has m rows and n columns with a vector that has n elements is a vector with m elements. If the matrix **A** is defined as having elements

$$
\begin{pmatrix}
a_{00} & a_{01} & \cdots & a_{0,n-1} \\
a_{10} & a_{11} & \cdots & a_{1,n-1} \\
a_{20} & a_{21} & \cdots & a_{2,n-1} \\
\vdots & \vdots & \ddots & \vdots \\
a_{m-1,0} & a_{m-1,1} & \cdots & a_{m-1,n-1}
\end{pmatrix}
$$

and the vector $\mathbf{b}$ has elements $b_0, b_1, b_2, \ldots, b_{n-1}$, then the product $\mathbf{c} = \mathbf{Ab}$ is a vector with the following elements:

$$
\begin{pmatrix}
c_0 = \sum_{i=0}^{n-1} a_{0i} b_i \\[2mm]
c_1 = \sum_{i=0}^{n-1} a_{1i} b_i \\[2mm]
c_2 = \sum_{i=0}^{n-1} a_{2i} b_i \\[2mm]
\vdots \\[2mm]
c_{m-1} = \sum_{i=0}^{n-1} a_{m-1,i} b_i
\end{pmatrix}
$$

For example, if we have the following two arrays

$$
\mathbf{A} = \begin{pmatrix} 3 & 2 \\ 4 & 1 \\ 7 & 9 \end{pmatrix}
$$

$$
\mathbf{b} = \begin{pmatrix} 2 \\ 1 \end{pmatrix}
$$

then the product $\mathbf{Ab}$ is given by

$$
\mathbf{Ab} = \begin{pmatrix} 8 \\ 9 \\ 23 \end{pmatrix}
$$

The C function called **mat_vec_mult()** (for matrix-vector multiply) below computes this type of product. Its arguments are a pointer to the first element of the matrix **a**, the vector **b**, the resultant product vector **c**, and **m** and **n**, the number of rows and columns in **A**. The user of this routine must make sure that the arguments **a**, **b**, and **c** are dimensioned correctly.

```
/* function to compute product of matrix and a vector */
#define A(I,J)  (*(a+(I)*n+(J)))
```

```
void mat_vec_mult(
  double *a,   /* pointer to first element in matrix  */
  double b[],  /*  vector */
  double c[],  /* result of  A*b */
  int m,       /* number of rows in A */
  int n)       /* number of columns in A */
{
  double sum=0.0;
  int i,j;
  for(i=0; i<m; i++) {
      for(j=0; j<n; j++)
        sum = sum + A(i,j) *  b[j];
      c[i] = sum;
    }
}


#undef A
```

The implementation uses a macro named **A** to access elements of the matrix.

To use the function **mat_vec_mult()**, you must pass the first element of the array **a**. For example, the following program multiplies an array with four rows and three columns by a vector with three elements, producing a vector with four elements.

```
/* use matrix times vector function */
void mat_vec_mult(double *,double *,double *,int,int);

main()
{

double mat[4][3] = {{3,2,1}, {5,6,4}, {8,4,2}, {2,1,2}};
double vec[3] = {1,2,3};
double result[4];

mat_vec_mult(&mat[0][0], vec, result, 4, 3);
}
```

The four elements in the array **result** will be 10, 29, 22, 10.

It is worth noting that the product of a matrix and a vector is *not* the same as the product of a vector and a matrix. More generally, operations involving matrix multiplication are not commutative.

Another example of matrix algebra is the multiplication of two matrices **A** and **B**, where **A** has m rows and n columns, and **B** has n rows and p columns. The product of **A** and **B** is a matrix which we shall call **D** that has m rows and p columns. The elements d_{ij} of **D** are given by the following formula:

$$d_{ij} = \sum_{k=0}^{n-1} a_{ik}b_{kj}$$

For example, if we have the matrices **A** and **B** as

$$A = \begin{pmatrix} 3 & 2 \\ 4 & 1 \\ 7 & 9 \end{pmatrix}$$

$$B = \begin{pmatrix} 2 & 3 \\ -1 & 4 \end{pmatrix}$$

then the product **AB** is

$$AB = \begin{pmatrix} 4 & 17 \\ 7 & 16 \\ 5 & 57 \end{pmatrix}$$

The function `mat_mult()` (for underline{ma}trix underline{mul}tiply) below computes the product of two matrices, placing the result in a third matrix. As with the function `mat_vec_mult()`, the user of the function must make sure that appropriately dimensioned arrays are provided as arguments.

```
/* function to compute product of two matrices */

#define A(I,J) (*(a + (I)*n + (J)))
#define B(I,J) (*(b + (I)*p + (J)))
#define C(I,J) (*(c + (I)*p + (J)))

void mat_mult(
  double *a, /* pointer to first element of A */
  double *b, /* pointer to first element of B */
  double *c, /* pointer to first element of A*B */
  int m,     /* number of rows in A */
  int n,     /* number of cols. in A & rows in B */
  int p)     /* number of cols. in B */

{
  double sum;
  int i,j,k;
  for(i=0; i<m; i++)
    for(j=0; j<p; j++){
      sum = 0.0;
      for(k=0; k<n; k++)
        sum +=  A(i,k) * B(k,j);
      C(i,j) = sum;
      }
}

#undef A
#undef B
#undef C
```

Other common matrix operations include:

- Transposition—constructing a matrix in which element ij replaces element ji.
- Addition—adding two matrices with the same number of rows and columns, with each element computed as the sum of the corresponding elements in the two original matrices.
- Operations on matrices that have a particular form—some matrices have a particular form that makes it possible to perform certain operations more efficiently. For example, a symmetric matrix is one where element ij equals element ji for all i and j. The transposition of a square symmetric matrix is trivial because transposition does not change the matrix at all.

Some specific cases of specialized matrix operations are given as exercises at the end of this chapter.

4.8 SIMULTANEOUS EQUATIONS

Systems of linear equations arise in virtually every area of engineering and science. In addition, many mathematical models in the social sciences produce systems of simultaneous linear equations. These systems are often quite large and can only be solved in reasonable amounts of time with a computer.

We consider here only the case where the number of linear equations is the same as the number of unknowns. We define the unknowns as $x_0, x_1, , \ldots, x_{n-1}$. Suppose that we have n equations with n unknowns. The jth equation of the system is of the form

$$a_{j0}x_0 + a_{j1}x_1 + \ldots + a_{j,n-1}x_{n-1} = b_j$$

Systems of linear equations are generally expressed in matrix form. Define a matrix $\mathbf{A}$ of coefficients in the form

$$
\mathbf{A} = \begin{pmatrix}
a_{00} & a_{01} & \cdots & a_{0,n-1} \\
a_{10} & a_{11} & \cdots & a_{1,n-1} \\
a_{20} & a_{21} & \cdots & a_{2,n-1} \\
\vdots & \vdots & \ddots & \vdots \\
a_{n-1,0} & a_{n-1,1} & \cdots & a_{n-1,n-1}
\end{pmatrix}
$$

and define two vectors, $\mathbf{x}$ and $\mathbf{b}$, with elements $x_0, x_1, , \ldots, x_{n-1}$ and $b_0, b_1, , \ldots, b_{n-1}$, respectively, then a system of linear equations can be written in the matrix form

$$\mathbf{Ax} = \mathbf{b}$$

4.8.1 Simple Gauss-Jordan Elimination

The basic method we will use to solve a system of linear equations is called *Gauss-Jordan elimination*. The method is based on two observations:

- Multiplying any equation in the system by a constant other than zero does not affect the solution. Since each row of the matrix $\mathbf{A}$ represents the coefficients of an equation in the system, we can multiply the jth row in $\mathbf{A}$ and the jth element in $\mathbf{b}$ by a constant without affecting the solution.

- Adding or subtracting any two equations in the system to does not affect the solution. Adding the ith equation to the jth equation corresponds to adding each element in the ith row of $\mathbf{A}$ to the corresponding values in the jth row, and adding the ith element in $\mathbf{b}$ to the jth element.

Gauss-Jordan elimination uses these operations to transform the original system of equations into one with the same solution, but where all the off-diagonal terms of the coefficients are zero. The right-hand side of the equation system after such a transformation divided by the diagonal terms is the solution to the system of linear equations. We present the method in two parts. First, we implement a simple (but slightly flawed) version of Gauss-Jordan elimination to show the basic steps of the method. In the next subsection we augment that method by a technique called *partial pivoting* to eliminate the flaw.

To see how these rules apply to a specific situation, consider a matrix $\mathbf{A}$ and a vector $\mathbf{b}$ as follows:

$$\mathbf{A} = \begin{pmatrix} 2 & 3 & 5 \\ 1 & 2 & 4 \\ 4 & 7 & 3 \end{pmatrix}$$

$$\mathbf{b} = \begin{pmatrix} 10 \\ 5 \\ 15 \end{pmatrix}$$

This represents the following system of equations:

$$2x_0 + 3x_1 + 5x_2 = 10$$
$$x_0 + 2x_1 + 4x_2 = 5$$
$$4x_0 + 7x_1 + 3x_2 = 15$$

Gauss-Jordan elimination proceeds by taking half the first equation and subtracting it from the second equation. The goal of these operations is to transform element a_{10} in the coefficient matrix $\mathbf{A}$ to zero. These transformations would yield the equations

$$2x_0 + 3x_1 + 5x_2 = 10$$
$$0x_0 + .5x_1 + 1.5x_2 = 0$$
$$4x_0 + 7x_1 + 3x_2 = 15$$

The next step would be to transform a_{20} to zero by taking twice the first equation and subtracting it from the third. This would reduce the system of equations to

$$2x_0 + 3x_1 + 5x_2 = 10$$
$$0x_0 + .5x_1 + 1.5x_2 = 0$$
$$0x_0 + 1x_1 - 7x_2 = -5$$

The effect of these transformations has been to reduce all off-diagonal coefficients in the first column of $\mathbf{A}$ to zero. We call the element on the diagonal used to transform the off-diagonal elements in the same column the *pivot element*.

The next step in Gauss-Jordan elimination is to use the diagonal element in the second row as a pivot to reduce all off-diagonal terms in the *second* column to zero. Taking 6 times the second row and subtracting it from the first row yields

$$2x_0 + 0x_1 - 4x_2 = 10$$

$$0x_0 + .5x_1 + 1.5x_2 = 0$$

$$0x_0 + 1x_1 - 7x_2 = -5$$

Taking 2 times the second row and subtracting it from the third row produces

$$2x_0 + 0x_1 - 4x_2 = 10$$

$$0x_0 + .5x_1 + 1.5x_2 = 0$$

$$0x_0 + 0x_1 - 10x_2 = -5$$

The last step is to use the third equation to eliminate off-diagonal terms in the final column. Taking .4 times the third equation and subtracting it from the first yields

$$2x_0 + 0x_1 + 0x_2 = 12$$

$$0x_0 + .5x_1 + 1.5x_2 = 0$$

$$0x_0 + 0x_1 - 10x_2 = -5$$

Taking .15 times the third equation and adding it to the second produces

$$2x_0 + 0x_1 + 0x_2 = 12$$

$$0x_0 + .5x_1 + 0x_2 = -.75$$

$$0x_0 + 0x_1 - 10x_2 = -5$$

The final solution is found by dividing the right-hand side by the diagonal coefficients, resulting in the solution $x_0 = 6$, $x_1 = -1.5$, and $x_2 = .5$. In vector notation, this solution is written as $\mathbf{x} = (6, -1.5, .5)$.

The example above generalizes by noting that Gauss-Jordan elimination proceeds by using the ith diagonal element (a_{ii}) to eliminate the off-diagonal elements in the ith column of $\mathbf{A}$. The basic transformation for each row is of the form

$$\text{row}_j = \text{row}_j \left(1 - \frac{a_{ji}}{a_{ii}}\right)$$

This algorithm is most easily implemented in C by creating a "working matrix" that contains all of the coefficients and the right-hand-side values. All transformations are done on the working matrix. This avoids changing values in the original arrays $\mathbf{A}$ and $\mathbf{b}$. The working matrix has n rows and $n + 1$ columns. The first n columns are the matrix $\mathbf{A}$, and the last column is $\mathbf{b}$. In our simple three equation example, the working matrix would be

$$\begin{pmatrix} 2 & 3 & 5 & 10 \\ 1 & 2 & 4 & 5 \\ 4 & 7 & 3 & 15 \end{pmatrix}$$

The C implementation copies values from **A** and **b** into the working matrix and then does the appropriate Gauss-Jordan elimination. It then computes the solution vector **x**. The function requires that the user define a working array with sufficient space. This working array is one of the arguments to the function. The implementation is as follows:

```c
/* Gauss-Jordan without partial pivoting */
#define A(I,J) (*(a + (I)*n + (J)))
#define WORK(I,J) (*(work + (I)*(n+1) + (J)))

void simple_gauss(
  double *a,      /* the coefficients in A */
  double b[],     /* the right-hand side b */
  double *work,   /* the working array */
  double x[],     /* the solution array */
  int n)          /* number of equations */

{
  double m;
  int i,j,k;

/* set up working matrix */
  for(i=0; i<n; i++) {
    for(j=0; j<n; j++)
      WORK(i,j) = A(i,j);
    WORK(i,n) = b[i];
  }

/* loop through the rows of the working matrix */
  for(i=0; i<n; i++)
/* perform elimination */
    for(j=0; j<n; j++)
      if(j != i) {
        m = WORK(j,i)/WORK(i,i);
        for(k=i; k<=n; k++)
          WORK(j,k) -= m*WORK(i,k);
      }

/* compute solution as rhs divided by diagonal */

  for(i=0; i<n; i++)
    x[i] = WORK(i,n)/WORK(i,i);
}

#undef A
#undef WORK
```

The implementation uses two macros for accessing elements in the matrix of coefficients and the working matrix. Note that the macro **WORK** is written somewhat differently from the macro **A** because working matrix has **n+1** rather than **n** columns.

The function prototype for `simple_gauss()` is

```
void simple_gauss(double *, double *, double *,
                  double *, int);
```

and a code fragment that uses the function to solve our sample three-equation linear system would be

```
/* code using simple_gauss() */
double coeff[3][3] = { {2,3,5}, {1,2,4}, {4,7,3}};
double rhs[3] = {10,5,15};
double place[3][4];
double answer[3];
simple_gauss(&coeff[0][0],rhs,&place[0][0],answer, 3);
printf("Solution is: %lf %lf %lf\n", answer[0],
       answer[1], answer[2]);
```

Note that the two matrices, `coeff` and `place`, are passed to `simple_gauss()` in the form `&coeff[0][0]` and `&place[0][0]` rather than as `coeff` and `mat`. This is because, as discussed in Section 4.6.2, `coeff` and `mat` are not pointers to `double`s, but are pointers to *arrays* of `double`s. The function `simple_gauss()` is written to accept pointers to `double`s, which are then used as the base addresses of the matrices. Many C compilers will accept either form for the arguments even though the use of the matrix names alone is technically incorrect.

4.8.2 Partial Pivoting

The implementation of `simple_gauss()` unfortunately has a major flaw. *In particular, the method fails if any of the pivot elements is zero.* In this case the algorithm will attempt to divide an element of the coefficient matrix by zero, producing a floating-point error.

In order to avoid division by zero, we need to select a nonzero pivot element at each step. The simplest method is based on the observation that exchanging two rows in the working matrix leaves the system of equations unchanged. Thus, before pivoting on a diagonal element, we can look for a row in the working matrix that would produce a nonzero pivot element. Once we find this row, we can exchange it with the row that would have yielded a zero pivot value. This approach is called *partial pivoting*.

At each step of Gauss-Jordan elimination, all the rows below the one currently being considered are candidates for pivot elements. The rows above the current one already have been used for pivot elements. They cannot be used again because moving them to a different row of the working matrix will place their nonzero diagonal element in a nondiagonal position.

In general, there will be more than one candidate row that yields a nonzero pivot element. The selection of which one to use turns out to be significant. This is because without an appropriate selection, it is possible to show that Gauss-Jordan elimination is numerically unstable. Roundoff errors tend to accumulate in ways that seriously compromise the accuracy of the method.

The best element to select on a theoretical basis is still unknown. However, the simple approach of selecting the pivot element with the greatest absolute magnitude tends to work well empirically. This is the method we will implement.

We also need to deal with the case where all of the candidate pivot elements are zero. This happens when the system of linear equations either has no solution or has an infinite number of solutions. One way to deal with this problem is to test whether the absolute value of the largest candidate pivot element exceeds zero. While this would work on a computer with infinite floating-point precision, a more useful test for real computers is to make sure that the largest candidate pivot element exceeds some tolerance that the user of the function specifies. This makes it possible to detect both cases where there is no solution or where the pivot element is so small that a numerically meaningful solution cannot be found. We will implement the latter technique by defining an argument **tol** which is the smallest allowed pivot element. Our algorithm will stop if a pivot smaller than **tol** in absolute value is encountered.

The basic steps of partial pivoting are as follows:

- **Step 1.** Set up a working matrix as in the simple version of Gauss-Jordan elimination.
- **Step 2.** For each row i (starting with row 0) in the working matrix:
  1. Check rows i through $n - 1$ for the one which yields the pivot element with the largest absolute value. Call that row k.
  2. Swap row i with k.
  3. Perform Gauss-Jordan elimination using element ii of the working matrix as the pivot.
- **Step 3.** For each row i compute solution x_i as element in of the working matrix divided by element ii of the working matrix.

The implementation of this method is as follows:

```
/* implementation of Gauss-Jordan elimination
   with partial pivoting */

#include <math.h>
#define TRUE 1

#define FALSE 0
#define A(I,J) (*(a + (I)*n + (J)))
#define WORK(I,J) (*(work + (I)*(n+1) + (J)))

int gauss_jordan(
    double *a,      /* the coefficients in A */
    double b[],     /* the right-hand side b */
    double *work,   /* the working array */
    double x[],     /* the solution array */
```

```
    int n,            /* number of equations */
    double tol)       /* minimum allowed pivot element */


{
  double m, max, temp;
  int i,j,k, swap;

/* set up working matrix */
  for(i=0; i<n; i++) {
    for(j=0; j<n; j++)
      WORK(i,j) = A(i,j);
    WORK(i,n) = b[i];
  }

/* loop through the rows of the working matrix */
  for(i=0; i<n; i++) {
    max = -1.0;
    for(k=i; k<n; k++)
      if(fabs(WORK(k,i)) > max) {
        max = fabs(WORK(k,i));
        swap = k;
      }
/* check if pivot element is "large enough" */
    if(max <= tol)
      return(FALSE);

/* swap rows */
    if(swap != i)
      for(k=i; k<=n; k++) {
temp = WORK(i,k);
        WORK(i,k) = WORK(swap,k);
        WORK(swap,k) = temp;
      }

/* perform elimination */
    for(j=0; j<n; j++)
      if(j != i) {
        m = WORK(j,i)/WORK(i,i);
        for(k=i; k<=n; k++)
          WORK(j,k) -= m*WORK(i,k);
      }

  }
/* compute solution as rhs divided by diagonal */

  for(i=0; i<n; i++)
    x[i] = WORK(i,n)/WORK(i,i);
  return(TRUE);
}
```

```
#undef A
#undef WORK
```

The function **gauss_jordan()** returns an **int** which is **TRUE** if it found a solution without encountering a pivot element smaller than the tolerance **tol**, and returns **FALSE** otherwise. A typical usage for the function is shown in the following **main()** program.

```
/* example program using Gauss-Jordan elimination */
#include <stdio.h>
int gauss_jordan(double *, double *, double *,
                 double *, int, double);

double coeff[3][3] = { {2,3,5}, {1,2,4}, {4,7,3}};
double rhs[3] = {10,5,15};
double place[3][4];

main()
{
  double answer[3];
  if (gauss_jordan(&coeff[0][0], rhs, &place[0][0],
                   answer, 3, .00001))
    printf("Solution is: %lf %lf %lf\n",
                   answer[0], answer[1], answer[2]);
  else
    printf("No solution found\n");
}
```

4.8.3 Solving Systems of Linear Equations with the Same Coefficients

The Gauss-Jordan method generalizes quite easily to the situation where there are several systems of linear equations of the form

$$\mathbf{Ax_0} = \mathbf{b_0}$$
$$\mathbf{Ax_1} = \mathbf{b_1}$$
$$\mathbf{Ax_2} = \mathbf{b_2}$$

$$\vdots$$

$$\mathbf{Ax_{M-1}} = \mathbf{b_{M-1}}$$

Here, each of the systems of equations has the same matrix of coefficients but the right-hand sides are different, so the solutions are different. Systems of equations such as these could be solved one at a time using the Gauss-Jordan method. However, they can be solved far more efficiently by altering the Gauss-Jordan method so that the working matrix consists of the matrix $\mathbf{A}$ augmented by M columns, $\mathbf{b_0}, \mathbf{b_1}, \ldots, \mathbf{b_{M-1}}$. The basic steps of Gauss-Jordan are then applied to the working matrix, transforming all the columns of the new working matrix. When the algorithm terminates, the solutions $x_0, x_1, \ldots, x_{M-1}$ can be found from the added columns in the working matrix.

As an example, consider the solution of the following two systems of simultaneous equations:

$$2x_0 + 3x_1 + 5x_2 = 10$$

$$1x_0 + 2x_1 + 4x_2 = 5$$

$$4x_0 + 7x_1 + 3x_2 = 15$$

and

$$2x_0 + 3x_1 + 5x_2 = 9$$

$$1x_0 + 2x_1 + 4x_2 = 4$$

$$4x_0 + 7x_1 + 3x_2 = 27$$

These equation systems have exactly the same coefficients but different right-hand sides. To solve these efficiently, we would create a working matrix that has the original coefficients *plus* one column per equation set. In the example above, this matrix would be as follows:

$$\begin{pmatrix} 2 & 3 & 5 & 10 & 9 \\ 1 & 2 & 4 & 5 & 4 \\ 4 & 7 & 3 & 15 & 27 \end{pmatrix}$$

We would then perform the steps in Gaussian reduction, operating on this working matrix at each step. Each step in the reduction would modify all the columns. For example, in a simple Gauss-Jordan elimination (without partial pivoting), the first step would take half the first row and subtract it from the second row, yielding the matrix

$$\begin{pmatrix} 2 & 3 & 5 & 10 & 9 \\ 0 & .5 & 1.5 & 0 & -.5 \\ 4 & 7 & 3 & 15 & 27 \end{pmatrix}$$

This process would proceed until the matrix was reduced to the following:

$$\begin{pmatrix} 2 & 0 & 0 & 12 & 8 \\ 0 & .5 & 0 & -.75 & 1 \\ 0 & 0 & -10 & -5 & 10 \end{pmatrix}$$

The two solutions are found by dividing the diagonal elements into the right-hand-side columns, producing the vectors (6, -1.5, .5) and (4, 2, -1) as solutions to the two systems of linear equations.

4.8.4 Improvements in Gauss-Jordan

A relatively minor improvement in the Gauss-Jordan method, called *implicit pivoting*, first rescales all the equations so they are all the same order of magnitude, and then uses partial pivoting. This requires a little additional computational effort and storage to find and store the scaling factors. In addition, the final solution must be rescaled back to the original units. The key advantage of this method is that the choice of the pivot element is independent of the scale of the independent variables.

A more sophisticated version of pivoting is called *full pivoting*. In this approach, exchanges of both rows *and columns* are considered in order to select the pivot element. Exchanging columns permutes the subscripts in the vector **x**. Implementing full pivoting therefore requires that the function keep track of which elements in the original vector **x** are stored in each column. The order of the independent variables must be updated each time two columns are swapped. The x's in the final solution are reordered to take into account the column swapping. Full pivoting makes it possible to select better pivot elements, thereby reducing the effects of roundoff errors.

The speed of all the pivoting methods can often be improved by a technique called *Gaussian elimination with backsubstitution*. This modification uses Gaussian elimination to reduce only the *lower triangle* of the system of equations to zero, reducing the original matrix of coefficients to one of the form

$$\begin{pmatrix} a'_{00} & a'_{01} & a'_{02} & \cdots & a'_{0,n-1} \\ 0 & a'_{11} & a'_{12} & \cdots & a'_{1,n-1} \\ 0 & 0 & a'_{22} & \cdots & a'_{2,n-1} \\ \vdots & \vdots & \vdots & \ddots & \vdots \\ 0 & 0 & 0 & \cdots & a'_{n-1,n-1} \end{pmatrix}$$

where the notation a'_{ij} denotes the coefficients of the equations after the Gaussian elimination. The original coefficients in the vector **b** are also transformed in the elimination process into a new vector $\mathbf{b} = b'_0, b'_1, b_2, \ldots, b'_{n-1}$.

Once the matrix is in this form, the solution can be found by working backward, solving first for x_{n-1} as

$$x_{n-1} = \frac{b'_{n-1}}{a'_{n-1,n-1}}$$

This can be used to solve for x_{n-2} as

$$x_{n-2} = \frac{b'_{n-2} - a'_{n-2,n-1}x_{n-1}}{a'_{n-2,n-2}}$$

The backward substitution proceeds solving for x_{n-j} with the general formula

$$x_{n-j} = \frac{b'_{n-j} - \sum_{k=n-j+1}^{n-1} a'_{n-j,k}x_k}{a'_{n-j,n-j}}$$

How backsubstitution works can be seen using the now-familiar system of equations

$$2x_0 + 3x_1 + 5x_2 = 10$$

$$1x_0 + 2x_1 + 4x_2 = 5$$

$$4x_0 + 7x_1 + 3x_2 = 15$$

If we create the working matrix

$$\begin{pmatrix} 2 & 3 & 5 & 10 \\ 1 & 2 & 4 & 5 \\ 4 & 7 & 3 & 15 \end{pmatrix}$$

and reduce it by only generating zeros in the lower triangle, we obtain the matrix

$$\begin{pmatrix} 2 & 3 & 5 & 10 \\ 0 & .5 & 1.5 & 0 \\ 0 & 0 & -10 & -5 \end{pmatrix}$$

This corresponds to the equation system

$$2x_0 + 3x_1 + 5x_2 = 10$$

$$0x_0 + .5x_1 + 1.5x_2 = 0$$

$$0x_0 + 0x_1 - 10x_2 = -5$$

This can be solved first for the values of $\mathbf{x}$ as follows:

$$x_2 = \frac{-5}{-10} = .5$$

$$x_1 = \frac{0 - 1.5(.5)}{.5} = -1.5$$

$$x_0 = \frac{10 - 5(.5) - 3(-1.5)}{2} = 6$$

There are even more sophisticated methods that are used to solve very large systems of linear equations. One group of methods involves various forms of decomposition of the matrix of coefficients (called *LU decomposition*). Another set of approaches are iterative in nature, converging to a solution that is close to the true one. All of these techniques are beyond the scope of this book. The reader is referred to [Press, William H. 88].

4.9 MATRIX INVERSION

One of the common uses of Gauss-Jordan elimination is to find what is called the *matrix inverse*. For any matrix $\mathbf{A}$ that has an equal number of rows and columns, the inverse of $\mathbf{A}$ (denoted by $\mathbf{A}^{-1}$) is the matrix such that the product $\mathbf{A}\mathbf{A}^{-1}$ is a matrix which has all ones along the diagonal and zeros for the rest of the elements. (A matrix with ones along its diagonal and zeros in its off-diagonal terms is called the *identity matrix*, and is usually denoted by $\mathbf{I}$.)

For example, if a 2 by 2 matrix $\mathbf{A}$ is

$$A = \begin{pmatrix} 1 & 2 \\ 4 & 3 \end{pmatrix}$$

then the reader can verify that the inverse of **A** is

$$\begin{pmatrix} -3/5 & 2/5 \\ 4/5 & -1/5 \end{pmatrix}$$

Gauss-Jordan elimination can be used to find the inverse of a matrix by structuring the problem of finding the elements of $\mathbf{A}^{-1}$ as the solution to a series of systems of simultaneous linear equations. Each system of equations defines the conditions for one of the rows of the inverse of **A**. To see this, define the elements of **A** as a_{ij} and denote the elements of $\mathbf{A}^{-1}$ as x_{ij}. Using this notation, the system of equations which provides the first row of $\mathbf{A}^{-1}$ is

$$a_{00}x_{00} + a_{01}x_{10} + a_{02}x_{20} + \ldots + a_{0,n-1}x_{n-1,0} = 1$$

$$a_{00}x_{01} + a_{01}x_{11} + a_{02}x_{21} + \ldots + a_{0,n-1}x_{n-1,1} = 0$$

$$a_{00}x_{02} + a_{01}x_{12} + a_{02}x_{20} + \ldots + a_{0,n-1}x_{n-1,2} = 0$$

$$\vdots$$

$$a_{00}x_{0,n-1} + a_{01}x_{1,n-1} + a_{02}x_{2,n-1} + \ldots + a_{0,n-1}x_{n-1,n-1} = 0$$

This can be written more compactly in matrix form by defining $\mathbf{I}^j$ as a vector with a one in the jth element and a zero in all other elements. $\mathbf{I}^j$ is the jth column of the identity matrix. We also define $\mathbf{x}^j$ as the jth column of $\mathbf{A}^{-1}$. Using this notation we can write the system of equations above as

$$\mathbf{A}\mathbf{x}^0 = \mathbf{I}^0$$

The other columns of $\mathbf{A}^{-1}$ can be solved with equation systems of the same form:

$$\mathbf{A}\mathbf{x}^1 = \mathbf{I}^1$$

$$\mathbf{A}\mathbf{x}^2 = \mathbf{I}^2$$

$$\vdots$$

$$\mathbf{A}\mathbf{x}^{n-1} = \mathbf{I}^{n-1}$$

This set of simultaneous equation systems is in exactly the same form as those discussed in the preceding section! It is a set of simultaneous equation systems where every equation system has exactly the same matrix of coefficients but where the right-hand sides of the systems differ. We can solve this using the same technique, creating a working matrix that has n additional columns, each corresponding to a column of the identity matrix. The resulting solutions will be the elements in the inverse of **A**.

To see how this would work, consider again the example matrix

$$A = \begin{pmatrix} 1 & 2 \\ 4 & 3 \end{pmatrix}$$

This matrix can be inverted by setting up two systems of simultaneous equations as follows:

$$1x_0^0 + 2x_1^0 = 1$$

$$4x_0^0 + 3x_1^0 = 0$$

and

$$1x_0^1 + 2x_1^1 = 0$$

$$4x_0^1 + 3x_1^1 = 1$$

These two systems of equations have the same coefficients, so they can be solved by performing Gauss-Jordan reduction on the following working matrix:

$$\begin{pmatrix} 1 & 2 & 1 & 0 \\ 4 & 3 & 0 & 1 \end{pmatrix}$$

The reader can verify that this matrix reduces to

$$\begin{pmatrix} 1 & 0 & -3/5 & 2/5 \\ 0 & -5 & -4 & 1 \end{pmatrix}$$

which implies solutions for x_0^0, x_1^0, x_0^1 and x_1^1 as follows:

$$x_0^0 = -3/5$$

$$x_1^0 = 4/5$$

$$x_0^1 = 2/5$$

$$x_1^1 = -1/5$$

or in matrix form, the inverse matrix is

$$\begin{pmatrix} -3/5 & 2/5 \\ 4/5 & -1/5 \end{pmatrix}$$

4.10 PROGRAMMING PROJECT: SHORTEST PATHS IN A NETWORK

While most of our discussion of arrays has focused on their application to linear algebra, the concept of an array in C is far more general. In this section we develop a complete program to solve what is called the *all-to-all shortest path problem*. This problem arises frequently in transportation systems and logistics planning.

The shortest path problem is what is called a *network* (or *graph*) problem. Basically, a network is a series of points (often called *nodes*) connected by a set of *links* (often called *arcs*). Each link or arc has associated with it some cost, which may be measured in dollars, time, or some more abstract measure of the difficulty of moving between the two points. In our formulation, each link will be unidirectional, allowing for the possibility that traveling from node i to node j may involve different costs than traveling from j to i.

The shortest path problem has numerous applications. For example, a trucking company may want to find the shortest path in the highway network to move goods from one point to another. Similarly, a telecommunications company may want to route phone messages on the least expensive lines. In these cases, the arcs represent physical entities such as highways or telephone cables.

Figure 4.7 depicts a sample network with five nodes numbered from 0 to 4 and a set of arcs. The label beside each arc is the cost associated with traversing it. For example, the arc connecting nodes 2 to node 3 has a cost of 2 units. Note that not all pairs of nodes have direct connections. For example, there is no arc connecting node 2 to node 4.

Networks are also used in more abstract ways. For example, the nodes might represent various stages in the completion of some construction project. Node 0 might represent the development site before any construction begins, and node 3 might represent the completed building. The arcs in the network might represent the costs of performing some element of the construction process, transforming the site from state i to state j. In this case, the shortest path from node 0 to node 3 would show the least expensive way to construct the building.

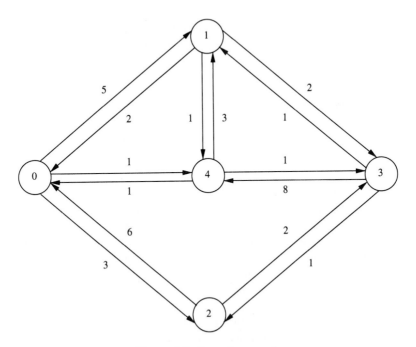

Figure 4.7 Example network.

4.10.1 The Floyd-Warshall Algorithm

Given a network, the all-to-all shortest path problem is to find the total cost of going
from every node to every other node in the network. For some pairs of nodes, this can
be found by inspecting the network. For example, the shortest way to get from node 4
to node 3 in Figure 4.7 is to traverse the arc connecting these two nodes, incurring a
cost of 1 unit. In a large network that may consist of tens of thousands of arcs, finding
the shortest path between various node pairs may be very complicated.

The method we will use to solve the all-to-all shortest path problem is called the
Floyd-Warshall algorithm [Bertsekas, Dmitri P. 89]. It uses a two-dimensional array
to represent the cost of traveling from every node to every other node. Each row
of the two-dimensional matrix corresponds to an originating node, and each column
corresponds to a destination node. For example, if we call the matrix of node-to-node
costs $\mathbf{C}$, the entries c_{ij} in $\mathbf{C}$ will hold the cost of traversing the shortest path from node
i to node j.

The Floyd-Warshall algorithm begins by initializing the entries in the cost matrix
with the costs of the arcs in the network. If we define n to be the number of nodes in
the network, this initialization is as follows

- Initialize the diagonal elements $c_{00}, c_{11}, \ldots, c_{n-1,n-1}$ to zero. This reflects the
  fact that travel from any node to itself is costless.
- Each arc in the network connects some node i and some node j. For each arc,
  initialize the value c_{ij} in the cost matrix $\mathbf{C}$ to the cost of that arc.
- All other entries in the array should be set to some large value that exceeds the
  total cost of any final path in the network. For now, we will denote that value
  as ∞.

The Floyd-Warshall algorithm then examines every pair of nodes ij ($i \neq j$), and
for each node pair, tests whether the current cost of going from i to j can be reduced
by using node 0 as an intermediate node. This corresponds to finding the following
minimum:

$$\min(c_{ij}, c_{i0} + c_{0j})$$

Once this is done for all ij pairs, the revised matrix $\mathbf{C}$ now holds the cost of
the shortest paths that use only node 0 as a possible intermediate node. The algorithm
then performs the same operation on all node pairs using node 1 as another potential
intermediate node. Nodes 2, 3, ..., $n - 1$ are each added, with the cost matrix updated
at each stage. When this is completed, the final cost matrix includes the possibility of
using all nodes as intermediates, and therefore contains the costs of the shortest paths
through the network.

To see how these steps in the algorithm work, consider again the simple network
shown in Figure 4.7. The initial cost matrix for this simple five-node network is as

follows:

$$
C = \begin{pmatrix}
0 & 5 & 3 & \infty & 1 \\
2 & 0 & \infty & 2 & 1 \\
6 & \infty & 0 & 2 & \infty \\
\infty & 1 & 1 & 0 & 8 \\
1 & 3 & \infty & 1 & 0
\end{pmatrix}
$$

After the initialization step, the algorithm would test alternative ways to get from every node i to every other node $j \neq i$ using node 0 as an intermediate node. For example, the initial cost of going from node 1 to node 2 is initialized to infinity because there is no arc in the network linking these nodes. The updating rule is to compare the current cost $c_{12} = \infty$ with $c_{10} + c_{02} = 2 + 3 = 5$. Since the use of node 0 as an intermediate node for getting from 1 to 2 reduces the current cost, the value 5 would replace c_{12}.

After all ij pairs are tested to see if using node 0 as an intermediate is less costly, the revised cost matrix would be as follows:

$$
C = \begin{pmatrix}
0 & 5 & 3 & \infty & 1 \\
2 & 0 & 5 & 2 & 1 \\
6 & 11 & 0 & 2 & 7 \\
\infty & 1 & 1 & 0 & 8 \\
1 & 3 & 4 & 1 & 0
\end{pmatrix}
$$

The algorithm then examines alternative paths using node 1 as an intermediate node. Since the cost matrix has already been revised using node 0 as an intermediate node, adding a test for node 1 yields the lengths of paths that can make use of *either* node 0 or node 1, or both. After all ij pairs are considered in this phase, the resulting cost matrix is

$$
C = \begin{pmatrix}
0 & 5 & 3 & 7 & 1 \\
2 & 0 & 5 & 2 & 1 \\
6 & 11 & 0 & 2 & 7 \\
3 & 1 & 1 & 0 & 2 \\
1 & 3 & 4 & 1 & 0
\end{pmatrix}
$$

The updating process continues by testing nodes 2, 3, and 4 as possible intermediate nodes. When all five nodes have been considered, the resulting cost matrix will contain the costs of the shortest paths in the network. The reader can verify that the resulting matrix will be

$$
C = \begin{pmatrix}
0 & 3 & 3 & 2 & 1 \\
2 & 0 & 3 & 2 & 1 \\
5 & 3 & 0 & 2 & 4 \\
3 & 1 & 1 & 0 & 2 \\
1 & 2 & 2 & 1 & 0
\end{pmatrix}
$$

There are several observations worth noting about the Floyd-Warshall algorithm:

- The Floyd-Warshall algorithm does not provide the actual paths that yield the lowest cost of getting between node pairs. It provides only the costs of those paths.
- The actual path that yields the least cost path may not be unique. For example, in the network shown in Figure 4.7, there are two paths between nodes 1 and 3 that each cost 2 units. The direct route uses the arc between nodes 1 and 3, while an indirect route uses node 4 as an intermediate node.
- The algorithm may not work when some of the arcs have negative costs. In particular, the algorithm requires that every series of arcs in the network that begins and ends at the same node have positive total cost. This condition is guaranteed when all arcs have positive costs.
- In some networks it may not be possible to reach every node from every other node. This will be detected in the algorithm because the initial infinite entries in the cost matrix will never be updated, leaving the value ∞ in the final cost matrix for such node pairs.
- The algorithm requires very large amounts of memory and computation time. The memory requirements grow as the square of the number of nodes in the network, and the computation time grows as the *cube* of the the number of nodes. Methods other than the Floyd-Warshall algorithm exist that are far more efficient for large networks, particularly for networks that have a relatively low ratio of arcs to nodes.

4.10.2 Implementation of the Floyd-Warshall Algorithm

Implementing the Floyd-Warshall algorithm in C is straightforward. We of course need to replace the value ∞ with some value. Since we will be using **int**'s for arc costs, we will select some positive integer value that is very large compared to the costs of arcs. The C header file **limits.h** has a defined constant **INT_MAX** (the largest representable integer). As explored in Exercise 4-22, the value **INT_MAX/2** is a reasonable choice for the "large value."

We begin the complete program with some **#include** directives, some **#define** directives, and function prototypes. These are as follows:

```
/* program to find the shortest path between all nodes
   in a network */

#include <stdio.h>
#include <limits.h>
#define MAXSIZE 100
#define LARGE_VALUE INT_MAX/2

/* prototype for Floyd_Warshall algorithm */
void floyd_warshall(int *, int, int);
```

```
int minint(int, int);     /* min of two ints */
void show_cost(int *, int, int); /* output matrix */
```

The value defined as **LARGE_VALUE** is used for infinity in the implementation. **MAXSIZE** is used to dimension the cost array; its value determines the largest network, measured in the number of nodes, that can be handled by the program. The three functions prototyped are:

- **floyd_warshall()**. This function implements the shortest path algorithm. Its arguments are a pointer to the first entry in the cost matrix, the number of rows in the cost matrix (declared in **main()**), and the number of nodes in the actual network.
- **minint()**. This function returns the minimum of its two **int** arguments.
- **show_cost()**. This function displays the cost matrix. Its arguments are the same as those for the function **floyd_warshall()**.

The next part of the program is a **main()** function that reads in the number of nodes in the network. This is followed by a series of **for** loops that initialize the cost matrix. The arcs in the network are then read in using **scanf()**, with each arc described by its beginning node, ending node, and cost. The **main()** function then invokes the function that implements the Floyd-Warshall algorithm, and then invokes a function that outputs the results.

The **main()** function for the program is as follows:

```
/* main() for Floyd-Warshall program */
main()
{
  int cost[MAXSIZE][MAXSIZE];  /* cost matrix */
  int i,j;                     /* subscripts */
  int flag = !EOF;   /* flag used in reading input */
  int arc_cost;      /* temporary variable */
  int nodes;         /* number of nodes in network */

/* read in number of nodes and
   initialize the cost matrix */
  scanf("%d", &nodes);

  for(i=0; i<nodes; i++)
    for(j=0; j<nodes; j++)
      if(i==j)
        cost[i][j] = 0;
      else
        cost[i][j] = LARGE_VALUE;

/* read in arcs in network */
  while(flag != EOF) {
```

```
      flag = scanf("%d %d %d", &i, &j, &arc_cost);
      if(flag != EOF)
        cost[i][j] = arc_cost;
  }


  /*  run Floyd-Warshall algorithm */

  floyd_warshall(&cost[0][0], MAXSIZE, nodes);

  /* output results */
    show_cost(&cost[0][0], MAXSIZE, nodes);


  }
```

Note that the function defines a cost array that has a maximum size **MAXSIZE**, which is set here to 100. This maximum value can be redefined to handle larger networks.

The core of the program is the function that implements the Floyd-Warshall algorithm. This function is as follows:

```
/* this function implements the Floyd-Warshall algorithm
   for the all-to-all shortest path problem */

#define M(I,J) (*(m + (I)*ncols + (J)))

void floyd_warshall(
   int *m,          /* pointer to beginning of matrix */
   int ncols,       /* number of columns in matrix */
   int nodes)       /* number of nodes */
{
   int i,j,k;

   for(k=0; k<nodes; k++)   /* test intermediate nodes */
     for(i=0; i<nodes; i++)
       for(j=0; j<nodes; j++)
         if(i != j)          /* check costs using node k */
           M(i,j) = minint(M(i,j), M(i,k)+M(k,j));
}
#undef M
```

The two remaining functions, **minint()** and **show_cost()**, are straightforward. **minint()** simply takes the minimum of its two integer arguments and returns that minimum value. Its implementation is

```
/* this function takes the minimum of two integers */

   int minint(int x, int y)
   {
```

```
    if(x<y)
      return(x);
    return(y);
}
```

The function **show_cost()** displays the resulting cost matrix. Because the cost matrix as defined in **main()** may have more rows than the number of nodes in the actual network, **show_cost()** must be able to display the square, upper left corner of the complete two-dimensional array. It therefore has as arguments a pointer to the first value in the array, the actual number of columns defined for the array, and the number of nodes in the network. As in the function **floyd_warshall()**, a macro is used to reference the actual elements within the array.

The code for **show_cost()** is as follows:

```
/* function to print matrix of integers */

#define MAT(I,J) (*(mat + (I)*ncols + (J)))

void show_cost(int *mat, int ncols, int nodes)
{
    int i,j;
    printf("Cost matrix is:\n");
    for(i=0; i<nodes; i++) {
      for(j=0; j<nodes; j++)
        printf("%5d ", MAT(i,j));
      printf("\n");
      }
}

#undef MAT
```

Our implementation of **show_cost()** has the unfortunate property of producing very long lines of output for large arrays. Exercise 4-11 at the end of this chapter explores the correction of this shortcoming.

4.11 PROGRAMMING PROJECT: SIMULATING A ROBOT IN A MAZE

In Chapter 1 we devised a hypothetical robot which was capable of executing eight distinct machine language instructions. In order to follow this programming project, the reader may wish to review the material in Section 1.5. The robot's machine language was used to write a program to find the way through a maze using the "right hand on wall" algorithm. In this section we develop a C program that simulates the machine language of the robot.

The idea of writing a program on one computer that simulates the machine language of another computer may at first seem somewhat odd. However, simulations of this sort are widely used in the design of software for processors which are under development. For example, one might want to experiment with developing programs for a processor which is still in the design stage in order to understand the probable performance of those programs. Writing a simulator allows you to work with the proposed machine language before you have to commit the design to fabrication.

In order to write this program, we will first have to define variables that describe the maze. Our maze will be coded using a grid of points on the (x, y) axes. The lower left-hand corner of the maze will be defined as point $(0,0)$. The line segments that define the walls of the maze will connect various coordinates on the grid. This geometry is illustrated in Figure 4.8.

As shown in Figure 4.8, each segment in the maze connects grid points with integer coordinates that are adjacent to each other. We will store these segments in a two-dimensional array called **walls**, with each row of the array holding a separate line segment. The **int** variable **nwalls** will store the total number of line segments that make up the maze.

Each row of the array **walls** will have four elements, corresponding to the (x, y) coordinates of the beginning and end of the segment. For example, if row 6 of the

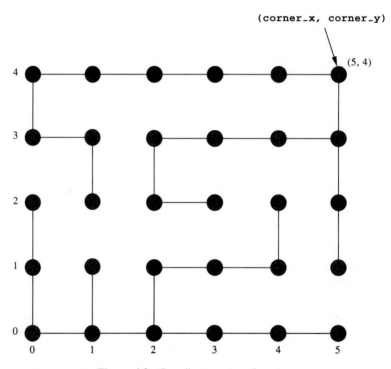

Figure 4.8 Coordinate system for maze.

array **walls** is used to store a horizontal line segment from point (2,1) to (3,1), then the following would be entered in the array:

```
walls[6][0] = 2;   /*x value for beginning of wall 6 */
walls[6][1] = 1;   /*y value for beginning of wall 6 */
walls[6][2] = 3;   /*x value for end of wall 6 */
walls[6][3] = 1;   /*y value for end of wall 6 */
```

By convention, the (x, y) values defining any wall of the maze will be ordered so that the starting value always is either below or to the left of the ending value. Thus, the wall connecting points (4,3) and (3,3) would have starting point (3,3) and ending point (4,3) because (3,3) lies to the left of (4,3) on the (x, y) plane.

We will also need variables to define the size of the maze. These will be stored in variables **corner_x** and **corner_y**, which will correspond to the (x, y) coordinates of the *upper right corner* of the maze.

The following variable definitions describe the geometry of the maze:

```
#define MAXWALLS 1000   /* max number of walls in maze */

int corner_x, corner_y;/* upper right corner of  maze */
int walls[MAXWALLS][4]; /* walls for maze */
int nwalls;             /* actual number of walls in maze */
```

The value **MAXWALLS** is used to define the maximum number of walls that will be allowed.

All these variables describing the maze will be defined *external* to any of the functions in our program. Their scope will therefore include all the functions in the program. This will avoid the need to pass their values as arguments to the functions that make up the complete program. The values of **corner_x, corner_y, nwalls** and the entries in the array **walls** will be read as inputs to the program.

We will also need to use the coordinate system to describe the position of the robot at any point in time. The robot moves between the squares defined by walls; we will refer to these squares as *cells*. Each cell of the maze will be labeled by the coordinates of its *lower left* corner of the grid points that define the square. For example, the lower left cell of the maze will be labeled as (0,0). We will use the variables **x** and **y** to hold the cell coordinates of the robot.

The robot also has a direction of forward movement. We will code this as one of four possible integer values defined by the following preprocessor directives:

```
#define NORTH 0   /* code for up direction in maze */
#define EAST 1    /* code for right direction in maze */
#define SOUTH 2   /* code for down direction in maze */
#define WEST 3    /* code for left direction in maze */
```

The integer variable **direct** will be used to store the direction the robot is heading. The initial values of **x**, **y**, and **direct** will be read as inputs to our program.

We will also use **#define** statements to code the eight possible machine language instructions. As with the values for the robot's direction of movement, these preprocessor definitions are not essential, but they improve the readability of the program significantly. The eight instructions are given by the following definitions:

```
#define FORWARD       1
#define IN_MAZE       2
#define WALL_AHEAD    3
#define COND_BRANCH   4
#define RIGHT         5
#define DISPLAY       6
#define BRANCH        7
#define HALT          8
```

For clarity, we will also use a preprocessor directive to define the value **FALSE** as 0 and the value **TRUE** as 1. These will be used in some of the functions that test whether there is a wall in front of the robot. These are provided in the following **#define** directives:

```
#define TRUE  1
#define FALSE 0
```

The robot simulator also requires storage to simulate the memory of the robot. We will define an array of **int**s named **ram**, which will have a maximum size **RAMSIZE**. The following definitions will be used:

```
#define RAMSIZE 100    /* maximum RAM of robot */
int ram[RAMSIZE];      /* simulated RAM of robot */
```

With all of the definitions above as preamble, our simulator will be developed using the following functions:

- **main()**. This will read the machine code for the robot's program, the maze size and geometry, and the initial position of the robot.
- **run_program()**. This will direct the actual simulation. Its arguments are the contents of the robot's memory, the location of the robot, and the direction of the robot.
- **wall_ahead()**. This will test whether there is a wall ahead of the robot, and return **TRUE** if there is such a wall, and **FALSE** otherwise. Its arguments are the array used to simulate the robot's memory, the initial (x, y) coordinates of the robot, and the robot's current direction.
- **search_walls()**. This function will be used by **wall_ahead()** to search the set of walls. Its arguments are the beginning and ending (x, y) coordinates of the segment being searched for.

- `still_in_maze()`. This checks if the robot is still inside the boundaries of the maze, and returns **TRUE** if it is, and **FALSE** otherwise. Its arguments are the current (x, y) coordinates of the robot.

The function prototypes for the functions other than `main()` are as follows:

```
/* simulator function */
void run_program(int [], int, int, int);

/* test for wall ahead */
int wall_ahead(int, int, int);

/* search through array of walls */
int search_walls(int, int, int, int);

/* check if still in maze */
int still_in_maze(int, int);
```

The relationships among the various functions are shown in Figure 4.9. As shown in this figure, `main()` invokes `run_program()`, which in turn invokes `still_in_maze()` and `wall_ahead()`. `wall_ahead()` invokes the function `search_walls()`. Diagrams such as this are often useful in understanding how the separate functions that make up a large program work together.

The function `main()` is responsible for reading the inputs to the program and calling the function `run_program()` to simulate the robot. The code for `main()` is as follows.

```
/* main() for robot simulation */
#include <stdio.h>

main()
{

  int ram[RAMSIZE];   /* simulated RAM of robot */
  int i;
  int x,y, direct;
  int num_inst;   /* number of instructions in program */

/* read in program */

  scanf("%d", &num_inst);
  for(i=0; i<num_inst; i++)
    scanf("%d", &ram[i]);

/* read in maze */

  scanf("%d %d %d", &corner_x, &corner_y, &nwalls);
```

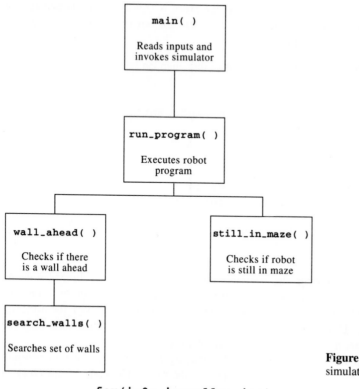

Figure 4.9 Functions used in robot simulator.

```
for(i=0; i<nwalls; i++)
    scanf("%d %d %d %d", &walls[i][0], &walls[i][1],
            &walls[i][2], &walls[i][3]);

/* read in initial position */
    scanf("%d %d %d", &x, &y, &direct);

/* run program */
    run_program (ram, x, y, direct);

}
```

The implementation of **main()** is based on the assumption that the inputs begin with the number of machine code instructions to be read, followed by the actual instructions. Following the example in Section 1.5, this portion of the inputs would be as follows:

```
25
1
2
4
```

18
5
5
3
4
15
10
5
5
5
7
6
1
7
1
6
4
15
14
5
0
8

These inputs are followed by the coordinates of the upper right corner of the maze and the number of walls in the maze. The walls in the maze are input as pairs of (x, y) coordinates. Figure 4.10 shows a very small maze and the initial position of the robot

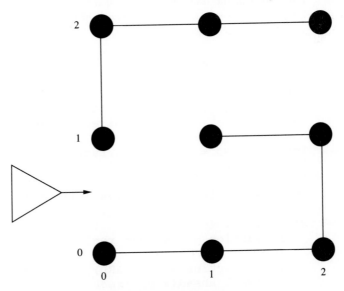

Figure 4.10 Small maze.

as a triangle. The small arrow shows the initial direction the robot is pointed in, which in this case is **EAST**. The input for this small maze would be as follows:

```
2 2 7
0 0 1 0
1 0 2 0
2 0 2 1
1 1 2 1
0 1 0 2
0 2 1 2
1 2 2 2
```

The final inputs are the initial (x, y) coordinates of the robot (which may be negative since the robot begins outside the maze), and an integer indicating the initial direction of the robot. For the robot shown in Figure 4.10, these values would be

```
-1  0  1
```

The next function is **run_program()**. This function simulates the actual execution of the robot machine code. Its arguments are:

- **ram**—the array containing the values in the memory of the robot
- **x** and **y**—the location of the robot
- **direct**—the direction the robot is pointing (**NORTH**, **EAST**, **SOUTH**, or **WEST**)

The function **run_program()** keeps track of the value in the instruction register of the robot in the variable **inst_reg** and the value of the general register in the variable **reg**. Most of the function consists of a large **while** loop that has a series of **if...else if...if** statements, one for each of the eight possible machine language instructions. The C code for the function follows.

```c
void run_program(
  int ram[],    /* memory of computer */
  int x,        /* initial x location of robot */
  int y,        /* initial y location of robot */
  int direct)   /* initial direction of robot */
{
  int inst_reg = 0;   /* instruction register */
  int reg = 0;        /* register */
  int j;
  int instruction;    /* holds current instruction */

  while(TRUE) {
    instruction = ram[inst_reg];

    if(instruction == FORWARD)    /* move forward */
      if(wall_ahead(x,y,direct)) {
        printf("Can't move forward;");
```

```
          printf("memory location %d\n",
                  inst_reg);
          return;
        }
      else {
        if(direct == NORTH)
          y++;
        else if(direct == SOUTH)
          y--;
        else if(direct == EAST)
          x++;
        else if(direct == WEST)
          x--;
        else {
          printf("Illegal direction--Program halted\n");
          return;
        }
        printf("Now at location (%d,%d).", x, y);
        printf("Facing direction %d\n", direct);
        inst_reg++;
      }

    else if(instruction == IN_MAZE) { /* in maze? */
      reg = still_in_maze(x,y);
      inst_reg++;
    }
    else if(instruction == WALL_AHEAD) { /* wall ahead? */
      reg = wall_ahead(x,y,direct);
      inst_reg++;
    }

/* conditional branch */
    else if(instruction == COND_BRANCH)
      if(reg == 0)
        inst_reg = ram[inst_reg+1];
      else
        inst_reg = ram[inst_reg+2];

    else if(instruction == RIGHT) { /* turn right */
      direct = (direct+1)%4;
      inst_reg++;
    }
    else if(instruction == DISPLAY) { /* message */
      printf("Message is ");
      for(j=1; j<=5; j++)
        if(ram[inst_reg+j] == 0)
          printf(" ");
```

```
              else
                  printf("%c", (char)ram[inst_reg+j]+'A'-1);
              printf("\n");
              inst_reg += 6;
          }

    /* unconditional branch */
          else if(instruction == BRANCH)
              inst_reg = ram[inst_reg+1];

          else if(instruction == HALT) { /* halt robot */
              printf("Machine halted\n");
              return;
          }
          else { /* illegal instruction code */
              printf("Illegal operation %d at location %d\n",
                     ram[inst_reg], inst_reg);
              return;
          }
      }
  }
```

Each possible machine instruction alters the value of the instruction register (stored
in the variable **inst_reg**) as well as possibly changing the values of **x, y, direct,**
or **reg**. Various **printf()** statements in the function report changes in the robot's
position or direction as well as possible errors that might be encountered during the
robot's simulation.

One new aspect of the C language that appears in the function **run_program()**
is the statement

```
printf("%c", (char)ram[inst_reg+j]+'A'-1);
```

This statement prints a single character from the simulated memory of the robot. The
cast in the form **char** converts the integer in the array **ram** to a **char**, the type
appropriate to the **%c** format in the control string. The part of the statement

```
ram[inst_reg+j]+'A'-1
```

takes the integer from 1 through 26 (which represents the uppercase characters from
A to Z in the robot's machine language) and adds the value of the character **'A'-1**
to convert it to the representation of uppercase letters in C. This takes advantage of
the fact that the characters from **A** to **Z** must be represented in C by sequential **char**
values that are in ascending order. On most computers, the ASCII character set is used,
in which the letter **A** is represented by the **char** value 65, the letter **B** is represented by
the value 66, etc. The reader should examine each of the **if ... else if** clauses to
understand how they simulate the various machine language instructions of the robot.

The function `wall_ahead()` returns an `int` which is either `TRUE` or `FALSE` depending on whether or not there is a wall in the maze ahead of the robot. Its arguments are the current location and direction of the robot. The code for `wall_ahead()` is shown below.

```
/* function to test if there is a wall ahead */

int wall_ahead(int x, int y, int direct)
{
  int rvalue;

  if(direct == NORTH)
    rvalue = search_walls(x,y+1,x+1,y+1);
  else if(direct == SOUTH)
    rvalue = search_walls(x,y,x+1,y);
  else if(direct == EAST)
    rvalue = search_walls(x+1,y,x+1,y+1);
  else
    rvalue = search_walls(x,y,x,y+1);
  return(rvalue);

}
```

`wall_ahead()` invokes the function `search_walls()`, which in turn searches the set of walls to find out whether or not one exists directly in front of the robot. The wall it looks for depends on the direction the robot is pointing. For example, if the robot is at location (1,1) and is pointing `NORTH`, then `wall_ahead()` invokes `search_walls()` looking for a wall connecting the point (1,2) with the point (2,2).

`search_walls()` is a straightforward search through the array `walls`. It loops through the entire array until it reaches the end of the set of walls or finds the one it is looking for. The C code is as follows:

```
/*  function to search list of walls */

int search_walls(int x1, int y1, int x2, int y2)
{
  int i=0;
  int found = FALSE;

  while(i<nwalls && !found) {
      found = (walls[i][0] == x1 && walls[i][1] == y1 &&
        walls[i][2] == x2 && walls[i][3] == y2);
      i++;
    }
  return(found);
}
```

The final function is `still_in_maze()`. This function has as arguments the current coordinates of the robot, and returns **TRUE** if the robot is in the maze and **FALSE** otherwise. The function simply checks whether the robot's current (x, y) coordinates are inside the rectangle bounded by the points $(0,0)$ in the lower left corner and `corner_y, corner_y` in the upper right corner. The C code is given below.

```
/* function to check if robot is still in maze */

int still_in_maze(int x, int y)
{
   return(x>=0 && y>=0 && x<corner_x && y<corner_y);
}
```

It should be noted that our robot simulation program is not particularly efficient. The procedure used to search through the list of walls, for example, could be improved significantly. One might consider ordering the entries in the array of walls in ascending values of the x coordinates of their starting points. This would reduce the time needed to search for a given wall because only the entries in the array `wall` with x values less than or equal to the one being searched for need be examined. If the array was sorted, once a wall in the array with starting x coordinate greater than the one being looked for is examined, you would know that the wall being looked for cannot be in the array. Efficient methods for sorting large numbers of items and searching for entries are explored in Chapter 6.

The other area for potential improvement in our robot simulation is the addition of further error checking. The program does not check whether the number of machine code instructions exceeds the value of **RAMSIZE** or if the number of walls in the maze exceeds **MAXWALLS**. Both of these checks should be added in a more robust implementation. Similarly, the program does not check whether the coordinates defining the walls have the starting point to the left or below the ending point. It assumes the user takes care to ensure that the input is valid. The program also does not check whether the first step forward actually moves the robot from outside the maze to inside the maze. (It does, however, make sure that any forward step does not pass through a wall.) The reader may wish to experiment with adding these and other error checks to the program.

4.12 SUMMARY OF CHAPTER 4

In this chapter we covered some of the important algorithms for solving linear algebra problems. In developing C implementations of these algorithms, we introduced the concept of arrays. In C, an array is a set of contiguous memory locations holding values of the same type.

Single-dimensional arrays in C are defined by giving the number of elements in the array in square brackets. The elements in the array are numbered starting with element zero. Thus, an array `c` defined as having size `n` has elements `c[0]`, `c[1]`, `..., c[n-1]`.

There is a close relationship between arrays and pointers. An array name is a synonym for the address of the first element in that array. Thus, if `c` is defined as an array, the notation `c[m]` and `*(c+m)` both reference the value in the element of `c` that is `m` elements beyond `c[0]`.

We also introduced the concept of pointer arithmetic. C allows the addition and subtraction of integer values to pointers, subtraction of two pointers, and comparisons of pointers of the same type. Operations such as increment and decrement by one (`++` and `--`) are allowed on pointers. Pointers are often used to loop through elements of an array.

Arrays are passed to functions in C by passing the address of the first element of the array. The entire array is not copied when an array is an argument to a function. The function receiving an array argument is free to treat the address it receives as either an array (using subscript notation) or as a pointer.

Several simple algorithms that operate on vectors were developed. These include vector dot product, vector product, and taking the length of a vector. Each of these algorithms can be implemented in C using either array subscripts or pointers.

Arrays were used in a programming project that developed a simple model to forecast the changes in a population. This model represented the population of men and women of different ages in an array, and predicted births and deaths in each time interval.

The idea of arrays in C extends to multiple dimensions. A two-dimensional array in C should be thought of as an array of arrays. Thus, if `mat` is a two-dimensional array of `int`s, then `mat[i]` is a one-dimensional array of `int`s.

Elements within multidimensional arrays can be referenced either through using multiple square brackets, as in `mat[i][j]`, or through pointers, as in `*(&mat[0][0] + i*ncols + j)`, where `ncols` is the size of the outer dimension of the array `mat`. Use of pointers and subscripts can be combined. For example, `*(mat[i]+j)` also references `mat[i][j]`.

Passing multidimensional arrays to functions presents some problems in C. The C language requires that all but the innermost dimension of array arguments be declared in order to reference elements with the array. This makes it awkward to use subscript notation for array arguments. A simple way around this shortcoming is always to pass array arguments as pointers to the address of their first element. Appropriate offsets from the starting address can be computed in the function to access elements of the array. The idea of *preprocessor macros* was introduced to make code that accesses array elements via pointers clearer.

One of the applications for multidimensional arrays is the solution of simultaneous linear equation systems. The Gauss-Jordan elimination method was described. This method reduces a system of equations to an equivalent one in which the matrix of coefficients has zeros in all its off-diagonal elements. At each stage of the algorithm, multiples of one row of the matrix are added to or subtracted from the other rows, reducing all the off-diagonal elements in a column to zero.

Gauss-Jordan elimination is implemented by creating a "working matrix" that consists of the original matrix of coefficients augmented by an additional column that contains the right-hand side of the equations. All operations such as addition and subtraction of multiples of rows of the equation system are performed on the working matrix.

A method called partial pivoting was described for choosing which row to use at each stage of the elimination process. When using partial pivoting, the row selected is the one that will provide the diagonal element with the greatest absolute value. This row is then swapped into the position where the pivot element is on the diagonal of the working matrix.

Enhancements to partial pivoting were discussed. These included exchanging both rows and columns (full pivoting) and scaling the rows so that the choice of which row to use is independent of the scale of the independent variables (implicit pivoting). In addition, a modified version of Gauss-Jordan elimination that makes use of back substitution was described. This approach reduces the computational requirements of the algorithm.

The use of Gauss-Jordan elimination to solve multiple systems of simultaneous equations with the same coefficients was illustrated. This involves constructing a working matrix that consists of the original array of coefficients and an additional column for the right-hand side of each system of equations. This approach is particularly useful for finding the inverse of a matrix.

Arrays in C have many uses other than for linear algebra. One application considered in this chapter is the *shortest path problem*, which involves finding the cost of the shortest route from one node to another in a network. The Floyd-Warshall algorithm uses a two-dimensional array to represent the network and the costs of going from every node to every other node. A second application was the simulation of the machine language of the robot first described in Chapter 1.

4.13 EXERCISES

4-1. Write a function that takes two arrays as arguments and computes the square root of the sum of squared differences in the arrays' elements. If each array has n elements, and the elements of the two arrays are x_j and y_j, respectively, the function should compute the square root of

$$\sum_{j=0}^{n-1}(x_j - y_j)^2$$

4-2. Consider a metal bar 1 meter in length, where the two ends of the bar are held at steady temperatures T^1 and T^2, respectively. Assume that except for the endpoints, the initial temperature of the bar is T^3. Over time heat will flow from the hotter portion of the bar to the cooler portions until the entire bar reaches a state of thermal equilibrium. We can approximate this process by dividing the bar into equal-size segments as shown in Figure 4.11. Using these subdivisions, we seek equilibrium values where, except for the endpoints (which are held to constant temperatures), the temperature of each segment is the average of its neighbors' temperatures.

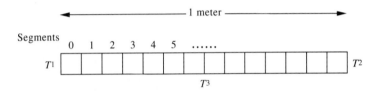

Figure 4.11 Dividing a rod into segments.

To compute this equilibrium, we can iterate through the segments, recomputing each segment's temperature as the average of its own temperature and that of its neighbors. These iterations continue until the temperature in each segment does not change more than some tolerance value. At this point, an approximate thermal equilibrium for the rod has been found.

If $T_n(i)$ is the temperature of segment i at iteration n, we can use the iteration formula:

$$T_{n+1}(i) = \frac{T_n(i-1) + T_n(i) + T_n(i+1)}{3}$$

or, as an alternative,

$$T_{n+1}(i) = \frac{T_{n+1}(i-1) + T_n(i) + T_n(i+1)}{3}$$

The first formula uses the old temperature for segment $i-1$ to compute the new temperature for segment i, while the second formula uses the new temperature for segment $i-1$.

Write a C program that implements both these methods. Run the program using 20 segments and initial values $T^1 = 200$, $T^2 = 10$, $T^3 = 20$. Use a tolerance value of .001. Which method requires the smaller number of iterations?

4-3. Create a C function that tabulates the frequency with which different ranges of values of a variable occur in some data. Your function should have as arguments an array of data values, integers giving the number of values in the array, the number of intervals the complete range of the data should be divided into for the purposes of tabulation, and an array of integers into which the tabulated frequencies are to be placed. The function should invoke a second function (which you should write) that computes the minimum and maximum data values that occur in the data array. These values should then be used to compute the width of each interval for the tabulation. The tabulation function should then loop through all the data values and count the number which fall into each interval. Write a `main()` function that reads in 20 values and outputs the tabulations for five intervals. Test the complete program on data you invent.

4-4. Write a program which uses `scanf()` to input a number as a string (e.g., it would input `1654` as "1654"), and then changes it into a integer value [e.g., (`int` 1654)].

4-5. Write a function that takes as input a string, then encodes that string and prints out the result. The coding of each character is as follows: first, take the original letter, and to its position in the alphabet (a = 1, b = 2, etc.) add its position in the string. Compute the resulting value modulus 26. Treat the resulting integer as a letter, with a = 1, b = 2, etc.

Then replace the existing letter with another one, based on the following relation:

```
a b c d e f g h i j k l m n o p q r s t u v w x y z   -- Original
m q p z n x w o l s a k t r u e c v b d y i j g h f   -- Replacement
```

You can assume that the initial string has only lowercase characters.

4-6. Write a quadratic equation parser. That is, write a function that has as one of its arguments a character string in the form

```
ax^2+ bx + c
```

where **a**, **b**, and **c** are floating-point values and the "caret" (^) denotes exponentiation. The function should ignore white space in the input string and place the values of **a**, **b**, and **c** in an array provided as one of the arguments.

Test this function by writing a **main()** function that will call the new function, then take the resulting coefficients and send them to the quadratic equation solver function you wrote for Exercise 3-4.

4-7. The transpose of any matrix is a matrix in which the rows and columns are interchanged. Thus, if **A** is a matrix with m rows and n columns, and each element of **A** is a_{ij}, the transpose of **A** has n rows and m columns, and has elements which are a_{ji}. Write a C function that has two arguments, one an original array and the other an array into which the transpose is to be placed. The function should create the transpose of the first matrix. It should not return a value.

4-8. Write a function which multiplies a matrix **A** that has the same number of rows as columns by itself. The function should have as arguments the original array, the number of rows (or columns) in the matrix, and an array into which **AA** will be placed.

4-9. A *square symmetric* matrix is defined as one that has an equal number of rows and columns where element ij equals element ji. When a matrix is symmetric, you can save storage space by keeping only either the upper or lower triangle of the matrix. The triangle can be stored in a one-dimensional array by rows. For example, if a 3 by 3 matrix with element a_{ij} could be stored in a one-dimensional array by keeping only the upper triangle as follows: $a_{00}, a_{01}, a_{02}, a_{11}, a_{12}, a_{22}$.

(a) Determine how many elements a one-dimensional array would need to store a square symmetric matrix with n rows and columns.

(b) Write a function that uses the representation discussed above that multiplies a square symmetric matrix by a vector.

(c) Write a function that uses the representation discussed above that multiplies two square symmetric matrices.

4-10. Write a function that computes the product of a vector, and a matrix. The arguments to the function should include the vector, a pointer to the starting address of the matrix, a vector into which the resulting product will be placed, the number of entries in the vector and the number of columns in the matrix. (The number of rows in the matrix must equal the number of entries in the vector for the multiplication to be defined.) Use **doubles** for the matrix, the vector, and the resulting product. After you have written the function, write a **main** () function that calls it with a sample vector and matrix.

4-11. Consider the function `show_cost()` in Section 4.10. This function is repeated below.

```
/* function to print matrix of integers */

#define MAT(I,J) (*(mat + (I)*ncols + (J)))

void show_cost(int *mat, int ncols, int nodes)
{
    int i,j;
    printf("Cost matrix is:\n");
    for(i=0; i<nodes; i++) {
      for(j=0; j<nodes; j++)
        printf("%5d ", MAT(i,j));
      printf("\n");
    }
}
```

This function is used to display a square matrix that is stored in the upper left corner of a larger two-dimensional array. Its arguments are:

- `mat`—the address of the first value (the zeroth row and column) of the array.
- `ncols`—the number of columns in the larger array from which the upper left corner is to be printed.
- `nodes`—the number of rows and columns in the square, upper left corner of the larger array that are to be displayed.

The function has the unfortunate property that it produces very long output lines when `nodes` is large. Rewrite the function so that long rows are properly divided to fit on an output device that can only have 80 characters on a line.

4-12. Write a program that extends the method described in Exercise 4-2 to determine the thermal steady state of a two-dimensional square plate being heated by a point source located at its center. To do this, you will need to set up a two-dimensional matrix of relatively small size (the range 10×10 to 20×20 is good), making the "outer edges" of the array represent the ambient temperature. As such, these values in the array should never change. To calculate the "new" temperature of a location in any given iteration, average that location's value with all four of its neighbor's values in the previous iteration. (Only adjacent regions sharing an edge are considered neighbors in this problem.) Run the program assuming that the outer edges are held to a temperature of zero degrees and that the point source holds the middle of the plate to a temperature of 400 degrees. Assume that the plate starts at a temperature of zero degrees.

4-13. Write a program that will set up a four-dimensional array which will be used to store the number of television viewers watching each network (FOX, ABC, NBC, CBS), in each age group (0–14, 15–25, 26–35, 36–45, 46–60, 61+), of each sex (male, female), for each time period of prime time (7 to 11:00, in half-hour increments).

The program should output information as requested by the user. The value to be output is determined from two user-provided inputs. These two inputs specify the dimensions to be *eliminated* from the four-dimensional table. If, for example, a user were to enter network and sex as inputs, the output would be a two-dimensional table with the age variable and the time slot. The number in each cell would be the number of viewers (male + female) who watched any of the networks for each age/time slot combination (e.g., 7 p.m., 15–25 yrs). Test your program on some hypothetical data you invent.

4-14. The game of *Life* is a simulation of population movement and fluctuation developed by John Conway of Cambridge University. The simulation takes place on a grid of locations, each of which can contain an "entity." Each such location has eight "neighbors." The state of each "generation" is determined by the state of the previous one according to the following two rules:

- An entity in a cell survives to the next generation if it has either two or three neighbors; otherwise, it dies.
- An empty cell which has exactly three neighbors has a new entity born in it.

Write a program that implements the rules of life for an area which is 25 by 25. Write the program such that wraparound can occur. That is, code the algorithm such that the left edge of the grid is considered "connected" to the right edge, and similarly, the top edge is considered "connected" to the bottom edge.

To do this, you'll need to set up two 25 × 25 arrays, one which will be the current grid, the other will be the grid into which you place the next generation. After each iteration you will need to copy the new array into the old one, print it out, and then start again.

You can either hard-code a starting configuration into the program, or prompt the user for one (which is the better way to do it). Try to make your program modular by creating functions that perform specific, well-defined operations.

4-15. It is standard practice to use computers to interpret "photos" taken by satellites in orbit around the earth. This enhancement is known as *image processing*. Any picture to be processed will be represented in the form of a grid of integers, with each value representing an intensity.

In this problem, we will be doing two things to a picture:

1. Noise reduction to reduce the amount of random noise in the picture.
2. Edge defining to increase the contrast in the picture.

Reducing the noise in a picture requires two steps. The first step is to determine whether the value in a particular location or *pixel* is noise, and the second is to replace the noise with something more meaningful. In this exercise, each pixel will contain a value from 0 to 9. A value will be considered noise if it differs from all eight of its neighbors by more than 2 (we will be ignoring the edges). For example, consider the following section of the grid:

```
68985
71639
65968
```

The '1' would be considered noise, while the '3' would not, since $5 - 3 = 2$. To replace the noisy value, take the average of all the neighbors, and use the result to replace the original value. In this example, then, we would replace the '1' with $(6 + 8 + 9 + 7 + 6 + 6 + 5 + 9)/8 = 7$.

To increase contrast is relatively simple, as it requires lumping values which are close in intensity together, and replacing all these values with a single value. In our exercise we will replace {0,1,2} with 1, {3,4,5} with 4, and {6,7,8,9} with 8.

Write a complete C program which has three functions: one should input a "raw" picture, one should eliminate noise, and the last should do the contrast adjustment. Your program should output the resulting picture. To test your program, use the following input picture:

```
76666888689869987887911599774798969467 67
36991373807800111278887817067387768896 86
77889188277252301997780666299667767887 78
69679865650220200097899688666685344697 708
87809847763027392219899776868854458697 98
89996876200111760920269662433455455554 76
77966899222216771011018799435344545335 66
96162788210687607608126866877054409789 49
89887615025696998686116186687840146668 67
98269601082210111092209268788976786797 40
78852112002911001270211100788977877677 68
87680120826990888787762021877976786688 88
78101166669846396668593610018676775676 48
78100097876677780678769611607626674118 99
77069289778729677898668769978688808878 09
```

4-16. It is sometimes convenient to be able to use one row of a two-dimensional matrix as an argument to a function since with only one row it is not necessary to declare the number of elements in a one-dimensional array used as an argument. To make it easy to do this, we can set up a one-dimensional array of pointers with each pointer pointing to the start of a row in the matrix. Suppose **a** is a two-dimensional array which has **NROW** rows and **NCOL** columns, and **row_a** is the array of pointers to the rows of **a**. We could use the following declarations:

```
double a[NROW][NCOL];
double *row_a[NROW];
```

with **row_a** is initialized in the following manner:

```
int i;
for(i=0; i<NROW; i++)
    row_a[i] = a[i];
```

This allows us to reference an element [i][j] of array **a** as either **a[i][j]** or ***(row_a[i]+j)**. If a function were to receive **row_a** as an argument, it would be declared in the argument list as

```
double **a;
```

or

```
double *a[];
```

(a) What are the advantages and disadvantages of this method of referencing arrays in functions?

(b) When would it be inappropriate to use this method?

(c) Rewrite the function `simple_gauss()` such that it takes advantage of the technique explained above.

4-17. Write a function that implements Gauss-Jordan elimination with backsubstitution. Compare the number of floating-point additions, multiplications, and divisions in your implementation for a system of three linear equations with three unknowns with the same values for the simplified Gauss-Jordan implementation given in Section 4.8.2.

4-18. Write a program that calls the function `gauss_jordan()` provided in the Section 4.8.2 to solve the following system of three linear equations with three unknowns:

$$2x_0 + 3x_1 + 5x_2 = 10$$

$$1x_0 + 2x_1 + 4x_2 = 5$$

$$4x_0 + 7x_1 + 3x_2 = 15$$

Your program should use array initialization to set up the matrix of coefficients and the right-hand side.

4-19. Since any numerical method for solving systems of linear equations must rely on floating-point arithmetic, any numerical solution will in general have some error. It possible to construct a second system of simultaneous linear equations to solve for the amount of the error, and then use this to adjust the original solution. This approach is called *iterative improvement*.

The original numerical solution can be written as $\mathbf{x} + \Delta\mathbf{x}$, where $\mathbf{x}$ is the true (and still unknown) solution and $\Delta\mathbf{x}$ is the error introduced by roundoffs by floating-point arithmetic. Similarly, we can write

$$\mathbf{A}(\mathbf{x} + \Delta\mathbf{x}) = \mathbf{b} + \Delta\mathbf{b}$$

or, equivalently,

$$\mathbf{A}\mathbf{x} + \mathbf{A}\Delta\mathbf{x} = \mathbf{b} + \Delta\mathbf{b}$$

After a single application of Gauss-Jordan elimination, the value of $\Delta\mathbf{b}$ is computable from terms we already know as $\mathbf{A}(\mathbf{x} + \Delta\mathbf{x}) - \mathbf{b}$. Since the original equation $\mathbf{A}\mathbf{x} = \mathbf{b}$ still holds, we can write the equation above as

$$\mathbf{A}\Delta\mathbf{x} = \mathbf{A}(\mathbf{x} + \Delta\mathbf{x}) - \mathbf{b}$$

Since both $\mathbf{A}$ and the right-hand side of the equation are completely known, we can solve the linear system of equations above for $\Delta\mathbf{x}$, and then subtract this value of $\Delta\mathbf{x}$ from the first solution $\mathbf{x} + \Delta\mathbf{x}$ to get a better estimate of the true solution, $\mathbf{x}$.

Write a function `iterative_gauss_jordan()` which uses this method. It should first invoke the function `gauss_jordan()` in Section 4.8.2 to get an initial solution. It should then compute the right-hand side to get the linear equations with $\Delta\mathbf{x}$ as the unknown and call `gauss_jordan()` again to solve these equations. Finally, it should compute the corrected solution vector.

4-20. The *determinant* of a 3 by 3 matrix **C** with elements c_{ij} is defined as

$$c_{00}(c_{11}c_{22} - c_{12}c_{21}) - c_{01}(c_{10}c_{22} - c_{12}c_{20}) + c_{02}(c_{10}c_{21} - c_{20}c_{11})$$

Write a C function that computes the determinant of a 3 by 3 matrix. The function should have the matrix as its argument and should return a `double` containing the determinant of the matrix. Then write a `main()` function that reads the nine values in the matrix from the user, and outputs the determinant of the matrix.

4-21. Cramer's rule is another way to solve simultaneous equations. Suppose that we have a system of three equations and three unknowns in the form

$$a_0x + b_0y + c_0z = d_0$$

$$a_1x + b_1y + c_1z = d_1$$

$$a_2x + b_2y + c_2z = d_2$$

Define the vector $\mathbf{a} = [a_0, a_1, a_2]$ and the vectors **b**, **c**, and **d** similarly. Define the notation [**a**, **b**, **c**] as a 3 by 3 matrix with columns **a**, **b**, and **c**. (By extension the notation [**d**, **b**, **c**] is a matrix with columns **d**, **b**, and **c**.) Cramer's rule states that we can solve the system of equations as follows:

$$x = \frac{\det[\mathbf{d}, \mathbf{b}, \mathbf{c}]}{\det[\mathbf{a}, \mathbf{b}, \mathbf{c}]}$$

$$y = \frac{\det[\mathbf{a}, \mathbf{d}, \mathbf{c}]}{\det[\mathbf{a}, \mathbf{b}, \mathbf{c}]}$$

$$z = \frac{\det[\mathbf{a}, \mathbf{b}, \mathbf{d}]}{\det[\mathbf{a}, \mathbf{b}, \mathbf{c}]}$$

where det [**a**, **b**, **c**] is the determinant of the corresponding matrix. (See Exercise 4-20.)

Write a function in C that implements this method for a system of three equations and unknowns. The arguments to the function should be a matrix containing the coefficients of the equations, a vector to hold the right-hand side of the equation system, a vector to hold the solution, and a tolerance value. The function should check if the absolute value of the determinant of the matrix [**a**, **b**, **c**] is less than the tolerance value, and if so, it should return a value of FALSE. The function should return TRUE if the determinant is not "too close" to zero.

Test your program on the following example system of equations.

$$2x_0 + 3x_1 + 5x_2 = 10$$

$$x_0 + 2x_1 + 4x_2 = 5$$

$$4x_0 + 7x_1 + 3x_2 = 15$$

4-22. As discussed in Section 4.10, the output of the Floyd-Warshall algorithm is the cost of the shortest path from every node in a network to every other node. Describe in words an algorithm that uses the initial cost matrix and the final cost matrix (as output by the

Floyd-Warshall algorithm) to find the actual shortest path from a given node i to another node j. Implement this algorithm in C and test it using the sample network shown in Figure 4.7.

4-23. In Section 4.10, when we implemented the Floyd-Warshall algorithm, we required a large integer to use in place of ∞. At first glance one might think that the standard value `INT_MAX` defined in the header file `limits.h` as the largest representable integer would be a good choice. Why doesn't this work correctly when used in the implementation shown in Section 4.10?

4-24. Write a C program that simulates the operation of the simple computer described in Exercise 1-5. Your program should have a `main()` function that reads the program into an array which simulates the computer's memory, and a second function that simulates the computer's execution. Use your simulator to test your answer to Exercise 1-5.

DATA STRUCTURES

5.1 INTRODUCTION

In this chapter we introduce the concept of *data abstraction*. By this, we mean the creation of units of information which have a well-structured form and which can be used in many different contexts. Such units of information are often called *data structures*. These differ from simple variables which can only store single values. We also use the term *data objects* to describe units of information that are composite groups of related items and a set of operations that can be performed on those composite groups.

The C programming language provides a range of capabilities that make it easy to create and operate on data structures. While in a sense, arrays can be viewed as data structures, they are limited to storing a group of values that are *all of the same type*. While these are useful in constructing algorithms to solve many problems, there are situations in which we need more sophisticated ways of organizing information.

Many interesting data abstractions are far more complicated than simple variables and arrays. Consider, for example, a large database used to store airline reservations. This database has information about passengers' names, flight times, the names of standby passengers, seat assignments, fares, and other items. While it is possible to construct a program to manage this database using just simple variables and arrays, it would be far more useful to think of the information as organized into larger units such as complete reservations (consisting of names, flight numbers, flight times, fare codes, etc.), flight manifests (consisting of the names of all passengers booked on a flight), standby lists (a list of names for each flight) and plane schedules (a list of flights for each plane in the fleet). We could then think about operations on these data abstractions such as, "add passenger p to flight y" or "assign seat q on flight f to passenger p."

Certain ways of organizing information have proven particularly useful in solving various information management problems. For example, many situations require creation of something called a *queue*. New entries are added to the end of a queue, and items are removed from the front of the queue. In the context of an airline management system, information about people waiting for standby seats might be organized as a queue, with people getting seats freed by cancellations on a first come, first served basis.

In order to implement various data structures, we will need to present some new elements in the C language. In particular, we will require the ability to define a composite of existing C data types called a **struct**. These units allow grouping together information of dissimilar types, such as an integer, an array of **double**s, and a character string. The entire group can be treated as a variable, and arrays of this type of variable can be created. We will also need the ability to create and destroy new data structures as a program executes. This feature is called *dynamic memory allocation*. C provides a library of routines that permit such memory usage.

We will also introduce features of C that make development and maintenance of data structures easier. We will, for example, adopt the approach of creating small *libraries* of functions which manipulate each type of data structure. Later in the chapter, we will show how these libraries can be kept in separate source code files from the functions that use the library. This approach is common in developing large programs, where keeping all the source code in a single file would be unmanageable.

Segregating the functions that create and manipulate the data structures into a separate library allows us to create data structures as abstract entities whose internal structure need not be known to other programmers. Only the functions that control the data structures need be known for the library to be useful. The partitioning of programming projects into separate units that communicate through function calls is crucial to effective implementation of large software systems.

After introducing some additional features of the C language, we will explore the most useful organizations of data structures. The particular forms we will study are:

- *Stacks*. These are data structures that organize information on a first in, last out basis. New items are added to the top of a stack, and items are removed from the top of the stack.
- *Ragged arrays*. This data structure is used to hold an array of arrays, where each of the arrays may have a different length. Ragged arrays are often used to hold multiple lines of text, where the number of characters in the lines varies.
- *Queues*. As discussed in the example above, queues are first in, first out data structures. New items are added to the end of the queue, and items are removed from the front.

- *Lists*. These are general-purpose data structures, with many different variants. Basically, a list is a group of data elements linked together in some way. We will develop a simple single linked list.
- *Trees*. These are also general-purpose data structures. Each element of a tree can have one or more elements linked to it. These linked elements are called its *children*. We will consider in detail the *binary tree*, where any element can have at most two children.

At the end of this chapter we develop some example applications that use many of the data structures. These programming projects will illustrate how data structures and the library of functions that operate on them can be used as building blocks to solve quite complicated problems. Using data structures as part of algorithms makes it possible to solve these problems in ways that are surprisingly straightforward.

5.2 THE BASICS OF C STRUCTURES

In this section we show how a **struct** is defined in the C language and illustrate how members of the **struct** are referenced. We also show a simple example of the use of **struct**s.

5.2.1 Creating a Structure in C

A **struct** in C is a variable which can consist of many components of different types. We can think of the creation of a **struct** in C as consisting of two steps. First, we define a *template* for the **struct**. A template declares a structure type, including what is in that structure type. The components of a **struct** are called its *members*. The template does not allocate any storage for a **struct**. The second step defines variables which are **struct**s of a particular type, allocating storage for them.

For example, suppose we want to define a **struct** that consists of information about some household, including an **int** for number of household members, a **float** for the household's annual income, and another **int** for the number of adults in the household. One way to do this in C is to define a template for a **struct** of this type as follows:

```
/* structure template declaration */

struct household {
   int total;      /* number of household members */
   float income;   /* household income */
   int adults;     /* number of adults */
   };    /* don't forget this last semicolon */
```

The template above does not create any new variables; it simply defines the format for **struct**s of type **household**. It declares that **struct**s of type **household** will contain three *members*: an **int** named **total**, a **float** named **income**, and an **int** named **adults**. The name **household** is called a *structure tag*.

Once the template for a **struct** is declared, we can define variables which are of type **struct household** as follows:

```
struct household a,b,c;
```

The statement defines three variables, **a**, **b**, and **c**, each of which is a **struct** of type **household**.

The two steps of declaration and definition can be combined in different ways. For example, C allows you to declare the template and define variables in a single statement, as in

```
/* template declaration and variable definition */

struct household {
  int total;       /* number of household members */
  float income;    /* household income */
  int adults;      /* number of adults */
  } a, b, c;
```

In this declaration, the structure tag **household** is declared and the variables **a**, **b**, and **c** are defined in a single statement.

You are also allowed to omit the structure tag entirely, as in the statement

```
/* variable definition  without tag */

struct {
  int total;       /* number of household members */
  float income;    /* household income */
  int adults;      /* number of adults */
  } a, b, c;
```

However, when you omit the declaration of the structure tag, you need to repeat the structure template when you want to define other variables of the same type. We will always use structure templates to identify tags and encourage you to do likewise.

C also allows you to create an array of structures. For example, once a template for a **struct** of type **household** has been declared, you can define a variable **harray** as an array of 10 **struct**s of type **household** as follows:

```
struct household harray[10];
```

The variable `harray` consists of elements `harray[0]`, `harray[1]`, ..., `harray[9]`, each of which is a `struct`. All the rules for using arrays in C discussed in Chapter 4 apply to arrays of `struct`s, including how arrays are passed to functions. We explore this in Section 5.2.6.

A `struct` in C can also have one or more `struct`s as members. If the tag `household` is defined earlier, then we could declare another `struct` which consists of a `household` and other elements. For example, we might have a student record that includes the identification number, age, and grade point average of a student along with the information about the student's household. A structure declaration for this would be as follows:

```
/* tag declaration of struct containing a struct */

struct student {
   struct household family;  /* household information */
   long int idnum;           /* id number */
   int age;                  /* student's age */
   float gpa;                /* grade point average */
   };
```

The structure type `student` contains a member `family` which itself is a structure of type `household`.

5.2.2 Accessing Members of a Structure

In addition to needing a mechanism for defining a `struct`, we need a way to access the members of the `struct` as variables. C provides the *dot operator* as one such mechanism. For example, the notation `a.income` is an expression which evaluates as the member `income` of `struct a`. Thus, assuming the structure tag `household` has been declared as above, the following are all legal C statements:

```
/* accessing members of a struct */

struct household a,b,c;
a.income = 54000.0;
b.adults = 2;
b.total = 7;
printf("Number of children is %d\n", b.total-b.adults);
scanf("%d %f %d", &c.total, &c.income, &c.adults);
```

The dot operator (along with parentheses denoting function calls, square brackets denoting array references, and a second mechanism for referencing members of a structure to be introduced shortly) have the highest precedence. Thus, in the expression `&c.total`, the member `total` of the `struct c` is evaluated first; the address operator (**&**) is then applied to create a pointer to the memory location where **c.total** is stored. In the example above, **scanf()** reads a floating-point value into that memory location.

The dot operator associates from left to right. Thus, if the structure tag **student** is defined as in Section 5.2.1, then the code fragment

```
struct student s;
s.family.adults = 2;
```

defines **s** to be a structure of type **student** and sets the member **adults** of the member **family** to 2.

The name of a member of a **struct** is local to that **struct**. Thus, we could define the template for another **struct** with the tag **staff**, and that **struct** could have as one of its members a variable called **idnum**. The member named **idnum** in the structure **staff** would be entirely different from the member with the same name in the structure **student**. The C compiler can always distinguish between the two members named **idnum** because references to a member always require the structure name as well as the member name. For example, if **a** is a **struct** of type **student**, and **d** is a **struct** of type **staff**, then **a.idnum** is a reference to member **idnum** in a **student** structure, while **d.idnum** is a reference to member **idnum** of a **staff** structure.

5.2.3 Initialization of a struct

A **struct** can be initialized in the same way as an array. For example, we could initialize a **struct** of type **household** along with its definition as follows:

```
struct household a={ 5, 35000.0, 2};
```

This definition initializes **a.total** to 5, **a.income** to 35000 and **a.adults** to 2. Similarly, a **struct** of type **student** could be initialized as

```
struct student s = { {5, 35000.0, 2}, 245323, 19, 3.54};
```

The inner curly braces enclosing the initialization of the **household** structure within the **student** structure are optional. We encourage their inclusion to make the composition of the members of the **struct** clear.

Arrays of structures get initialized just as any other array. For example, we could initialize an array of **household** structures as

```
struct household h[] = { {4, 20000.0, 1},
                         {7, 29000.0, 2},
                         {1, 35000.0, 1},
                         {5, 95000.0, 2}
                       };
```

As with other array initialization, the C compiler will automatically set the number of entries in an array of structures to the number of initializers if the size is omitted.

5.2.4 Structure Pointers and the Member Access Operator

As with any object in C, you can create a *pointer* to a `struct`. The definition

```
struct household *p;
```

defines the variable **p** as a pointer to a `struct` of type household. This definition makes sense only if the template for the structure tag `household` has already been declared.

A pointer to a `struct` can be used like any other pointer. For example, if **a** has been defined as a `struct` of type `household`, then the statement

```
p = &a;   /* p set to address of struct a */
```

sets the value of **p** to the address of **a**. Once **p** is set to the address of **a**, we can use the *member access operator* as another way of accessing the members of a structure. This operator, also called the *arrow operator*, is denoted as `->` (a hyphen followed immediately by a greater than symbol). Thus, assuming that the variables **a** and **p** are declared as above and **p** is assigned the address of **a**, the statements

```
/* fragment showing use of pointer to struct */

p->total = 3;
p->adults = 1;
printf("Number of adults is %d\n", p->adults);
scanf("%f", &p->income);
```

are all valid in C.

You can also use pointer arithmetic with pointers to structures. For example, the following fragment of C code would read in values for 10 different households into an array of structures.

```
/* fragment using address arithmetic with
   pointer to structure */
/* tag household is assumed to be declared earlier */

struct household harray[10];
struct household *p;

for(p=harray; (p-harray)<10; p++)
  scanf("%d %f %d", &p->total, &p->income, &p->adults);
```

You can also use the dereferencing operator (`*`) with a pointer to a **struct**. For example, if **p** points to a **struct** of type **household**, then the statement

```
(*p).total =   7;
```

sets the member **total** of the structure pointed to by **p** to 7. The parentheses are necessary because the dot operator(`.`) has higher precedence than the dereferencing operator (`*`). Omitting the parentheses is an error because the dot operator requires that the left-hand side be a structure, not a pointer to a structure.

In fact, the notation

```
(*p).total
```

is entirely equivalent to

```
p->total
```

The arrow notation is used far more often than the combination of the dereferencing and dot operators because it is more compact, clearer, and avoids the potential for forgetting the parentheses.

The member access operator is in the group of operators with the highest precedence. It associates from left to right. For example, suppose that we have two structures defined as follows:

```
/* two structure templates */

struct type1 {
     double a;
     double b;  };

struct type2 {
     int c;
     struct type1 *d;};
```

In this example, member **d** of **struct type2** is a pointer to a **struct** with template **type1**. In this case, we might have the following C fragment:

```
/* fragment using member access operator */

struct type1 s;     /* a type1 struct */
struct type2 t;     /* a type2 struct */
struct type2 *pt;   /* a pointer to a type2 struct */

pt = &t;              /* pt is address of t */
t.d = &s;   /* member d of t assigned address of s */
pt->d->a = 17.5;    /* equivalent of s.a = 17.5 */
```

The three variable definitions create two variables which are structures and a pointer to one type of structure. The first assignment statment in this example assigns **pt** the address of the **type2** structure **t**. The member **d** of structure **t** is then assigned the address of **s**. Thus, member **d** in **t** points to structure **s**. The third assignment statement assigns member **a** of **struct s** the value 17.5. This is equivalent to the statement

```
s.a = 17.5;   /* equivalent to pt->d->a = 17.5 */
```

5.2.5 Allowable Operations on Structures

While C allows you to define a variable that is a **struct**, not all operations can be performed on such variables. More specifically, C allows you to perform only the three following operations on **struct**s:

- Accessing a member of a structure.
- Taking the address of a structure.
- Copying a structure for the purposes of:
  - Assigning one structure to another of the same type.
  - Passing a structure as an argument to a function.
  - Returning it as the result of a function.

The third of these allowed operations, copying a structure, allows you to have a **struct** on the left-hand side of an assignment statement. For example, imagine that we are using the **student struct** defined earlier in a program that keeps records of all students registered at a university. Assuming that the template for **student** were already defined, we might have two such structures called **old_student** and **new_student**. If the variable **new_student** is to be used to store information about the sister of the **old_student**, then much of the data about the **old_student** could be used in filling in the members of the **new_student**. For example, we might use the code fragment

```
/* code fragment showing assignment of structs */

struct student new_student, old_student;
     .
     .
     .
new_student.family = old_student.family;

scanf("%d %d %f", &new_student.idnum, &new_student.age,
        &new_student.gpa);
```

The statement assigning the **struct household** from **old_student.family** to **new_student.family** copies all the members of the structure **old_student.family** into the corresponding members of **new_student.family**. This avoids the need to write separate statements to copy each member one at a time. It also allows us to change the template for the **household struct** and still have this fragment of code do what we want.

We explore the use of **struct**s as function arguments and returned values in the next subsection.

5.2.6 Using Structures as Function Arguments and Returned Values

Note that C does not allow you to do arithmetic or logical operations on **struct**s even when such operations make sense. For example, we could define a template for a **struct** which is a point in three dimensions as follows:

```
/* struct template for a point in three dimensions */

struct point3D {
   double x;    /* x coordinate */
   double y;    /* y coordinate */
   double z;    /* z coordinate */
   };
```

Given two structures **p1** and **p2**, the operation **p1+p2** makes logical sense but is not allowed in C.[1]   Instead, you would have to write a function in C that had two **point3D** structures as arguments and returned a **struct** of type **point3D**. You could then invoke this function whenever you wanted to add two points together as shown in the following example. (The code below assumes that the structure template for **point3D** has already been declared.)

```
/* function that adds two structs representing
      3D points and returns the sum as a struct */

struct point3D add_points(
   struct point3D a,
   struct point3D b)
{
   struct point3D sum; /* holds sum of points */
   sum.x = a.x + b.x;   /* add x coordinates */
   sum.y = a.y + b.y;   /* add y coordinates */
   sum.z = a.z + b.z;   /* add z coordinates */

   return(sum);         /* return sum */
}
```

[1]C++, an extension of the C language, provides direct support for defining operations such as **p1+p2**. This is discussed in Chapter 9.

This function could then be used as in the following program. For brevity we have not repeated the declaration of the template for the **struct point3D** and the function **add_points()**.

```
/* main() function showing use of function
   involving structs */

#include <stdio.h>

   /* code for template of point3D and the
      implementation of add_points() assumed
      to be here */

/* function prototype for add_points() */
struct point3D add_points(struct point3D,
                          struct point3D);

main()
{

/* two points to be added */
   struct point3D p1  = {4.0, 5.0, 7.4};
   struct point3D p2 =  {-3.5, 7.2, 1.6};

   struct point3D result;  /* result of addition */

   result = add_points(p1, p2);
   printf("Result is (%lf,%lf,%lf)\n", result.x,
          result.y, result.z);
}
```

When a **struct** is used as an argument to a function, the *entire contents of the structure* are copied during the function invocation. This is quite different from how arrays are passed as arguments, where only the address of the first element is passed. Thus, the function **add_points()** above receives a complete copy of each of the two structures that are its arguments. If it modified these copies (which it does not), the changes would not affect the values of the arguments in the function which called **add_points()**.

Copying the entire contents of a **struct** as part of the function invocation process can be time consuming, particularly if the **struct** has many members. Frequently, a function that has one or more **struct**s as its arguments does not need complete copies. For this reason, it is far more common for functions to use *pointers* to a **struct** rather than a **struct** itself as arguments. It is almost always faster to pass a single pointer to a function than it is to pass a complete copy of a structure.

For example, the function **add_points()** could be implemented using pointers to structures for the arguments. A revised version, named **add_points_new()**, would

be as follows:

```
/* function uses two pointers to structs representing
      3D points and returns the sum as a struct */

struct point3D add_points_new(
   struct point3D *pa,   /* first pointer to struct */
   struct point3D *pb)   /* second pointer to struct */
{
   struct point3D sum; /* holds sum of points */
   sum.x = pa->x + pb->x;   /* add x coordinates */
   sum.y = pa->y + pb->y;   /* add y coordinates */
   sum.z = pa->z + pb->z;   /* add z coordinates */

   return(sum);             /* return sum */
}
```

The function prototype for this new version and a typical invocation are given in the following code fragment.

```
/* code fragment showing passing pointers to structs */

/*function prototype */
struct point3D add_points_new(struct point3D *,
                              struct point3D *);

/* typical use of new function */
struct point3D p1  = {4.0, 5.0, 7.4};
struct point3D p2 =  {-3.5, 7.2, 1.6};

struct point3D result;  /* result of addition */

result = add_points_new(&p1, &p2);
```

Note that the address operator (&) is used in the function invocation to create a pointer to each of the **structs**. Also, the type of each argument given in the function prototype is a pointer to a **struct** of type **point3D**.

5.3 PROGRAMMING PROJECT: A STACK

In this section we describe and implement a simple version of a data structure called a *stack*. This is probably the simplest form of data structure that is widely used. Stacks are data structures to which entries can be added or removed. Adding an entry to a stack is referred to as *pushing* it on the stack. Removing an entry is referred to as *popping* the stack. Stacks use *last in, first out* discipline to determine the order in which previously pushed entries are popped.

Figure 5.1 illustrates how a stack works. Part (a) of the figure shows a stack containing three names: **"Deborah"**, **"Amy"**, and **"David"**. Part (b) shows what happens when the stack is popped: the most recently entered name, **"Deborah"**, is removed from the stack. Part (c) of the figure illustrates the pushing of **"John"** onto the stack. Since **"John"** is the last name added, it would be the first one removed if the stack were popped.

In the somewhat contrived example in this section, we will consider a situation where airline passengers arrive at an airport to board some flight. When these passengers check in, their arrival is assumed to be recorded in a computer system. Because the flight may be overbooked, we may need to *bump* some passengers off the flight after they have arrived and checked in. For the purposes of this example, we assume that the passengers who checked in last are the ones bumped off the flight.

While this is not exactly how airlines operate in overbooking situations, we will use it as an example of a programming problem where a stack might be useful. We will use a stack to store the arriving passengers. When a passenger checks in, he or she will be pushed onto the stack. At boarding time, we might then have to pop off the

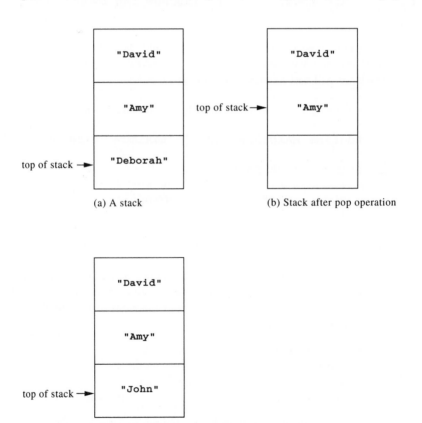

(a) A stack   (b) Stack after pop operation

(c) Stack after push operation

Figure 5.1 Example of a stack.

passengers who arrived most recently to reduce the total number of passengers to the number of seats on the aircraft.

We begin our implementation by declaring the template of a **struct** named **pass** to hold passenger information. We will store the first 80 characters of the passenger's name, the number of items of luggage (up to the allowed limit of two pieces), and the tag numbers of the luggage. This will allow us to unload the luggage of the bumped passengers from the aircraft. We will assume that luggage tag numbers are always positive, so that values of zero are entered for the tag numbers when there is no luggage. The template for this **struct** is as follows:

```
/* template for passenger struct */

struct pass {
  char name[80];    /* name of passenger */
  int pieces;       /* number of pieces of luggage */
  int tag1;         /* luggage tag number 1 */
  int tag2;         /* luggage tag number 2 */
  };
```

Another **struct** will be used to store the actual stack. The stack will have some maximum capacity which we will call **MAXSTACK**. The template for this **struct** (which we will call **stack_pass**) is given below.

```
/* template for a stack of passengers */

#define MAXSTACK 300   /* maximum  size of stack */

struct stack_pass {
  int count;  /* number of entries in stack */
  struct pass entries[MAXSTACK];
  };
```

The member **count** is a count of the number of elements in the stack. It should be initialized to zero, denoting an empty stack. (We show a more elegant way to initialize data structures in Section 5.9.) The array named **entries** is an array of **struct**s of type **pass**. It will be used to hold the information about passengers in the stack.

The next step is to implement a set of functions that manipulate the stack. We will develop four distinct functions:

- **init_stack()**—initializes the stack
- **push()**—pushes a new passenger on the stack
- **pop()**—pops a passenger from the stack
- **give_count()**—returns the number of passengers on the stack

The four functions will all have a pointer to a stack as their first argument. Using a pointer rather than the stack itself will vastly reduce the amount of work done in copying the arguments when the functions are invoked. **give_count()** will return an

int which is the number of items currently on the stack. push() will have a pointer to a struct of type pass to be pushed on the stack as an additional argument and will have no returned value. pop() will return a struct of type pass that was popped off the stack.

Both push() and pop() have to check for error conditions. It is not permissible to try to pop something from a stack which is empty or to push something on a stack that is full. In this implementation we will treat attempts at illegal pushes and pops as fatal errors and exit from the program. In Section 5.9 we develop a more general implementation that handles these situations in a much more elegant way.

The implementations of push(), pop() and give_count() are listed below. They assume that the templates for pass and stack_pass are as given above.

```
/* function to initialize the stack */
void init_stack(struct stack_pass *s)
{
  s->count = 0;
}


/* function to give count of stack entries */
int give_count(struct stack_pass *s)
{
  return(s->count);
}

/* function to pop from stack */

struct pass pop(struct stack_pass *s)
{

/* If stack isn't empty, pop it */
  if(s->count > 0) {
    s->count--;
    return(s->entries[s->count]);
  }
  else {      /* Output error message and exit */
    printf("Error-Attempt to pop empty stack\n");
    exit(-1);
  }
}

/* function to push on stack */

void push(struct stack_pass *s, struct pass *p)
{

/* If stack isn't full, push item on it */
  if(s->count < MAXSTACK) {
```

```
      s->entries[s->count] = *p;
      s->count++;
   }
   else {    /* output error message*/
      printf("Error-Attempt to push on full stack\n");
      exit(-2);
   }
}
```

A few things are worth noting about these implementations. The function **exit()** is part of the standard C library. It causes a program to terminate. The value of its integer argument is returned to the operating system, or what is often referred to as the *command shell*, which processes operating system commands. In some operating systems, the value returned by **exit()** can be used by the command shell to handle error conditions in some way.

When an item is popped from the stack, **s->count**, the count of the number of entries in the stack, is first decremented by one. The element **s->count** in array of passenger structures is returned in the statement

```
   return(s->entries[s->count]);
```

The decrement of the count is done first because array subscripts in C begin with 0. Information about the passenger who arrived first is stored in element 0 of the array, not element 1.

In the implementation of **push()**, the pointer to the passenger structure is dereferenced in the assignment statement

```
   s->entries[s->count] = *p;
```

The right-hand side of this assignment, ***p**, is the dereferencing of the pointer **p**, which produces a **struct** of type **pass**. This is assigned to element **s->count** of the array **s->entries**.

The last step in the program development is to create the **main()** program that accepts the input of the passengers as they arrive using **scanf()** and pushes them on the stack. The user is first prompted to input the capacity of the airplane. The user then enters information for each passenger who checks in; each passenger is pushed onto a stack. When the arrival gate for passengers is closed, the user of the program enters the appropriate keystrokes so that **scanf()** returns **EOF**, the "end of file" indicator (see Section 2.14). The program then checks if it is necessary to bump passengers off the flight. If so, it uses **pop()** to list the passengers who arrived last.

The implementation of **main()** along with the appropriate **#include** statements and function prototypes are given below. We assume that the templates for the **pass** and **stack_pass** structs have already been declared.

```
   /* function prototypes for stack management */
   void init_stack(struct stack_pass *);
```

```
int give_count(struct stack_pass *);
void push(struct stack_pass *, struct pass *);
struct pass pop(struct stack_pass *);

/* main program for example */
main()
{
  struct pass p;     /* holds a single passenger */
  struct stack_pass stack; /* the stack */
  int flag=!EOF;     /* indicator when EOF reached */
  int seats;         /* number of seats on plane */

/* initialize stack and get capacity of aircraft */

  init_stack(&stack);
  printf("Enter number of seats on plane:\n");
  scanf("%d", &seats);

/* read in the passengers until EOF found */

  while(flag != EOF) {
      flag = scanf("%s %d %d %d", p.name, &p.pieces,
                  &p.tag1, &p.tag2);
      if(flag != EOF) push(&stack, &p);
  }

/* pop passengers who are bumped */

  while(give_count(&stack) > seats) {
    p = pop(&stack);
    printf("Passenger %s is bumped. Remove luggage
          %d and %d\n", p.name, p.tag1, p.tag2);
  }
}
```

The **main()** program initializes the stack and reads in the capacity of the aircraft. It then reads in the data for the various passengers. If there are fewer than two items of luggage, it is assumed that zeros are entered for the corresponding tag numbers. The variable **flag** is used to test whether the end-of-file is reached. Once **scanf()** returns the end-of-file indicator **EOF**, the extra passengers are popped off the stack until the number allowed to board is less than or equal to the seating capacity of the aircraft.

5.3.1 An Aside on Modularity in Software Design

Note that the functions used to initialize and manipulate a stack in the example above are quite simple. One might reasonably ask, "Why bother to create separate functions for these operations rather than using statements in the **main()** program that access the internal structure of the stack?" The answer to this question is crucial to understanding the usefulness and importance of building large software systems out of simple, well-defined modules.

By using only functions to initialize and manipulate the data structure, we can separate the *use* of the stack functions from the *internal structure* of the stacks. As long as we keep the function names and arguments unchanged, we are free to alter how the data structure is implemented. While this may seem artificial in our simple example, it is extremely important in larger software systems. It allows one programmer to work on the implementation of a data structure while other programmers use these data structures in their parts of the software. As long as the two parts of the programming team agree on the functions that control the data structure, the implementer of the data structure library is free to change the implementation at any time. In effect, the functions become a *contract* between the data structure implementer and the rest of the programming team. How that contract is fulfilled can change without affecting the rest of the team as long as the functions do what is agreed upon.

Figure 5.2 illustrates how this separation of function interface and implementation works. One part of the programming team (Group A in the figure) defines a set of functions that operates on the data structure. The other part of the team (Group B) operates on the data structures *only* by using the interface functions. This allows changes in the internal details of the implementation to be made by Group A independently from the rest of the software development team. However, it requires that programmers of the data structure functions provide a complete and reliable set of interface functions, and that the other part of the team avoid the temptation to make use of the internal structure of the current implementation of the data structure. This discipline is crucial to the software design and implementation process for large projects. Failure to enforce such discipline is a major reason why software projects often take longer than projected and have unexpected errors.

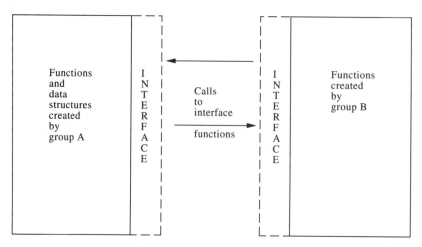

Figure 5.2 Programming interfaces in software design and implementation.

Even when a software project is small enough to be done by a single individual, the discipline of "walling off" some aspects of a program and defining a function interface to it can be invaluable. It allows a programmer to focus his or her attention on one aspect of a large program without worrying about the other aspects. It also makes detection of errors and later maintenance of the software far easier. We will encourage this style in our examples throughout this and subsequent chapters.

5.4 DYNAMIC MEMORY ALLOCATION AND VOID POINTERS

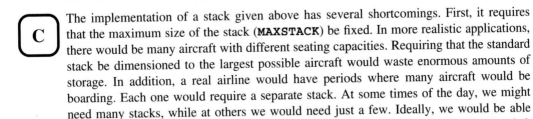

The implementation of a stack given above has several shortcomings. First, it requires that the maximum size of the stack (**MAXSTACK**) be fixed. In more realistic applications, there would be many aircraft with different seating capacities. Requiring that the standard stack be dimensioned to the largest possible aircraft would waste enormous amounts of storage. In addition, a real airline would have periods where many aircraft would be boarding. Each one would require a separate stack. At some times of the day, we might need many stacks, while at others we would need just a few. Ideally, we would be able to create stacks *dynamically* and have those stacks be as large or as small as needed. This will require what is called *dynamic memory allocation*.

In all the programs up until this point in the book, arrays and structures had to be declared as part of the program. Memory for these variables was allocated prior to the program's execution. The amount of storage needed by these variables had to be specified before the program was executed or was allocated automatically when functions were invoked. Dynamic memory allocation allows you to *control* the allocation of memory while the program is running. In this way, the amount of storage you need can reflect inputs from the user. In addition to permitting you to allocate memory as a program executes, you can also free up memory that you previously allocated but no longer need. This allows the memory to be reused for other purposes later in the program's execution.

One way to think of dynamic memory allocation is to imagine that there is a pool of unused memory available to a C program while it is executing. This pool is managed by a group of functions in the standard C library. Every C compiler provides these functions for dynamic memory allocation. Of course, the size of the memory pool and the internal details of how it is managed will vary across different computers and compilers. All the C programmer needs to care about is the programming interface to the library of functions used to access this pool. In this section we explore the most useful functions in this library.

5.4.1 Void Pointers and malloc()

Most pointers in C point to objects of a particular type, such as an int, a float, an array, or a struct with some known template. C also allows you to define a general-purpose pointer called a **void** *pointer*. Pointers to **void** are used extensively by the library functions that manage dynamically allocated memory. A pointer to **void** can be declared just like any other pointer, as in the declaration

```
void *vp;
```

The standard library function **malloc()**, the simplest dynamic memory function, returns a pointer to **void** that is the starting address of the allocated memory. You give as an argument the number of bytes of memory you want, and **malloc()** returns a **void** pointer to that memory. If it cannot allocate the memory requested, **malloc()** returns the pointer value **NULL**. The memory provided by successful invocations of **malloc()** is uninitialized. This means that its contents are entirely indeterminate.

Pointers to **void** can be assigned to pointers of any type. For example, the following code fragment calls **malloc()** to allocate 1000 bytes of memory, and assigns the **void** pointer returned by **malloc()** to a pointer to an **int**. For the moment, we assume that each **int** occupies four bytes. (In the next subsection we show how to avoid the need to make such machine-dependent assumptions.) It then reads 250 **int**s, using pointer arithmetic to compute the address into which each **int** should be read. The **void** pointer returned by **malloc()** will automatically be converted to a pointer to an **int** by the assignment operator.

```
/* example using void pointer */

#include <stdio.h>
#include <stdlib.h>

int *pn;           /* pointer to int */
int i;             /* an int used as a counter */

pn = malloc(1000);

if(pn != NULL)
  for(i=0; i<250; i++)
    scanf("%d", pn+i);
```

The header file **stdlib.h** contains the function prototypes for the dynamic memory allocation functions. Thus, any program using dynamic memory allocation should use the preprocessor directive

```
#include <stdlib.h>
```

before any of the memory management functions are invoked. We will place this directive at the beginning of our source code files along with the other **#include** directives.

Note that we check whether **malloc()** was successful in allocating the requested memory by making sure that the pointer it returned is not **NULL**. Attempting to access memory that was not allocated successfully is a grievous error, resulting in symptoms ranging from programs that abort abruptly to those that bring the entire computer to a halt. *You should always check to make sure that the memory you requested could be provided before you attempt to access that memory.*

Pointers to **void** can be thought of as generic pointers. They are often used when you have to manage pieces of memory without knowing the type of object that will be stored in it.

5.4.2 The sizeof Operator

C provides a special operator to assist in computing the amount of memory you will need to allocate for a particular purpose. For example, C does not standardize how many bytes are used to store an **int** or a **double**. If you want to allocate enough memory to hold **n int**s, you need to know how many bytes a single **int** requires. The **sizeof** operator provides this.

For example, suppose that you wanted to generalize the code fragment in the preceding subsection to make it into a function that allocates space for **n int**s and reads values using **scanf()** into those **int**s. The function could then return a pointer to the beginning address of the array of **int**s. This pointer could then be used just the way you might use the beginning address of a regular array. The advantage is that with an array you have to know the size of the array when you write the program. Using dynamic memory allocation, you can create the array during the program's execution.

You can use the **sizeof** operator and **malloc()** to accomplish this as follows:

```
/* function to allocate n ints
   and read values into them */

#include <stdio.h>
#include <stdlib.h>

int *make_ints(int n)
{
  int *pn;              /* pointer to int */
  int i;

/* allocate memory */
  pn = malloc(n*sizeof(int));

/* read values into the allocated memory */
  if(pn != NULL)
    for(i=0; i<n; i++)
      scanf("%d", pn+i);

return(pn);
}
```

Note that we again check whether `malloc()` returned a `NULL` pointer indicating that it failed to allocate the requested memory.

We explore the potential application of dynamic memory allocation and the `sizeof` operator in generalizing some of the linear algebra functions from Chapter 3 in the exercises at the end of this chapter.

The `sizeof` operator can be used with any C type, including any pointer or `struct` template. You can also use `sizeof` to find the number of bytes occupied by any defined variable, including arrays or structures. For example, the fragment

```
double mat[20][40][10];
printf("Bytes in mat = %d\n", sizeof(mat))
```

will output the number of bytes in the array.[2]

The `sizeof` operator has lower precedence than the structure member (`.`), array element (`[]`), function invocation (`()`), and member access (`->`) operators. The parentheses after the `sizeof` keyword are optional when the operand referenced by `sizeof` is a variable rather than a variable type such as `int` or `float`.

The `sizeof` operator is extremely useful in creating programs that can be moved across different computers without having to be rewritten. It automatically accounts for differences in the storage required for objects, avoiding the need to code the number of bytes a particular machine uses to store any given data type.

5.4.3 calloc(), realloc(), and free()

There are three other functions in the standard library used in managing memory dynamically. The first of these is `calloc()`. It has two arguments: the number of elements to allocate and the size (in bytes) of each element. It allows you to allocate arrays in a more straightforward fashion than using `malloc()`.

If possible, `calloc()` allocates sufficient memory to hold the requested number of elements. It returns a pointer to `void` that points to the starting address of the requested memory. If `calloc()` cannot provide this memory, it returns the value `NULL`. Unlike `malloc()`, the memory provided by successful invocations of `calloc()` is initialized to all zero values.

For example, if you wanted to allocate an array of 25 `struct`s of type `point3D` as defined in Section 5.2.6, you would do so in the following fragment of code:

```
/* allocating an array of 25 structs */

#include <stdlib.h>

/* struct template for a point in three dimensions */
```

---

[2]As a technical matter, the value provided by the `sizeof` operator [as well as integer arguments to the library functions `malloc()`, `calloc()`, and `realloc()`] are of an unsigned integer type called `size_t`. This issue is discussed in Appendix A (see Section A.12).

```
struct point3D {
  double x;    /* x coordinate */
  double y;    /* y coordinate */
  double z;    /* z coordinate */
  };

/* declare pointer to structure of type point3D */
struct point3D *p;

p = calloc(25, sizeof struct point3D);
```

The pointer **p** could then be used as the starting address of an array of 25 **struct**s each of type **point3D**.

The library function **realloc()** changes the size of a previously allocated piece of memory. It has two arguments: a pointer to the beginning address of the previously allocated memory, and the new size (measured in bytes) requested. It returns a pointer to **void**, which is the starting address of the new memory.

realloc() will not change the entries in the existing part of memory up to the minimum of the old and new sizes. For example, if you had previously allocated memory for 10 **double**s and then invoked **realloc()** requesting space for 5 **double**s, the first five entries in the memory pointed to by the value returned from **realloc()** would be the same as the first five entries in the original memory. Similarly, if you used **realloc()** to get space for 15 **double**s, the first 10 entries in the memory returned would be the same as in the original memory.

If the requested size of memory is larger than the old size, then the additional memory provided by **realloc()** is not initialized. If **realloc()** cannot provide the new memory, it leaves the old memory unchanged and returns **NULL**.

Suppose that we had allocated memory for 25 **struct**s of type **point3D**, and we later needed to store the coordinates for 30 points. If **p** pointed to the memory originally allocated in the fragment above, we could increase the size of this in the following statement:

```
struct point3D *q;

q = realloc(p, 30*sizeof struct point3D);
```

Note that if **realloc()** is successful, the first 25 entries in the memory pointed to by **q** will be the same as those pointed to previously by **p**. Also, it is important to check whether **q** is **NULL** before we attempt to use it in case **realloc()** was unable to provide the requested memory. When **realloc()** fails, the original memory pointed to by **p** is unchanged. As with **malloc()**, the functions **calloc()** and **realloc()** always provide a block of contiguous memory locations. This memory can therefore be treated as an array.

The last memory allocation function is **free()**. It deallocates memory that was previously allocated by **malloc()**, **calloc()**, and **realloc()**. It has a single argument which is a pointer to the memory allocated previously. **free()** does not return a value.

For example, if you no longer needed the memory pointed to by **q** in the example above, you could return it to the memory allocation system for later reuse with the following statement:

```
free(q);
```

It is an error to try to use the functions **free()** or **realloc()** on a segment of memory that was not previously allocated.

5.5 RAGGED ARRAYS IN C

One data structure that gets widely used in text processing is called a *ragged array*. Consider, for example, an application in which we need to store a series of words. Since words vary in length, it would be inefficient to create an array of character arrays each long enough to store the longest possible word. Instead, we generally create a data structure to hold the words. This data structure is an array of pointers to **char**. Each pointer in the array points to a character array that is allocated dynamically when the size of the word to be stored is known. Figure 5.3 illustrates how such an array would be organized.

To create a ragged array from a series of words input by a user, we use a character array (called a *buffer*) with some fixed length equal to the longest string we are likely to encounter (plus one additional array element for the null character). After we input a word into the buffer, we determine its length using the standard library function

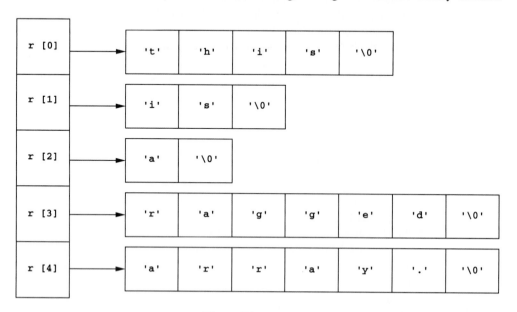

Figure 5.3 Ragged array.

strlen(), allocate memory for the word using **malloc()**, and then copy the word from the buffer into the newly allocated memory.

The function **ragged_array()** given below creates a ragged array from a series of input words (separated from each other by white space). It has as arguments **r_array**, a pointer to the beginning of the array of character pointers, and **maxwords**, the greatest number of words to be read into the array. The function returns an **int** equal to the number of words actually read into the array.

```
#include <stdio.h>  /* input/output library */
#include <stdlib.h> /* memory allocation library */
#include <string.h> /* string library */

#define LONGWORD 80 /* longest allowed word */

/* function to create ragged array of strings */
int ragged_array(
  char *r_array[], /* array of character pointers */
  int maxwords)    /* max number of words to be read */
{
  int nwords=0;       /* counter of words read */
  int flag;           /* flag for end of file */
  char buffer[LONGWORD+1];   /* buffer */

/* read in first word up to maximum allowed length */
  flag = scanf("%s", buffer);

/*loop until end of file reached */
  while(flag != EOF && nwords < maxwords) {
    r_array[nwords] = malloc(strlen(buffer)+1);
    if(r_array[nwords] != NULL){
        strcpy(r_array[nwords], buffer);
        nwords++;
    }
    else
        flag = EOF;
  }
  return(nwords);
}
```

The crucial statements in this function are

```
        r_array[nwords] = malloc(strlen(buffer)+1);
```

and

```
        strcpy(r_array[nwords], buffer);
```

The first of these uses **malloc()** to allocate sufficient space for the string in the buffer. Note that we add one to the value returned by **strlen()** to have space for the null character. The pointer returned by **malloc()** is assigned to the next free element of the array of character pointers, **r_array**. The second key statement uses the library function **strcpy()** to copy the contents of the buffer into the next element of the ragged array.

5.6 ARGUMENTS TO main()

Up until this point, we have written complete programs as though the function **main()** did not have any arguments. In fact, **main()** can have two arguments that are used to pass information between the command interpreter (or shell) being used to invoke programs and the C program itself. For example, some computer systems have a command for printing a file of the form

```
print filename
```

where **filename** is the name of the file to be printed. If the **print** command is implemented in C, there needs to be some way for the name of the file to be printed to be communicated to that C program.

A **main()** function in C actually has two arguments, which by custom are named **argc** and **argv**. The value of **argc** passed to **main()** is an **int** equal to the number of strings that appeared on the command line invoking the C program, including the name of the command program. In the foregoing example of a **print** command, the value passed to **argc** would be 2. (Each string is a series of characters not separated by white space.) The argument **argv** is a ragged array (i.e., an array of pointers to strings). This ragged array contains the values of the separate strings in the command line. In the example above, the first element in the ragged array would be the string **"print"** and the second would be **"filename"**.

The following program shows how the arguments to **main()** might be used. It simply prints out the values of the arguments to **main()**.

```
/* program to print out arguments to main() */

#include <stdio.h>

main(
    int argc,        /* number of arguments to main */
    char *argv[])    /* ragged array    */
{
    int i;           /* used for looping */
    printf("Number of arguments to main is %d\n", argc);
```

```
/* loop through elements in ragged array */
  for(i=0; i<argc; i++)
    printf("String %d is %s\n", i, argv[i]);
}
```

A more realistic use would be to pass the program user's selections among various options such as the files to be operated on. For example, many C compilers are themselves written in C. The names of the files to be compiled, the various libraries to be used, and the name of the executable file to be created are often options passed using the **argc** and **argv** arguments.

The memory in which the ragged array is stored is allocated by the command processor, not by the C program itself. All of the entries in the ragged array are complete strings, including the terminating null character.

5.7 THE typedef STATEMENT

Another feature of C that makes it more convenient to create and use libraries of functions that operate on data structures is the language's ability to give a name to a new type of data, and then to use that derived data type in the same way as the standard types C provides. The **typedef** statement allows you to create and name derived data types.

Suppose, for example, that you wanted to define a new data type called **Complex** to hold a complex number consisting of real and imaginary parts. We might first create a template for a **struct** for this data object as follows:

```
/* struct to hold complex number */
struct real_and_imaginary {
  double real;       /* real part */
  double imag; /* imaginary part */
  };
```

Following this declaration, we could use a **typedef** statement to declare that **Complex** refers to objects of this type:

```
typedef struct real_and_imaginary Complex;
```

Once these statements appear in a source code file, we are then free to use the data type **Complex** just as we could use any other data type. For example, all of the following would be allowed:

```
/* using Complex data type */

/* prototype for function */
Complex add_complex(Complex, Complex);
```

```
/* function adding two Complex values */
Complex add_complex(Complex a, Complex b)
{
  Complex sum;
  sum.imag = a.imag + b.imag;
  sum.real = a.real + b.real;
  return(sum);
}

/* fragment dynamically allocating space
   for a Complex value */

Complex *p;  /* pointer to a Complex value */

/* use malloc to get memory */
p = malloc(sizeof (Complex));
if(p != NULL){
    p->real = 1.0;
    p->imag = 0.0;
}
```

While not required, we will adopt the convention that data types created by the **typedef** mechanism will always have names that begin with a capital letter and have the remainder of their name in lowercase. This will distinguish them from values created using **#define** preprocessor directives.

The most valuable aspect of the **typedef** capability is that it allows you to define new data types and then use them without being overly concerned with their internal structure. This is particularly useful for creating libraries of functions that manipulate data structures when the library will be used by others. You can give a library's users the appropriate **typedef** statements and let them use variables with types such as **Stacks** or **Lists** in their code. We will demonstrate the usefulness of this approach in Section 5.9 by reimplementing the stack functions in a more elegant fashion.

5.8 C PROGRAMS WITH MULTIPLE SOURCE FILES

C allows the programmer to combine source code from multiple files to create a single executable program. These source files (formally termed *translation units*) can contain different parts of the complete program, thereby facilitating development of large programs by more than one programmer. In addition, the programmer can compile each of the source code files separately and link them together into a single executable program at a later stage. Several rules apply to programs that are spread across multiple files.

First, variables that are defined *external* to any function can be referenced in other source files. However, since each file can be compiled independently, you must inform the compiler that the variable is "defined elsewhere" and you must declare the type of the variable. For example, suppose that you have one source file named **a.c** with an external variable **i** defined as

```
/* definition of i in file a.c */
int i;
```

If you wanted to use that variable in another source file **b.c**, then you would have to include the following declaration in that file.

```
/* declaration of i in file b.c */
external int i;
```

When file **b.c** is compiled, there would be no memory allocated to store the value of variable **i**. Instead, the compiler generates an *external reference* to **i** which would be found in some other source code module. The location of **i** would be resolved when the complete executable program was linked together from the separately compiled parts.

Second, all functions are by default considered to be external. This means that you can use these functions in other source code files. You should, however, include the function prototype in each source code file. This is often done by creating a separate **#include** file that is included with each source code file. For example, you might have a **#include** file named **c.h** which has all the function prototypes for the complete program. This would typically be kept in the same directory as the source code files. You would then have the preprocessor directive

```
/* include file in the same directory */
#include "c.h"
```

at the beginning of each source code file that made up the complete program. Note that the name **c.h** is enclosed in quotes rather than less than and greater than symbols. This indicates that the file **c.h** is not one of the standard header files, and that the file's name should be found by whatever file naming conventions are used by your computer's operating system.

The third rule allows some functions not to be treated as external. To do this, you define the function to be **static**, as in the following example:

```
/* declaration of a function which
   will not be external */
static double squares(double x)
{
  return (x*x);
}
```

Functions that are defined as static can be used only in the source code file in which they are defined. In effect, they are "hidden" from the other source code files.

Such functions are most often used when you are creating libraries of functions for someone else and you do not want that person to invoke some of the functions you use internally in your library.

5.9 PROGRAMMING PROJECT: STACKS REVISITED

We can now use the dynamic memory allocation functions, the **typedef** feature, and the ability to create separately compiled collections of functions to create a more general stack manipulation library. In particular, the new implementation will allocate memory for stacks dynamically and will automatically extend the size of those stacks when needed. In addition, the stack library will return error codes when unexpected conditions arise rather then simply terminating. This allows the programmer using the library to take whatever action is appropriate in the application.

The code for the stack manipulation is more complicated than the example presented in Section 5.3. The additional complexity of the implementation is offset by added generality of the stack functions. This tradeoff is often favorable because data structure manipulation functions can be used in many parts of a large software project. It therefore makes sense to invest the time to code these functions in a very general style.

Our implementation will create a separate header file **stack.h** and a file named **stack.c** containing the functions to manipulate the stack. The assumption is that users of the library will **#include** the header file in their programs, eliminating the need for reentering the various structure template declarations and the function prototypes. The following is a listing of the contents of the header file **stack.h**.

```
/*  header file stack.h */

/* template for passenger struct */
struct pass {
  char name[80];   /* name of passenger */
  int pieces;      /* number of pieces of luggage */
  int tag1;        /* luggage tag number 1 */
  int tag2;        /* luggage tag number 2 */
  };

/* template for a stack of passengers */
struct stack_pass {
  int count;   /* number of entries in stack */
  int size;    /* maximum size of stack */
  int inc;     /* increment by which stack grows */
  struct pass *entries; /* pointer to the last */
  };                    /* item in stack */

/* typedef for stack of passengers */
typedef struct stack_pass * Stack;
```

```
/* prototypes for stack functions */
Stack make_stack(int, int);
int give_count(Stack);
int push(Stack, struct pass *);
int pop(Stack, struct pass *);
void destroy_stack(Stack);

#define TRUE 1
#define FALSE 0
```

The **struct** with the template **pass** is the same as in our earlier implementation. However, the **struct** template for **stack_pass** now has four entries:

- **count**—the number of items in the stack.
- **size**—the maximum number of items that currently can be held in the stack.
- **inc**—the number of items by which the stack should grow if it needs to be extended.
- **entries**—a pointer to an array of structures of type **pass** containing the information about stacked passengers.

Figure 5.4 illustrates how the stack structure is organized. It shows a stack that has capacity for 50 passengers. There are three passengers named **"Jefferson"**, **"Hancock"**, and **"Adams"** currently in the stack, with **"Adams"** at the top of the stack. The stack will be incremented by enough space to hold 10 additional passengers each time it fills up.

The **typedef** statement defines a **Stack** to be a pointer to a **struct** of type **stack_pass**. This will allow us to declare variables as **Stack**s in our programs.

The header file also gives the function prototypes for the five stack manipulation functions. These functions are as follows:

- **make_stack()**. This function has two integers as its arguments. The first gives the initial size of the stack and the second is a *growth* increment describing how many additional spaces in the stack should be added when the stack grows. **make_stack()** returns a newly created **Stack** if it can successfully allocate memory for it or the value **NULL** if it fails to allocate the requested memory.
- **give_count()**. Takes a **Stack** as its argument and returns the number of items currently in a **Stack**.
- **push()**. This function pushes a new passenger on a **Stack**. Its two arguments are the **Stack** onto which the passenger is to be pushed and a pointer to a **struct** of type **pass** holding the data for the passenger. **push()** returns an **int** which will have a value which is **TRUE** (i.e., nonzero) if the item is pushed on the **Stack** successfully, and **FALSE** (i.e., zero) otherwise.
- **pop()**. This function pops an item off a stack. Its first argument is a **Stack** from which the passenger is popped. Its second argument is a pointer to a **struct** of type **pass** into which the passenger data is placed. **pop()** returns an **int** which will have a value that is **TRUE** (i.e., nonzero) if an item can be popped from the **Stack**, and **FALSE** (i.e., zero) otherwise.

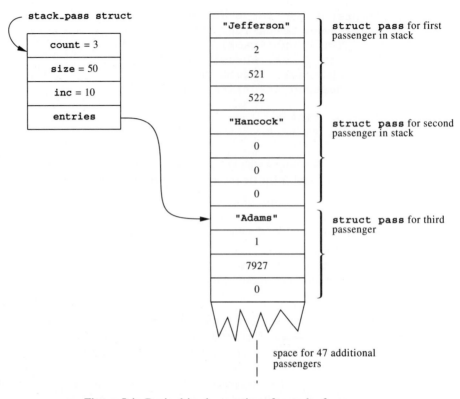

Figure 5.4   Revised implementation of a stack of passengers.

- **destroy_stack()**. Destroys a **Stack**. This function has as its argument the **Stack** to be destroyed and does not return a value.

The next file is the actual implementation of the stack functions. This is in the file **stack.c**. The implementation begins with the following **#include** statements:

```
/* #include statements for stack manipulation functions
       in file stack.c */

#include <stdio.h>
#include <stdlib.h>
#include "stack.h"
```

The C code for the function **make_stack()** follows.

```
/* function to make a stack */
Stack make_stack(
    int initial_size,    /* initial size of stack */
    int increment)       /* growth increment */
```

```
{
  Stack s;

/* allocate memory for stack */
  s = malloc(sizeof(struct stack_pass));,
/* check if stack can be allocated */
  if(s != NULL) {
/* allocate memory for data in stack */
    s->entries=calloc(initial_size,sizeof(struct pass));
    if(s->entries == NULL) { /* check allocation */
      free(s);
      s = NULL;
      }
    else {
      s->size = initial_size;
      s->inc = increment;
      }
  }
  return(s);
}
```

This function begins by allocating memory for a **Stack**. If this is successful, then it allocates sufficient memory for an array of **initial_size** structures of type **pass**. Each one of these array entries can hold information about a passenger. If this memory allocation fails (as indicated by **calloc()** returning a **NULL** value), then the memory allocated for the **Stack** is freed and the **NULL** value is returned. Otherwise, the size of the stack and the size of the increments to be added when the stack fills up are set, and the **Stack** is returned.

The second function, **give_count()** is essentially unchanged from the version described in Section 5.3. The C code is as follows:

```
/* function to give count of stack entries */
int give_count(Stack s)
{
  return(s->count);
}
```

The third function, **pop()**, first checks if the stack is empty. If not, then the item is popped from the stack and the value **TRUE** is returned. Otherwise, **FALSE** is returned.

```
/* function to pop from stack */
int pop(
  Stack s,            /* stack to pop */
  struct pass *p)     /* pointer to where popped */
  {                   /* data should be put */
```

```
   /* if stack isn't empty, pop it */
   if(s->count > 0) {
     s->count--;
     *p = s->entries[s->count];
     return(TRUE);
   }
   else
     return(FALSE);   /* stack was empty */
}
```

Note the statement

```
*p = s->entries[s->count];
```

Since **p** is a pointer to a structure, the value of ***p** is a structure. Thus the statement assigns the complete contents of the structure **s->entries[s->count]** to the structure pointed to by **p**.

The fourth function, **push()**, must deal with the possibility that the stack is full. In this case, it must use the library function **realloc()** to extend the size of the array **entries** in the stack. As with any other memory allocation function calls, care must be taken to make sure that the additional memory could be allocated. The implementation of **push()** is as follows.

```
/* function to push on stack */
int push(
   Stack s,         /* stack to push data on to */
   struct pass *p)/* pointer to data to push on stack */
{
   struct pass *temp;
/* if stack if full,increase size of allocated memory */
   if(s->count == s->size) {
     temp = realloc(s->entries,
                    (s->size+s->inc)*sizeof(struct pass));
     if(temp == NULL)
       return(FALSE);
     else
       s->entries = temp;
   }
   s->entries[s->count] = *p; /* add to stack */
   s->count++;
   return(TRUE);
}
```

The last function destroys a **Stack** by freeing the previously allocated memory. This must be done in two steps. First, the memory allocated for the array **entries** must be freed. Then the memory for the structure containing the stack can be freed. The code for this is provided below.

```
/* function to destroy stack */
void destroy_stack(Stack s)
{
  free(s->entries); /* free memory for data */
  free(s);          /* free memory for stack */
}
```

Note that it would be an error to first free the memory pointed to by **s**. Once **s** is freed, the reference **s->entries** is no longer valid.

Once this library is complete, we can then write other programs that make use of it. A realistic application would make stacks for each arriving airplane and keep adding passengers to these stacks as they checked in. Below we show the simpler case introduced in Section 5.3 using the stack library for a single flight.

```
/* using a stack for airline passengers */

#include <stdio.h>
#include "stack.h"

main()
{
  struct pass p;      /* holds a single passenger */
  Stack   s;          /* the stack */
  int flag1=!EOF;     /* indicator when EOF reached */
  int flag2;          /* indicator for illegal push */
  int seats;          /* number of seats on plane */

/* initialize stack and get capacity of aircraft */

  printf("Enter number of seats on plane:\n");
  scanf("%d", &seats);
  s = make_stack(seats, 10);

/* read in the passengers until EOF found */

  while(flag1 != EOF) {
    flag1 = scanf("%s %d %d %d", p.name, &p.pieces,
                  &p.tag1, &p.tag2);
    if(flag1 != EOF)
      if(!push(s, &p))
        printf("Can not add passenger to stack\n");
  }

/* pop passengers who are bumped */

  while(give_count(s) > seats) {
    pop(s, &p);
```

```
        printf("Passenger %s is bumped. Remove luggage ");
        printf("%d and %d\n", p.name, p.tag1, p.tag2);
    }
}
```

5.10 LINEAR LINKED LISTS

A *linear linked list* consists of a series of items (often called *nodes*), where each node contains a pointer to the next node. Such data structures are frequently used in situations where the number of items to be stored varies as the program executes. A linear linked list can grow as needed, with new items added to either the front or the end of the list. When some items on the list are no longer needed, they can be removed, allowing the list to shrink. Figure 5.5a to d show how a linear linked list is organized. The figure shows a sequence of operations on an initial list, with items added to the beginning and end of the list, and an item deleted from the list.

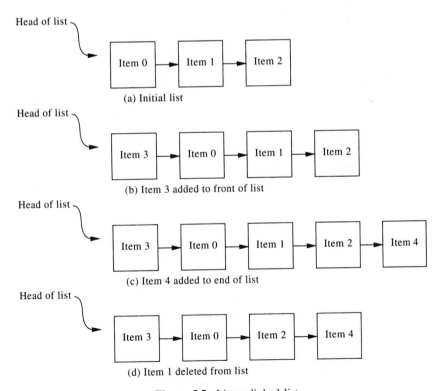

Figure 5.5   Linear linked list.

In this section we develop a library of functions for manipulating a linked list. The example we use to motivate the basic operations on linked lists is the representation of a list of students. Each element of the list will store the name of a student as a character string.

5.10.1 Self-Referential Data Structures

Linked lists in C generally use **struct**s to store the nodes in the list. However, in order for this to work, one member of the **struct** must be a pointer to the next node on the list. This requires that the **struct** have a member which is a *pointer to a* **struct** *of the same type*. Structures that do this are allowed in C; they are referred to as *self-referential* data structures.

Consider as an example a list of names of students. In this example we could represent a node in the list with a **struct** using the following template:

```
/* template for a list node
     representing student in list */
struct list_node {
  char name[80];              /* name of student */
  struct list_node *next;     /* pointer to next */
  };                          /* list element */
```

By convention, the last node on the list will have the member **next** set to the **NULL** pointer.

The member declared as **struct list_node *next** is a pointer to a **struct** of type **list_node**. At first, this may seem to be a circular definition. The definition is not circular because the template for **struct list_node** includes only a *pointer* to the same structure type, not the actual structure itself.

While not essential, it will be convenient to use the **typedef** mechanism in C to define the type **List**. The statement

```
typedef struct list_node * List;
```

defines **List** to be a pointer to a node in the list. After this statement, a definition such as

```
List p1, p2, p3;
```

would define the variables **p1**, **p2**, and **p3** as **List**s.

In our implementation, a variable which is a **List** will point to the first node in the list. Note that the pointer member **next** in any list is itself of type **List**. Data structures that have this property are said to be *recursively defined*.

The fact that linked lists are recursively defined means that any function that can operate on a list can also be applied to the pointer **next** in any node on that list.

Suppose, for example, that the function **show_names()** prints the name of a student in a list. Assuming that the **struct list_node** and the type **List** are defined as above, this function might be implemented as follows:

```
/* function to output names in a list */

#include <stdio.h>

void show_names(List p)
{
   if(p != NULL) {
      printf("Student name:%s\n", p->name);
      show_names(p->next);   /* recursive invocation */
   }                         /* of show_names() */
}
```

The recursive implementation of **show_names()** exploits the recursive definition of the list structure.

5.10.2 Implementation of Operations on Lists

In this section we implement C functions that perform some of the common operations on lists. We use the example of a list of students' names throughout. The generalization of the functions to more realistic situations where each node contains more complicated data is straightforward. We examine the generalization of our list manipulation functions to avoid the need to rewrite many of the functions in the list library later in Section 5.14.

Following the approach used in our stack function library shown in Section 5.9, we will create a separate header file **list.h** for the structure template declarations, **typedef** statements, and function prototypes. The C code for the list operations will be in a file named **list.c**.

The function prototypes and a brief description of what each function does are given below.

- **List init_list (void)**—returns an empty list.
- **int empty_list(List)**—returns **TRUE** if a **List** is empty, **FALSE** otherwise.
- **List add_to_front(List, char *, int *)**—puts a new student at the front of the **List**, returning the revised **List**. The first argument is the **List** to be added to, the second is a pointer to a string containing the student's name, and the third is a pointer to an **int** that the function will set to **TRUE** if the addition is successful and **FALSE** otherwise.
- **destroy_list(List)**—destroys a **List**, freeing all the allocated memory.
- **List delete_from_list(List, char *, int *)**—deletes a student from the **List**, returning the revised **List**. The first argument is the **List**

from which the student's name is to be deleted, the second is a pointer to a string containing the student's name, and the third is a pointer to an **int** that the function will set to **TRUE** if the deletion is successful and **FALSE** otherwise.

Figure 5.6 illustrates the effects of these functions on a list. In part (a), a list named **slist** is initialized. Parts (b) and (c) of the figure show the effects of invoking **add_to_front()** and **add_to_end()**, respectively. Part (d) shows the result of invoking **delete_from_list** using the string **"John Smith"** as the character string to be deleted.

The header file **list.h** for the list manipulation library is given below. The prototype for the function **show_names()** given earlier is also included.

```
/*----------------list.h--------------------*/

#define TRUE 1
#define FALSE 0
#define MAXNAME 80   /* longest allowed name */

/* template for a list node containing a name */
struct list_node {
   char name [MAXNAME+1];    /* name of student */
   struct list_node *next;   /* pointer to next */
   };                        /* list element */

typedef struct list_node * List;

/* prototypes for list functions */
List init_list(void);
int empty_list(List);
List add_to_front(List, char *, int *);
void destroy_list(List);
List delete_from_list(List, char *, int *);
void show_names(List);
```

The file **list.c** containing the code for the five list manipulation functions begins with the following **#include** statements.

```
/* ----------------list.c----------------------*/

/* include files for student list manipulation */

#include <stdio.h>
#include <stdlib.h>
#include <string.h>
#include "list.h"
```

```
slist = NULL
```

(a) Result of `slist =init_list( );`

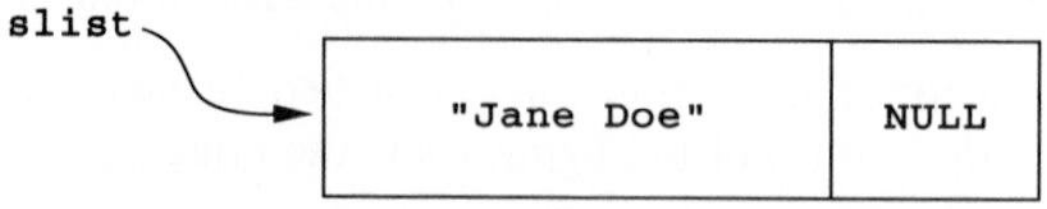

(b) Result of `slist =add_to_front(slist, "Jane Doe", &flag);`

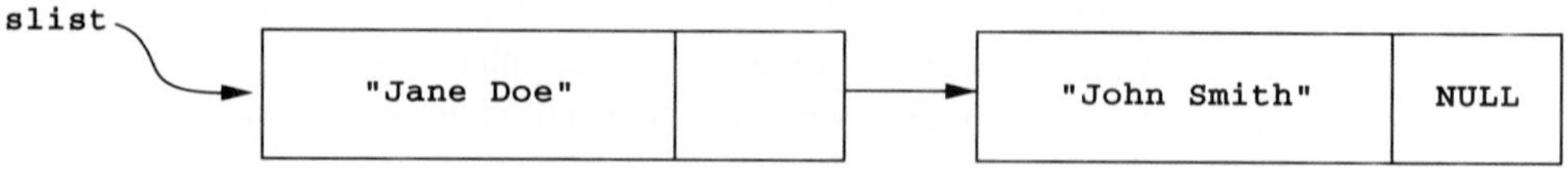

(c) Result of `slist = add_to_end(slist, "John Smith", &flag);`

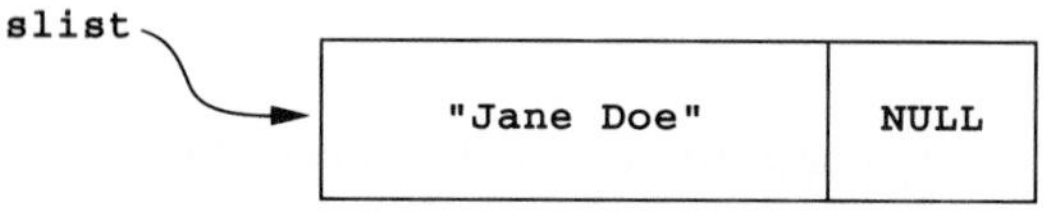

(d) Result of `slist =delete_from_list(slist, "John Smith", &flag);`

Figure 5.6 List operations.

The functions `init_list()` and `empty_list()` are extremely simple. `init_list()` returns a **NULL** pointer, and `empty_list()` checks whether its argument is **NULL**, returning **TRUE** if this is the case and **FALSE** otherwise. The code for these functions is as follows:

```
/* this function initializes list */
List init_list(void)
{
   return(NULL);
}

/*this function tests if list is empty */
int empty_list(List slist)
{
   if(slist == NULL)
      return(TRUE);
   return(FALSE);
}
```

The function `add_to_front()` is more complicated. It must use `malloc()` to allocate memory for a new node and check whether `malloc()` was successful. If so, it must then copy the student's name (passed as an argument) into the new node and link the new node into the list. Finally, it returns the appropriate flag value indicating whether or not it was successful. The implementation is given below.

```
/* this inserts a name on the front of the list */
List add_to_front(List slist, char *student, int *flag)
{
    List node;

/* allocate memory for a node and check if successful*/
    node =  malloc(sizeof(struct list_node));
    if(node == NULL)
      *flag = FALSE;

    else {   /* put node on list */
      strncpy(node->name, student, MAXNAME);
      node->next = slist;
      slist = node;
      *flag = TRUE;
    }
    return(slist);    /* return list after addition*/
}
```

The function **destroy_list()** is interesting because it exploits the recursive nature of the list structure. (Exercise 5–4 explores an iterative implementation.) The function tests for whether its argument is an empty list. If not, it calls itself using the pointer to the next node in the list as the argument, and then frees the memory allocated for the node. When invoked, the function will work its way to the end of the list, and then free the nodes starting with the last node first. The code for this function is given below.

```
/* this destroys a list */

void destroy_list(List slist)
{
  if(!empty_list(slist)) {
    destroy_list(slist->next);
    free(slist);
  }
}
```

The fifth list function, **delete_from_list()**, removes a specific entry from the list. This is the most complicated list operation we will consider. In order to delete an item, the function must first find it by working its way down the list until it locates the name to be deleted or reaches the end of the list. If the item to be deleted is found on the list, then it must be removed from the list. In doing so, we must ensure that the **next** pointers are set so that the list remains correctly structured. Finally, the function should free the memory for the deleted node. The code for **delete_from_list()** is as follows.

```
/* this deletes a node from the list */
List delete_from_list(
  List slist,       /* list from which name is deleted */
  char *str,        /* pointer to name to be deleted */
  int *flag)        /* set TRUE if deletion successful */
{
  List temp;        /* temporary List */
  List prev;        /* pointer to node before one
                       to be deleted */

/* find item to be deleted by working through list */
  *flag = FALSE;
  temp=slist;

  while(!empty_list(temp) && ! (*flag))
    if(!strcmp(temp->name, str))  /* name found */
      *flag = TRUE;
    else {  /* name still not found */

      prev = temp;
      temp = temp->next;
    }

/* if item was found, delete it from list */
  if(*flag) { /* check if item is first on list */
    if(temp == slist)
      slist = temp->next;
    else        /* if item not first, set next pointer
                   from previous node */
      prev->next = temp->next;
    free(temp); /* free memory for deleted node */
    }
  return(slist);  /* return list after deletion */
}
```

The **while** loop uses the variable **temp** to work its way through the list, starting at the beginning node, until either the name to be deleted is found or the end of the list is reached. One of the keys to implementing **delete_from_list()** correctly is not only to keep track of the node to be deleted, but also to maintain a pointer to the preceding node on the list. The pointer to the preceding node is kept because we need to relink the list after we delete a node. In the code above, the variable **prev** is set to the node before the one to be deleted. Note also that the section of code that deletes a node must deal with two cases. The first is where the node to be deleted is the first on the list. In this case, the **List** returned by **delete_from_list()** must be modified. (Recall that variables of type **List** are actually pointers to the first node on the list.) The second case is where the item to be deleted is not the first in the **List**.

5.11 QUEUES

A *queue* is a data structure that can be used to store information that needs to be accessed in a *first in, first out* manner. This contrasts with a stack, where the first item pushed on the stack is the last item popped. Queues occur very often in service systems such as bank teller lines or aircraft waiting for permission to take off or land at airports. In computer systems, queues are often used to hold tasks awaiting services such as the use of a disk drive or a printer. Queues are used very frequently in computer simulations of complex systems such as traffic moving through a bottleneck.

Figure 5.7 illustrates some standard operations on a queue. Following the example of the preceding section on lists, each item in the queue is the name of a student. (A more general queue could have any set of information in the nodes, including complete `struct`s.) Part (a) of the figure shows an initial queue of items. Figure 5.7b and c show the queue after a new item has been added and an item has been removed. While the figure shows the queue as a linked list, any data structure that operates with the first in, first out discipline could be used as a queue.

5.11.1 Implementing a Queue

In theory, one could use a simple linked list to hold a queue. Items could be removed from the front of the list and added to the end of the list, thus assuring that items will be removed in the same order in which they were added. The major shortcoming of doing this is that while it is simple to remove data from the front of a list, adding something to the end of a simple linked list requires starting at the beginning and tracing through all the pointers until the end of the list is reached.

A more efficient strategy is to store the data for a queue in a linked list, but keep track of both the front and the rear of the list. This is the approach we will implement.

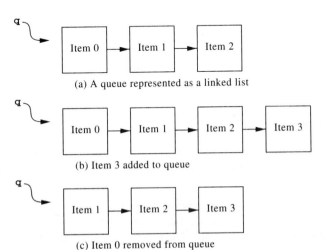

(a) A queue represented as a linked list

(b) Item 3 added to queue

(c) Item 0 removed from queue

Figure 5.7 Example of a queue.

We will use the **struct** template, the functions, and the **typedef** statements for Lists as presented in Section 5.10.1 and will add the following template and **typedef** statements.

```
/* queue definition */
#include "list.h"

struct queue_struct {
  List front;
  List rear;
  };

typedef queue_struct * Queue;
```

We rely on the header file **"list.h"** to provide the definition of **List**s and the prototypes for the functions that manipulate lists. The data structure template **queue_struct** has two **List**s as members. The first **List**, **front**, is used as a pointer to the beginning node of the linked list in which the data will be stored. The second **List**, **rear**, is a pointer to the last node in the queue. (Recall that the data type **List** is itself a pointer to a node on a list.) The **typedef** statement allows us to define variables which are **Queue**s as pointers to a structure containing the two **List** pointers. Figure 5.8 illustrates how the queue is implemented.

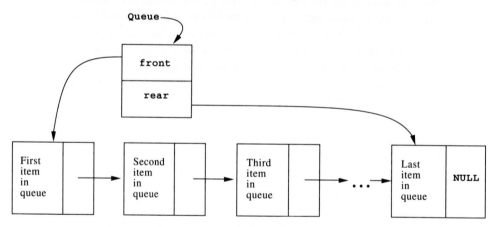

Figure 5.8 Organization of a queue.

We will provide three functions that operate on a queue and will make extensive use of the list operations we created in the preceding section. The three functions we implement are as follows:

- **make_queue(void)**. This function returns an empty **Queue**. An empty queue is defined as one in which both the **List**s are empty (i.e., where both pointers to the nodes on the list are **NULL**). The function returns a **NULL** pointer if the **Queue** could not be created.

- **add_to_queue(Queue, char *)**. This function adds a new item to a queue. The first argument is the **Queue** to be added to, and the second argument is a pointer to the name of the student to be added. The function returns an **int** set to **TRUE** if the addition was successful, and **FALSE** otherwise.
- **remove_from_queue(Queue, char **)**. This function removes an item from the queue. The first argument is the **Queue** from which an item is to be removed, and the second argument is a pointer to the character string which, after the item is removed, will hold the name of the student removed. (Since this argument is a pointer to a string, which itself is a pointer to array of **char**, its type is **char ****. In words, this is a pointer to a pointer to a **char**.) The function returns an **int** set to **TRUE** if the **Queue** had an item which could be removed, and **FALSE** if the **Queue** was empty.

The full header file for a queue is given below.

```
/* ------------queue.h------------*/

#include "list.h"  /* relies on list data structure */

/* structure template and typedef statement */
struct queue_struct {
  List front;
  List rear;
  };

typedef struct queue_struct * Queue;

/* function prototypes */
Queue make_queue(void);
int add_to_queue(Queue, char *);
int remove_from_queue(Queue, char **);
```

The file **queue.c** which will hold the code implementing these functions begins with the needed **#include** statements.

```
/* include files required for queue manipulation */

#include <stdio.h>
#include <stdlib.h>
#include <string.h>
#include "queue.h"
```

The function **make_queue()** is given below. It uses **malloc()** to allocate memory for the **queue_struct**. If **malloc()** is successful, the members **front** and **rear** are initialized to the **NULL** pointer, indicating an empty queue.

```
/* function to make a new queue */
Queue make_queue(void)
{
  Queue q;
/* allocate memory for queue structure */
  q = malloc(sizeof (struct queue_struct));
/* if malloc successful, set members of structure */
  if(q != NULL) {
    q->front = NULL;
    q->rear = NULL;
  }
  return(q);   /* return queue */
}
```

The second function, **add_to_queue**(), makes use of the list processing functions developed in the preceding section. It initializes a new **List** by calling **init_list**(), and then adds the character string containing the student's name to that **List**. It then adds that new **List** to the existing one that forms the queue.

```
/* function to add name to queue */
int add_to_queue(
  Queue q,    /* queue to be added to */
  char * str)/* pointer to string to be added */
{
  int flag;   /* flag indicating successful addition */
  List node;

/* add item to rear of queue */
  node = init_list();
  node = add_to_front(node, str,&flag);
/* if addition successful, check if queue was
    initially empty */
  if(flag)
    if(empty_list(q->rear))
      q->front = q->rear = node;    /* if empty, set
                                        front & rear */

    else{ /*add item to list and update rear of queue*/
      q->rear->next = node;
      q->rear = node;
    }
  return(flag);
}
```

Note that **add_to_queue**() must deal with two distinct cases. If the queue to which an item is being added is empty, then both the **front** and **rear** pointers must be updated. If the queue already has items in it, then the **rear** pointer must be updated, but the **front** remains unchanged.

The final queue manipulation function, `remove_from_queue()`, first checks if there is anything in the queue to be removed by seeing if the list is empty. If there is something in the queue, it allocates memory for the character string (including the terminating null character) and copies the name at the front of the queue into the newly allocated memory. It then deletes the item from the queue. If after the removal the queue is now empty, `remove_from_queue()` resets the `rear` pointer to `NULL`.

```
/* function to remove item from front of queue */
int remove_from_queue(
   Queue q,     /* queue from which item to be removed */
   char **str) /* pointer to string in which name */
{                /* will be stored */
   int flag=FALSE;

/* check if queue is empty to begin with */
   if(!empty_list(q->front)) {
/* allocate memory and copy name at front of
   queue into it */
     *str = malloc(strlen(q->front->name)+1);
     if(*str != NULL) {
       strcpy(*str, q->front->name);
       q->front = delete_from_list(q->front,
                       q->front->name, &flag);
     }
/* if removal leaves queue empty, reset rear pointer */
     if(empty_list(q->front))
         q->rear = NULL;
   }
   return(flag);
}
```

Note that the implementation of `remove_from_queue()` checks whether the memory for the string has been successfully allocated by `malloc()`. If `malloc()` fails, then the value returned by the function is `FALSE`. This is the same value as returned when the queue is empty. A more sophisticated implementation might return a special indicator for this situation.

5.11.2 Using Queues

To show how the queue manipulation functions work, we consider a case where orders arrive at a product distribution center. The center handles 20 different products, with different groups responsible for each product. Orders are filled by each group on a first come, first served basis.

We will use a queue for each of the 20 products. As new orders come in, they are entered into one of the 20 queues. Our program will accept orders and put them in the appropriate queue. For simplicity, the products will be coded with an integer between 1 and 20, and the orders will be represented by a simple string, which might contain the name of the company placing the order or an order code. We assume that the product groups in the company use the simple string to access the orders, which in turn is used by some other program that gives them detailed information about the shipping address and the quantity of goods ordered. In an actual application, the items in the queue would probably consist of more complete information about the order.

The program needs to read in the item number and the string representing the order. It then must put the item on the appropriate queue using **add_to_queue()**. When no more orders are to be processed, it will output the queues by removing items one at a time (using **remove_from_queue()**) for each product.

The implementation is as follows:

```
/*-----------example program using queues ----------*/


#include <stdio.h>
#include <string.h>
#include "queue.h"

#define NITEMS 20

main()
{
  Queue order_queues[NITEMS]; /* array of queues */
  char order_name[80];     /* buffer for order names */
  int i, item_no, flag, test;
  char *out;              /* pointer to character array */


/* initialize queues */
  for(i=0; i<NITEMS; i++)
    order_queues[i] = make_queue();

/* read in orders and put on correct queues */
  test = scanf("%d %s", &item_no, order_name);
  while(test != EOF) {
    flag = add_to_queue(order_queues[item_no-1],
                        order_name);
    test = scanf("%d %s", &item_no, order_name);
  }

/* output the queues */
  for(i=0; i<NITEMS; i++) {
    printf("Queue of orders for item %d:\n", i+1);

    flag = remove_from_queue(order_queues[i], &out);
    while(flag) {
      printf("%s ", out);
```

```
    flag = remove_from_queue(order_queues[i], &out);
      }
    printf("\n");
  }
}
```

A real-world application of this type would have to do considerably more error checking. For example, this program will accept a product number outside the range 1 through 20. In the version shown above, this will generally produce an error during the program's execution. Production-quality applications of this type need to perform error checks on all the inputs and provide their users with messages requesting correct inputs. These checks significantly increase the length of programs and are often the most time-consuming part of a program to write.

5.12 TREES

The last general data structure we will consider is the *tree*. A tree is a series of connected nodes in which there exists exactly one path between every node pair. Trees have one node, called the *root*, which has no entering connections. Figure 5.9 illustrates a tree with the root node shown at the top. As with lists and stacks, each node can contain any set of data appropriate to the problem at hand.

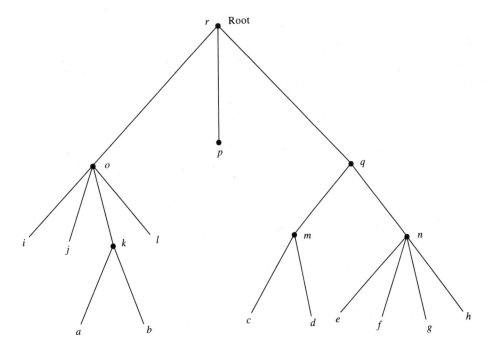

Figure 5.9   Tree.

Trees are flexible data structures for holding large numbers of nodes where the order in which nodes need to be accessed is not a simple, fixed rule such as first in, first out. We often put some structure on the ordering of nodes based on their content. One common organization is called a *binary search tree*. This type of tree requires that a single value in each node be used as a *key*, and that keys have some natural ordering. If, for example, the keys are names of people, the ordering might be alphabetical. Every node in a binary search tree has at most two nodes at the next level below it. Moreover, binary search trees require that every node added to the tree has the value of the key for its left branch less its own key and the value of the key for its right branch greater than its own key. Figure 5.10 illustrates a binary search tree containing the social security numbers and names of people. The social security numbers are used as the key for the organization of the tree. We explore the uses of such trees much further in Chapter 6.

Trees that have specific structures are widely used to store and retrieve information. For example, many database programs rely on trees to organize the data so that it can be accessed efficiently. Searching a linked list of N items can require examination of as many as N nodes. If those nodes are properly organized as a tree, we can find items by examining on the order of $\log(N)$ nodes. When N is large, the difference between $\log(N)$ and N can be enormous.

Another common use of trees is to represent moves in a game such as checkers or chess. Each node is a state of the chess board, and the nodes below it are the legal moves from that current node. We will use a tree for this purpose in Section 5.13.

5.12.1 Terminology for Trees

There is a fairly standard set of terminology for trees that is widely used. For example, if there is a direct connection, called a *branch*, from node *a* to node *b* (where node *b* is one level "down" from node *a*), then node *b* is referred to as the *child* of node *a*. Some texts use the terminology *son* or *daughter* for such nodes. Similarly, node *a* is called

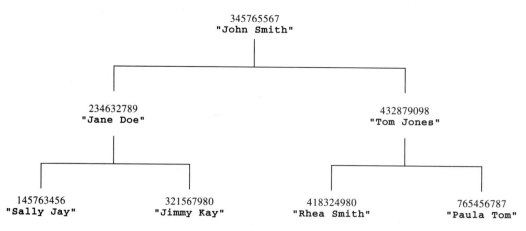

Figure 5.10   Binary search tree.

the *parent* of *b*. In a tree, all nodes except the root node have exactly one parent. Nodes that share a common parent are called *siblings*. For any node *a* the nodes which are its children, its children's children, etc. are referred to collectively as the *descendants* of *a*, and the nodes which are its parent, it parent's parent, etc. are called its *antecedents*.

Using this terminology, the root node is the one node in a tree that has no parent. A node which has no children is called a *leaf node*. The *level* of a node *a* in a tree is the number of antecedent nodes between *a* and the root. By this definition, the root is at level 0 and the children of the root are at level 1. Figure 5.11 illustrates these relationships.

There are many different variants of trees. For example, trees can be structured so that every node has at most *k* children. These are called *k-ary* trees, so when *k* equals two or three, the trees are called binary and ternary, respectively. Trees can also be *balanced*, meaning that the leaf nodes are all either at the lowest or next-to-lowest levels. Figure 5.12a and b illustrate both an unbalanced and a balanced ternary tree.

5.12.2 Implementing a Binary Tree

Binary trees are by far the most commonly used type of tree. In this subsection we describe one way this structure can be represented in C. Because the functions that operate on a binary tree often depend on the purpose for which the tree is being used,

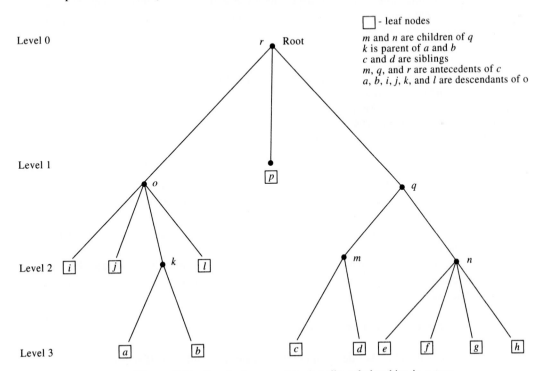

□ - leaf nodes

m and *n* are children of *q*
k is parent of *a* and *b*
c and *d* are siblings
m, *q*, and *r* are antecedents of *c*
a, *b*, *i*, *j*, *k*, and *l* are descendants of o

Figure 5.11 Terminology used to describe relationships in a tree.

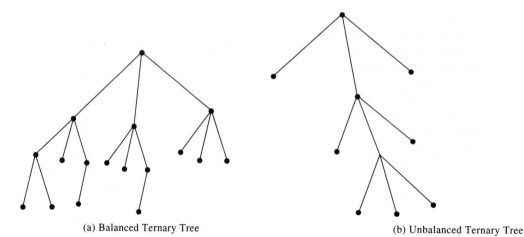

(a) Balanced Ternary Tree   (b) Unbalanced Ternary Tree

Figure 5.12   Unbalanced and balanced ternary tree.

we reserve the discussion of functions that manipulate binary trees until Chapter 6. There we explore binary search trees in detail.

As in our earlier examples with lists and queues, we assume that each node in the tree contains some character string, with the understanding that in real applications, a node might contain a data structure with many types of information in it. Each node in a binary tree will be represented by a **struct**. The template for this **struct** will be named **tnode**. The template declaration for this is as follows:

```
/* struct template for a node in a binary tree */
struct tnode {
  char name[80];        /* student's name */
  struct tnode *left;   /* pointer to left child */
  struct tnode *right;  /* pointer to right child */
};
```

Note that this data structure is self-referential. Each node contains two pointers named **left** and **right** which point to a structure of type **tnode**. These two members point to the left and right children of the node. If a node does not have a left or right child, then the values of the respective pointers are set to **NULL**. Leaf nodes have both pointers set to **NULL**.

Following the pattern established in earlier sections, we will use the **typedef** mechanism in C to define a data type called a **Tree** as a pointer to a **tnode**. The statement

```
typedef struct tnode * Tree;
```

accomplishes this. We define an empty **Tree** as simply a **NULL** pointer.

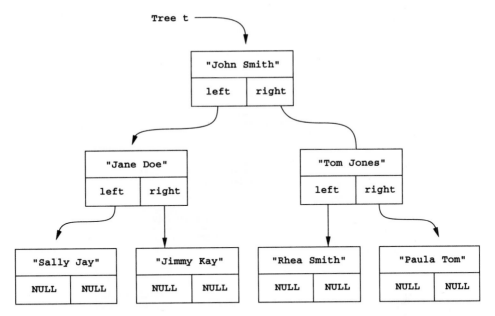

Figure 5.13 Representation of a binary tree.

The template, the **typedef** statement, and the function prototypes for the tree manipulation functions would normally be put in a header file. This header file would be included in any source code file that makes use of the tree library.

Figure 5.13 shows a binary tree and the pointers in the data structure. Note that when represented in the form above, a tree is a recursive data structure. If some variable **t** is a **Tree**, then both **t->left** and **t->right** are **Tree**s.

In the degenerate case, a tree can also be a linked list. This occurs when every node except one (the last in the list) has exactly one child, as shown in Figure 5.14. Thus, linked lists are special cases of trees.

While it is usual for trees to be implemented with pointers from the parent node to the child nodes, this form is not essential. In the next section we use a tree with exactly the reverse structure.

5.13 PROGRAMMING PROJECT: THE TILE PUZZLE PROBLEM

In this section we apply many of the concepts in data structures to solve a common children's game. This game was invented by Samuel Lyod in 1827.[3]   It consists of 15 tiles numbered from 1 through 15 arrayed in a square tray that can hold 16 tiles. One space in the tray is left empty. The object of the game is to transform an initial

---

[3]The puzzle example described in this section is based on an algorithm described in [Horowitz, Ellis and Sartj Sahni 78].

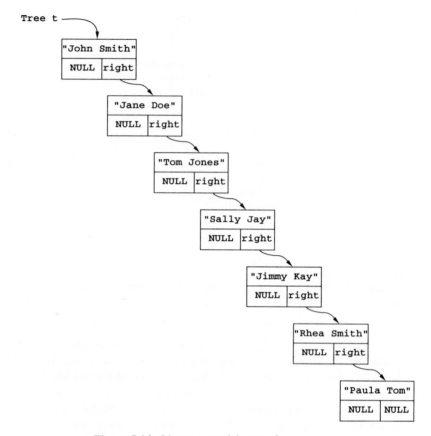

Figure 5.14 List as a special case of a tree.

arrangement of the tiles into one where the tiles are arranged in ascending order from left to right, with the empty spot in the lower right-hand corner. The arrangement of tiles is altered by moving any of the tiles that are adjacent to the empty area into that area. Figure 5.15(a) and (b) illustrates a typical initial position and the puzzle in a winning position.

There are 16! (almost 21 million million) possible arrangements of the tiles in the puzzle. It can be proved that half of these "states" correspond to initial tile configurations which cannot be solved through a series of legal moves.[4] Even discounting these illegal initial states, an exhaustive search of all possible arrangements is not a particularly attractive solution strategy. Instead, we will develop an algorithm that structures the search in a reasonable, though certainly not optimal way. Such an algorithm is called a *heuristic*. The algorithm we show here has at least one notable flaw that will be eliminated when we revisit this problem in Chapter 6.

[4]See Exercise 5-17 for a description of a method to determine whether a puzzle is solvable.

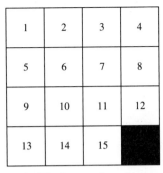

(a) Initial puzzle position   (b) Winning puzzle position

Figure 5.15   The 15 tile puzzle.

5.13.1 Organizing the Solution as a Tree

In order to solve the puzzle, we will organize states of the puzzle as a tree. The initial state will be the root of the tree, and the children of each node will be the allowable moves from that node. We will build the tree move by move, seeking a node that solves the puzzle. Once such a node is reached, the steps to solve the puzzle can be found by tracing the path through the tree from the root to the goal state of the puzzle. For example, Figure 5.16 shows a tree in which the circled node is the goal state for the puzzle. The moves from the initial state (the root of the tree) that solve the puzzle are drawn as heavy lines from the root to the goal state.

Note that the maximum number of children any node in the tree can have is four. This corresponds to shifting the empty spot up, down, left, or right. In cases where the empty position is along the edges of the puzzle, only two or three legal moves are possible. Our algorithm must take these situations into account.

Building the tree that simply enumerates all possible moves in a haphazard way is likely to take an unacceptably long time. Instead, we will create some measure that indicates which moves seem the most promising and build the tree by focusing attention on these promising nodes. We will construct a rough measure of how close any arrangement of the tiles in the puzzle is to the goal. Our algorithm will always add to the tree from the node that appears closest to the solution.

The measure we will use is the number of tiles in their correct positions. For example, Figure 5.17 shows the first steps from an initial position. The root of the tree generates four new arrangements, labeled **A**, **B**, **C**, and **D**. The integer next to each of the board positions is the number of correctly placed tiles. In this example, the board position labeled **C** has the highest value of 12. This is the node which is examined further, creating three new child nodes, labeled **E**, **F**, and **G**. (Note that there is no purpose in moving the blank upward from node **C**, since this would just recreate the original starting position.) Of all the nodes still not expanded (**A**, **B**, **D**, **E**, **F**, and **G**), node **E** has the greatest number of correctly placed tiles. It would therefore be the next node examined. The algorithm follows this simpleminded process until the goal state is reached.

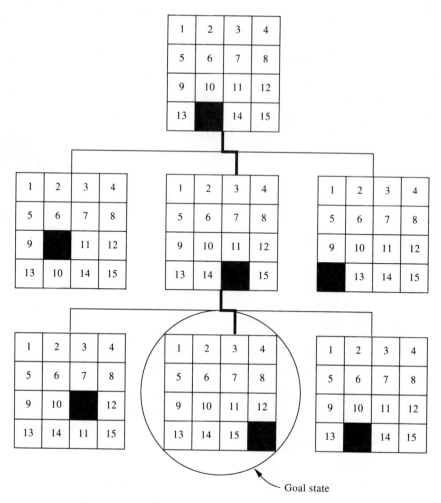

Figure 5.16   Using a tree to represent the 15 tile puzzle.

The algorithm always adds to the tree by creating the legal moves from a leaf of the tree. Since finding the leaves of a tree can require examining all the tree's nodes, we will maintain a list of leaf nodes. The next move will be made from one of the nodes on this list. Once the children of this selected node are generated, the node will be removed from the list. Because this list contains all nodes which are currently candidates for further consideration, we will refer to it as the *active list*.

There is a simple way to reduce the number of nodes in the tree generated by our algorithm. If we are moving from some node x, it makes no sense to make a move that generates the same board configuration as the parent of x. For example, if we move a tile up to generate a new puzzle configuration, it makes no sense to move that same tile down in the next move. Eliminating such simple cycles reduces by one the number of nodes generated at each step in the algorithm except when moves from the root node are considered.

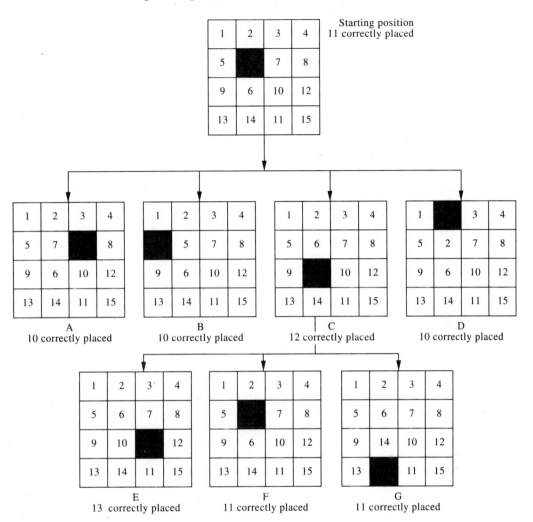

Figure 5.17   First steps in algorithm to solve the 15 tile puzzle.

By a logical extension of the argument above, it makes sense to eliminate *all* cycles in the algorithm. This extension requires significantly more code, which will be added in Section 6.7.

Given the discussion above, the algorithm we will use is as follows:

- Step 1. Read the initial state into the root of a tree. Start a list consisting of that node. Call that node "best".
- Step 2. while("best" isn't a solution) {

    Generate all legal children of node "best" except the child that is the same as its parent's parent.

    Remove "best" from the list.

    Add all the children of "best" to the list.

Scan the list to find the node on the list with the greatest number of correctly positioned tiles. Call that node "best".
```
}
```
- Step 3. Trace steps in solving puzzle from the solution to the root of the tree, pushing each step on a stack.
- Step 4. Pop steps in the solution off the stack, outputting each one, until the stack is empty.

Step 3 is needed in this algorithm because the pointers in the tree go from each node to its parent. Thus, once the solution is reached, the only way to trace the sequence of steps in the tree is to go from the solution node to the root. In order to get the steps output in the correct order, we push each move from the solution to the root of the tree on a stack. When we pop off items from this stack, the order of the steps is reversed, providing the moves in the correct order.

5.13.2 Implementing the Puzzle Algorithm

One way to think about the puzzle is to consider the empty slot as a special tile, which we will number tile zero. A legal move consists of exchanging the tile labeled zero with its neighbors. We will store the state of the puzzle in an array of **char**s named **values**. We use **char**s because they require less memory than **short int**s (or other integer data types) and the range of values to be stored is only from 0 to 15. Each entry in the array corresponds to one of the places in the puzzle. The order of items in the array corresponds to the arrangement of the tiles in the puzzle from left to right by rows. This representation is illustrated in Figure 5.18. The figure shows an example board configuration and the values in the array which represent that position.

We begin the description of the implementation by defining a **struct** to hold the nodes of the puzzle tree. Each node will contain the following five items:

- **values**—the array that describes the state of the puzzle.
- **parent**—a pointer from the node to its parent.
- **correct**—the number of correctly placed tiles in the node.
- **direction**—the direction the empty slot was last moved to reach this state.
- **active**—a pointer to the next leaf node on the "active" list of candidate nodes for the next move. This is set to **NULL** if the node is either not on the active list or is at the end of that list.

The implementation begins with the necessary **#include** directives and the template for the **struct** that will be used to define a puzzle position. We will also use a **typedef** statement to define a pointer to one of these **struct**s as a **Puzzle**. The following code does this.

```
/* header files */
#include <stdio.h>
#include <stdlib.h>
```

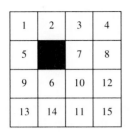
Puzzle

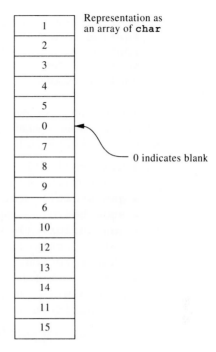
Representation as an array of **char**

0 indicates blank

Figure 5.18   Representation of puzzle with an array.

```
/* structure template for node in the board */
struct board {
  char values[16];  /* values of tiles on board */
  struct board *parent; /* pointer to parent board */
  struct board *active; /* next on active list */
  char correct;    /* count of correctly placed tiles */
  char direction; /* direction of move from parent */
  };

/* typedef for a Puzzle */
typedef struct board * Puzzle;
```

The values for **direction** will be coded in a special way. Since moving a tile corresponds to changing its position in the **value** array, we will encode **direction** with the number of positions in the array corresponding to a move. For example, moving a tile to the left shifts its position in the array downward one. Therefore, a leftward move will be coded as -1. Similarly, moves to the right, up, or down will be coded as +1, -4, and +4, respectively. For convenience, we will use four **#define** directives for these values (and an additional one to define the value of the blank tile) as follows:

```
/* define statements for the move
   directions and blank tile */
```

```
#define LEFT     -1
#define RIGHT     1
#define UP       -4
#define DOWN      4
#define BLANK     0
```

The program uses eight functions in addition to **main()**. These functions perform well-defined, narrow operations on the board tree or the active list. Unless stated otherwise, all the functions have no return value. The functions are as follows:

- **scan_active()**—scans the active list and returns the node that has the greatest number of tiles in the correct place.
- **get_start()**—reads in the starting position for the puzzle.
- **show_board()**—outputs a node in the tree.
- **gen_children()**—generates the children of a node.
- **delete_active()**—deletes a node from the active list.
- **show_solution()**—outputs the solution to the puzzle in the correct order.
- **eval()**—returns the number of tiles in the correct position for a node.
- **make_new()**—makes a new node in the tree. This function is invoked by **gen_children()**.

The prototypes for these eight functions are given below.

```
Puzzle scan_active(void); /* scans active list */
void get_start(Puzzle);   /* reads starting position */
void show_board(Puzzle); /* displays a board position */
void gen_children(Puzzle); /* generates children */
void delete_active(Puzzle); /* removes from active list */
void show_solution(Puzzle); /* shows solution */
int  eval(Puzzle);          /* evaluates a position */
void make_new(Puzzle, char, char); /* makes new board */
```

For efficiency and convenience, the root node of the tree and the pointer to the beginning of the active list are defined as external variables. This makes it possible for all functions to reference these variables without passing them as arguments. Thus, the definitions

```
/* external variables */
Puzzle active_list;        /* head of active list */
struct board root_node;    /* root node */
```

are placed before the beginning of the **main()** function.

With the above as preamble, the **main()** function implements the algorithm, invoking the other functions as needed. The code for **main()** is given below.

```
/* main routine controlling solution of puzzle */
main()
```

```
{
  Puzzle best;               /* current best state */
  Puzzle root=&root_node;    /* root of tree */


/*initialize start of puzzle */
  get_start(root);
  best = root;
  active_list = root;

  /* main loop to solve puzzle */

  while(best->correct < 15) {
    gen_children(best);
    delete_active(best);
    best = scan_active();
  }
    show_solution(best);
}
```

The steps in **main()** follow the algorithm given in Section 5.13.1. The function **get_start()** is called to read in the initial arrangement of tiles. The **active_list** is initialized to be the **root**. Since it is the only node on the solution tree, it must be the current **best**. The **while** loop continues until the current best solution has all 15 tiles in their correct places. Until this is true, the child nodes of the current **best** node are created using **gen_children()**, the node that was the best is deleted from the active list using **delete_active()**, and the new best node is found using **scan_active()**. Once a solution node is reached, **show_solution()** is invoked to output the moves in the correct order.

The details of how each of the eight service functions work will not be described here. The reader is encouraged to examine the code below, simulating an example puzzle problem. While the connections among nodes in the tree are complex, the basic logic of each step is relatively straightforward. The most difficult parts of the code to follow are probably in the function **gen_children()**, where some cumbersome logic must be used to determine what moves of the empty space are legal. Most of this logic involves checking whether the empty space is on any of the four perimeter rows and columns of the puzzle.

Another tricky aspect of our implementation is the reuse of the active list pointers in the function **show_solution()** to create the stack used to reverse the order of the nodes from the solution to the root of the tree. This avoids creating an entirely new data structure once a solution is found.

The complete code for the eight service functions is given below.

```
/* This routine displays a board state */

void show_board(Puzzle p)
```

```
      {
        int i;
        printf("Puzzle state is:");
        for(i=0; i<16; i++) {
          if(i%4 == 0) printf("\n");
          printf("%3d",p->values[i]);
        }
        printf("\n");
      }
```

```
/* This routine deletes a node from the active list.
   It goes through the active list until it finds the
   item to delete. It then resets pointers on the active
   list to skip the found item. */
```

```
void delete_active(Puzzle item)
   {
     Puzzle t,b;
     for(b=t=active_list; t != item; t = t->active)
       b = t;
     if(t == active_list)          /* check if item */
       active_list = t->active; /* is head of list */
     else
       b->active = t->active;
   }
```

```
/* This routine reads starting state of puzzle
   and initializes the root node
   of the search Puzzle */
```

```
void get_start(Puzzle b)
   {
     int i;

     for(i=0; i<16; i++)
       scanf("%d", &(b->values[i]));
     b->active = NULL;
     b->parent = NULL;
     b->correct = eval(b);
     b->direction = 0;
   }
```

```
/* This routine evaluates the number of correctly
   placed tiles on board */
```

```
int eval(Puzzle b)
   {
     int i;
```

```
    b->correct = 0;
    for(i=0; i<16; i++)
      if(b->values[i] == i+1) (b->correct)++;
    return(b->correct);
  }

/* This routine scans the active list to
   find best active node */

Puzzle scan_active(void)
  {
    int best_value;
    Puzzle b = active_list;
    Puzzle  t;

    for(best_value = -1; b!=NULL; b = b->active)
      if (b->correct > best_value) {
        best_value = b->correct;
        t=b;
      }
    return(t);
  }
/* This routine generates the children of a node */

void gen_children(Puzzle b)
  {
    int i;
/* look for blank tile */
    for(i=0; b->values[i] != BLANK; i++)
      ;

/*generate legal moves of blank to left */
    if (i%4 !=0 && b->direction != RIGHT)
      make_new(b,i,LEFT);
/* generate legal moves of blank up */
    if(i>3 && b->direction != DOWN)
      make_new(b,i,UP);
/* generate legal moves of blank to right */
    if((i+1)%4 != 0 && b->direction != LEFT)
      make_new(b,i,RIGHT);
/* generate legal moves of blank down */
    if(i<16-4 && b->direction != UP)
      make_new(b,i,DOWN);
  }

/* This routine makes a new node in Puzzle */

void make_new(Puzzle b, char blank, char move)
```

```
    {
      Puzzle new;
      int i;

  /*allocate a new node */
      new = malloc(sizeof(struct board));

  /* copy parent tile configuration */
      for(i=0; i<16; i++)
        new->values[i] = b->values[i];

  /* swap tiles from parent */
      new->values[blank+move] = b->values[blank];
      new->values[blank] = b->values[blank+move];
      new->parent = b;
      new->correct = eval(new);
      new->direction = move;
      new->active = active_list;   /* put new node on */
      active_list = new;           /* active list */
    }
  /* This routine displays solution path backwards */

  void show_solution(Puzzle b)
    {
  /* make stack of solved puzzles */
      for(b->active = NULL;
          b->parent != NULL;b = b->parent)
        b->parent->active = b;
  /* output solution */
      for( ;b != NULL; b = b->active)
        show_board(b);
    }
```

5.14 POLYMORPHISM IN DATA STRUCTURES

Note to Reader: The material in this section can be skipped without loss of continuity.

In this chapter, all of the data structures we have implemented and the functions which operate on them rely on a **struct** that contains both the data of interest and one or more pointers to other such data structures. For example, in our implementation of linked lists, we declared a structure template for nodes on a list of students as follows:

```
    /* template for a list node containing a name */
    struct list_node {
      char name[80];              /* name of student */
      struct list_node *next;     /* pointer to next */
      };                          /* list element */
```

We also used a **typedef** statement of the form

```
typedef struct list_node * List;
```

to allow us to declare variables as **List**s in a convenient way.

One of the weaknesses of this approach is that if we wanted to store anything but a character string in each node of the list, we would have to recode the structure template for the nodes. For example, if we wanted to create a list of **double**s, we would have to declare an entirely new template and **typedef** statement such as

```
/* template for a list node containing a double */
struct list_double {
  double value;                /* double value in list */
  struct list_double *next;   /* next list element */
  };

typedef struct list_double * List_of_Doubles;
```

This aspect of our data structure implementation makes our library of functions for data structures far less general than we would want. In our implementation up to this point, lists containing different types of data need to be coded separately.

In this section we rectify this shortcoming by implementing a data structure that can manage information of any type. Such data structures are called *polymorphic*. In a polymorphic data structure, we separate the structure into two parts: an element that contains the needed pointers, and the actual content of the nodes. Using this approach, we will be able to create general data structures and manipulation functions that, with some additional coding, work with any data.

While we will use the problem of adding to the front of linked lists as our working example, the basic concepts in this section generalize to all of the other operations and data structures discussed in this chapter. Readers interested in exploring how data structures other than lists can be made polymorphic are referred to Exercises 5-19 and 5-20 at the end of the chapter.

The key to implementing polymorphic data structures is to create elements of the data structure that contain a *pointer* to the data in the element rather than the data itself. Since the elements in the data structure must be able to deal with data of any type, we must have a pointer which can point to any type of data object in C. Fortunately, C provides the *pointer to void*, **void ***, which can serve this purpose. As discussed in Section 5.4.1 the key feature of pointers to **void** in C is that they can point to data of *any* type. Pointers to specific types can be freely assigned to pointers to **void** without losing any information.

In the case of linked lists, each element of the linked list could be a **struct** with the following template:

```
/* template for a polymorphic list node */
struct poly_list {
```

```
void *data;
struct poly_list *next;
};

typedef struct poly_list * List;
```

Using this approach, all the list manipulation functions would be written to operate on the polymorphic lists. The major difference is that we will pass and return a pointer to **void** as one of the arguments to the functions rather than a pointer to some specific data type. This data can point to any information, including a **struct** containing a number of items.

For example, the function **add_to_front()** which adds a new item to the front of a list would have as one of its arguments a pointer to the data we want to add to the list rather than a string containing the name of a specific student. We assume the file **"poly_list.h"** contains the header information for the polymorphic lists, including the structure definition, the **typedef** statement, and the function prototypes. A polymorphic implementation of **add_to_front()** would be as follows:

```
#include <stdio.h>
#include <stdlib.h>
#include "poly_list.h" /* header file for lists */
                                 polymorphic lists */

/* this inserts an item on the front
   of a polymorphic list */
List add_to_front(List slist, void *info, int *flag)
{
    List node;

/* allocate memory for a node and check if successful*/
    node =  malloc(sizeof(struct poly_list));
    if(node == NULL)
      *flag = FALSE;

    else {   /* put node on list */
      node->next = slist;
      node->data = info;
      slist = node;
      *flag = TRUE;
    }
    return(slist);   /* return list */
}
```

This function can be used to add a node to any list. For example, suppose that we wanted to create a list of student records, each containing up to 80 characters of the student's name, year (1, 2, 3, or 4), age, and the amount owed the university. We could store this information in a **struct** of type **s_record** with the template

```
/* structure to hold a student record */
struct s_record {
  char name[80];
  int year;
  int age;
  double balance_owed;
  };
```

The following fragment of code would read in information about 10 students and add each of them to a **List**.

```
/* fragment to add a student record to a List */

/* include statements */
#include <stdio.h>
#include <stdlib.h>
#include "poly_list.h"


     .
   . /* omitted section of code */
     .
List slist;          /* list to be added to */
struct s_record *s;  /* pointer to a student record */
int i,flag;

slist = init_list();  /* initialization of list */


/* read in items and put on list */
  for(i=0; i<10; i++) {
    s = malloc(sizeof (struct s_record));
    if(s != NULL) {
      scanf("%s %d %d %lf", s->name,&s->year, &s->age,
            &s->balance_owed);
      slist = add_to_front(slist, (void *) s, &flag);
      }
  }
```

Note that the invocation of **add_to_front()** in the statement

```
slist = add_to_front(slist, (void *) s, &flag);
```

has **s**, the pointer to the structure containing the student's record, cast as a pointer to **void**. We have included this in the code to emphasize that the information in a polymorphic list is passed as a pointer to **void**. This cast is not really needed since the header file **poly_list.h** would normally have the function prototype for **add_to_front()**. The prototype would indicate that the second argument to **add_to_front()** is of type **void ***, so the transformation of the pointer to a structure of type **s_record** to a pointer to **void** would be done automatically.

5.15 SUMMARY OF CHAPTER 5

In this chapter we introduced the concept of organizing aggregates of information into *data structures*. One can view such structures as distinct *objects* that can be created, queried, altered, and destroyed through a library of data manipulation functions.

Additional components of the C language were introduced to make implementation of data structures feasible. The most important idea is a **struct**, a unit of information that can hold variables of dissimilar data types. A **struct** can hold variables, arrays, or other **struct**s. A *template* for a **struct** can be declared to define the types and names of the members of a type of **struct**.

C provides the *dot operator* to access a member of a **struct**. C also allows variables which are pointers to a **struct**. Such a pointer can be used with the *arrow operator* to access a member of a **struct** to which a pointer is pointing. C also allows definition of arrays of **struct**s and permits pointer arithmetic on elements of such arrays.

A **struct** in C can be assigned to another **struct** of the same type. This results in the values of all the members of the **struct** on the right-hand side of the assignment statement being copied to the corresponding members in the **struct** on the left-hand side. A **struct** may also be passed as an argument to a function or returned from a function. As with all arguments in C, when a **struct** is an argument to a function, a complete, local copy of that **struct** is made whenever the function is invoked; the function operates on the copy, not on the original **struct**. A more common way to access a **struct** from a function is to pass a pointer to it as an argument.

A **struct** that includes a pointer to a **struct** of the same type is termed *self-referential*.

Dynamic memory allocation was also introduced. Four functions in the standard C library that allow the programmer to allocate and deallocate memory were described. The functions that allocate memory return a *generic pointer* called a pointer to **void**, declared as **void ***. A pointer to **void** can be assigned to any other pointer type. The prototypes for the dynamic memory allocation functions are in the standard header file **stdlib.h**.

Five different types of data structures were presented. These were as follows:

- *Ragged arrays*. This structure is typically used to hold text strings, each of which may be a different length. It consists of an array of pointers, each of which points to an array of characters containing a string.
- *Stacks*. These are used to manage information on a *first in, last out* basis. Elements are *pushed* onto a stack and *popped* from the top of the stack.

- *Linear linked lists*. Each element in a linear linked list contains a pointer to the next element on the list. The elements in a linear list must be accessed by starting at the first element and tracing the pointers down the list.
- *Queues*. A queue is used to manage information on a *first in, first out* basis. Elements are added to the rear of the queue and removed from the front of the queue.
- *Trees*. A tree is a general-purpose data structure in which each element other than the *root* has one other element as its *parent*. Elements of the tree which are not the parent of any other elements are called *leaves*, or *leaf nodes*.

A programming project that used a tree, a list, and a stack to solve a puzzle in which 15 tiles must be rearranged into numerical order was presented. This problem relied on a *heuristic algorithm* in which the state of the puzzle was represented as a node in a tree. Legal moves from any node were represented as child nodes. The algorithm always explored moves from the leaf node that had the most tiles in their correct positions.

In the last section of the chapter we described the concept of *polymorphism* in data structures. In a polymorphic data structure, we separate the structure into two parts: an element that contains the needed pointers, and the actual content of the nodes. This allows us to define generic data structures and libraries of functions that manipulate those structures without specifying the type of elements in the structures.

5.16 EXERCISES

5-1. Write a function that has as its two arguments pointers to the starting elements of two arrays of `doubles` and an `int` that gives the number of elements in both the arrays. The function should dynamically allocate memory to hold an array of `doubles` that sums the two arrays element by element, and return a pointer to the first element of that allocated array. Thus, if a and b are two arrays with elements $a_0, a_1, \ldots, a_{n-1}$ and $b_0, b_1, \ldots, b_{n-1}$, the function should return a pointer to a newly allocated array with elements $a_0 + b_0, a_1 + b_1, \ldots, a_{n-1} + b_{n-1}$.

5-2. It is not uncommon for high school math textbooks to introduce complex numbers of the form $a + bi$. If we think of a complex number as a vector, this is the rectangular representation of complex numbers. An alternative method of representing complex number vectors is the polar representation, where each complex number has a magnitude and an angle.[5]

Given two complex numbers z_1 and z_2, the easiest way to add them is by using the rectangular representation and doing vector addition:

$$\text{real part}(z_1 + z_2) = \text{real part}(z_1) + \text{real part}(z_2)$$

$$\text{imag part}(z_1 + z_2) = \text{imag part}(z_1) + \text{imag part}(z_2)$$

The product of two complex numbers is the vector obtained by stretching one complex number by the length of the other and then rotating it through the angle of

[5]This exercise is based on a problem in [Abelson, H., Sussman, G. and Sussman, J. 85].

the other. This is easiest to perform in polar coordinates, where a vector consists of a magnitude and an angle.

$$\text{magnitude}(z_1 * z_2) = \text{magnitude}(z_1) * \text{magnitude}(z_2)$$

$$\text{angle}(z_1 * z_2) = \text{angle}(z_1) + \text{angle}(z_2)$$

Since the rectangular and polar representations are both useful, any function which uses complex numbers should ideally be able to use complex numbers stored using either representation. The easiest way to do this is to set up a `struct` that contains a variable which will be set to one value if the struct contains a number in a rectangular representation and a different value if the `struct` contains a number in polar coordinates, as well as two variables to actually hold the appropriate values.

Using all of the information above, write a library of complex number functions that will perform arithmetic operations on complex numbers represented in either rectangular or polar form. Your library should include a template for a `struct` that holds a complex number, functions to make new complex numbers from values in either polar or rectangular form, functions to convert from polar to rectangular, and vice versa, as well as addition, subtraction, and multiplication functions.

5-3. Write a function named `add_to_end()` that adds a student's name to the end of the linear linked list described in Section 5.10.2. This function should take three arguments. The first argument is the `List` to be added to, the second is a pointer to a string containing the student's name, and the third is a pointer to an `int` that the function will set to `TRUE` if the addition was successful and `FALSE` otherwise. If a student's name is already in the list, your function should not add that name to the list again. Make sure that your implementation handles the case where the initial list is empty.

5-4. Write an iterative version of the function `destroy_list()` shown in Section 5.10.2.

5-5. Suppose that you have two linear linked lists, each storing integers in ascending order. Write a function that creates a third list that merges the two original lists. The new list should have all the entries appearing on both the original lists in ascending order. You may assume that the entries in the original lists are all unique. The function should have the two original lists as arguments and return the new, merged list without destroying the original lists. Write a complete program that reads in data, creates the two lists, invokes the function that merges them, and outputs the merged list.

5-6. Suppose that you have two linear linked lists, each storing character strings in their nodes. Write a function that creates a third list that contains the *intersection* of the original lists (i.e., contains only those character strings which appear on both the lists). The function should have the two original lists as arguments and return the new list without destroying the original lists. Write a complete program that reads in the two lists, invokes the function that takes their intersection, and outputs the new list.

5-7. Answer Exercise 5-6, replacing the intersection of two lists with their *union*, creating a new list that has nodes which appear in either or both the original lists, but does have any duplicate nodes.

5-8. Consider a polynomial such as

$$3.2x^7 + 2.6x^3 + 6.0x + 4.5$$

One way to represent such a polynomial is as an ordered list. Each element in the list could represent a term in the polynomial using a `double` for the coefficient and an `int` for the exponent. The terms would always be stored in descending order, so that the highest-order term in the polynomial is at the head of the list.

Answer the following questions about the use of lists to represent polynomials.

(a) What is that advantage of using a linked list to represent a polynomial of order n over an array that has one element for each possible term in an nth-order polynomial?

(b) Write a template for a struct for an element of a list that could be used to store a polynomial.

(c) Write a typedef statement that will allow you to define variables of type Poly in your programs, where Poly is a polynomial represented as a linked list.

(d) Write a function that creates a polynomial in list form. The function should read in the number of terms in the polynomial and a set of pairs containing the coefficients and the order of each term. For example, the polynomial given above would be input with the following values:

```
4 3.2 7 2.6 3 6.0 1 4.5 0
```

This function should return a variable of type Poly.

(e) Write a function that evaluates a polynomial represented in list form at some value of x. The polynomial (represented by a variable of type Poly) and value of x at which the polynomial is to be evaluated should be arguments to the function. The function should return the numerical value of the polynomial for the value given as the argument.

(f) Write a function that adds two polynomials represented in list form. This function should have two variables of type Poly as arguments and return a value of type Poly which is the sum of the two arguments.

5-9. In many numerical analysis problems involving matrices, the matrices are relatively *sparse* (i.e., they have many zero entries). It is often possible to store such matrices using lists or other data structures rather than using two-dimensional arrays. For example, one might store each row of a sparse matrix as a list, with each node in the list corresponding to a nonzero element in the matrix. The nodes in the list need to include the column numbers for their respective entries. For example, the matrix

$$\begin{pmatrix} 0.0 & 3.5 & 2.3 & 0.0 \\ 0.0 & 0.0 & 2.1 & 1.3 \\ 1.2 & 0.0 & 0.0 & 0.0 \\ 0.0 & 0.0 & 1.1 & 0.0 \end{pmatrix}$$

could be stored as an array of lists as shown in Figure 5.19.

Using the foregoing idea, do the following:

(a) Rewrite the struct template for a node in a List as described in Section 5.10.2 so that each node can store a double corresponding to an element in an array and an int corresponding to a column number.

(b) Using the typedef for a List, create a typedef for a Sparse_Matrix that is a pointer to an array of Lists.

(c) Write a function make_sparse_matrix() that has as an argument the number of rows in a sparse matrix. This function should initialize the matrix to all zeros.

(d) Write a function that reads in elements in a sparse array as groups of three values: an element's value, its row number, and its column number. Put these elements into the

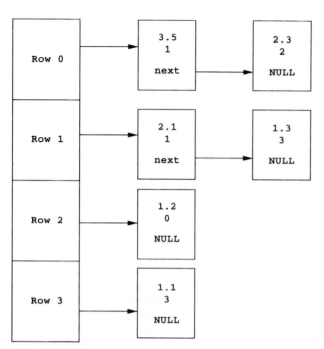

Figure 5.19 Matrix as an array of lists.

array as they are each read in. You may create variants of the list library developed in Section 5.10.2 as a starting point for some of this code.

(e) Write a function that multiplies two sparse matrices. It should have the two matrices as its arguments and return a new matrix as its product.

(f) Write a **main()** program that tests your solution to part (e). It should read in two matrices, compute their product, and then output the resulting matrices.

5-10. There are some situations where items in a data structure are deleted and added very frequently. Since adding and deleting items requires calls to the memory allocation functions which may take a significant amount of computer time, it is often simpler to use what is called *lazy deletion*. With this approach, an item is deleted by setting its key value to some predefined code rather than by actually removing it from the data structure. When an element is added, it can be put into the data structure in any node that has its key value set to the predefined code. (In effect, the predefined code signals that the node is "not in use.") Functions that manipulate the data structure check nodes for the predefined value, treating nodes with that value as unused. Reimplement the list library presented in Section 5.10.2 using this approach. Use the string **"zzzzzz"** as the special code.

5-11. A *circular* list has the same structure as a linear linked list except that the "last" node contains a pointer back to the "first" node. It is common to access a circular list by having a pointer point to the last node in the list. This has the advantage that you can always find the front of the list as the node to which the **next** pointer at the rear of the list is pointing. Create a library of functions for a circular list in which each node contains a string. Your implementation should include a template for a **struct** for an element of the list, a **typedef** statement defining a pointer to an element as a **Circular_List**, and functions to:

- Add a new element to the end of the list.
- Add a new element to the front of the list.
- Search for an element in the list and delete it.

5-12. A *doubly linked list* is a list where each element has two pointers, one to the preceding element on the list and one to the following element. Having pointers in each direction allows one to move forward or backward through the list with equal ease. An example of a doubly linked list containing three elements, `data1`, `data2`, and `data3`, is shown in Figure 5.20.

    (a) Write a structure template for an element of a doubly linked list where each element contains an integer. Write a `typedef` statement that will allow you to declare a variable which is a doubly linked lists as a `Dlist`.

    (b) Write a function `make_dlist()` which creates an empty doubly linked list.

    (c) Write a function `add_to_dlist()` which puts a new integer on the front of a doubly linked list. This function should allocate memory for the new element. Make sure that it checks for possible error conditions and signals errors back to the function which invoked it.

    (d) Write a function `delete_from_dlist()` which removes an element with a particular integer in it from a doubly linked list. The function should have the integer value as one of its arguments. It should check whether there is an element with that value to be deleted.

    (e) Write a function `insert_in_dlist()` that inserts a new integer into a doubly linked list. The new value should be inserted immediately after some particular integer in the list. This integer should be one of the function's arguments. If the value after which the new element is to be inserted does not appear in the current list, the function should put the new value at the end of the list.

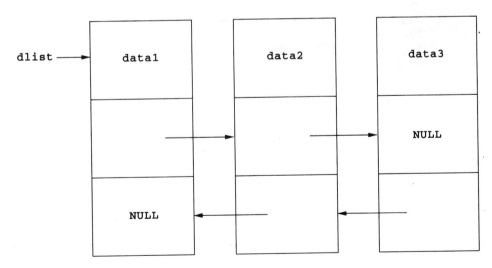

Figure 5.20 Doubly linked list.

5-13. In some situations the maximum number of elements that need to be stored in a queue is known in advance. For example, in a simulation, we might know that no more than n customers can ever be in a queue for some service. In these cases it is often more efficient to use an array to store the items in the queue rather than a list. We might, for example, define a template for a `struct` to hold a queue of 100 characters as follows:

```
/* structure for a queue of 100 characters */
struct queue_of_char{
   int front;  /* index of item in front of queue */
   int rear; /* index of item one beyond end of queue */
   char items[101];  /* array to hold items in queue */
   };
```

An empty queue would be indicated by having the value of `front` equal to the value of `rear`. These two values can be initialized to zero when the queue is first initialized. The array `items` has 101 elements in order to distinguish the situation where the queue is empty from one where it is full.

Using this representation, we would usually add a new character to the queue by placing that character in element `items[rear]` and adding one to the value of `rear`. The only situation where this wouldn't work is when the value of `rear` exceeded 100. In this case, we would "wrap around" the end of the array, setting the value of `rear` to zero. Similarly, the item at the head of the queue would be element `items[front]`. When an item is removed from the queue, we would add one to `front`, again "wrapping around" the array if the value of `front` exceeded 100.

Using this representation, do the following:

(a) Write a function that initializes a queue. This should allocate memory for a `struct` of type `queue_of_char` and return a pointer to this memory. The function should return the `NULL` pointer if the memory allocation fails.

(b) Write a function that adds a character to the end of a queue. This function should have a pointer to a `struct` of type `queue_of_char` and a `char` to be added as its arguments. The function should return a value equal to `TRUE` if the item could be added or `FALSE` if the queue was already full.

(c) Write a function that deletes a character from the queue. This function should have as its arguments a pointer to a `struct` of type `queue_of_char` and a pointer to a `char` where the character removed from the queue is to be stored. The function should return a value equal to `TRUE` if the item could be removed or `FALSE` if the queue was empty.

5-14. In a complete, balanced binary tree, it is possible to store all the nodes in a single array by adopting a standard convention for the ordering of the nodes. Let node 0 be the root of the tree. Starting at the root, number the nodes at each level from left to right. Thus, the left child of the root would be node 1 and the right child would be node 2. Similarly, the four nodes at the next level would be numbered 3, 4, 5, and 6. Using this schema, we can store each node in the position in an array corresponding to its node number. For example, a tree containing floating-point values in each of its nodes, such as the one shown in

Figure 5.21, could be stored in an array of `float`s with seven elements as follows:

$$\begin{pmatrix} 37.56 \\ 27.35 \\ 98.32 \\ 11.23 \\ 25.32 \\ 54.87 \\ 99.03 \end{pmatrix}$$

Assume that the general, complete binary tree has n levels. Answer the following questions about this storage approach.

(a) How many elements must an array have to store all the nodes of a complete binary tree with n levels?

(b) What is the index number in the array of the parent of node i?

(c) What is the index number in the array of the left child on node i?

(d) What is the index number in the array of the right child of node i?

(e) Write a function that has as its argument an `int` equal to the number of levels in the complete, binary tree of `float`s and that returns a pointer to an appropriate size array to store that tree. The function should use dynamic memory allocation to create the array. Make sure that your code has the appropriate `#include` directives for the header files. The function should return the `NULL` pointer if the memory allocation fails.

(f) Write three separate functions that return the value stored in of the parent, the left child and the right child of a node, respectively. These three functions should have three arguments: an array of `float`s that store a complete, binary tree, an `int` equal to the node number for which the parent, left child, or right child is being found, and an `int` equal to the number of levels in the tree. These functions should return the value -1 if the node under consideration does not have a parent, left child, or right child.

(g) Write a function that takes an an array of `float`s used to store a complete binary tree and adds enough elements to that array to hold an additional level. It should have as its arguments the original array and the number of levels in the tree represented

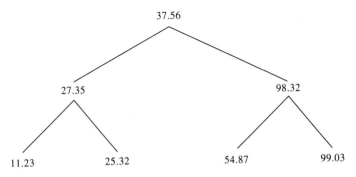

Figure 5.21   Tree to be stored in array.

by that array. Make sure to provide some way for the user of your function to detect when the attempt to allocate the additional memory needed to store the new level of nodes fails. *Hint: Your function should use the dynamic memory allocation function* `realloc()`.

5-15. Consider a binary tree, where each element stores an integer, a pointer to a left child, and a pointer to a right child. Modify the `struct` template and the `typedef` in Section 5.12 to declare an element in such a tree, and do the following:

    (a) Write a function named `listify()` that makes the `Tree` into a `List`. The function should have the `Tree` as its argument and return the `List`. Make sure that you check for failures in attempts to allocate memory.

    (b) Write a function `treeify()` that makes a `List` into a balanced binary `Tree`. The function should have the `List` as its argument and return the `Tree`. Make sure that you check for failures in attempts to allocate memory.

    (c) Check the functions you have written by developing a `main()` program that loads entries into a `Tree`, prints out the `Tree`, converts the `Tree` to a `List`, prints out the `List`, converts the `List` back into a `Tree`, and prints out the `Tree`.

5-16. Consider the puzzle problem described in Section 5.13. Start with the tiles in the goal state. Now exchange the position of the tiles numbered 14 and 15. (This cannot be done through a series of legal moves.) Develop an argument as to why the puzzle in this initial state cannot be solved.

5-17. Horowitz and Sahni [Horowitz, Ellis and Sartj Sahni 78] describe a method for determining whether the any particular initial state of the tile puzzle described in Section 5.13 is solvable. The method is easiest to describe if we relabel the blank tile as number 16 rather than zero. The method defines a vector of 16 entries p, where entry p_i is the position number of the tile labeled i. Thus, if the tile labeled 7 was in position 11 in the puzzle, then p_7 would be 11. The vector p can be used to create another vector with 16 entries which we will call q, where q_i is the count of the number of tiles $j < i$, where $p_j > i$. One can show a necessary and sufficient condition for a puzzle to be solvable is as follows:

    • If the empty tile is one of the shaded positions in shown in Figure 5.22, then the sum of the entries in q must be odd.

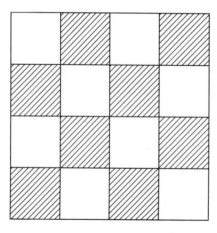

Figure 5.22 Different initial positions for blank tile.

- If the empty tile is one of the unshaded positions in shown in Figure 5.22, then the sum of the entries in q must be even.

Write a C function that has a vector of puzzle entries as its inputs and which returns a value which is TRUE if the puzzle is solvable and FALSE otherwise. Then write a `main()` function which reads in a puzzle value using the function `get_start()` shown in Section 5.13 and outputs a message as to whether that puzzle is solvable. Create at least one example of a solvable and an unsolvable initial puzzle state.

5-18. The algorithm implemented in Section 5.13 avoids simple cycles by making sure that no node in the tree replicates the state of its grandparent. For example, if we are generating moves from any given node, then the move which reverses the move that created the node is not generated. This approach does not eliminate longer cycles. For example, a cycle which moves the blank space LEFT, UP, RIGHT, and then DOWN can occur. Modify the algorithm used to generate moves so that it avoids cycles of four moves. This will require you to check board states four levels upward in the tree.

5-19. Redesign the implementation of a stack and the library of stack manipulation functions so that they are polymorphic. Recode all the functions shown in Section 5.9 using a polymorphic form of the stack. Show how the general stack functions could be used to manage a stack of character strings.

5-20. Redesign the implementation of a queue and the library of queue manipulation functions so that they are polymorphic. Recode all the functions shown in Section 5.11 using a polymorphic form of the queue. Show how the general queue functions could be used to manage a queue of character strings.

5-21. Suppose that you have been hired by an instructor to write a program for her which will store and retrieve grades. She wants to be able to access the information in several different ways. First of all, for any given student, she wants to be able to reference that student's grades on homework, tests, and the final, as well as averages of homework and test scores. She also wants to be able to see how well the class did overall on any given assignment or test. Describe at least two data storage schemes that will be efficient given these requirements, and list some pros and cons of each. Pick the most efficient scheme and implement any data structures necessary, as well as writing the three routines necessary to:

- Store a grade in the appropriate structure(s)
- Retrieve all relevant entries for a student
- Retrieve all student's scores for a particular assignment or test

CHAPTER

6

SORTING AND SEARCHING

6.1 INTRODUCTION

A significant aspect of many problems solved using computation involve *sorting* and *searching*. Sorting is generally used to organize large volumes of data such as billing records, where having information sorted makes it easy to combine data from different sources. Sorting is also frequently used as the first step in searching for a particular item. Both searching and sorting algorithms play important roles in the implementation of computer databases.

While searching and sorting are essentially trivial for very small problems, they become time consuming for realistically sized problems, where thousands or millions of pieces of information must be organized. Knuth[Knuth, Donald E. 73a], for example, has estimated that up to a quarter of all computation time is spent on sorting. In this chapter we introduce several of the more common sorting algorithms and show how they can be implemented efficiently in C.

While sorting is an important component in solving many problems, searching is of even more obvious value. For example, in the airline reservation problem described in Chapter 5, rapid access to information on available seats on a particular flight, as well as the reservation information for specific passengers, is essential. This capability depends on fast and flexible searching algorithms. In this chapter several approaches to the searching problem are presented, including the use of a particular type of tree called a *binary search tree*. Another technique, called *hashing*, is also described. This method uses some additional computer memory beyond the minimum necessary to speed up searching significantly.

Because searching and sorting involve processing large volumes of information that are most often to be stored permanently, it is natural to introduce the idea of *files* in this chapter as well. Files make it possible to process quantities of data that are too large to be kept in a computer's memory. This is often the case for computer databases. In addition, files are often used to store results of algorithms in a form suitable for further processing by other programs.

Files are used to represent information most commonly written to and read from secondary storage devices such as floppy or hard disks. The C programming language provides a rich set of library functions for the creation and manipulation of files. The most useful portions of this library are discussed in Section 6.2.

Sections 6.3 and 6.4 cover some of the most widely used algorithms for sorting and searching, respectively. Section 6.5 describes the use of binary search trees as data structures for rapid retrieval of information. In Section 6.6 we present an introduction to hashing methods. This is followed by a programming project in Section 6.7, where hashing is used to extend the algorithm for solving the 15-tile puzzle introduced in Chapter 5 to eliminate the possibility of cycling.

6.2 FILES IN C

Files allow the storage and processing of large amounts of data typically associated with most real problems. Beyond having capacity considerably in excess of the memory on most computers, data in files also has the property of *persistence*. That is, because files are written to secondary storage devices, data stored in files is maintained even when the computer is shut off.

Up until this point in this book we have relied on the standard C library functions `printf()` and `scanf()` to obtain input from the keyboard for our programs and to output the results. As will be made clearer below, these functions are simply restricted versions of the general file processing functions which are available in C. For example, many applications require dealing with several files simultaneously. C provides considerable flexibility in reading and writing to different files which are active at the same time.

In C a file is treated as a *stream* of characters which are processed sequentially. In addition to other, less important operations, the standard C library provides functions that allow the programmer to operate on a file in any of the following ways:

- Open it. Opening a file establishes a link between the program and the file. The open operation generally will create the file if it does not already exist. If the file exists, the open operation will determine whether the user running the C program has access privileges to the file.

- Read from it. A read operation closely parallels what happens when the **scanf()** function is invoked except that input is taken from the file rather than from the keyboard.
- Write to it. A write operation closely parallels what happens when the **printf()** function is invoked except that output is directed to the file rather than to the display.
- Close it. This breaks the link between the program and the file. Further reading or writing from the file after it is closed is not allowed unless the file is opened again.

Access to any file for these operations is through something called a *file pointer*. The file pointer data type (denoted by **FILE *** in a C variable definition) is defined in the header file **stdio.h**, most often through a **typedef** statement. In most cases, the file pointer points to a **struct** which is also defined in the **stdio.h** header file. This **struct** contains information on the file itself, including the current place in the stream of characters where processing(reading or writing) is taking place.

Since the **FILE struct** is defined in **stdio.h**, this header file must be included whenever a program includes file processing. So, for example, two file pointers, **fpin** and **fpout**, could be declared in the following code fragment:

```
#include <stdio.h>   /* defines FILE pointer */
   .
   .
   .
FILE *fpin, *fpout; /* two FILE pointers */
```

After this fragment the variables **fpin** and **fpout** can be used to access files. Each of the principal functions that operate on files is described below. All of the prototypes for these functions are in **stdio.h**.

6.2.1 Opening a File

Before we can do anything with a file, we must first open it by making use of the standard C library function **fopen()**. **fopen()** returns a file pointer and takes two arguments:

- A character string which is the name of the file to be opened and subsequently processed.
- A character string indicating the *mode* in which the file may be operated on. The three most common modes of use are:
  - **"r"** opens the file for reading, beginning at the start of file.
  - **"w"** opens the file for writing.
  - **"a"** opens the file for appending (i.e., adding to the end of the file).

The effect of **fopen()** depends on several factors, including whether or not the file already exists. The most important rule in using **fopen()** is that *opening an existing file for writing results in the erasure of the current contents of the file*. One of the most common ways to delete a file accidentally is to open it for writing when you really intended to open it either for reading or appending.

If a nonexistent file is opened for writing, then a new file with that name will be created. **fopen()** may be unsuccessful in opening the file referred to by the first argument. For example, an attempt to open a nonexistent file for reading will always fail. Another possible reason for a file opening to fail is that on some larger computer systems, one must have the correct permissions in order to open a file.[1] In these cases **fopen()** will return the **NULL** pointer. Before making use of the file pointer returned by **fopen()** it is essential to check whether the attempt to open the file has been successful.

The following fragment of code shows how to open three files, one for reading, one for writing, and one for appending:

```
/* fragment showing use of fopen() */
#include <stdio.h>
    .
    .
FILE *fpi, *fpo, *fpa;
char input[80];

/* read name of data file into input */
scanf ("%s", input);


fpi = fopen( input, "r");
if (fpi == NULL)
    printf("File error, unable to open file %s\n",input);
    exit (-1);
    }
fpo = fopen("results", "w");
if (fpo == NULL)
    printf("File error, unable to open file results\n");
    exit (-2);
    }
fpa = fopen("output", "a");
if (fpa == NULL)
    printf("File error, unable to open file output\n");
    exit (-3);
    }
    .
    .
```

As shown, this code reads in the name of a file and opens that file for reading. It then opens a file named **"results"** for writing and a file named **"output"** for

---

[1]Personal computer systems such as IBM PCs, PC-compatibles, and Apple computers do not generally enforce permissions except in the case of floppy disks, which can be "write locked." All multiuser computer systems, including UNIX workstations, have file access systems.

appending. As with any other variables, the file pointers **fpi**, **fpo**, and **fpa** can be reassigned values later in the program once processing the file has been completed and the file has been closed.

When a C program is started three "files" are opened automatically: **stdin, stdout**, and **stderr**. These are the standard devices used for input, output, and error messages, respectively. Normally, the keyboard is the standard input file and the screen is the standard output and standard error message file.

6.2.2 Reading from a File

Reading from a file is accomplished with the function **fscanf()** which is identical to **scanf()** except for the inclusion of the file pointer as a new first argument. [2] Thus, if the preceding code fragment also included the following declaration:

```
int a[100]; /* array of integers */
int i;      /* a counter */
```

we could read integer data from the file named in the character string **input** simply by adding the following code to the example above:

```
int test;  /* used as a value to test for end of file */

for (i=0; i<100; i++) {
  test = fscanf(fpi, "%d", &a[i]);
  if(test == EOF)    /* check if EOF is reached */
    exit(-4);
  }
```

As with **scanf()**, the function **fscanf()** returns an integer which is the number of items read successfully from the input file. It is important to check this integer to determine whether the end-of-file value (**EOF**) is returned from **fscanf()**. This occurs when a read operation would go beyond the last item in the file.

6.2.3 Writing to a File

Writing to a file is accomplished through the function **fprintf()**. We add a new first argument, the file pointer for the file to be written to. [3] To illustrate using the preceding code fragments, if we add the declaration

```
double b[100], c[100];
```

---

[2]In fact, **scanf()** is generally defined with a preprocessor macro that uses **fscanf()** with the file pointer set to **stdin**.

[3]As with reading from a file, **printf()** is usually defined by a preprocessor macro that uses **fprintf()** with the file pointer set to **stdout**.

we could write to the two files **results** and **output** by adding the following code after these files are opened successfully:

```
for (i=0; i<100; i++){
   fprintf(fpo, "%lf \n", b[i]);
   fprintf(fpa, "%lf \n", c[i]);
   }
```

As with **printf()**, the function **fprintf()** returns an integer which is the number of characters successfully written to the file or a negative value if an error occurred. The fragment above ignores these returned values.

6.2.4 Closing a File

When operations on a file have been completed, the file can be closed with the **fclose()** function with the single argument being the file pointer for the appropriate file. After a file has been closed the pointer can be recycled to access another file. Any open files are closed automatically when the program's execution ends. Referring back to the previous code, the input file could be closed by using the following statement:

```
fclose(fpi);
```

The file-closing function returns an integer which is set to **EOF** if some error occurs. This returned value is often ignored by programmers.

6.2.5 An Example Using Files

These basic file operations described above are illustrated in the following function, which simply copies one file into another on a character-by-character basis. The names of both files are passed as string arguments to the function. The function returns an **int** whose value indicates whether or not the copying has been successful.

```
/* copy in_file into out_file,
   returning an integer flag
            = 0 for a successful copy
            = 1 for failure to open in_file
            = 2 for failure to open out_file */

#include <stdio.h>

int copy_text(
  char *in_file,      /* name of input file */
  char *out_file)     /* name of output file */
{
 FILE *fpi, *fpo;
 char c;
```

```
/* open input file */
 fpi = fopen(in_file, "r");
 if (fpi == NULL) {
    printf("ERROR: couldn't open input file\n");
    return(1);
    }

/* open output file */
 fpo = fopen(out_file, "w");
 if (fpo == NULL) {
    printf("ERROR: couldn't open output file\n");
    return(2);
    }

/* copy input file to output file */
 while (fscanf(fpi, "%c", &c) != EOF)
    fprintf(fpo, "%c", c);

/* close files */
 fclose(fpi);
 fclose(fpo);
 return(0);
}
```

Note that the function **copy_text()** checks only for problems in opening files.
A more rigorously coded version should check for reading and writing errors as well.
For example, the function **fprintf()** may fail because the disk to which it is writing
is full.

6.3 SORTING

Sorting is required in the solution of many computational problems, but perhaps its
most obvious use is to facilitate searching. Without prior sorting any search must be on
a sequential, item-by-item basis; this is known as a *linear search*. While a linear search
may be acceptable in terms of computation time for some very small problems, it will
be extremely inefficient for most applications—hence the need to sort.

Before presenting specific sorting algorithms we will define some basic terminology
to be used throughout this chapter and distinguish among alternative sorting contexts
which can influence choice of sorting algorithm. First some definitions:

- *Records.* These are the items to be sorted, generally data structures which
  include several pieces of information. In many cases these structures will be
  quite complex. For example, records in an airline reservation system might
  include: the passenger's name, home and work telephone numbers, the number
  of passengers traveling together, origin city, destination city, flight number,

and fare paid as well as information on associated flight legs. The size and complexity of a record can influence the best approach to sorting.

- *Keys.* These are the data attributes which are used for sorting. The *primary key* is the first attribute used in the sort, while *secondary keys* are those used to resolve ties based on the primary key. For example, in a mailing list the primary sort key might be the zipcode and the name of the individual might be the secondary key used to organize records with the same zipcode.

In this discussion we focus on *internal sorts*, in which all records to be sorted are stored in random access memory, as distinct from *external sorts*, which involve secondary storage. Our focus on internal sorting is because with the rapid decline in the cost of random access memory, more problems are now solvable with internal sorting algorithms. In addition, consideration of the bottleneck caused by the movement of data between memory and secondary storage is outside the scope of an introductory textbook.

It is also important to recognize other characteristics of sorting problems beyond the obvious issues of number of records and their individual composition. One of these characteristics is whether or not there is some structure in the initial data set. For example, a database which is being frequently updated through the addition of new records, with sorting following each new set of additions, presents a much easier problem than a one-time sort through a randomly ordered database. This type of problem structure can have a significant impact on the efficiency of different algorithms.

Finally, we come to the sorting algorithms themselves. In this book we do not attempt to be comprehensive in our treatment. Rather, we present several of the more useful approaches at different levels of complexity. (See [Knuth, Donald E. 73a] or [Sedgewick, Robert 90] for more comprehensive treatments of sorting algorithms.) It is usual to distinguish between *elementary* and *advanced* sorting methods on the basis of their relative complexity as well as their efficiency for large, randomly ordered data sets.

- Elementary methods. These methods:
  - Usually require on the order of n^2 steps to sort n randomly arranged records.
  - Are suitable for small files (i.e., less than about 50 records).
  - Are suitable for larger, partially sorted files.
- Advanced methods. These usually require on the order of $n \log n$ steps to sort n randomly arranged records.

It is customary to use "Big-O" notation to denote how performance of an algorithm varies with the size of a problem. Thus, elementary sorting methods in which the computation time increases with the square of the number of records to be sorted are said to be $O(n^2)$, while advanced are $O(n \log n)$. The difference between elementary and advanced sorts is not trivial. Particularly for the very large data sets that characterize many commercial applications, algorithms which require $O(n^2)$ can be *much* slower than those which take $O(n \log n)$. The following table compares the values of these two functions for different values of n. For values of n over 100,000, the ratio of the times is nearly a factor of 10^4.

COMPARISON OF COMPUTATION TIMES

n	n^2	$n \log n$
10	100	23.0259
100	10,000	460.517
1,000	10^6	6,907.76
10,000	10^8	92,103.4
100,000	10^{10}	1.15129×10^6

In the remainder of this section we present insertion sort, shellsort, and selection sort as examples of elementary methods, and quicksort as an advanced method.

6.3.1 Insertion Sort

Insertion sort is a very simple but flexible algorithm which, as with the remaining elementary methods, can be implemented with data organized either in an array or in a linked list. For ease of presentation, we focus on the array implementation, although several linked list examples are also presented.

Insertion sort moves through the array record by record, at each iteration inserting the new record in the appropriate place in the already sorted subarray. This is analogous to the way many people sort a hand of playing cards.

Figure 6.1 illustrates how an array of eight integer values changes as it is insertion sorted. The initial array is unaffected in the first iteration because the first two values (65 and 70) are in the correct order. At iteration 2, the value 50 is inserted as element

Initial Array: 65   70   50   85   55   80   45   90

Iteration	State of Array							
1	65	70	50	85	55	80	45	90
2	50	65	70	85	55	80	45	90
3	50	65	70	85	55	80	45	90
4	50	55	65	70	85	80	45	90
5	50	55	65	70	80	85	45	90
6	45	50	55	65	70	80	85	90
7	45	50	55	65	70	80	85	90

Figure 6.1   Insertion sort.

zero because it is the minimum of the first three entries in the array. At each subsequent iteration, the next element in the array is inserted into the sorted subarray.

Two implementations of this algorithm are shown below. The first implementation operates directly on the array of records, moving each element into its correct position. This is presented first to show clearly the structure of the method. The example sorts an array of **double**s in ascending numerical order.

```
/* function for insertion sort directly moving records.
   Sort is in ascending numerical order */

void insertion_sort_direct(
  double data[],      /* array to be sorted */
  int n)              /* number of elements in array */
{
 int position,index;
 double value;

/* outer loop over all records (except first) */

 for (position = 1; position < n; position++){
    /* value of record to be inserted */

    value = data[position];

/* inner loop over previously sorted records
   to find  place for insertion of new record */

    for(index=position; index>0 && data[index-1]>value;
         index--)
      data[index] = data[index-1];
    data[index] = value;
  }
}
```

A useful approach to attempt to improve the efficiency of this function is to focus on the inner loop, which will, of course, be executed most frequently. In this case part of the test for whether the loop should terminate could be eliminated by reversing the direction of the outer loop [i.e., starting from the last array element rather than the first and setting a *sentinel marker* as the $(n + 1)$th element of the array]. The sentinel value would be set high enough to be greater than the highest possible value of any record.[4] Thus the sentinel would automatically terminate the inner loop when the **index** reached $n + 1$ without having an explicit test for the value of **index**. In some cases this would be straightforward since a value could readily be found beyond the range of the other records, but in other cases this would not be so easy. Here we see the classic tradeoff

---

[4]The value **DBL_MAX**, the largest representable **double**, defined in the standard header file **float.h** is an obvious choice for the sentinel value in this example.

between writing general functions which will work for a wide range of applications versus writing special functions which will work more efficiently for limited cases. In general we prefer to present code which can have multiple uses even if some price is paid in efficiency.

Our second implementation of insertion sort uses an array of pointers to access the records in the array, and the sort occurs on the pointers rather than on the records directly. This will be preferred in many cases for several reasons. First, we will frequently want to sort the same data set using different keys and use the sets of sorted lists simultaneously in later phases of the larger program. This is obviously impossible following the strategy of directly reorganizing the list unless we create duplicate lists. Duplication, however will consume large amounts of memory in the case where the records are large data structures. Duplication of an array of pointers which can then be sorted on different keys will usually be much more efficient. Second, again in the case of large structures, using pointers enables us to avoid the extra computation time associated with shifting these records around during the insertion sorting process. The final reason applies when the data is stored as a linked list. In this case the sorted array of pointers can be used to access the correct record in a search without scanning the linked list.

The example below assumes that the set of records to be sorted are character strings.

```
/* insertion sort of character strings
      using array of pointers to access records */

#include <stdio.h>
#include <string.h>

void insertion_sort_indirect(
  char *array[], /* array of pointers to character strings*
  int n)         /* number of elements in array */
{
 int position, index;
 char *value;

/* loop over all records (except the first) */
  for (position = 1; position < n; position++){
    value = array[position];

/* inner loop of sort */
    for(index = position; index > 0 &&
        strcmp(array[index-1],value) > 0; index--)
      array[index] = array[index-1];
    array[index] = value;
  }
}
```

With this code we have overcome the problem of moving the records around in memory, but there are still several other obstacles to overcome before we have a general-purpose implementation of insertion sort. First, we have used arrays of records to be sorted, with each record consisting of only a single variable; in general, we need to be able to sort data structure records which are stored as linked lists as well as arrays. Second, we have "hard-wired" into the code the variable on which to sort. Of course, when the record is a single variable there is no choice in the sorting key. Each of these limitations is dealt with in the following generalized implementation of insertion sort.

6.3.2 General Insertion Sort

In this implementation we start with a linked list of known length **num** with each node defined to have the following structure:

```
struct list_node {
        int x;
        int y;
        struct list_node *next;
        };

typedef struct list_node * List;
```

When sorting a linked list it is usual to set up an array of pointers with each pointer assigned the address of one record in the list. The sorting occurs in the array of pointers, which can then be used in any subsequent search to locate the appropriate record without the linked list itself ever having been altered. The following fragment of code uses **calloc()** to obtain the memory necessary to set up the pointer array and then initializes this array:

```
#include <stdlib.h>

List *record; /* used to store the address of the array
                        of pointers once memory is allocated */
List present, head;
int num, i /* number of records and counter */
.
.


/* allocate memory for elements of List, where num
   is the number of nodes in the linked list */
record =  calloc(num,sizeof(List));
.
.


/* initialize array of pointers to access each record */
present = head;
```

```
for(i = 0; present != NULL; i++){
  record[i] = present;
   present = present->next;
     }
```

The function **insertion_sort_general()** shown below can be used to sort the records on either key **x** or **y**. The function uses a pointer to a function called **key()**, which compares two records and returns an integer which is TRUE if the first record is "greater" (i.e., higher in the sorting order) than the second record and FALSE otherwise. The code for this generalized insertion sort is as follows:

```
/* generalized insertion sort */
void insertion_sort_general(
  List record[],            /* array of pointers */
  int num,                  /* number of records */
  int (*key)(List, List) )  /* pointer to function
                               which takes Lists
                               as arguments
                               and returns an int */
{
  List old_node;
  int position, index;

  /* loop through all entries */
  for (position = 1; position < num; position++) {
      old_node = record[position];

  /* find correct positions */
      for (index = position; index > 0 &&
              key(record[index-1], old_node);index--)
          record[index] = record[index-1];
      record[index] = old_node;
  }
}
```

The arguments to **insertion_sort_general()** include the array of pointers to the nodes on the linked list and a pointer to a function **key()**. The second component of the logical test for termination of the inner loop of the sort uses the pointer to **key()** to generalize the record key comparison.

To show how this could be used, the following fragment of **main()** code together with the two functions would result in the linked list being sorted twice, first by key **x** in ascending order and second by key **y** in descending order:

```
{
/* fragment of main */
int by_x (List, List);
int by_y (List, List);
```

```
void insertion_sort_general (List[], int,
     int (*) (List, List));
   .
   .
   .
/* sort by x in ascending order */
insertion_sort_general(record, num, by_x);
   .
   .
/* sort by y in descending order */
insertion_sort_general(record, num, by_y);
   .
   .
}


/* by_x compares the x values of two structs,
   returning TRUE if first value exceeds second */

int by_x( List node1, List node2)
{
   return ( node1->x > node2->x);
}
/* by_y compares the y values of two structs,
   returning TRUE if first value is less than second */

int by_y(List node1, List node2)
{
   return ( node1->y < node2->y);
}
```

This approach can be followed to generalize any of the remaining sorting algorithms, which, for the sake of clarity, will be presented for arrays of single key records.

6.3.3 Shellsort

Insertion sort is not very efficient, except for partially ordered data sets, because it exchanges only adjacent records. So, for example, if the initial data set of n items is reverse ordered, it will take n cycles through the inner loop to place the last record in its correct place. Shellsort is a simple extension which can considerably improve the efficiency of insertion sort by exchanging records which are farther apart. The approach is to sort all records which are h records apart. If, for example, $h = 13$, records 0,13,26... will be sorted after the first pass through the array. After completion of all iterations for $h = 13$, all sequences of records separated by h will be sorted (including sequences 1,14,27..., and 2,15,28..., etc.). In subsequent iterations, h is systematically reduced until the $h = 1$ iteration is completed. At this point the data set will be fully sorted.

The following implementation of shellsort sorts an array of *n* **double**s:

```
/* this function sorts an array of n doubles with
   the gap size being halved at each iteration  */

void shell_sort(
  double data[],   /* array to be sorted */
  int n)           /* number of entries in array */
{
  double temp;
  int h, i, j;   /* h is gap size at each iteration */

/* outer loop varies gap size */
  for (h = n/2; h > 0; h /= 2) {

/* middle loop covers all sequences for a gap size h */
    for (i = h; i < n; i++) {

/* inner loop uses a simple exchange sort */
      for(j=i-h; j>=0 && data[j]>data[j+h]; j -= h) {
        temp = data[j];
        data[j] = data[j+h];
        data[j+h] = temp;
        }
      }
    }
}
```

Figure 6.2 shows how shellsort works on an array of eight integers. The state of the array after each execution of the outer loop is illustrated.

While the principle of shellsort is well illustrated with the code and example above, the actual sequence of values of *h* used in the outer loop is far from ideal. Sedgewick [Sedgewick, Robert 90] notes that a much better sequence for *h* is the reverse of the sequence 1,4,13,40,121,... . In this sequence the $(i + 1)$th number is given by $h_{i+1} = 3h_i + 1$. For a given problem size *n*, the sequence of values of *h* would start with the second largest number in the given sequence that is smaller than the array size.

As an aside, when $h = 1$, shellsort is often called a *bubble sort*.

Initial Array:	65	70	50	85	55	80	45	90
After h = 4	55	70	45	85	65	80	50	90
After h = 2	45	70	50	80	55	85	65	90
After h = 1	45	50	55	65	70	80	85	90

Figure 6.2 Shellsort.

6.3.4 Selection Sort

The final elementary sorting method presented is selection sort, which follows a straightforward strategy of finding the minimum value among the record keys and making that the first record, then finding the minimum of the remaining elements and making that the second record, etc. Selection sort is implemented for an array of integers in the following function.

```
/* this function implements selection
   sort for array of ints */

void selection_sort(
  int data[],       /* array to be sorted */
  int n)            /* number of elements in array */
{

  int min, i ,j;
  int temp;

/* outer loop over all array elements */
  for (i = 0; i < n; i++) {
    min = i;

/* loop over remaining elements to find minimum value */
    for (j = i + 1; j < n; j++)
      if (data[j] < data[min])
        min = j;

/* insert minimum at correct place */
    temp = data[min];
    data[min] = data[i];
    data[i] = temp;
  }
}
```

Figure 6.3 illustrates the major steps in a selection sort on the same array of eight integers used in earlier examples. After the first iteration, the minimum value in the array (45) is moved to the element zero. In the second iteration the next smallest value is moved to element one of the array. This process continues until the last array element is reached. In this particular example, the array is completely sorted after the fourth iteration. However, the remaining iterations would still be executed.

6.3.5 Quicksort

The only advanced sorting algorithm we will present is *quicksort*, which is perhaps the most widely applied sorting method for large problems. Quicksort was developed by C.

Initial Array: 65   70   50   85   55   80   45   90

Iteration	State of Array							
1	45	70	50	85	55	80	65	90
2	45	50	70	85	55	80	65	90
3	45	50	55	85	70	80	65	90
4	45	50	55	65	70	80	85	90
5	45	50	55	65	70	80	85	90
6	45	50	55	65	70	80	85	90
7	45	50	55	65	70	80	85	90

Figure 6.3   Selection sort.

A. R. Hoare[Hoare, C.A.R. 62] in the early 1960s and is the classic embodiment of a "divide and conquer" algorithmic strategy.

The central idea in quicksort is to partition the data set into two parts and sort them independently. This partitioning process is repeated until all the subproblems are of size one, when they are, by definition, sorted. The key to this method is to find an efficient way to partition a data set into two parts such that:

- Everything in one subarray is smaller than a known value called the *pivot element*.
- Everything in the other subarray is greater than the pivot value.

Assuming that the records are stored in an array, the quicksort partitioning method works as follows:

- Choose an element in the array to be the pivot element. For convenience we will choose the first element in the array.
- Start one integer array index (**lowindex**) at the second element of the array and another index (**highindex**) at the last element.
- Decrease **highindex** until an element is found with value *less than* the pivot value or **highindex** equals **lowindex**. Increase **lowindex** until an element *greater than* the pivot is found or until the value **highindex** is reached. We refer to this process as *scanning*.
- If the two array indices **highindex** and **lowindex** are different, the two array elements are out of place and are exchanged. Repeat the previous step, resuming the two scans where they had been interrupted.

• If the two indices are the same and the value in the array they both reference is *less than* the pivot value, exchange the pivot element and the array element. The array is now partitioned by the element referenced by **highindex** (or **lowindex**). The current location of the pivot element separates the array into a portion less than the pivot and a portion greater than the pivot. Moreover, the pivot element is in its correct place in the array once it is fully sorted.

The following example illustrates this partitioning process. Suppose that the original array consists of the following eight elements:

65 70 50 85 55 80 45 90

The pivot element will be 65 (element zero in the array), and the scans will first be halted at elements one and six of the array (45 and 70), which will then be exchanged. After this first exchange the array will be as follows:

65 45 50 85 55 80 70 90

The scan will next be halted at elements three and four of the array (85 and 55), which will then be exchanged to produce

65 45 50 55 85 80 70 90

The scan will next be stopped with both indices referencing element three (55), which is then exchanged with the pivot element (since it is smaller than it) to produce

55 45 50 65 85 80 70 90

This array is now partitioned about the original pivot value (65), which is in its correct position in the final, sorted array. The partitioning process can now be applied to the subarray

55 45 50

as well as to the subarray

85 80 70 90

The recursive nature of quicksort is clear from this simple example. We can apply the partitioning recursively to each subarray until each subarray has only a single element. At this point, the complete array will be sorted. This structure will be used in the implementation of quicksort below.

The code for quicksort uses three distinct functions. Function **quicksort()** executes the basic recursion, invoking **partition()** to partition the array and then invoking **quicksort()** again for each of the subarrays created. The function **exchange()** is used to interchange two elements of the array. The arguments to **quicksort()** are the array to be sorted and the number of elements in the array. The code for sorting an array of integers is as follows:

```
/* quicksort for an array of num ints */
```

```
/* function prototypes */
void quicksort (int [], int);
void partition (int *,int,int *([]),
                int *,int *([]),int*);
void exchange (int [], int, int);

void quicksort(
     int data[], /* data is array of ints to sort */
     int num)    /* number of elements in data */
{
  int *low, *high;
  int numlow, numhigh;

  if (num > 1) /* a subarray of size one is solved */
  {
    partition(data, num, &low, &numlow,
              &high, &numhigh);
    quicksort(low, numlow);
    quicksort(high, numhigh);
  }
}
```

The second function, **partition()**, has six arguments. The first two, **array** and **num**, are the array to be partitioned and the number of elements in that array. The remaining four arguments are all pointers. They are used to return the results of the partitioning to the function which invokes **partition()**. The pointer **low** points to the beginning of the first subarray (the one containing all values lower than the pivot element after the partitioning is complete). The argument **numlow** is a pointer to the number of elements in the array pointed to by **low**. The argument **high** points to the second subarray created by partitioning (the one with all values greater than the pivot) and the argument **numhigh** points to the number of elements in this subarray.

partition() scans the elements in the array, invoking the function **exchange()** to exchange elements which are out of place. The C code is as follows:

```
/* partition() applies the partitioning method
     to an array with num elements */

void partition(
  int *array,     /* array to be partitioned */
  int num,        /* number of elements in array */
  int *(low[]),   /* pointer to the left subarray */
  int *numlow,    /* pointer to the number of
                     elements in the left subarray */
  int *(high[]),  /* pointer to the right subarray */
  int *numhigh)   /* pointer to the number of
                     elements in the right subarray */
```

```
/*   values resulting from the partition
     returned using pointers */
{
   int lowindex, highindex, pivot;
/* initialize pivot value and array subscripts */
   pivot = array[0];
   lowindex = 1;
   highindex = num - 1;

/* highindex scans down and lowindex
     up the array until stopped */
   while (lowindex < highindex) {
     while (highindex > lowindex &&
            array[highindex] > pivot)
       highindex--;
     while (lowindex < highindex &&
            array[lowindex] <= pivot)
       lowindex++;
 /* if needed exchange the two out of place elements */
     if (highindex > lowindex)
        exchange (array, lowindex, highindex);
   }

/* see if pivot and value pointed
        to by should be exchanged */

   if (pivot > array[lowindex]) {
     exchange(array, 0, lowindex);
     highindex++;
   }

/* set return values */
   *low = &(array[0]);
   *high = &(array[highindex]);
   *numlow = lowindex;
   *numhigh = num - highindex;
 }
```

The third function used to implement a quicksort is **exchange()**, which exchanges two elements of an array. Its arguments are the array where the exchange is to take place and the subscripts of the two elements to be exchanged. The code is as follows:

```
/* exchange()swaps two array elements */
void exchange(
     int array[], /* array to be operated on */
     int index1,  /* index of one exchange element */
     int index2)  /* index of other exchange element */
```

```
{
  int temp;
  temp = array[index1];
  array[index1] = array[index2];
  array[index2] = temp;

}
```

While this implementation presents the basic quicksort algorithm, there are many ways to improve its performance (see Sedgewick [Sedgewick, Robert 90] for a full discussion of these options). Several of the more important ones are discussed briefly below.

- Selection of pivot element. Ideally, the array to be sorted would be partitioned into approximately equal-size subarrays at each partition stage, since this will minimize computation time. One reasonably straightforward way to improve on the "take the first element as the pivot" rule is to select the *median* of three elements to be the partition element. For example, one could take the median of the first, last, and middle elements in the array, exchange this median with the first element (if necessary), and proceed as before. This approach would tend to make the subarrays closer in size.
- Order of subarray processing. In the recursive implementation of quicksort there is no preference given to short subarrays in the processing sequence. However, such a priority could minimize the number of `quicksort()` invocations active concurrently. Since an executing C program must allocate memory for the arguments and local variables for every active invocation of a function, this approach will reduce the memory required by the quicksort algorithm.
- Sorting of small subarrays. Although quicksort is efficient for larger data sets, each step in quicksort takes considerable computational effort, making it less efficient than simpler methods for small data sets. This deficiency in quicksort can be corrected by using a simple sorting method on subproblems smaller than a given size.

Implementation of these improvements is explored in Exercise 6-9.

6.4 SIMPLE SEARCHING METHODS

As stated earlier, one of the most common reasons for sorting is to improve the efficiency of subsequent searches of the data. The objective of any search is to locate a specific record identified through one or more keys. Making searches more efficient is of practical importance whenever large databases are involved, particularly when access to the record must be very fast. Examples of this include telephone reservation systems, such as for a chain of hotels or for an airline. These searches are often characterized by the need to use more than one key as alternative means to identify a specific record.

For example, in the hotel reservation case, a reservation record would include the hotel name and location, the customer name and associated data, the date of the booking, and the room rate. The record will also be uniquely identified by a reservation number. It should be possible to access a specific record through any one of several keys, so it would be unwise to design the search process to work efficiently for one key but inefficiently for others.

In other software systems this may be a less severe problem. For example, in a bank there may be a strong reason to make accessing information on an account difficult to protect the privacy of the customer. In this case the data structure may be set up specifically to allow access only through the account number. If such a restriction is included, it may result in a much more efficient data storage design and corresponding search process.

The characteristics of any specific problem will clearly have a major role in determining the organization and content of the database as well as the appropriate search algorithm to be employed. Among the important problem characteristics are:

- Frequency of accessing any record. If records are likely to be accessed only infrequently, then the efficiency of the search process becomes less important.
- Stability of the database. In the airline reservation case, for example, reservations are likely to be changed frequently, whereas in the banking application, information about owners of accounts will be quite stable.
- Nature of the access process. This includes whether or not there is a maximum acceptable time for access to information and the type of processing required after a record being searched for is found.

We will return to the appropriateness of each data organization option and each search strategy at the end of this chapter.

Sorting and searching are strongly interrelated. The type of sort implemented must be consistent with the type of search to be used. In the preceding section the focus was on producing a sorted array of data structures or a sorted array of pointers to nodes on a linked list. As will be shown in this section there are other approaches to searching which require a radically different type of data organization than sorting. In all cases, however, we will assume that each record consists of a data structure which includes the *search key* along with other information. A basic principle in searching is first to organize the database in such a way that the search can quickly be focused on the part of the database which is likely to contain the record of interest. As will be shown, this general objective can be pursued through very different strategies.

Many tasks which do not initially appear to be searches do, in fact, require search as an element. For example:

- Inserting a new record in an already structured database. If the structure of the database is to be preserved for future processing, then the correct location for the insertion must be determined. This requires a search of the existing records.
- Deleting an existing record. First the correct record must be found as a result of a search.

These different types of search-related activities impose different demands on the search process, depending upon the organization of the data. For example, record deletion in an array is more difficult than in a linked list, as is inserting a new record. Hence the more dynamic the database, the greater the attraction of a linked list implementation. Search techniques can be classified into elementary and advanced, with the main distinction being the access time for very large databases. Elementary methods include binary search and binary search trees, both of which are presented in this section. For the sake of completeness we start with a short discussion of linear search.

6.4.1 Linear Search

Linear search is the sequential process of scanning through the records, starting at the first record, until either a match is found or the search is completed unsuccessfully. Linear search is the only option if the records are in random order or if the data is stored in a linear linked list for which no pointer array has been established. This approach may be appropriate if the size of the data set is guaranteed to be small and the content of the database is highly dynamic. In this case the effort of continually sorting the list may *not* be justified. However this is an extremely artificial scenario, particularly when one recognizes that a highly dynamic small database implies frequent deletion of records, which is itself a task requiring a search.

The following function implements a linear search on an array of data structures which include the following members:

```
/* structure template for typical data record */
struct node {
  int phone_num;
  char name[80];
  .....              /* other variables in the record  */
  .....              /*    would go here               */
};
```

The search will use either the telephone number (**phone_num**) or the name (**name**) as the key, depending on the value of a flag which is passed as one of the search function's arguments. Because the type of item to be searched for may be either an integer or a character string, we use a **void** pointer as an argument to the searching function. This **void** pointer contains the address of the item to be searched for. The value pointed to by this pointer is cast as an **int** when the search is for a phone number, and as a character string when the search is for a name.

If the item being searched for is found, then the linear search function returns the subscript in the array of records of the found item. If the item is not found, then the linear search returns the special code **NOT_FOUND**, which is set to negative one. The implementation of the linear search is as follows:

```
/* linear search method */

#include <string.h>

#define SEARCH_BY_PHONE 0
#define SEARCH_BY_NAME  1
#define NOT_FOUND -1     /* indicates value not found */

int lin_search(
    struct node data[], /* array of structs to search */
    int n,              /* number of elements in array */
    int flag,           /* type of  search key */
    void *target)       /* pointer to search target */
{
  int i = 0;

/* loop through all records */
  for(i=0; i<n; i++)
    if(flag == SEARCH_BY_PHONE &&
       (data[i].phone_num == *(int *)target))
      return(i);
    else if(flag == SEARCH_BY_NAME &&
       !strcmp(data[i].name, target))
      return(i);

  return(NOT_FOUND);
}
```

Note that the header file **string.h** is included. This provides the function prototype for **strcmp()**, the string comparison function in the standard library. The prototype for this library function automatically casts the argument **target** from a pointer to **void** to a pointer to **char** when **stremp()** is invoked.

A second aspect of the linear search function worth noting is the expression ***(int *)target** used in the **if** statement. This construction casts the **void** pointer **target** as a pointer to an integer, and then uses the indirection operator (*****) to find the integer value pointer to by **target**. It would be incorrect to code this expression as **(int)*target** because the indirection operator cannot be applied to a **void** pointer.

The approach of using flags and void pointers can be used to write more general functions for any type of sorting or searching method, but for the sake of clarity in presentation, for the remainder of this section we assume that search is based on a single key, either an **int** or a string. Some of the exercises at the end of the chapter explore generalizations of the functions in the text to allow searching for items of different types.

Before leaving the rather pedestrian linear search method for more efficient approaches, we should note that for an array of *n* items linear search requires on average $(n + 1)/2$ comparisons for a successful outcome and $n + 1$ comparisons for an unsuccessful search. Given the availability of more efficient algorithms, linear search is unattractive for all but the smallest problems.

6.4.2 Binary Search

Binary search is a straightforward procedure for locating an element in an already sorted array. It is directly analogous to the bisection method for root finding presented in Section 3.5.2, proceeding by systematically halving the search domain at each iteration until either the correct record is found or the search concludes unsuccessfully.

The function **bin_search()** shown below implements a binary search using the integer key **phone_num** in the array of data structures of type **struct node** used in the preceding subsection. The three arguments to the function are the array of records to be searched, the number of elements in the array, and the phone number being searched for. **bin_search()** returns an integer equal to the index in the array where the record with the requested phone number is found or a special code (set to negative one in the example below) when the record cannot be found. As with any application of the binary search method, we assume that array of records is sorted on the search key.

```
#define NOT_FOUND -1    /* indicates value not found */

int bin_search(
   struct node data[], /* array to be searched */
   int n,              /* number of elements in array */
   int target)         /* value being search for */
{
   int low,high,middle;

   low = 0;
   high = n-1;

/* terminate search when either we have narrowed to
   a single record or when we have found target */

   while (low <= high) {
     middle = (low+high)/2;
     if (target < data[middle].phone_num)
       high = middle-1;
     else if ( target > data[middle].phone_num)
       low = middle+1;
```

```
    else
      return(middle);   /* search was successful */
  }
    return (NOT_FOUND);   /* search unsuccessful */
}
```

Binary search is much more efficient than linear search since it requires $O(\log n)$ iterations in the worst case when there is no match. It is an attractive approach to searching when the database is reasonably stable but large and when many searches are required. On the other hand, if the database is subject to frequent modification while the search itself is still efficient, the need to resort the array as records are added and deleted detracts seriously from its appeal. In such situations a method which does not require maintaining a sorted array would be much more attractive. In the remainder of this chapter we present several such approaches.

6.5 BINARY SEARCH TREES

In Section 5.12 we introduced the *binary search tree* as a special type of tree with the following properties:

- Each node has at most two nodes at the next-lower level (this is a requirement for any binary tree).
- Every node in the left subtree has a key value *no larger than* the root node; every node in the right subtree has a key value *no smaller than* the root node. This property applies recursively to each subtree of the complete tree.

Binary search trees allow a search process which retains the efficiency of the binary search method but overcomes some of the disadvantages of requiring data representation in array form. However, the basic deficiency of binary search (that the array remain sorted) is replaced with another problem with binary search trees: how to maintain trees that satisfy the properties listed above as records are added to, and removed from, the data set. A second problem that is introduced is due to the multiplicity of binary search trees which can represent the same data set. Figure 6.4 illustrates this characteristic of binary search trees. All three trees satisfy the properties of a binary search tree, and all contain the same key integer data. Tree a is a balanced tree since all the leaf nodes exist at the lowest two levels, whereas tree c is a degenerate form of tree which is also a linked list since each node has at most a single descendant. Tree b is intermediate in terms of the number of levels at which nodes exist.

Figure 6.4 also illustrates several other important properties of binary search trees. First, the smallest key of a binary search tree is found in the node farthest to the left in the tree, and the largest key is found in the node farthest to the right. Note that these minimum and maximum key nodes may be at any level in the tree, depending on the tree structure. So in tree a the maximum node is at the lowest level, whereas in c, it is at the highest level. Second, the efficiency of a search in a binary search tree

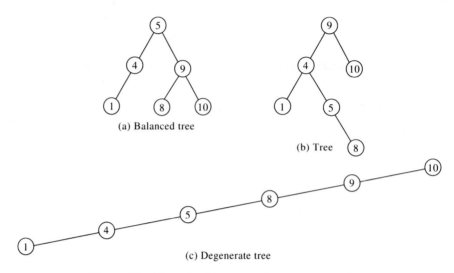

Figure 6.4 Alternative binary search tree representations.

will depend on the tree structure. For a given number of nodes, n, the most efficient tree structure will be a balanced tree which will have $\log_2(n + 1)$ levels. In this case the computation time for a search will be $O(\log n)$, compared with $O(n)$ in the fully degenerate case. Thus an important issue to address is how to obtain a tree which has a balanced structure initially. A second issue relevant if the data in the tree changes is how to maintain balance in the face of subsequent additions and deletions. While it is not essential to obtain a fully balanced tree, it is important to achieve a structure more like that of tree a than tree c in Figure 6.4.

A key characteristic of binary search trees which can greatly facilitate writing functions that operate on them is their highly recursive nature. This is because the subtree of any node in a binary search tree is itself a binary search tree. This can readily be seen by reference to any of the example trees in Figure 6.4. To illustrate the value of this property, we will show how a sorted list can easily be obtained from any binary search tree.

Any systematic process of visiting all nodes in a tree is referred to as a *traversal* of the tree. To obtain a sorted list of all nodes in a binary search tree we apply an *inorder* traversal, which means that for any subtree the nodes are visited in the order

- Left node
- Root node
- Right node

In this, and subsequent, examples of binary search trees we will use the following data structure, in which we define only the node pointers and the search key, in this case an individual's social security number:

```
/* structure template for binary tree nodes */
struct node {
  int soc_sec;
  struct node *left;
  struct node *right;
};

typedef struct node * Bin_tree;
```

The following function would execute an in-order traversal of a binary search tree. It prints the social security numbers in ascending order. The function **empty_tree()** simply tests for an empty tree as did the function **empty_list()** for lists in Chapter 5.

```
#include <stdio.h>
#define TRUE 1
#define FALSE 0

/* prints sorted items in a binary tree */

void tree_print(Bin_tree t)
{
  /* first check for an empty tree */
  if (! empty_tree (t)){
     tree_print(t->left);
     printf("%d\n",t->soc_sec);
     tree_print(t->right);
  }
}

/* determines if tree is empty */

int empty_tree (Bin_tree b)
{
  if (b == NULL)
     return (TRUE);
  return (FALSE);
}
```

In order to use binary search trees we need to develop algorithms that accomplish the following tasks:

- Search for a record with a specific key value
- Add a node to an existing tree
- Delete a node from an existing tree

These functions are presented in the following subsections.

6.5.1 Searching in a Binary Search Tree

The result of a successful search in a binary search tree will be a pointer to the record sought. This is different from the array-based searches, in which an array index is used to identify the record in question. In fact, most binary search tree processing functions will communicate with the calling function through pointers to nodes in the tree. The search process takes advantage of the structure of the binary search tree in the following steps:

1. Check to see if the root node is empty. If so, return.
2. Compare the search key with the root key.
3. If it matches, end the search.
4. If it is smaller, search the left subtree.
5. Otherwise, search the right subtree.

Eventually, the search will either conclude with a match or reach a leaf node without a match, in which case the search has been unsuccessful. Our implementation of **find_node()** has as arguments the tree to be searched and the integer value to be searched for. It returns a pointer to the node in the tree where the item is located or **NULL** if the item is not found. The function takes advantage of the recursive structure of the tree, calling itself recursively as it works its way from the root to the item being searched for. The code is as follows:

```
/* finds a node in a binary search tree */

Bin_tree find_node(
   Bin_tree t,        /* tree to be searched */
   int value)         /* value to search for */
{
   if (empty_tree(t)) /* tree is empty */
      return(t);
/* check the node */

   else {
      if(t->soc_sec == value) /* match has been found */
         return(t);
      else if(t->soc_sec > value) /* search left subtree */
         return(find_node( t->left, value));
      else                        /* search right subtree */
         return(find_node( t->right, value));
   }
}
```

As with any function that returns a pointer which may be **NULL**, it is essential that the calling function check to see if a **NULL** pointer has been returned before further processing is done. Again, while this function will eventually find a match if it exists, its efficiency will depend on the tree structure, so we turn next to the topics of building and modifying binary search trees.

6.5.2 Adding a Node to a Binary Search Tree

The most straightforward operation on an existing binary search tree is to add a new node. In this case we cannot drastically affect the degree of balance of the tree, since there will be only a single node added. One simple approach is to add the node as a child of some existing node without shifting anything else in the tree. This strategy could also be used repeatedly to build a tree from scratch, but in this case there needs to be some consideration of the impact of the sequence of additions on the tree structure. We reserve consideration of this problem to Section 6.5.3.

Given an existing tree, there will be just one location at which the new node can be added which preserves the properties of the binary search tree. The task of the function **add_node()** is to find this location and set up the information associated with the new node. To preserve the binary structure of the tree, the new node must be added as a child of a node which has at most one existing child. The value of the search key for the new record is used to find the correct location for the new node. In the following implementation of **add_node()** we assume that the **struct** to hold the new node has already been set up, including initialization of its right and left pointers to **NULL**.   A pointer to this node is passed to **add-node()** as an argument.

```
    /* adds a new node to a binary search tree */

    void add_node(
      Bin_tree t,          /* root of the tree */
      Bin_tree new_node) /* struct to be added to tree */
    {
      Bin_tree prev;   /* used to access new node's parent */

    /* find correct place for new node */
      while(t != NULL) {
        if(new_node->soc_sec < t->soc_sec) {
          prev = t;
          t = t->left;
        }
        else {
          prev = t;
          t = t->right;
        }
      }

    /* next set up new node pointer in parent node */
        if(new_node->soc_sec < prev->soc_sec)
          prev->left = new_node;
```

```
    else
      prev->right = new_node;
}
```

This function chains down the appropriate branch from each node until it finds a **NULL** pointer where the new node should be added. Figure 6.5 illustrates this process for the addition of a new node with key value 7 to an existing tree. The arrows in the figure show the path through the tree followed by the algorithm when searching for the proper location to add the new node.

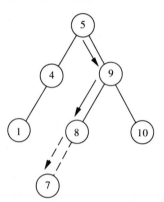

Figure 6.5 Example of node addition.

6.5.3 Construction of a Binary Search Tree

If a binary search tree has to be constructed from scratch, the most straightforward approach would simply be to create a root node and then apply the **add_node()** function repeatedly until all nodes have been added to the tree. The major problem with this method is that the structure of the resulting tree will depend heavily on the sequence in which the nodes are added. For example, if the records happen to be in sorted order, then the resulting tree will be the degenerate case of a linked list, an extremely inefficient binary search tree. To obtain a balanced tree from an initially sorted list, the order of assignment should follow a process in which the children of any node are the midpoints of the intervals above and below that node in a sorted array containing the records.

To illustrate this process, consider the problem of transforming a sorted array of records into a binary search tree. Initially, each record has **NULL** pointers for both the left and right children. The function **create_bst()** presented below could be used to set up the correct pointers in all records:

```
    Bin_tree create_bst(
      Bin_tree data, /* sorted array of records */
      int n)         /* number of elements in data */
    {
      int mid;
```

```
/* check if array has no elements */
  if(n == 0)
    return (NULL);

  mid = n/2;
  (data + mid)->left = create_bst (data, mid);
  (data + mid)->right = create_bst (data+mid+1,n-mid-1);
  return (data + mid);
}
```

This recursive function will set up the node pointers for a binary search tree as shown in the example in Figure 6.6. The function works from the root of the tree down, dividing the array (or subarray) into two equal parts with the middle element being the root of the tree. The two pointers for the root node are the midpoints of each subarray, as determined by further invocations of **create_bst()**.

The tree creation function will work only with an initially sorted array of data structures. The more general problem of creating balanced trees from an initial data set is beyond the scope of this book. [5]   More general approaches check the efficiency of a binary search tree created through repeated addition of nodes. One way to do this is to maintain a count of the number of levels in the tree, which would be checked and revised as necessary after each node addition, and compare this count with the minimum number of levels required to hold the n nodes in the tree. This minimum number is simply $\log_2(n + 1)$. The ratio of the actual number of levels to the minimum number gives a good indicator of the efficiency of the tree; the lower this ratio, the better.

---

[5]Sedgewick [Sedgewick, Robert 90] provides a detailed discussion of this problem.

Element in **data**		Values in **data**	
	value	**left** pointer	**right** pointer
0	37	NULL	NULL
1	40	data	data+2
2	48	NULL	NULL
3	51	data+1	data+5
4	55	NULL	NULL
5	63	data+4	NULL
6	70	data+3	data+9
7	74	NULL	NULL
8	77	data+7	NULL
9	80	data+8	data+11
10	96	NULL	NULL
11	91	data+10	NULL

Figure 6.6   Organizing array as binary search tree.

One point to note about this implementation is that the memory used to store elements of the tree it creates is organized in array. This differs from the trees described in Section 5.12, where memory for the tree was allocated using **malloc()** one node at a time. Because the tree created by **create_bst()** is built from an array of elements, the memory for individual nodes in it cannot be freed even if nodes were to be deleted, since any deleted node would be an element in an array. Consequently, some tree manipulation functions, including the node deletion function presented in the next subsection, cannot be used in conjunction with **create_bst()** without modification.

6.5.4 Node Deletion

Deletion from a binary search tree is a more complex process than node addition. The first step in node deletion is to locate the node. This can be accomplished through the **find_node()** function presented earlier in this section. If the node is a leaf node, deletion is straightforward since the basic structure of the tree will not be modified by the node's removal. However, if the node is an internal one (i.e., it has one or two child nodes), the task becomes more complicated. Figure 6.7 shows the three locations a node to be deleted may have in a tree:

1. A leaf node, for example the node with a key value of 37 in Figure 6.7. Any leaf node can be removed with the only adjustment in the remaining tree being setting the corresponding pointer in the parent node to **NULL**.
2. A node with only one child, for example the node with a key value of 40 in Figure 6.7. Any such node can be removed and replaced with its child node. As a result, all nodes on the subtree move up one level. As with the case of a leaf node, only a single pointer must be changed, that of the parent node.
3. A node with two children, for example node 80 in Figure 6.7. In this case there are two options for replacement of the deleted node:
   - Replace it with the *largest* node from the *left* subtree, or
   - Replace it with the *smallest* node from the *right* subtree.

While the first two cases do not need further discussion, the final one does. To preserve the structure of the binary search tree, a deleted node must be replaced by

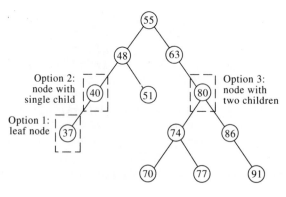

Figure 6.7 Node deletion in a binary search tree.

either the next largest node (the one with the value 86 in Figure 6.4) or the next smallest node in the entire tree (the one with the value 77). The next largest node will be located in the right subtree. A simple procedure to find it would be to chain down the leftmost branches of the right subtree until the **NULL** pointer is found. This last node encountered is the candidate node for the replacement. Similarly, the next smallest node will be located at the end of the rightmost branch of the left subtree.

Having found the candidate replacement nodes, one is selected and used to replace the deleted node. However, this in itself is a deletion from the tree, which will require further modification to the tree. This second modification is straightforward because the replacement node is certain to be either a leaf node or a node with only one child.

Putting all these possible deletion cases together results in the function we call `delete_node()`. The function relies on four other functions as follows:

- `find_parent()`. This function finds a node *and its parent node* in a binary search tree. The parent node is required in order to delete a node efficiently. Its arguments are the tree to be deleted from, a pointer to where the parent of the found node is to be placed, and the integer key value to be found. It returns a pointer to the node where the integer value in the tree was found or the **NULL** pointer if the value is not found.
- `delete_leaf()`. Deletes a leaf node of the tree. Its arguments are the tree from which the node is to be deleted, a pointer to the parent of the node to be deleted, and a pointer to the node to be deleted. It returns the modified binary search tree.
- `delete_one_child()`. Deletes a node that has one child. Its arguments and returned value are the same as those for `delete_leaf()`.
- `delete_two_children()`. Deletes a node that has two children. Its arguments are the tree from which the node is to be deleted and a pointer to the node to be deleted. It does not return a value.

The function prototypes for `delete_node()` and the four functions it uses are as follows:

```
/* function prototypes for delete_node() and the
        four functions it uses */

Bin_tree delete_node(Bin_tree, int, int *);
Bin_tree find_parent(Bin_tree, Bin_tree *, int);
Bin_tree delete_leaf(Bin_tree, Bin_tree, Bin_tree);
Bin_tree delete_one_child(Bin_tree, Bin_tree, Bin_tree);
void delete_two_children(Bin_tree, Bin_tree);
```

Given the four functions described above, the C code for `delete_node()` is straightforward. The function has three arguments: the tree from which a node is to be deleted, the value of the key for the item to be deleted, and a pointer to an integer used as a flag to indicate whether or not the key was in the tree to begin with. The integer pointed to by the flag is set TRUE if the deletion is successful and FALSE otherwise.

`delete_node()` returns the revised binary tree. The implementation is as follows:

```
/* delete a node from a binary search tree */
 #include <stdlib.h>
#define TRUE 1
#define FALSE 0

Bin_tree delete_node(
  Bin_tree t, /* root of the tree */
  int value,  /* soc_sec number of record to delete */
  int *flag)  /* flag set FALSE if node not found */
{
  Bin_tree parent, node;

/* find parent of node to be deleted */
  node = find_parent(t, &parent, value);
  if(node == NULL) {  /* node not in tree */
    *flag = FALSE;
    return(t);
  }

/* is it a leaf node? */
  if((node->left == NULL)  && (node->right == NULL))
    t = delete_leaf(t, parent, node);

/* has it a single child ? */
  else if ((node->left == NULL) || (node->right == NULL))
    t = delete_one_child(t, parent, node);

/* it has two children */
  else
    delete_two_children(t,node);

  *flag = TRUE;
  return(t);
}
```

The function `find_parent()` is a generalization of `find_node()` developed earlier. The major change is that it keeps track of the parent of the node being searched for as well as the node itself. The parent is returned to the function invoking `find_parent()` through a pointer argument. (This pointer is set to **NULL** if the key value is in the root node, which by definition has no parent.) The C code is as follows:

```
/* find node and its parent in tree */

Bin_tree find_parent(
  Bin_tree t,      /* tree to search */
```

```
    Bin_tree *parent, /* points to parent of found node */
    int value)        /* value to search for */
{
  *parent = NULL;
  while(t != NULL && value != t->soc_sec) {
    *parent = t;
    if(value < t->soc_sec)
      t = t-> left;
    else
      t = t-> right;
  }
  return(t);
}
```

Deleting a leaf node is the simplest case. The function **delete_leaf()** deals with three possible situations:

1. The leaf node to be deleted is the root of the tree. The function should free the memory for the node and return a **NULL** pointer. After the deletion the tree is empty.
2. The leaf node to be deleted is the right child of its parent. The right pointer of the parent should be set to the **NULL** pointer and the memory for the node should be freed.
3. The leaf node to be deleted is the left child of its parent. The left pointer of the parent should be set to the **NULL** pointer and the memory for the node should be freed.

The following code handles all three of these cases.

```
/* delete a leaf node */

Bin_tree delete_leaf(
  Bin_tree t,        /* tree where deletion to occur */
  Bin_tree parent,   /* parent of node to be deleted */
  Bin_tree node)     /* node to be deleted */
{
  if(parent == NULL)    /* root node to be deleted */
    t = NULL;
  else if(parent->soc_sec < node->soc_sec)
    parent->right = NULL;
  else
    parent->left = NULL;
  free(node);
  return(t);
}
```

The case of a node with only one child is also straightforward. The situation where the node to be deleted is the root must be handled specially so that the tree returned by the function is whichever of the root's children is not empty. For nodes other than the root, the child of the node to be deleted must be made a child of the parent of the deleted node. The C code for **delete_one_child()** is given below.

```
/* delete node with one child */

Bin_tree delete_one_child(
  Bin_tree t,        /* tree where deletion to occur */
  Bin_tree parent,  /* parent of node to be deleted */
  Bin_tree node)     /* node to be deleted */
{

  if(parent == NULL) {   /* root node to be deleted */
    if(node->left == NULL)
      node = t->right;
    else
      node = t->left;
    free(t);
    return(node);
  }

/* node to be deleted is not root */
  if(node->left == NULL)
    if(parent->soc_sec < node->soc_sec)
      parent->right = node->right;
    else
      parent->left = node->right;
  else
    if(parent->soc_sec < node->soc_sec)
      parent->right = node->left;
    else
      parent->left = node->left;
  free(node);
  return(t);
}
```

The last case is when the node to be deleted has two children. The implementation given below always uses the next largest node in the tree when replacing an internal node with two children. As discussed earlier, this will always be the leftmost node of the right subtree of the node to be deleted. Once this replacement node is found, it can be eliminated from its current position in the tree using either **delete_leaf()** or **delete_one_child()** (depending on whether the replacement is a leaf or has only one child). The key originally in the replacement node can then be stored in the node which originally had the key to be deleted.

The C code for `delete_two_children()` is as follows:

```
void delete_two_children(
  Bin_tree t,        /* tree where deletion to occur */
  Bin_tree node)     /* node to be deleted */
{
  int temp;
  Bin_tree small, small_parent;

/* find the smallest node in the right subtree */
  small = node->right;
  small_parent = node;
  while (small->left != NULL) {
    small_parent = small;
    small = small->left;
  }

 /* call either delete_leaf() or delete_one_child()
      to eliminate node replacing one deleted */
  temp = small->soc_sec;
  if(small->left == NULL && small->right == NULL)
    delete_leaf(t, small_parent, small);
  else
    delete_one_child(t, small_parent, small);
 /* move replacement to deleted node */
  node->soc_sec = temp;
}
```

As with adding nodes, when nodes are deleted from a binary search tree it may become unbalanced. Other functions could be written to rebalance the tree if it becomes badly out of balance. Algorithms for doing this are beyond the scope of this book, but readers interested in exploring this topic further should see Sedgewick [Sedgewick, Robert 90].

6.6 HASHING

All of the methods so far presented for searching have involved examining records in a systematic sequence until either the record in question is found or the search is concluded unsuccessfully. The efficiency of the search depends directly upon the size of the data set as well as the method used to organize the records and move from record to record in the search process. For very large data sets even an efficient search method will require looking at many records and may become computationally burdensome.

An alternative approach to searching is to use the search key itself to access the element of an array which should correspond to the record being sought. To generalize this approach, some transformation of the search key is used to access an element of the array containing all the records. This approach to search is called *hashing* and is commonly used for applications such as automated telephone directories and on-line dictionaries. The fundamental design tradeoff with a hash scheme is that of computer memory versus access time. Whereas the other search methods presented use memory efficiently by allocating space only for data records and essential pointers, hash schemes allocate more memory than is required. This additional memory can both reduce the number of records examined to find the match and ease the processes of addition and deletion of records, which, as we saw, can be troublesome for the other methods.

The principal elements in any hashing scheme are introduced in this section, and some common hash designs are then presented. The array of active records is called a *hash table*, which will also include free space for the insertion of new records. An entry in this hash table may be either a data structure containing all information on the entity, or simply a pointer to a data structure. Because hash tables are designed to leave space for future additions, there is a considerable advantage to storing just the pointer to a structure in the table, particularly for large data records, so this is the more common approach.

A *hash function* is used to map the record key into the appropriate array index. The aims of the hash function are to spread the records fairly evenly over the hash table, and to minimize the number of *duplicate hashes* (or *collisions*) which occur when more than one key is mapped into the same array index. Any efficient hash function will, however, produce some duplicate hashes, so the final element required is a *collision resolution process* to resolve these situations.

6.6.1 Hash Functions

To illustrate the basics of hashing, consider the following two situations:

1. There are 1000 customers of a shop, each of which has an account for charging purchases, with information on the account kept in a record. There is an unusually stable clientele, so each customer has been assigned an account number between 0 and 999. Simply by setting up an array of 1000 elements, we can use the account number directly to access the individual account information.

2. There are 1000 employees of a company, with each employee record accessed through the social security number. A social security number is a unique nine-digit identifier, so there are 10^9 possible numbers. In this case, short of having an array with 10^9 elements, we need to develop a hash function which will map each possible employee social security number into an index in a reasonably sized array.

The first example is highly artificial both in terms of the supposed stability of the customer base and the assumption that the account numbers will be a suitable basis for accessing records. However, it does clearly show the advantage of using the key to access directly the record sought. The second example is the more typical case in which we want to take advantage of direct access, but must use a hash function if the hash table required is going to be of a feasible size.

A hash function, $h(key\_value)$, performs some computation on the value of the key to produce an integer between 0 and $M - 1$, where M is the size of the hash table. The simplest hash function makes use of the modulo operator (%). For an integer key, the function

$$h(key\_value) = key\_value \% M$$

will provide an index in the desired range. If the search key is a string, then the same hash function can be used with key_value defined to be the sum of values of the characters in the string. In this method the hash table size, M, should be prime to improve the chances of obtaining randomly distributed entries in the array.

To illustrate the hashing process, consider a set of 10 students in a small college, each of whom has a three-digit identification number. To build a hash table of these student records we must first select a hash table size, M. Clearly, if all the records are to be accommodated directly in the table, M must be at least size 10. The higher the value of M, the more memory is wasted, but the lower the probability of obtaining duplicate hashes, which decrease the efficiency of the search process. Suppose that M is set at 17. Then applying the modulo hash function, a set of table indices can be produced for a set of student IDs, as shown in Figure 6.8. Several of the unique student ID numbers map into the same hash table indices. This result of obtaining duplicate hashes for unique key values is inherent in any efficient hash scheme and can be resolved in several ways, including *linear probing*, *double hashing*, and *chaining*. Each approach to collisions is described below.

Student ID number	Hash index (ID % 17)
062	11
101	16
304	15
330	7
562	1
579	1
614	2
777	12
823	7
914	13

Figure 6.8 Hash table.

6.6.2 Linear Probing

Linear probing is the simplest method to resolve collisions. It involves entering the hash table at the index produced by the hashing function and moving down the array until either the record with the matching key is found or an unused location is found. In the first case the search is concluded successfully, and in the second it has been unsuccessful. Linear probing takes advantage of the empty locations in the hash table to store duplicate hash codes as close as possible to, but after, the location produced by the hash function. In the discussion below we assume that the hash table size is larger than the number of items to be included, so we omit the error checks. Our actual implementation includes checking whether the table is full.

To set up a hash table based on linear probing, the following algorithm can be used:

1. Declare an array of the appropriate size, with each element a pointer to the type of data structure being searched for.
2. Initialize all elements in the array to **NULL**.
3. For each item to be hashed:
   - Compute the hash index using a hash function.
   - If the hash table entry for the index computed by the hash function is **NULL**, set that entry in the hash table to point to the item.
   - Otherwise, scan the hash table entries starting at the index to find the first **NULL** entry. If the last entry in the hash table is reached before a **NULL** entry is found, wrap around to the first entry in the hash table and continue.

Once the hash table has been created, a search can be conducted in it for an item as follows:

1. Compute the hash index using the hash function.
2. Check if the hash table entry for the index points to the item. If so, end the search successfully. If the hash table entry for the index is **NULL**, the search is unsuccessful. Otherwise, scan subsequent entries until:
   - A **NULL** entry is found; the search is therefore unsuccessful.
   - The pointer points to the item being searched for. The search was successful.

The functions **make_hash()** and **hash_search()** implement the steps listed above to create a hash table and then to search it. For convenience, we also create a third function, **init_hash()**, which allocates an initial, empty hash table.

We assume that the records to be hashed are in a linked list form, with each record having just an integer key and a pointer to the next record. Below are the preprocessor directives, structure template for a record, and the function prototypes for this example.

```
#include <stdlib.h>
#include <stdio.h>
```

```
#define TABLE_FULL -1  /* indicates full hash table */

/* structure template for records */
struct node {
   int soc_sec;
   struct node * next;
   };

typedef struct node * List;

/* function prototypes */

List *init_hash(int);
List *make_hash (List , int);
int hash_search (List *, int, int);
```

init_hash() has an integer, which is the desired hash table size, as its sole argument. It allocates memory for an array of pointers using **calloc()** and initializes that array to **NULL** pointers. The C code is as follows:

```
List *init_hash(
   int n)          /* hash table size */
{
  List *hash_table;
  int i;

/* allocate memory for hash_size pointers */
  hash_table = calloc(n, sizeof(List));

/* check if allocation was successful */
  if (hash_table == NULL) {
    printf ("Can't allocate memory for hash table\n");
    exit(-1);
  }

/* initialize all pointers in the hash table to NULL */
  for (i = 0; i < n; i++)
      *(hash_table + i) = NULL;

  return(hash_table);
}
```

Function **make_hash()** receives as arguments a pointer to the linked list containing the data records and the size of the hash table. It returns a pointer to the hash table it has created. It first invokes **init_hash()** to allocate memory for the

hash table and then invokes function **hash_search()** to determine where in the hash
table the pointer for each node should be stored. The code is as follows:

```
/* make hash table from a linked list */

List *make_hash(
  List data,        /* linked list containing data */
  int hash_size) /* hash table size */
{
  List *hash_table;
  int j;

/* allocate initial, empty hash table */
  hash_table = init_hash(hash_size);

/* chain down linked list using hash_search()
   to find an empty slot */
  while ( data != NULL){
    j = hash_search(hash_table, hash_size, data->soc_sec);
    if (j == TABLE_FULL) {
       printf ("Hash table too small for the data\n");
       exit(2);
       }

/* if hash table pointer is not NULL
   record exists with same key */
    if (*(hash_table +j) == NULL)
      *(hash_table + j) = data;
    else
      printf ("Record duplicate exists\n");
    data = data->next;
  }
  return (hash_table);
}
```

The function **hash_search()** takes as arguments a pointer to the hash table,
the size of the hash table, and the key value of the record to be located. It returns the
index for the pointer to the record of interest. In the event of a collision for the last
entry in the hash table, the **%** operator is used to reset the index to the first entry in the
hash table.

```
/* used both to set up hash table and to search it */

int hash_search(
  List table[], /* hash table */
  int size,     /* hash table size */
  int num)      /* key of record sought */
```

```
    {
      int entry = num % size;
      int count = 0;

  /* count is used to see if hash table is full */

      while((count<size) && (table[entry] != NULL) &&
            (table[entry]->soc_sec != num)) {
        entry = (++entry) % size;
        count++;
      }

      if (count == size) /* table is full, return flag */
          return (TABLE_FULL);
      return (entry);
    }
```

hash_search() is used to set up the hash table, but care must be exercised to make sure that the size of the hash table is not exceeded by the number of items in the data set. This same function can be used to search for an item in the hash table. In this case the calling function would interpret the fact that the entry in the hash table at the element returned by hash_search() is NULL to mean that no match was found. (A returned value of TABLE_FULL would also indicate an unsuccessful search.)

The hash table size must always be larger than the data set. As the ratio of the hash table size to the data set size approaches 1, the efficiency of the search process declines. Values of this ratio in excess of 1.5 result in very efficient searches.

6.6.3 Double Hashing

Another approach to collision resolution is to repeat the hashing process itself with a second hash function to obtain an increment which is added to the original index to produce the new hash table index. This second hash function should have similar properties to the first but with the additional constraint that it should never produce a zero. (Obviously, if the second hash function produced a zero, the new index would not change from its old value.) A common method of ensuring a nonzero outcome for an integer key is to use the following second hash function, where the hash table size is M and the key value is k:

$$h'(k) = M - 2 - k\%(M - 2)$$

The value of the second hash function would then be added to the first hash function to produce the new hash table index, wrapping around to the beginning of the hash table array as needed.

If double hashing were used with the second hash function above, instead of linear probing, the previous function make_hash() could be used with the following version of `hash_search()`:

```
/* hash_search now is based on double probing */
int hash_search(
    List * table,  /* pointer to the hash table */
    int size,      /* size is the hash table size */
    int num)       /* num is the key of record sought */
{
    int entry, count;
    entry = num % size;

/* count limits the number of attempts
   to resolve the collision */

    for (count = 0; (count < size) &&
        (*(table + entry) != NULL) &&
        ((*(table + entry))->soc_sec!= num); count++)

/* Use of % operator handles index wrap around */

        entry = (entry + (size-2) - num % (size-2)) % size;
    if (count == size) /* give up after "size" attempts */
        return (TABLE_FULL);
    return (entry);
}
```

One comment is needed here. The use of `count < size` to limit the number of hash attempts does not necessarily mean that the hash table is full in this case. Depending on the choice of hash table size, a cycle of indices in which not all indices are attempted may occur. So if `hash_search()` returns the value `TABLE_FULL`, it really means that with this particular set of hash functions, no available slot can be found.

6.6.4 Chaining

The third option for resolving collisions is to set up a linked list whenever a duplicate hash is encountered (see Figure 6.9). In this way the hash table itself can be kept short, but the efficiency of any search will depend on the length of the typical linked list. The length of the linked lists should be kept short enough that a simple linear search of any one list will be adequate to resolve duplicate hashes.

The principle of chaining can be illustrated using the example given for linear probing. Since the records were originally in the form of a linked list, the chaining can be accomplished simply through reassigning pointer values. The previous functions `hash_search()` and `make_hash()` can be modified as shown below to accommodate chaining.

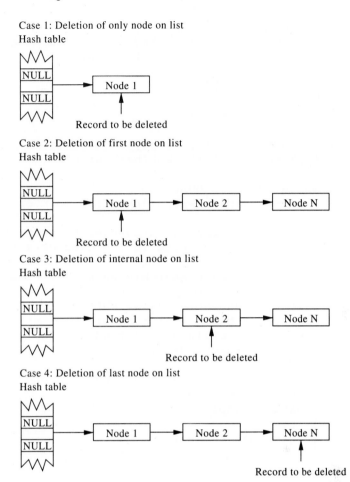

Case 1: Deletion of only node on list
Hash table

Record to be deleted

Case 2: Deletion of first node on list
Hash table

Record to be deleted

Case 3: Deletion of internal node on list
Hash table

Record to be deleted

Case 4: Deletion of last node on list
Hash table

Record to be deleted

Figure 6.9 Deletion of record with separate chaining.

Our implementation reorganizes the original list of records, changing their pointers so that the original list is transformed into an array of lists. All items on each of the transformed lists have identical hash values. In this implementation the **next** pointer in the original linked list gets reused as the pointer in one of the hash chains. For this reason **hash_chain_search()** will modify the **next** pointers, so the original pointer value has to be stored in **make_chain_hash()** before each node is processed through **hash_chain_search()**.

The code for **make_chain_hash()** is given below

```
/* make hash table from a linked list using chaining */
```

```
List *make_chain_hash(
  List data,      /* linked list containing data */
  int hash_size) /* hash table size */
{
List *hash_table;
int i,j;
List temp,  prev;

/* allocate initial, empty hash table */
  hash_table = init_hash(hash_size);

  while (data != NULL) {
    temp = data->next; /*save old pointer in list */

/* pass the address of a pointer to store the address
   of the previous node in the case of a collision */

     j = hash_chain_search(hash_table, hash_size,
          data->soc_sec, &prev);
     if (*(hash_table +j) == NULL)
       *(hash_table + j) = data;
     else  /* collision occurred */
       prev->next = data;

/*  we need to indicate this node is end of chain */
     data->next = NULL;
     data = temp;
  }
  return(hash_table);
}
```

The function **hash_chain_search()** is modified such that collisions are resolved by chaining down the list of duplicate hash nodes.

```
/* hash search will both return the hash table
   entry, and set prev to a pointer to the previous
   node on the linked list of duplicates for that
   hash table entry */

int hash_chain_search(
    List table[], /* hash table */
    int size,     /* hash table size */
    int num,      /* key of record sought */
    List * prev)  /* used to return address of
                    node preceding the target node */
```

```
{

    int entry;
    List  temp;
    entry = num % size; /* compute hash function */
    temp = table[entry];

 /* chain down the linked list  */
    while ( (temp != NULL) && (temp->soc_sec != num)) {
 /* set up the address of the previous node */
      *prev = temp;
      temp = temp->next;
      }
    return (entry);
}
```

In the function **hash_chain_search()** we need to keep track of both the entry in the hash table and, in the case of a duplicate hash, the node in the linked list which precedes the target node. The standard way to handle this, which we adopt here, is to return one value and use a pointer in the argument list to return the other value. In this case we pass the address of a pointer (i.e., a pointer to a **List**), **prev**, which is then assigned the address of the preceding node on the hash list.

While the code itself is more complicated than for the linear probing or double hashing methods, separate chaining avoids the problems of having too many records for the hash table size. For this reason, if there is a lot of uncertainty about the problem size, chaining may be the preferred approach.

6.6.5 Deleting a Record

With any dynamic data set it should be easy to remove a record from the list. As has already been shown, this can be difficult with the other approaches to searching. In the case of hashing, removing a record is relatively straightforward, although we must be careful to preserve the structure of the hash table.

For both linear probing and double probing, when a record is removed it must be replaced with a non-**NULL** entry in the hash table to permit searches for duplicate hash records lying beyond the removed record to continue. The simplest way to do this is to set up a dummy record which has a unique key not replicated by any real record. The hash table pointer can then be set to the address of this dummy node whenever a record is deleted. An additional complication is that we need to distinguish between searches which are to add new records and those to find an existing record in the hash table. In the first case the search should be terminated when the first **NULL** or dummy entry is located, while in the second case it would terminate unsuccessfully only if a **NULL** entry is found.

In the case of separate chaining, record deletion is identical to removing a node from a linked list, and the same special cases have to be dealt with:

1. The node to be deleted is the only one on the list.
2. The node to be deleted is the first node on the list.
3. The node to be deleted is an internal node on the list.
4. The node to be deleted is the last node on the list.

Each of these cases is shown in Figure 6.9. In all cases the trick is to ensure that the pointers are reset correctly in both the hash table itself (affected only in cases 1 and 2), and in the preceding (cases 3 and 4) and following nodes (cases 2 and 3).

6.7 PROGRAMMING PROJECT: THE TILE PUZZLE REVISITED

A good example of using a hashing scheme is in the tile puzzle problem introduced in Section 5.13. The algorithm presented in Section 5.13 could pursue solutions which had already been generated. In other words, the algorithm could waste computational effort in searching for the solution. In this section we use hashing to eliminate this wasted effort in an efficient way. In this enhancement to the previous algorithm, whenever a new node in the solution tree is generated, a search is made to see if this puzzle state has already been generated. If so, the node is not added to the tree. Only if the puzzle state is new is it added to the tree.

Because of the uncertainty about the number of distinct states which might be generated in the course of solving the puzzle, separate chaining is an attractive approach to resolving duplicate hashes. The hash table will be an array of pointers to a data structure **hash_element** which contains two pointers: one to the puzzle data structure describing the corresponding puzzle state, and the other to the next **hash_element** node with the same hash index. The structure template for the **hash_element** is defined as follows:

```
/* structure template for element on hash lists */
struct hash_element{
  struct board * board_state;
  struct hash_element * next;
};
```

The hash table itself simply consists of an array of pointers to **hash_element** structures. We declare the array holding the hash table as external to any functions so that it can be referenced from any function without passing it as an argument. The pointers in the hash table are initialized to **NULL** as part of the overall initialization process as follows:

```
/* array for hash table pointers */
```

```
#define HASHSIZE 1973 /* hash table size */
struct hash_element * hash_table[HASHSIZE];


/* initialize hash table pointers to NULL */
void init_hash_table(void)
{
  int i;
  for (i = 0; i < HASHSIZE; i++)
      hash_table[i] = NULL;
}
```

We will use the modulus operator to obtain the hash index as discussed in the preceding section with a prime number (1973 in the example above) being selected as the hash table size. There are many possible ways to obtain an integer key from the puzzle state stored in the array **values**. In this example we treat each row of the puzzle as a base 16 number and sum the rows and use the modulus operator to compute the hash table index. The resulting function to compute the hash table index is shown below.

```
/* finds the hash table index
   for the new puzzle state */

int hash_compute(
  char tiles[]) /* array describing puzzle state */
{
  int i,j;
  int power = 1;
  unsigned cum = 0;

/* loop over each column indexed by j,
   starting with last */

  for ( j = 3; j >= 0; j--) {

/* loop over each row adding the
   column value for that row */

    for ( i = 0; i < 4; i++)
      cum += tiles [j + 4*i] * power;
    power = power * 16;
  }
   return (cum % HASHSIZE);
}
```

The final function needed invokes **hash_compute()** to check whether the current puzzle state is really new, and if so, adds the board to the appropriate linked list in the hash table. Adding a new puzzle state to the hash table involves allocating new memory for the required **hash_element** and setting the list's pointers appropriately. The function **is_new()** has a **Puzzle** state as its argument and returns TRUE if that state is new and FALSE if that state has already been examined.

```
#include <string.h>

/* returns TRUE if the state is
   new and FALSE otherwise */
int is_new(Puzzle b)
{
  int index;
  struct hash_element *temp;
  int flag;

/* obtain the hash table index */
  index = hash_compute (b->values);
  temp = hash_table[index];

/* chain down linked list from hash table */
  for(flag=TRUE; temp != NULL && flag; temp=temp->next)
      flag = strncmp(b->values,
                  (temp->board_state)->values, 16);

/* if the state is new, set up a
        new hash element struct */
  if(flag) {
    temp = malloc(sizeof (struct hash_element);
    if(temp == NULL) {
      printf("Unable to allocate hash table node.\n");
      exit(3);
    }
/* put new hash element at front of list */
    temp->next = hash_table[index];
    temp->board_state = b;
    hash_table[index] = temp;
  }
    return (flag);
}
```

In **is_new()** the string library function **strncmp()** is used to compare the strings describing puzzle states. **strncmp()** returns a zero (FALSE) if the two strings in the argument list are identical. The function **strncmp()** differs from **strcmp()** in that only the first **n** characters of the two strings are compared, where **n** is the third argument to the function. **strcmp()** compares characters in the strings until a null character is reached. The prototype for **strncmp()** is included in the **string.h** header file.

In a revised implementation of the puzzle solver, the function `is_new()` would be called from the existing function `make_new()` with a specific puzzle state before adding a new board to the tree and to the active list.

6.8 SUMMARY OF CHAPTER 6

In this chapter we have explored some of the fundamental tasks frequently associated with large data sets. Whenever we deal with realistically sized data sets we require convenient ways to read and output data other than through the terminal. C provides these capabilities through *files*, which can be thought of as streams of characters processed sequentially. The standard C header file `stdio.h` provides definitions for *file pointers* which can be used as arguments to functions which read, write, and close files.

Before being operating on, any file must be *opened* using `fopen()`, a standard C library function. `fopen()` takes as arguments the name of the file and the mode of processing on the file; it returns a pointer to the file which is used for subsequent access. A file can be opened for reading from, writing to, or appending to. More than one file can be opened for processing simultaneously.

Reading from a file is accomplished through `fscanf()` in a manner directly analogous to `scanf()`, with the addition of the file pointer as the first argument. Similarly, writing to a file is done using the library function `fprintf()`, which is a generalized version of `printf()`. If a file is opened for appending, writing to it using `fscanf()` will result in the new output being added to the end of the file.

When processing of a file has been completed, the file should be *closed* using `fclose()`, with the single argument being the file pointer. After a file has been closed the file pointer can be reused to process another file.

Sorting is one of the most basic and common processing functions for data sets. Typically, the data to be sorted is in the form of data structures (or records), with sorting done on a single attribute, the *key*. The relative efficiency of sorting algorithms is sensitive to the degree of structure in the initial database and the size of the records.

Elementary sorting methods are appropriate for small files and for files which are already partially sorted. *Insertion sort* moves through the array of records (or pointers to records) sequentially, at each iteration inserting one more record at the correct place in the already sorted subarray. Insertion sort is inefficient, except for small data sets, since it exchanges only adjacent records. *Shellsort* is a simple extension of insertion sort which improves its efficiency by comparing, and exchanging when appropriate, records which are farther apart in the array. Thus, large amounts of disorder are quickly eliminated from the data set. In general, the computation time required for these elementary sorting algorithms is proportional to n^2 for a set of n randomly arranged records.

Advanced sorting methods are more appropriate for large data sets and are characterized by computation time that is proportional to $n\log n$ for n randomly arranged records. *Quicksort*, one of the most widely used sorting methods, partitions the original array into two subarrays, and sorts these subarrays independently. The partitioning is achieved so that every record in one subarray has a key value smaller than the partition element, and every record in the other subarray has a key value greater than the partition element. Quicksort can be implemented in a recursive manner using a series of exchanges to position the partition element in its correct place in the array.

Searching for a particular record is necessary whenever a record is to be modified, deleted, or added to the data set. Many search methods depend on the data set being organized in a specific manner, with sorting being only one of the interesting options. If the data set is in the form of an unsorted linked list or array, the only search method which can be applied directly is *linear search*. In this case each record is examined until the key value is found. This method is extremely inefficient except for the smallest data sets.

Two other elementary searching methods which are of greater utility are *binary search* and *binary search trees*. Binary search is a straightforward method for searching in an already sorted data set. It proceeds by sequentially halving the search interval at each iteration, keeping the search key value in the active half for the next iteration. Binary search is attractive when the database is large but reasonably stable. If the database is more dynamic, however, the need to add to and delete records from the database while maintaining the sorted order detracts seriously from any method which depends on sorting.

Search in a binary search tree can be as efficient as binary search, but reduces the overhead associated with a dynamic database. A binary search tree is a tree in which every node has at most two nodes at the next lower level, and every node in the left subtree has a key value no larger than the root node, and every node in the right subtree has a key value no smaller than the root node. Search in this type of tree proceeds from the root, always proceeding down the branch which would contain the search record if it exists in the tree. The efficiency of search in a binary search tree depends on the balance of the tree. In a balanced tree, when all the leaf nodes are at the lowest two levels, search through a binary search tree is as efficient as a binary search process. However, if the tree is highly unbalanced, search can be much less efficient. In the worst case, where the tree degenerates to a linked list, searching a binary search tree will be the same as a linear search.

Adding a node to a binary search tree is reasonably straightforward, as is tree construction without worrying about the difficult issue of obtaining a balanced tree. However, node deletion can become complex, particularly in the case of internal nodes with two child nodes. Despite the complexities of node deletion, binary search trees are easier to maintain than sorted arrays if the database changes frequently.

The last search method described is *hashing*, which is a radically different approach to search. Hashing uses some transformation of the key value to obtain an index to a hash table. The *hash table* consists of an array of pointers to structures in which the records are stored. A *hash function* is used to transform the record key into an array index. The simplest hash function makes use of the modulus operator to obtain an index ranging from zero to one less than the hash table size.

There are several different ways to resolve duplicate hashes, called *collisions*, which occur when different key values produce the same hash table index. In *linear probing*, a duplicate hash is stored in the first free array element after the hash function index. The efficiency of this method will depend on the utilization level of the hash table; the higher the utilization level of the table, the lower the efficiency of the overall search process. Another way to resolve duplicate hashes, called *double hashing*, is to use a second hash function to obtain a new index if the first hash table entry is already occupied. Again this method will be inefficient if the hash table utilization level is high.

The final way to resolve duplicate hashes is to create a linked list of records having the same hash function index. This method, known as *separate chaining*, uses linear search to locate a record within the linked list. In this approach the hash table size is reduced but the number of records which must be examined to find the correct record may be increased. Because of the relative inefficiency of linear searches it is strongly recommended that the average linked list should have no more than 10 to 15 nodes.

Hashing was used in a programming project to extend the basic algorithm presented for the tile puzzle to eliminate investigation of puzzle states which have already been defined.

6.9 EXERCISES

6-1. Write a C function that counts the number of words and letters in a text file. This function should prompt the user for the name of the file, open the file, read each word in it, close the file, and output the word and letter count. Your function should treat any set of consecutive characters separated by white space as a word. Write a `main()` function that tests your word and letter counter.

6-2. Suppose you have two files that contain integer values, and each file is sorted in ascending order. Write a C function that opens the files and *merges* their contents, creating an output file in ascending order. The function should have as arguments the names of the two input files and the name of the output file. It should return an integer value which has codes for the following possible conditions:

   a. The files were merged successfully.
   b. The first of the input files could not be opened for reading.
   c. The second of the input files could not be opened for reading.
   d. The output file could not be opened for writing.

   Write a `main()` function that tests your file merging function on two files you create.

6-3. Generalize your answer to Exercise 6-2, creating a function that merges *n* files. Your new function should have as arguments a ragged array of character strings, providing the input file names, an integer giving the number of input files to be merged, and a string with the name of the output file. It should return an integer to report error conditions. (Think through what possible error conditions your function might encounter.) You may use the answer to Exercise 6-2 in your solution to create a temporary file that merges two files, and then merges that temporary file with the next input file, etc.

   Create a `main()` function that merges four files you create. You should print out the contents of each of the input files and the final output file.

6-4. Write a new version of insertion sort that uses a secondary key to "break ties" between records that have the same primary key. Assume that the records to be sorted are in an array of **struct**s that include both a **double** and an **int**. Use the **double** as the primary key, the **int** as the secondary key. Write a **main()** function that reads values from a file into the array, sorts the array in descending order, and prints out the records after they are sorted.

6-5. Simulate the execution of quicksort by hand on the following array:

> 11   15   21   45   12   22   17   9   5   17

Show the state of the array after each partitioning and after each invocation of quicksort during its recursive execution. Count the number of times entries are exchanged in the execution of quicksort for this array.

6-6. Recode the quicksort implementation in Section 6.3.5 so that it uses pointers rather than array subscripts to scan through the array.

6-7. Modify the version of **quicksort()** described in the Section 6.3.5 so that it sorts records rather than simply integer values. Create an implementation that has as its arguments an array of **struct**s that include three **double** values which are (x, y, z) coordinates of a point and sorts these values based on their Euclidean distance from the origin. Write a **main()** function that reads in coordinate values for points and tests your revised quicksort function.

6-8. It is possible to implement **quicksort()** (or for that matter, any other recursive function) without using any recursion. The general approach is to create a stack to hold values to be operated on. In this case you could create a stack holding the array indices of the lower and upper subarrays after you do a partitioning. The next subarray to be partitioned would be the one on the top of the stack. Each partitioning should push the indices for the two resulting subarrays onto the stack unless the subarray has only one entry. The stack should start with the indices of the beginning and ending elements of the array to be sorted on the stack. The algorithm terminates when the stack is empty.

Implement a new quicksort that uses an explicit stack rather than recursion. Write a **main()** function that tests this revised quicksort.

6-9. The end of Section 6.3.5 suggested three improvements in the version of **quicksort()** developed in the text. Implement an improved version of **quicksort()** that incorporates these algorithmic improvements.

6-10. Discuss the performance of selection sort, insertion sort, and quicksort as implemented in the chapter for the cases where the items to be sorted are already in the correct order and where they are in the reverse of the correct order.

6-11. Write a C function that sorts a linear linked list in ascending order. Each element on the list should be a **struct** containing a **float**, a **double**, a character string, and a pointer to the next element on the list. Write another function that outputs the values in the list, with each value on a single line. The sorting function should have as its arguments the list to be sorted and a code indicating which of the three fields to sort on. It should return the list in the correctly sorted order. Then write a **main()** function that creates an initial list from input provided by the user, outputs the list, and then sorts the list in all three orders, outputting each ordering.

6-12. Given a file that consists entirely of text, write a C program that sorts the words in the file in alphabetical order and eliminates all duplicates. For the purposes of this assignment, a word is any consecutive sequence of non-white-space characters. The function should output the set of unique words into a file.

6-13. Write an implementation of a generalized version of a binary search procedure that can search for any variant of C integers and floating-point values. The function should have the following arguments:

- A pointer to the key being searched for. This should be a pointer to `void` so that any type of C variable can be used.
- The array to be searched. This can be an array of any type. To make this possible, this argument should be a pointer to `void`. You should assume that this array is already sorted.
- An integer equal to the number of elements in the array.
- A code indicating the type of value stored in the array, with codes defined for a `short int`, `int`, `long int`, `float`, `double`, and `long double`.

The function should return an integer subscript which is the element of the array where the item was found or a special code indicating that the item was not found.

Remember that you will want to cast both the array and the value being searched for to the appropriate C type before comparing items during the binary search on the array.

6-14. A *ternary search* is identical to a binary search except that at each step the array being searched is divided into three parts rather than two. The parts should be as equal in size as possible. Write a ternary search function that searches an array of character strings that is sorted. The function should have the array and the number of elements in the array as arguments and should return the index of the found value in the array or a special code if the item is not in the array.

Write a C function that reads a sorted file, loads the strings in the file into a ragged array, and then prompts the user for a value to be searched for. It should output the index of the found string or a message stating that the string is not in the array. The input file should have the number of strings in the file as its first line and then each string on a separate line.

6-15. Write a function that has as input a binary search tree and which returns another binary search tree with the same records but is balanced. Make sure that your function has a way to report problems such as a failure to allocate needed memory through some sort of error flag. Write a `main()` function that creates an unbalanced tree, uses the rebalancing function to create a new tree, and then outputs the contents of the rebalanced tree.

6-16. It is often useful to organize data so that more than one binary search tree is represented. Consider, for example, data organized as nodes on two distinct trees, where each node is a `struct` that has the following members:

- An `int`
- A `double`
- A character string
- Pointers to the left and right subtrees of a binary search tree in which the `int` is the key value

- Pointers to the left and right subtrees of a binary search tree in which the **double** is the key value

  Do the following:

  (a) Write a C function that starts with an array of such **struct**s where the pointers are all initially set to **NULL** and which sets the pointers so that it creates two binary search trees. This function will have as its arguments the initial array of **struct**s, the number of elements in that array, and two pointers to binary search trees. The function should set the values of these last two arguments to the roots of the two binary search trees it creates. It should not return a value.

  (b) Write a C function that traverses either of the two trees in descending order of the key. This function should have as arguments the tree being traversed and an integer code indicating which member of the **struct** (the **int** or the **double**) is the basis for the traversal. It should output the elements of the tree in the order they are visited in the traversal.

  (c) Write a **main()** function that reads a set of data you invent from a file into the initial array, calls the tree creation function, and outputs the elements in each of the two trees in order.

6-17. Another approach to deleting entries in binary search trees is called *lazy deletion*, where deleted nodes are kept in the tree but marked as unused with some special code. For example, the key for deleted nodes might be set to some special value which is known not to occur in the real data. Alternatively, the **struct** used to store the node could have a separate variable that is set to TRUE or FALSE depending on whether the node had been "lazy deleted."

Modify the binary search tree functions for node addition, searching, and deletion so that lazy deletion is used. Assume that a special value, established in a **#define** statement, for the key can be used to mark deleted nodes.

6-18. A *3-tree* is a ternary search tree where each node has two keys and as many as three children. In each node, all items on the left subtree are less than the first key, all items on the middle subtree are between the two keys, and all items on the right subtree are greater than the second key. Figure 6.10 illustrates a possible 3-tree.

Write a C function that searches a 3-tree that contains integer keys. Write a **main()** function that tests your 3-tree search using the tree in Figure 6.10. Try test cases where the item being searched for is the root node, a leaf node, a nonleaf node, and where it is not in the tree.

6-19. An alternative to binary search trees uses values of the keys directly to determine which branch of a tree to follow. For example, if the keys are three-digit integers, we could use the last digit to determine which branch from the root to search in a 10-ary (10 branches per node) tree. The second digit would be used at the next level and the third digit for the following level. This is called *radix searching*. This type of search is efficient when the keys have a well-defined structure such as for part numbers in a catalog.

Implement a set of functions that create and manage a radix search tree for three-digit integers. Make sure you think through the appropriate **struct** to use for each node in the tree. You should create a function that adds new three-digit values to the tree as well as one that searches for values. Write a **main()** function that creates a new tree, loads some values into it from a file, prompts the user for some value to be searched for, and reports whether or not that value is in the file.

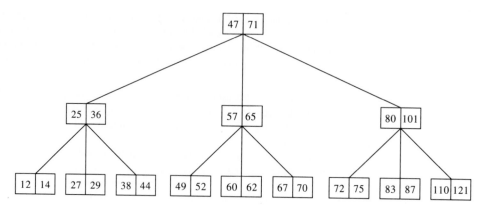

Figure 6.10 3-tree with integer keys.

6-20. Suppose that we have a hash table for integer keys and use linear probing to resolve collisions. Assume that the table has a maximum of 11 entries and that the hash function is $h(k) = k\%11$.

  (a) Write a C function that places x randomly drawn integer keys into the hash table. You can use the standard C library function **rand()** introduced in Section 2.9 to generate a random integer. (The function prototype for **rand()** is in the header file **stdlib.h**.)

  (b) Write a C function that searches the hash table for 1000 randomly drawn keys and determines the average number of hash table entries that need to be examined per search.

  (c) Write a **main()** function that outputs the average number of hash table entries examined per search when there are 2, 4, 6, 8, and 10 entries in the table. Use 1000 randomly drawn numbers in each case.

  Plot your results with the number of entries in the hash table on the horizontal axis and the average number of entries examined per search on the vertical axis.

6-21. Extend the linear probing implementation in Section 6.6.2 to handle deletion of entries. You should modify the hash table searching function and create a new function for deletion of hash table entries. You should indicate deleted entries by setting the hash table entry of the deleted item to the address of the hash table itself. (This is guaranteed to be a non-**NULL** pointer which cannot be a pointer to a valid data item that is in the hash table.) Write a C function that will add a new entry to the hash table so that the deleted items will be reused.

6-22. Reimplement the hash table search functions that use linear probing (see Section 6.6.2) so that the hash table can grow by a fixed amount when the hash table gets full. You should design the function that creates the initial hash table so that the hash table is a **struct** which contains the size of the table, the growth increment, and the array of pointers that is the table itself. The function that creates the initial hash table should be written to create this **struct**. Write a **main()** function that tests this revised hashing implementation making sure that you test its ability to increase the size of the hash table as needed. [Hint: You will need to use the C library function **realloc()** in solving this exercise.]

6-23. Suppose that you have an engineering database containing the part descriptions for the components of an automobile engine. Each part has a unique identification number (an

integer), a name (a character string), and a cost (represented as a floating-point value). This information is in a file, where each line of the file has the values associated with a single part. Engineers using this database will want to be able to retrieve the complete record for a part by either part number or name. Write a C program that has the following components:

- A function that prompts the user for the part he or she is looking for. This function should read in the requested part as a character string and determine if it is a part number or a part name by checking the first character and determining if it is a number or character.
- A function which opens the file containing the part list and reads the values in the database into a linked list. Each item in the list should be a **struct** that you define.
- A function which creates two hash tables from the linked list. These hash tables should use linear probing. One table should use the part number as the key value and the other should use the part name.
- A function that uses the hash tables to retrieve the complete part description given either the part number or name. This function should return a pointer to the **struct** that contains the part information.
- A **main()** function that uses all the other functions to provide the user with a general part searching program.

You may need to write other functions (such as hash functions) as part of your complete program.

CHAPTER

7

GRAPHICS

7.1 INTRODUCTION

One of the most significant problems in making effective use of computation for problem solving is that computers and their human users deal with information in entirely different ways. Humans process information most effectively in visual form, while computers operate directly on individual bits of data. Computer graphics try to bridge the gap between computers and their users by structuring information visually, allowing users to interact with information in ways that make better use of humans' visual processing capabilities.

Computer graphics is a vast and rapidly growing area, and no single chapter in an introductory textbook could possibly introduce all the important concepts and methods. For this reason, the treatment of computer graphics in this chapter is intentionally selective. We focus on the most important areas of computer graphics and present some of the more interesting algorithms.

We begin with a discussion of graphics devices. Although graphics devices were originally peripherals that were added on to existing computers, they are now standard parts of most of the personal computers and virtually all of the engineering workstations now on the market. Many computers come equipped with both a graphics display and some form of graphical input device, usually a mouse.

The distinctions among types of graphics devices determine why particular algorithms are used. In particular, we distinguish between graphics displays that operate on line segments (or vectors), and those in which the display consists of small squares called *pixels* (for picture elements). Displays that work with pixels are called *raster devices*.

After introducing graphics hardware, we describe some low-level graphics algorithms. These are methods which work in what is called *device coordinates*, the coordinate system of the graphics device itself. For example, in Section 7.3 we consider seemingly simple problems such as drawing a straight line segment between two points or a circle on a raster device.

We then turn to representation of graphical information in more general coordinate systems. Techniques used to transform objects drawn in one coordinate system to another are discussed. These coordinate transformations are used extensively in virtually all graphics software, such as drawing programs and computer-aided design systems. The ability to transform graphical objects from one coordinate system to another is so important that manufacturers of high-performance computer graphics hardware often build the algorithms for coordinate transformation into their products' hardware. We introduce the key methods used in coordinate transformations in two dimensions, and then extend the results to three-dimensional coordinate systems.

In the following section we develop methods to represent curves in two-dimensional space. We introduce the concept of *parametric functions* where both the x and y values of a function are themselves functions of a single variable. This form makes computing points on the function and many other geometric relationships straightforward.

The last topic covered in the chapter deals with *geometric algorithms*. This includes seemingly simple problems such as finding whether two line segments intersect, determining whether some point is inside or outside a closed polygon, and finding a subset of points which, when connected to make a polygon, enclose a larger set of points. One of the consistent themes in this section is that it is often quite difficult to write algorithms to do what humans can do almost without thinking.

7.2 GRAPHICS DEVICES AND TERMINOLOGY

One of the striking characteristics of graphics devices is the range of designs and capabilities that manufacturers offer. In this section we discuss some of the major categories of input and output graphics devices that are in use. Our goal is not to describe how the hardware actually works, but rather to give the reader a sense of the key features of different devices and the tradeoffs inherent in choosing among them.

7.2.1 Graphics Displays

We first consider graphics displays. Most of these devices use cathode ray tubes, or CRTs, in which a focused beam of electrons excites a phosphor, causing it to glow. More recently, liquid crystal, gas plasma, and light-emitting-diode technologies have

been used as alternatives to CRTs. All these devices share many properties, though their costs, performance, and other characteristics vary widely.

The earliest such graphics display were *storage tube* displays. In these early devices, once a line was drawn with an electron beam the phosphor remained excited for up to an hour. Lines could be erased only by applying a voltage to the entire display surface, erasing everything drawn on it. The inability to erase specific lines limited the usefulness of storage tubes, and they are no longer manufactured.

A second class of graphics device is a *refresh graphics* display. These devices use phosphors that emit light for only a short interval of time after they are excited by an electron beam. Lines and other figures drawn on such displays must be constantly refreshed at a rate of at least 30 times per second to avoid annoying flicker. These devices are also referred to as *calligraphic refresh graphic displays*, *vector refresh displays*, and *random scan displays*. They typically require a segment of memory, called the *display buffer*, in which all the information needed to refresh the entire screen is stored. For example, the display buffer might contain a list of vectors (line segments) which need to be redrawn in each refresh cycle. The graphics device constantly scans through the display buffer and redisplays the buffer's contents in each refresh cycle.

The advantage of refresh displays is that it is straightforward to change what appears on the screen. If you want to remove a vector from what appears on the display, you simply delete the vector from the display buffer. The next time the display hardware scans the display buffer, the deleted vector will not be drawn. This makes it possible to show the motion of objects on the screen.

The third type of display is called a *raster device*. These devices constitute the majority of the displays used on personal computers and virtually all displays used on engineering and scientific workstations. In a raster device, the entire usable surface of the display is divided into small rectangles call *pixels* (for picture elements). These rectangles are usually square, and each is a uniform color at any instant in time. In a simple monochrome display, each pixel is either light or dark.

The color displayed in each pixel is determined by the contents of an area of memory called the *frame buffer*. In a simple monochrome raster display, the frame buffer has one bit per pixel; this bit is typically set to 1 if the pixel is dark and 0 if it is light. Figure 7.1 shows the contents of a hypothetical frame buffer for a portion of a monochrome display and the corresponding pattern of pixels that would appear on the device.

What appears on a raster display is determined by the contents of the frame buffer. The display is constantly refreshed by scanning the display buffer and updating the pattern of pixels. This often requires that a special type of memory be used to allow the CPU of the computer to change values in the buffer while that memory is being scanned to update the display. As in the case of refresh displays, raster displays are generally updated completely at least 30 times per second. High-quality display may be updated much more frequently.

Because raster displays can only control the color of pixels, they cannot in general draw lines that are completely smooth. While vertical and horizontal lines drawn with pixels yield smooth lines, oblique line segments must be made up of patterns of squares

Portion of
frame buffer

Corresponding
portion of display

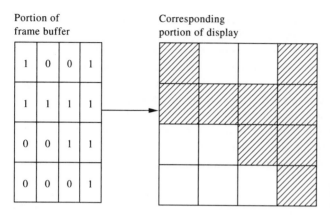

Figure 7.1 Frame buffer and raster display.

which best approximate a smooth line. This jagged appearance of line segments on a raster display is called *aliasing*. On a display in which all pixels are either light or dark, the extent to which any line segment will appear smooth depends on the density of pixels and the angle of the line. On more sophisticated displays, it is possible to use colors and shades of gray to improve the overall appearance of lines. This is referred to as *anti-aliasing*. We consider algorithms that render lines and other simple geometric figures on raster displays in Section 7.3.

7.2.2 Color Displays and Color Maps

Color displays generally use CRTs that have separate phosphors for red, green, and blue. These are often referred to as *RGB displays* (for "red, green, and blue"). Their frame buffers allocate one or more bits for each of these colors for each pixel. The total number of bits used to encode the colors of each pixel is called the *depth* of the display. The bits in a frame buffer can be viewed as organized into *planes*. A single plane can be thought of as an array of bits with the same number of rows and columns as the pixels on the display.

The value of the bits associated with each color determines the relative intensity with which the pixel will be "lit up" in that color. For example, a simple three-plane color display would have one bit for red, green, and blue associated with each pixel. If the bits for red and green are set to one and the bit for blue is set to zero, the pixel would appear to be yellow. With three bits, it is possible to construct eight distinct color combinations. Similarly, if the frame buffer allocates eight bits for the intensities of red, green, and blue per pixel, then a total of 2^{24} (or over 16 million) colors could be displayed. This is approximately the limit of the ability of the human eye to distinguish colors, and displays with frame buffers that have 24 or more planes are often referred to as providing *true color*. On a large format display that might have on the order of 1 million pixels, the frame buffer for such a display would require at least 24 million bits (or 3 million bytes) of memory.

Because frame buffer memory is expensive, many display manufacturers use considerably less than 24 bits per pixel. In order to avoid limiting their displays to showing only a subset of the full color spectrum, many of these displays use what is called a *color map*. The method used by a frame buffer with a color map is shown in Figure 7.2.

Suppose, for example, that only eight bits per pixel are available in the frame buffer. Rather than having each combination of these eight bits correspond to some fixed color, the eight bits can be used to create an integer index into another part of memory where the color map is stored. This color map holds $2^8 = 256$ distinct entries. Each entry in the color map describes a combination of red, green, and blue with enough accuracy to define a color uniquely. (This is usually 24 or 32 bits.) The display would be limited to showing only 256 colors at any one time. However, by changing the entries in the color map you can alter which 256 colors are shown.

The number of bits in each entry of the color map determines what is called the *palette* of the display, while the number of bits per pixel in the frame buffer determines the number of colors which can be *displayed simultaneously*.

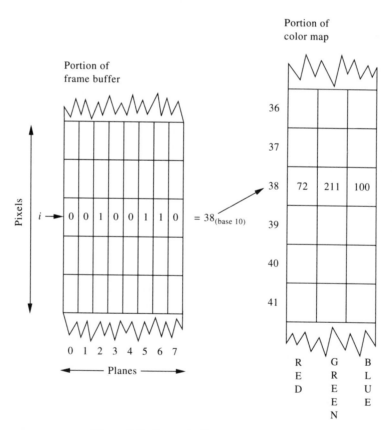

Figure 7.2 Frame buffer with color map.

7.2.3 Graphics Input Devices

Computer applications that use graphics often require input in some non-character based form. For example, a computer-aided drafting program generally allows the user to position objects drawn on the screen by selecting points on the screen with some form of input device other than a keyboard.

Computer input devices can be classified into the following five logical categories [Foley, James D. 90]:

- *Keyboard*—used for character-based input.
- *Locator*—a device with one or more buttons used to specify coordinates on the display screen.
- *Pick*—to select something displayed on the screen.
- *Valuator*—to input a single real number.
- *Choice*—to select among possible alternatives.

Most computer systems rely on keyboard and locator devices. Since the use of a keyboard is obvious, we discuss only locator devices here.

The most commonly available locator device is a *mouse*. The user moves the mouse along some horizontal surface. Sensors in the mouse detect the motion, transmit it to the computer, and cause a corresponding movement of a cursor on the output display. Points on the screen or graphical objects are selected by clicking one or more buttons on the mouse. There is no standard number of buttons on a mouse, though the vast majority have between one and five.

The *trackball* can be viewed as an upside-down mouse. The rotation of a ball is mapped to movements of the cursor. Trackballs often come with buttons, or in some cases, the trackball itself can be pressed to activate a button.

A mouse or trackball can only be used to indicate relative location. The movement of the cursor is activated by movement of the mouse or the trackball; the absolute position of the mouse or trackball at any point in time is unknown to the computer. In contrast, *data tablets* convey information about absolute locations. These devices usually consist of a special surface and a *stylus* or small *puck*. Electrical sensors determine the location of the stylus or puck on the tablet. The technologies used to sense this location vary quite widely.

A *joystick* is a shaft that can be moved both side to side and backward and forward. The direction the joystick is moved controls the movement of the cursor on the display. Joysticks can have buttons in their shafts to indicate selections.

Other, less frequently used locator devices include *lightpens* and *touch panels*. Both of these devices can be used to detect absolute locations. However, their precision is often quite limited, making them more useful for selecting among alternatives (i.e., as choice devices) than as locators.

7.2.4 Graphics Hard Copy Devices

Hard copy devices produce graphic images on paper, photographic film, transparencies, or other surfaces. The devices vary widely depending on the size of the image to be created, the level of detail that needs to be rendered, and whether they provide output in color. We consider here only a subset of the devices available.

Laser printers are raster output devices that provide relatively high resolution, typically at 300 or more dots per inch. These devices are widely used for both text and graphics. The basic technology used in laser printers closely parallels the xerographic processes used in photocopiers. As with photocopiers, most low- and moderate-priced laser printers are black and white only. However, the cost of full-color laser printers has been dropping steadily.

The key shortcoming of most laser printers is that they can produce graphic displays of relatively modest size. This is often inadequate for engineering and architectural drawings, where a great deal of detail must be displayed on large sheets of paper. *Plotters* of various types are typically used to produce such drawings.

Plotters range in size and complexity from low-cost versions capable of handling the same-size paper as laser printers to very large plotters capable of producing output tens of feet wide and long. These plotters often move a pen of some type along the surface of the paper, move the paper with respect to a fixed pen, or use some combination of both types of movement. They often have the capability to switch colors by mechanically exchanging the pens.

The movement of the pen and the paper is generally controlled by motors capable of small, fixed steps. In that sense, most plotters are raster devices. The minimum step size may be .001 inch or smaller, yielding much finer resolution than that of most laser printers.

Specialized plotters replace the pen with various cutting tools or other components. These devices can be used to cut fabrics (for sails or clothing) or to expose a photographic plate.

Other hard copy technologies include *ink jet printers*, *thermal plotters*, and *dot matrix printers*. Ink jet printers spray very small drops of ink on the printing surface. Full-color images can be created by blending different colors of ink. Thermal plotters use heat sensitive paper or use heat to transfer ink from a special ribbon to the paper. Dot matrix printers transfer ink from a ribbon by striking the ribbon against the paper with an array of small pins, much as ink is transferred from a ribbon on a typewriter. The number and pattern of the pins determine the resolution of the graphics.

7.3 GRAPHICS ALGORITHMS IN DEVICE COORDINATES

The first graphics algorithms we will study are methods for drawing simple geometric shapes on a raster display. We will assume that each pixel on the display is referenced by an (x, y) integer coordinate, starting with pixel $(0, 0)$ in the *upper left* corner of the display. This coordinate system, called *device coordinates*, is shown in Figure 7.3. Note that any given coordinate is *not* a point, but a square area on the display screen.

While this coordinate system is clearly different from the usual convention adopted for axes in the real plane, it is widely used to describe the location of pixels in raster graphics displays. We will assume that our pixels are all squares, and that any attempt

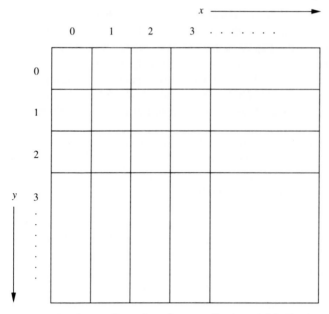

Figure 7.3 Device coordinates for a raster display.

to change the color of a coordinate outside the boundaries of the display will simply be ignored by the graphics hardware.

We begin with the simple problem of drawing a line segment (or what is termed a *vector* in the graphics literature) on a display which has only two colors, black and white. We assume that all the pixels on the portion of the display we are plotting on are initially all one color, called the background color. Our algorithm will draw the vector in the other color (called the foreground).

Because graphics hardware varies so widely, there is no C language standard for performing graphics. Different raster graphics systems use completely different ways to control the contents of their respective frame buffers. Rather than present algorithms intended for any particular machine, we will assume that there exists a function called **plot_pixel()** that has as its arguments the x and y coordinates of the pixel that will be "painted" in the foreground color. We assume that someone else has implemented this function for the computer on which we are working and provided it to us. This will enable us to write our graphics algorithms in a machine-independent way.

The prototype for **plot_pixel()** is

```
void plot_pixel(int, int);
```

where the first integer argument is the x coordinate of the pixel to be painted in the foreground color, and the second integer is the pixel's y coordinate.

7.3.1 Bresenham's Algorithm for Vector Drawing: Restricted Case

The algorithm we present will select the pixels to be painted in the foreground color to best approximate a line segment between some starting pixel (x_1, y_1) and an ending pixel (x_2, y_2). The method we show is called Bresenham's algorithm. While it was originally developed to control plotters, it is now widely used in raster displays.

The easiest way to present Bresenham's algorithm is to begin with the special case where the slope of the line is between 0 and 1 and where $x_1 < x_2$. An example of coordinates that satisfy these conditions is shown in Figure 7.4. The straight line connecting the centers of pixels (x_1, y_1) and (x_2, y_2) would be the "true" line segment in a vector display. The problem Bresenham's algorithm solves is finding which pixels best approximate that ideal line.

Bresenham's algorithm begins by "painting" the pixel (x_1, y_1). Since the line segment has slope less than 1, we know that the pixel $(x_1, y_1 + 1)$ cannot be part of the set of pixels that best approximate the true line. Moreover, if we increment x_1 by 1, there are only *two* possible candidates for which pixel should be colored. Either the point $(x_1 + 1, y_1)$ or $(x_1 + 1, y_1 + 1)$ should be part of the approximating vector.

We select which of these two candidates to color by finding the one closest to the true line segment. To derive an appropriate measure of the error for each candidate point, we define

$$\Delta x = x_2 - x_1$$
$$\Delta y = y_2 - y_1$$

Any point on the "ideal" line segment must satisfy

$$\frac{x - x_1}{y - y_1} = \frac{\Delta x}{\Delta y}$$

or, put in another form, the "ideal" line should satisfy

$$(x - x_1)\Delta y - (y - y_1)\Delta x = 0$$

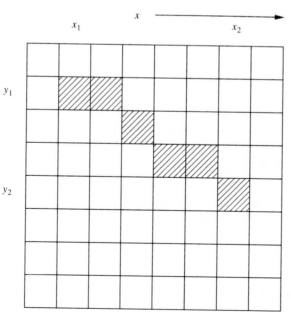

Figure 7.4 Drawing a line in device coordinates.

Because we are restricted to only integer values of x and y, the pixels we paint for the line will in general not satisfy the last equation above. We can use the amount by which $(x - x_1)\Delta y - (y - y_1)\Delta x$ differs from zero as a measure of the error associated with using any pixel (x, y) as part of the segment. Using this measure, we can compare the two candidates $(x_1 + 1, y_1)$ and $(x_1 + 1, y_1 + 1)$ to determine which results in the smaller error.

The point $(x_1 + 1, y_1)$ will be either on the line or "above" it. The amount of the error for this point is

$$\text{error}_y = (x_1 + 1 - x_1)\Delta y - (y_1 - y_1)\Delta x = \Delta y$$

Since Δy is greater than or equal to zero, the value of error_y will always be nonnegative. Stated another way, the point $(x_1 + 1, y_1)$ will always be on the ideal line or above it. (Recall that in the device coordinates the value of y *increases* as we move from the top of the screen to the bottom.) By a similar argument, the point $(x_1 + 1, y_1 + 1)$ will either be on the line or below it. The amount of error for this point is always nonpositive and is given by

$$\text{error}_{y+1} = (x_1 + 1 - x_1)\Delta y - (y_1 + 1 - y_1)\Delta x = \Delta y - \Delta x$$

The difference between these two errors is simply Δx. Thus, if the point $(x_1 + 1, y_1)$ produces an error smaller than $\Delta x/2$, then it must be the correct pixel to be plotted. If the error for $(x_1 + 1, y_1)$ produces an error which exceeds $\Delta x/2$, then the correct point to be plotted is $(x_1 + 1, y_1 + 1)$.

This basic idea of selecting between two candidate points on the basis of their error measures can be used for finding the appropriate pixel for $x_1 + 2$, $x_1 + 3$, $\ldots$, x_2. At each step we check if the error associated with not incrementing y by one is smaller than $\Delta x/2$. If it is smaller than $\Delta x/2$, we do not increment y; otherwise, we increment y.

The implementation of this limited form of Bresenham's algorithm in C is surprisingly simple and computationally efficient. The   function below   named **bresenham_special()** shows the C code.

```
/* Bresenham's line drawing algorithm for special
      case where slope is <= 1 and x1 < x2 */

void bresenham_special(
   int x1,   /* x coordinate of first pixel */
   int y1,   /* y coordinate of first pixel */
   int x2,   /* x coordinate of second pixel */
   int y2)   /* y coordinate of second pixel */
{
   int error = 0;          /* accumulated error */
   int deltay = y2-y1;   /* delta y */
   int deltax = x2-x1;   /* delta x */
   int criterion = deltax/2;
```

```
/* loop through all values of x from x1 to x2 */
  while(x1 <= x2) {
        plot_pixel(x1,y1);
        x1++;
        error = error + deltay; /* compute error if */
        if(error > criterion) { /* y isn't incremented*/
                error = error - deltax;
                y1++;
                }
        }
}
```

Note that the value of the variable `criterion` in our implementation is defined as an **int**. When **deltax** is odd, the value computed for `criterion` in the initialization

```
int criterion = deltax/2;
```

will be truncated to the nearest integer *less than* **deltax/2**. This is why the check as to whether to elect the candidate pixel with y incremented is a strict inequality in the statement

```
if(error > criterion) {
```

For example, if **deltax** were 5, then `criterion` would be 2. We increment **y1** when **error** is any integer greater than 2, but not when it equals 2.

The implementation also assumes that the points (x_1, y_1) and (x_2, y_2) are valid pixel coordinates. A more complete, robust implementation would check this before attempting to render the line.

7.3.2 Bresenham's Algorithm for General Line Segments

In the preceding subsection we developed Bresenham's algorithm for a restricted class of vectors. Here we extend that result to deal with any line segment.

First consider cases where $x_1 \geq x_2$. In this situation, we can adapt the logic of the restricted version of Bresenham's algorithm by *decrementing* x_1 rather than incrementing it. We could alternatively just exchange the points (x_1, y_1) and (x_2, y_2).

A second case is where the slope of the line is between 0 and -1. We can adapt our restricted implementation to handle this situation by checking whether or not to *decrement* y at each step of the algorithm rather than checking whether to increment it.

Dealing with cases where the absolute value of the slope of the line segment exceeds 1 is only slightly more difficult. In this case we need to reverse the roles of the x and y coordinates in the restricted version of the algorithm. Rather than incrementing x at each step and checking whether we need to increment y, we instead increment along the y axis and check whether x needs to be incremented.

With these three minor changes, the algorithm generalizes straightforwardly to deal with any line segment. The algorithm first determines whether steps along the x and y axes should be increments or decrements. It then checks the slope of the line to determine whether it should always increment x (if the absolute value of the slope is less than or equal to 1) or always increment on y (if the absolute value of the slope exceeds 1). Each of these two cases results in a separate **while** loop.

The C code for the function **bresenham()** follows.

```
/* general version of Bresenham's
   algorithm for line  drawing */

void bresenham(
   int x1,  /* x coordinate of first pixel */
   int y1,  /* y coordinate of first pixel */
   int x2,  /* x coordinate of second pixel */
   int y2)  /* y coordinate of second pixel */
{
   int error, criterion, deltax, deltay, xstep, ystep;

   error = 0;
   deltax = x2 - x1;

/*  determine whether steps on x axis should
                 be increments or decrements */
   if(deltax < 0) {
        deltax = -deltax;
        xstep = -1;
        }
   else
        xstep = 1;

/*  determine whether steps on y axis should
                 be increments or decrements */
   deltay = y2 - y1;
   if(deltay < 0) {
        deltay = -deltay;
        ystep = -1;
        }
   else
        ystep = 1;

/* handle case where magnitude of slope <= 1    */
   if(deltay <= deltax) {
        criterion = deltax/2;
        while (x1 != x2+xstep) {
          plot_pixel(x1,y1);
          x1 += xstep;
```

```
            error += deltay;
            if(error > criterion) {
              error -= deltax;
              y1 += ystep;
            }
        }
      }
   /* handle case where magnitude of slope > 1 */
   else {
           criterion = deltay/2;
           while(y1 != y2 + ystep) {
           plot_pixel(x1,y1);
           y1 += ystep;
           error += deltax;
           if(error > criterion) {
               error -= deltay;
               x1 += xstep;
           }
       }
     }
}
```

One interesting aspect of Bresenham's algorithm is that it does not use any floating-point arithmetic. Moreover, there are no integer multiplications, and only one integer division for any given vector.[1] Given that most computers can perform integer addition and subtraction much faster than any floating-point operations, Bresenham's algorithm tends to execute very quickly. A further speedup can often be achieved by using **short int**s for all values because pixel coordinates can almost always be stored in a C variable of this type.

7.3.3 Bresenham's Algorithm for Circles

The basic concept used in Bresenham's algorithms can be generalized to draw other simple, two-dimensional geometric shapes in device coordinates. For example, suppose that we wanted to draw a circle centered at some pixel coordinate (x_c, y_c) with radius r. We assume that r is measured in pixels and is therefore an integer value.

Because circles are symmetric around their center, we can simplify the drawing problem by constructing an eighth of the circle, relying on symmetry to select the appropriate pixels for the other seven-eighths. Figure 7.5 shows the complete circle we will construct.

---

[1]Note that the division by 2 can be eliminated on most computers by right-shifting the bits in the integer value being halved.

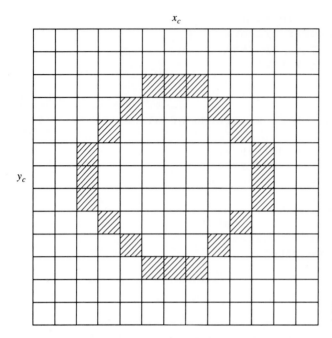

Figure 7.5 Drawing a circle in device coordinates.

Our algorithm computes the pixels on the circle as though the circle is centered at the pixel (0,0). We will then translate each pixel to be plotted by an amount (x_c, y_c). This will simplify the derivation of the best pixel to be plotted.

Since the equation of a circle centered a (0,0) is

$$x^2 + y^2 = r^2$$

we can measure the error associated with using any pixel (x, y) as

$$\text{error}(x, y) = x^2 + y^2 - r^2$$

Suppose that we have just plotted pixel (x, y) as part of drawing the circle. The *next* pixel will either be at coordinate $(x, y + 1)$ or $(x - 1, y + 1)$. These two candidate points have the following respective errors:

$$\text{error}(x, y + 1) = x^2 + y^2 + 2y + 1 - r^2$$
$$\text{error}(x - 1, y + 1) = x^2 - 2x + 1 + y^2 + 2y + 1 - r^2$$

These errors always differ by $2x - 1$. Thus, we need only compute the error associated with plotting $(x, y + 1)$ and check if it is less than x. If so, then $(x, y + 1)$ should be plotted; otherwise, $(x - 1, y + 1)$ should be plotted.

The algorithm begins at the point $(r, 0)$. This pixel is known to lie on the circle, so the accumulated error starts at zero. After we plot the pixel $(r, 0)$ [appropriately translated to (x_c, y_c)], we increment y by 1. The two possible candidates for the next pixel to be plotted are $(r, 1)$ and $(r - 1, 1)$. If the first of these candidates has error less than x, we plot it (appropriately translated) and add its error to the accumulated total. If the point $(r, 1)$ produces an incremental error greater than x, we plot the second candidate and add its error to the accumulated total.

This process of incrementing y and checking if x should be decremented is used at each step to solve for all the pixels in the first octant of the circle. The complete circle is drawn by plotting symmetric points in each of the seven other octants as the algorithm executes.

The implementation of this algorithm in C is as follows:

```c
void pixel_circle(
   int xc,   /* x coordinate of center of circle */
   int yc,   /* y coordinate of center of circle */
   int r)    /* radius of circle

{
/* initialize variables at point (r,0)   */
   int x = r;
   int y = 0;
   int error = 0;

   int sqrx_inc = 2*r -1;
   int sqry_inc = 1;

/* loop through first octant of circle */

   while(y <= x) {

      plot_pixel(xc+x,yc+y);    /* plot points in */
      plot_pixel(xc+x,yc-y);    /*   in each      */
      plot_pixel(xc-x,yc+y);    /*     octant     */
      plot_pixel(xc-x,yc-y);
      plot_pixel(xc+y,yc+x);
      plot_pixel(xc+y,yc-x);
      plot_pixel(xc-y,yc+x);
      plot_pixel(xc-y,yc-x);

      y++;
      error += sqry_inc;
      sqry_inc = sqry_inc + 2;
      if(error > x) {
         x--;
         error -= sqrx_inc;
         sqrx_inc -= 2;
      }
   }
}
```

The implementation of `pixel_circle()` exploits the fact that the values of $2y + 1$ can be computed at each point in the first octant of the circle by initializing an integer to 1 and increasing the value by 2 each time y is incremented. Similarly, the values of $2x - 1$ can be computed by starting at $2r - 1$ and decrementing this value by 2 each time x is decremented. This saves a multiplication operation for each time x or y is changed.

7.4 COORDINATE TRANSFORMATIONS IN TWO DIMENSIONS

Many software packages that rely on graphics must be able to move items drawn on the screen quickly. For example, computer-aided drafting systems often allow the user to enlarge or contract elements of a drawing by selecting them with a mouse and "dragging" one part of the drawn item to a new position on the screen. The software must be capable of redrawing the object fast enough so that the illusion of dragging it across the screen is sustained. Similarly, many computer systems such as the Apple Macintosh allow the user to reposition rectangular areas (called *windows*) from one position on the screen to another.[2]

In this section we discuss algorithms for moving objects on a graphics display. We focus entirely on transformations in two dimensions. The extension of the methods we develop to three dimensions is discussed in Section 7.6.

The coordinate transformations we consider in this section are:

- *Translation*—relocation of each point (x, y) to some other point $(x + T_x, y + T_y)$.
- *Scaling*—corresponds to stretching or contracting the x and y axes by factors S_x and S_y, respectively.
- *Rotation around the origin*—moving each point (x, y) some angle θ around the origin.

These three basic operations can be used in combination to create still more complex transformations. For example, to rotate something around a point (x_r, y_r) other than the origin, you can first translate the object so that (x_r, y_r) is moved to the origin, do the rotation, and then translate the object back to its original position.

7.4.1 Coordinate Systems

Moving or resizing objects drawn on a graphics display from one place on a screen to another requires transforming the coordinates of objects from one frame of reference to another. In this section we develop algorithms that work in what is called *world coordinates*. By this we mean that the coordinates we will operate with are not tied to any particular hardware, but are instead the "natural" coordinates for the problem at hand. We will assume that the underlying graphics software handles the translation from these world coordinates to the device coordinates of the graphics hardware.

[2]Macintosh is a trademark of Apple Computer, Inc.

This separation of function from an abstract, problem-specific coordinate system to a concrete, hardware-dependent one is quite common in graphics software. Graphics software systems often introduce still another coordinate system, called *normalized device coordinates*. In this coordinate system, the entire graphics screen is represented as being 1 unit long on both the *x* and *y* axes. For example, a pixel that is in the middle of the screen would correspond to the normalized device coordinate (.5, .5).

Writing software in world or normalized device coordinates enables us to analyze coordinate transformations using real values instead of integers. It also makes it possible to develop algorithms that are independent of any particular graphics hardware. However, the reader should be aware that world and normalized device coordinate systems are always mapped to the device coordinates by some layer of software. This software layer is often provided as part of the graphics system.

7.4.2 Translation

Translation is the simplest case. We define any point *P* as the coordinate position (x, y) and consider the translation of *P* by an amount $T = (T_x, T_y)$. The new point, called P', is given by the vector $P' = T + P$. For example, if *P* is originally the point (2,3) and we translate it by 1 unit along the *x* axis and 2 units along the *y* axis, then $T = (1,2)$, and $P' = P + T = (2,3) + (1,2) = (3,5)$.

Figure 7.6 illustrates the translation of a simple five-sided polygon. Each vertex of the original polygon is a point in (x, y) coordinates. Figure 7.6a shows the polygon before it is translated. Figure 7.6b shows the polygon after it is translated by 2 units along the *x* axis and 3 units along the *y* axis. The translated polygon is found by adding

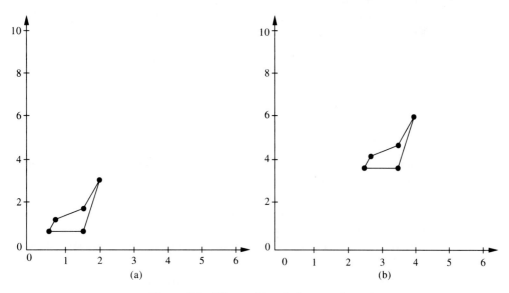

Figure 7.6   Effects of translation transformation.

the vector (2,3) to each vertex of the original polygon, and redrawing the line segments that connected the vertices.

7.4.3 Scaling

Rescaling the x and y axes is also straightforward. Suppose that we wish to rescale the x axis by some amount S_x and the y axis by some amount S_y. Any point $P = (x, y)$ would be transformed to a new point $P' = (xS_x, yS_y)$.

For reasons that will be become clearer later, it is convenient to be able to express the scaling operation as the result of multiplying a vector representing P by a matrix representing the transformation. (See Section 4.7 for a description of an algorithm to multiply a vector by a matrix.) To do this, we will define the matrix S as follows:

$$\mathbf{S} = \begin{pmatrix} S_x & 0 \\ 0 & S_y \end{pmatrix}$$

In this notation, the scaling of a point can be written as $P' = P\mathbf{S}$.

As an example, consider rescaling the point (2,3) by 2 along the x axis and .5 along the y axis. The rescaled point would be

$$P' = (2, 3) \begin{pmatrix} 2 & 0 \\ 0 & .5 \end{pmatrix} = (4, 1.5)$$

Scaling the axes by equal amounts corresponds to the case where $S_x = S_y = k$. This is called *uniform scaling*. After a uniform scaling, any line segment between two points will be k times longer than it was in the original coordinate system.

If $S_x > S_y$, then objects in the transformed coordinates will appear more squat in the new coordinates. Conversely, if $S_x < S_y$, transformed objects will appear thinner in the new coordinates. Both these cases are called *differential scaling*.

Figure 7.7 illustrates the effects of scaling a polygon three different amounts. Figure 7.7a shows the original figure. Figure 7.7b shows the same polygon after a uniform scaling by 2. Figure 7.7c and d show the effects of scaling when $S_x > S_y$ and $S_x < S_y$, respectively.

7.4.4 Rotation Around the Origin

The third coordinate transformation requires rotating any point (x, y) around the origin by some angle θ. The effects of this rotation are easiest to derive in polar coordinates. The point (x, y) can be written as $(r \cos \alpha, r \sin \alpha)$, where r is the length of the vector from the origin to (x, y), and α is the angle between the vector and the x axis. Figure 7.8 shows the geometry of this transformation.

If we rotate the point $(r \cos \alpha, r \sin \alpha)$ by some angle θ, the coordinates of the new point $P' = (x', y')$ are given by the following equations:

$$x' = r \cos(\alpha + \theta) = r \cos(\alpha) \cos(\theta) - r \sin(\alpha) \sin(\theta)$$

$$y' = r \sin(\alpha + \theta) = r \cos(\alpha) \sin(\theta) + r \sin(\alpha) \cos(\theta)$$

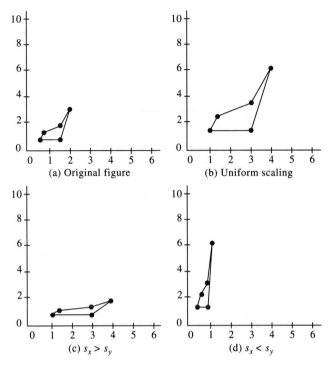

(a) Original figure

(b) Uniform scaling

(c) $s_x > s_y$

(d) $s_x < s_y$

Figure 7.7 Effects of scaling transformation.

If we now substitute $x = r \cos(\alpha)$ and $y = r \sin(\alpha)$ into the equations above, we obtain

$$x' = x \cos(\theta) - y \sin(\theta)$$

$$y' = x \sin(\theta) + y \cos(\theta)$$

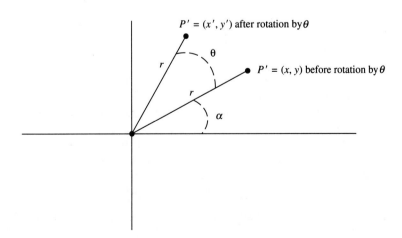

$P' = (x', y')$ after rotation by θ

$P' = (x, y)$ before rotation by θ

Figure 7.8 Geometry of rotation around the origin.

This transformation can also be expressed in matrix form. Define the matrix **R** as

$$\mathbf{R} = \begin{pmatrix} \cos(\theta) & \sin(\theta) \\ -\sin(\theta) & \cos(\theta) \end{pmatrix}$$

In this notation, the rotation of a point around the origin can be written as $P' = P\mathbf{R}$.

To illustrate how rotation around the origin works, consider a point $P = (2,3)$. Suppose that we rotate this point by 30 degrees ($\pi/6$ radians). The matrix **R** for this rotation is

$$\mathbf{R} = \begin{pmatrix} .86603 & .50000 \\ -.50000 & .86603 \end{pmatrix}$$

The new point $P' = P\mathbf{R}$ is

$$P = P\mathbf{R} = (2, 3) \begin{pmatrix} .86603 & .50000 \\ -.50000 & .86603 \end{pmatrix} = (.23206, 3.59809)$$

Figure 7.9 shows the effects of rotating an entire polygon around the origin by 30 degrees. As with the earlier transformations, the rotation of the entire object can be achieved by rotating the vertices and connecting them with line segments.

7.4.5 General Transformations

The three basic operations of translation, scaling, and rotation about the origin can be combined to produce still more complicated coordinate transformations. Consider a situation where we want to rotate the polygon used in the earlier examples by 60 degrees around the point (1,1), scale the x axis by 2 and the y axis by .5, and translate

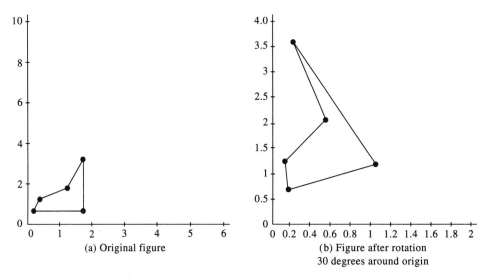

(a) Original figure

(b) Figure after rotation
30 degrees around origin

Figure 7.9   Rotation of polygon around the origin.

the polygon by -2 in the x direction and -1 in the y direction. These steps can be accomplished by relocating each vertex as follows:

1. Translate the point P so that $(1,1)$ is the origin of a transformed coordinate system by adding the vector $T_0 = (-1, -1)$. The new point is $P' = P + T_0$.
2. Rotate the point 60 degrees around the origin by multiplying it by the matrix

$$\mathbf{R} = \begin{pmatrix} \cos(60) & \sin(60) \\ -\sin(60) & \cos(60) \end{pmatrix} = \begin{pmatrix} .50000 & .86603 \\ -.86603 & .50000 \end{pmatrix}$$

The new point is $P' = (P + T_0)\mathbf{R}$.
3. Translate the point back to the original coordinate system by subtracting the vector T_0. The new point is $P' = (P + T_0)\mathbf{R} - T_0$.
4. Scale the x axis by 2 and the y axis by .5 by multiplying the point by the scaling matrix

$$\mathbf{S} = \begin{pmatrix} 2 & 0 \\ 0 & .5 \end{pmatrix}$$

The new point is $P' = ((P + T_0)\mathbf{R} - T_0)\mathbf{S}$.
5. Translate the point by the vector $T_1 = (-2, -1)$. The new point is $P' = (((P + T_0)\mathbf{R} - T_0)\mathbf{S}) + T_1$.

Consider the application of these steps to the point $(2,3)$. Applying each of the steps in turn results in the following sequence of transformations:

1. Translate the point $(2,3)$ so that $(1,1)$ is the origin by adding the vector $T_0 = (-1, -1)$. The new point is $P' = (1,2)$.
2. Rotate the point 60 degrees around the origin by multiplying it by the matrix $\mathbf{R}$ given above. The new point is $P' = (-1.23206, 1.86603)$.

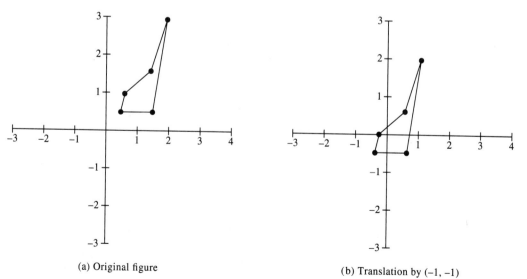

(a) Original figure   (b) Translation by $(-1, -1)$

Figure 7.10   Results of multistep transformation.

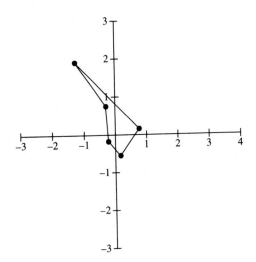

(c) Rotation 60 degrees around origin

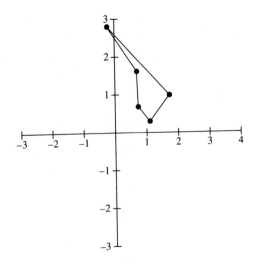

(d) Translation by (1, 1)

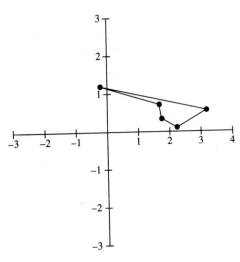

(e) Scaling by (2, .5)

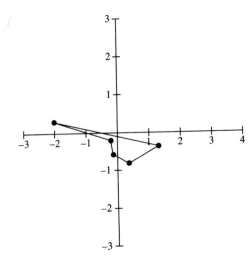

(f) Translation by (−2, −1)

Figure 7.10   (continued)

3. Translate the point back to the original coordinate system by subtracting the vector $T_0 = (-1, -1)$. The new point is $P' = (-.23206, 2.86603)$.
4. Scale the x axis by 2 and the y axis by .5 by multiplying the point by the scaling matrix S given above. The new point is $P' = (-.46412, 1.43302)$.
5. Translate the point by the vector $T_1 = (-2, -1)$. The new point is $P' = (-2.46412, .43302)$.

Figure 7.10 shows the results of these transformation on the original polygon used in our earlier examples. Each vertex has been transformed through the steps above, and the resulting transformed vertices have been connected with line segments.

7.5 HOMOGENEOUS COORDINATES IN TWO DIMENSIONS

The example of the complicated transformation given in Section 7.4 illustrates a subtle shortcoming of our method for coordinate transformation. Because translation is an *additive* vector operation, while scaling and rotation are the result of multiplying a vector by a matrix, the steps in a complicated transformation have to be repeated for each point in any geometric figure. It would be far simpler if the steps were either all additive or all multiplicative. In this case, all the transformation steps could be reduced to a single operation that was the sum or product of each of the original steps. In this section we show how this goal can be achieved.

The approach uses what are called *homogeneous coordinates*. In this coordinate system, each point (x, y) in two dimensions is represented by *three* elements in homogeneous coordinates: the original x and y, and an additional, arbitrary constant which we shall choose to be 1. Thus, in homogeneous coordinates, a point (x, y) is represented by the triple $(x, y, 1)$.

The addition of a third coordinate makes it possible to express translation, scaling, and rotation about the origin all as matrix multiplications. For example, to translate a point $P = (x, y, 1)$ by amounts T_x along the x axis and T_y on the y axis, you simply multiply the point's representation in homogeneous coordinates by the matrix

$$\mathbf{T} = \begin{pmatrix} 1 & 0 & 0 \\ 0 & 1 & 0 \\ T_x & T_y & 1 \end{pmatrix}$$

A new point $P' = P\mathbf{T}$ would be the product of $(x, y, 1)$ and $\mathbf{T}$, or $(x + T_x, y + T_y, 1)$.

For example, if we want to translate the point (2,3) by 1 unit on the x axis and 2 units on the y axis, we would compute the product

$$(2, 3, 1) \begin{pmatrix} 1 & 0 & 0 \\ 0 & 1 & 0 \\ 1 & 2 & 1 \end{pmatrix} = (3, 5, 1)$$

Similarly, scaling a point by S_x and S_y can be achieved by multiplying the point in homogeneous coordinates by the matrix $\mathbf{S}$ defined as

$$\mathbf{S} = \begin{pmatrix} S_x & 0 & 0 \\ 0 & S_y & 0 \\ 0 & 0 & 1 \end{pmatrix}$$

For example, to scale the point (2,3) by $S_x = 2$ and $S_y = .5$, we would compute the product

$$(2, 3, 1) \begin{pmatrix} 2 & 0 & 0 \\ 0 & .5 & 0 \\ 0 & 0 & 1 \end{pmatrix} = (4, 1.5, 1)$$

Finally, the rotation of a point in homogeneous coordinates by some angle θ can be achieved by multiplying the point by the matrix $\mathbf{R}$ defined as

$$\mathbf{R} = \begin{pmatrix} \cos(\theta) & \sin(\theta) & 0 \\ -\sin(\theta) & \cos(\theta) & 0 \\ 0 & 0 & 1 \end{pmatrix}$$

For example, a rotation around the origin of the point (2,3) by 30 degrees would be computed as

$$(2, 3, 1) \begin{pmatrix} .86603 & .50000 & 0 \\ -.50000 & .86603 & 0 \\ 0 & 0 & 1 \end{pmatrix} = (.23206, 3.59809, 1)$$

We illustrate how homogeneous coordinate systems make complicated transformations simpler by considering again the case of transforming the polygon by shifting its vertices. We will again rotate the polygon used in the earlier examples by 60 degrees around the point (1,1), scale the x axis by 2 and the y axis by .5, and translate the polygon by -2 in the x direction and -1 in the y direction. The steps are as follows:

1. Translate the point P so that (1,1) is the origin by multiplying it by the matrix

$$\mathbf{T_0} = \begin{pmatrix} 1 & 0 & 0 \\ 0 & 1 & 0 \\ -1 & -1 & 1 \end{pmatrix}$$

The new point is $P' = P\mathbf{T_0}$.

2. Rotate the point 60 degrees around the origin by multiplying it by the matrix

$$\mathbf{R} = \begin{pmatrix} \cos(60) & \sin(60) & 0 \\ -\sin(60) & \cos(60) & 0 \\ 0 & 0 & 1 \end{pmatrix}$$

$$= \begin{pmatrix} .50000 & .86603 & 0 \\ -.86603 & .50000 & 0 \\ 0 & 0 & 1 \end{pmatrix}$$

The new point is $P' = P\mathbf{T_0}\mathbf{R}$.

3. Translate the point back to the original coordinate system by multiplying it by the vector $\mathbf{T_1}$, defined as

$$\mathbf{T_1} = \begin{pmatrix} 1 & 0 & 0 \\ 0 & 1 & 0 \\ 1 & 1 & 1 \end{pmatrix}$$

The new point is $P' = P\mathbf{T_0}\mathbf{R}\mathbf{T_1}$.

4. Scale the x axis by 2 and the y axis by .5 by multiplying the point by the scaling matrix

$$\mathbf{S} = \begin{pmatrix} 2 & 0 & 0 \\ 0 & .5 & 0 \\ 0 & 0 & 1 \end{pmatrix}$$

The new point is $P' = P\mathbf{T_0}\mathbf{R}\mathbf{T_1}\mathbf{S}$.

5. Translate the point by the vector by multiplying it by the matrix $\mathbf{T}_2$ defined as

$$\mathbf{T}_2 = \begin{pmatrix} 1 & 0 & 0 \\ 0 & 1 & 0 \\ -2 & -1 & 1 \end{pmatrix}$$

The new point is $P' = P\mathbf{T}_0\mathbf{RT}_1\mathbf{ST}_2$.

The usefulness of the homogeneous coordinates becomes clearer when you note that the matrix product $\mathbf{M} = \mathbf{T}_0\mathbf{RT}_1\mathbf{ST}_2$ can be computed just once and then applied to *any* point in the object being transformed. Once the series of matrix multiplications to compute this product is performed, the resulting 3 by 3 matrix can then be applied to any point of interest. Each point P can be transformed by the matrix equation $P' = P\mathbf{M}$.

In the example above, the matrix $\mathbf{M}$ is equal to

$$\mathbf{M} = \begin{pmatrix} 1.00000 & .43302 & 0.00000 \\ -1.73206 & .25000 & 0.00000 \\ .73206 & -1.18302 & 1.00000 \end{pmatrix}$$

The reader can verify that if we multiply the point $(2,3,1)$ by this matrix we obtain exactly the same result as obtained from the series of steps in Section 7.4.5.

When using matrix multiplication for coordinate transformation it is important to remember that matrix multiplication is not in general commutative. In general, the matrix product $\mathbf{AB}$ is not the same as the product $\mathbf{BA}$. Thus, some care should be exercised when computing any general transformation matrix from a series of simpler transformations to ensure that the matrices are multiplied in the correct order.

Another interesting aspect of using homogeneous coordinates is that no matter how complicated the series of transformations, they can all be reversed by multiplying the transformed point (in homogeneous coordinates) by the *inverse* of the complete transformation matrix $\mathbf{M}$. (See Section 4.9 for a discussion of computing the inverse of a matrix.) This can be seen by noting that a transformed point is found through the equation $P' = P\mathbf{M}$. If we now multiply P' by the inverse of $\mathbf{M}$, which we shall denote as the matrix $\mathbf{M}^{-1}$, then the new point is $P'' = P'\mathbf{M}^{-1} = P\mathbf{MM}^{-1} = P\mathbf{I}$, where $\mathbf{I}$ is the identity matrix. Since any vector times the identity matrix is simply the original vector, we have $P'' = P$, the original point.

7.6 COORDINATE TRANSFORMATIONS IN THREE DIMENSIONS

Note to Reader: The material in this section can be skipped without loss of continuity.

All of the concepts involved in transforming points in two dimensions extend naturally to three-dimensional coordinates. In particular, the idea of homogeneous coordinate systems makes it possible to use matrix multiplication for the operations of translation, scaling, and rotation. Aside from the addition of another dimension in the coordinate system, the concept of rotation must be extended from the two-dimensional notion of rotation about a point to the three-dimensional analog of rotation about a line.

In regular three-dimensional coordinates, the translation of a point $P = (x, y, z)$ by some amount $T = (T_x, T_y, T_z)$ is found by computing the point $P' = P + T$. Using homogeneous coordinates, we represent P as a *four*-dimensional quantity

$$P = (x, y, z, 1)$$

A translation matrix in homogeneous coordinates would be written as

$$\mathbf{T} = \begin{pmatrix} 1 & 0 & 0 & 0 \\ 0 & 1 & 0 & 0 \\ 0 & 0 & 1 & 0 \\ T_x & T_y & T_z & 1 \end{pmatrix}$$

A new point $P' = P\mathbf{T}$ would be the product of $(x, y, z, 1)$ and $\mathbf{T}$, or $(x + T_x, y + T_y, z + T_z, 1)$.

For example, if we want to translate the point (2,3,5) by 1 unit on the x axis, 2 units on the y axis, and -1 units on the z axis, we would compute the product

$$(2, 3, 5, 1) \begin{pmatrix} 1 & 0 & 0 & 0 \\ 0 & 1 & 0 & 0 \\ 0 & 0 & 1 & 0 \\ 1 & 2 & -1 & 1 \end{pmatrix} = (3, 5, 4, 1)$$

Similarly, scaling a three-dimensional point by S_x, S_y, and S_z on the x, y, and z axes, respectively, can be achieved by multiplying the point in homogeneous coordinates by the matrix $\mathbf{S}$ defined as

$$\mathbf{S} = \begin{pmatrix} S_x & 0 & 0 & 0 \\ 0 & S_y & 0 & 0 \\ 0 & 0 & S_z & 0 \\ 0 & 0 & 0 & 1 \end{pmatrix}$$

For example, to scale the point $P = (2,3,5)$ by $S_x = 2$, $S_y = .5$, and $S_z = 3$, we would compute the product $P' = P\mathbf{S}$ as follows:

$$(2, 3, 5, 1) \begin{pmatrix} 2 & 0 & 0 & 0 \\ 0 & .5 & 0 & 0 \\ 0 & 0 & 3 & 0 \\ 0 & 0 & 0 & 1 \end{pmatrix} = (4, 1.5, 15, 1)$$

The third transformation, rotation, requires somewhat more thought. In two dimensions it makes sense to conceive of rotation about an arbitrary point. The simplest way to describe this mathematically is first to translate the point to be rotated to a coordinate system in which the point about which the rotation was to be done is the origin. Rotation is then a simple matrix transformation. To position the point back in the original coordinate system after rotating it about the origin, we simply reversed the original translation. In homogeneous coordinates, this series of three operations (translation, rotation, and reversed translation) can be reduced to computing the product of the three transformation matrices.

The same basic strategy of performing a rotation by making it a series of simpler operations applies in three dimensions except that the rotation transformation is defined as rotation around a *line* rather than a *point*. As we will show shortly, rotation about an arbitrary line will require the ability to rotate a point around any of the three axes (x, y, or z) of a coordinate system. We will show these simpler rotations first and then use them as building blocks for more complex rotations.

Consider first a rotation of a point around the z axis as shown in Figure 7.11. As a convention, we define rotation in the positive direction using the *right-hand rule*. This means that if you point the thumb of your right hand in the positive direction along the z axis and curl your fingers, then positive angles are measured in the direction of your fingers.

If we define θ as the angle of rotation, then one can show that a point $P = (x, y, z, 1)$ in homogeneous coordinates is rotated an amount θ around the z axis by the transformation $P' = P\mathbf{R}_z$, where $\mathbf{R}_z$ is the matrix defined as follows:

$$\mathbf{R}_z = \begin{pmatrix} \cos(\theta) & \sin(\theta) & 0 & 0 \\ -\sin(\theta) & \cos(\theta) & 0 & 0 \\ 0 & 0 & 1 & 0 \\ 0 & 0 & 0 & 1 \end{pmatrix}$$

This can be shown by generalizing the rotation in two dimensions. The matrix $\mathbf{R}$ has the effect of rotating the point in the (x, y) plane, leaving the value of the z coordinate unchanged.

Rotation around the x or z axes follows the same rules except that the terms reflecting the rotation appear in different rows and columns of the transformation matrix. Thus, a rotation around the x axis by an angle θ corresponds to multiplying the point P

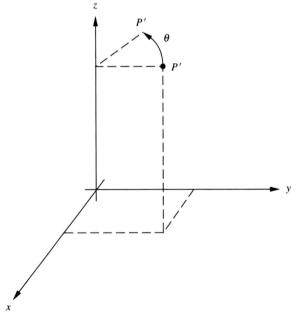

Figure 7.11 Rotation around the z axis.

by a matrix $\mathbf{R}_x$ given as

$$\mathbf{R}_x = \begin{pmatrix} 1 & 0 & 0 & 0 \\ 0 & \cos(\theta) & \sin(\theta) & 0 \\ 0 & -\sin(\theta) & \cos(\theta) & 0 \\ 0 & 0 & 0 & 1 \end{pmatrix}$$

Similarly, rotation around the y axis corresponds to multiplication by the matrix $\mathbf{R}_y$ given as

$$\mathbf{R}_y = \begin{pmatrix} \cos(\theta) & 0 & \sin(\theta) & 0 \\ 0 & 1 & 0 & 0 \\ -\sin(\theta) & 0 & \cos(\theta) & 0 \\ 0 & 0 & 0 & 1 \end{pmatrix}$$

Given the results above, we can now consider the more general problem of rotating a point around a line connecting any two points. Suppose that the line about which the point P is to be rotated connects points P_0 and P_1. The effects of this type of rotation are depicted in Figure 7.12. The rotation of the point is done in the plane that is perpendicular to the segment connecting P_0 and P_1 that passes through the point P.

The rotation of a point around a line can be performed through the following steps.

1. Translate P and P_1 by the amount needed to put P_0 at the origin of the coordinate system. Call the translation matrix $\mathbf{T}$.

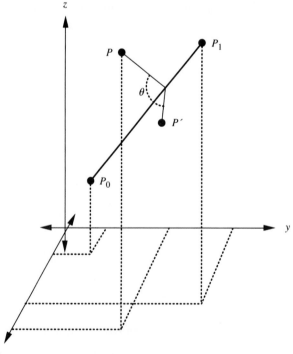

Figure 7.12 Rotation around a line.

2. Rotate the points P and P_1 around the z axis by an amount ϕ_1 needed to put P_1 in the yz plane. Call the rotation matrix $\mathbf{R}_1$.
3. Rotate the point P_1 around the x axis by an amount ϕ_2 needed to place it on the z axis. Call the rotation matrix $\mathbf{R}_2$.
4. Rotate the point P an angle θ around the z axis. Call the rotation matrix $\mathbf{R}_3$.
5. Undo the translation in step 1 and the rotations in steps 2 and 3. This can be done in a single step by computing the inverse of the matrix $\mathbf{TR}_1\mathbf{R}_2$.

It is worth noting that the complete sequence of steps listed above can be combined into a single transformation. This can be done by computing the matrix product of the various transformation matrices as

$$\mathbf{M} = \mathbf{TR}_1\mathbf{R}_2\mathbf{R}_3(\mathbf{TR}_1\mathbf{R}_2)^{-1}$$

As a numerical example, consider rotating the point $(2,3,5)$ by $\theta = 60$ degrees $(\pi/3$ radians) around a line connecting the points $P_0 = (1,1,1)$ and $P_1 = (3,4,4)$. This initial condition is depicted in Figure 7.13a. The computational steps are as follows:

1. Translate P_0 to the origin by multiplying its coordinates by the matrix

$$\mathbf{T} = \begin{pmatrix} 1 & 0 & 0 & 0 \\ 0 & 1 & 0 & 0 \\ 0 & 0 & 1 & 0 \\ -1 & -1 & -1 & 1 \end{pmatrix}$$

In homogeneous coordinates, this results in $P = (1,2,4,1)$ and $P_1 = (2,3,3,1)$. P_0 is at the origin, as shown in Figure 7.13b.

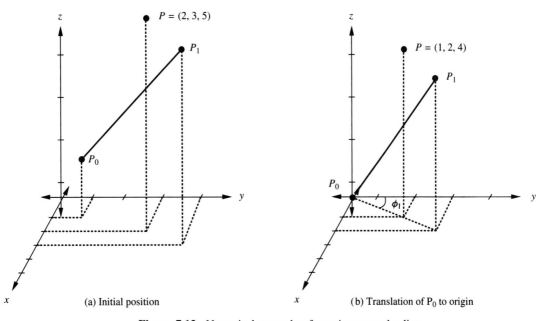

(a) Initial position   (b) Translation of P_0 to origin

Figure 7.13 Numerical example of rotation around a line.

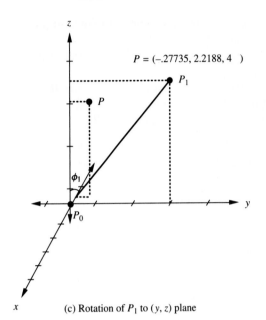

(c) Rotation of P_1 to (y, z) plane

$P = (-.27735, 2.2188, 4\quad)$

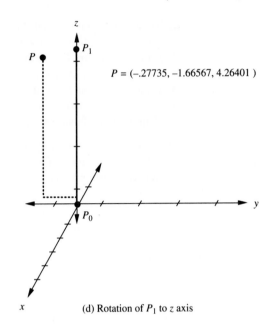

(d) Rotation of P_1 to z axis

$P = (-.27735, -1.66567, 4.26401)$

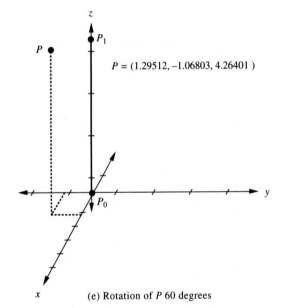

(e) Rotation of P 60 degrees

$P = (1.29512, -1.06803, 4.26401)$

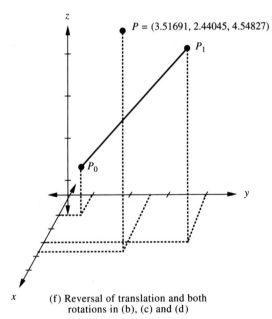

(f) Reversal of translation and both rotations in (b), (c) and (d)

$P = (3.51691, 2.44045, 4.54827)$

Figure 7.13   (continued)

2. To rotate point P_1 around the z axis to put in the yz plane, we need to find the cosine and sine of ϕ_1, the appropriate angle of rotation. Figure 7.13b shows the basic geometry of this rotation. In this case, the required angle ϕ_1 must satisfy

$$\cos(\phi_1) = \frac{3}{\sqrt{13}}$$

or approximately .83205 and

$$\sin(\phi_1) = \frac{2}{\sqrt{13}}$$

or approximately .55470. The matrix $\mathbf{R}_1$ is given by

$$\mathbf{R}_1 = \begin{pmatrix} \cos(\phi_1) & \sin(\phi_1) & 0 & 0 \\ -\sin(\phi_1) & \cos(\phi_1) & 0 & 0 \\ 0 & 0 & 1 & 0 \\ 0 & 0 & 0 & 1 \end{pmatrix}$$

or approximately

$$\mathbf{R} = \begin{pmatrix} .83205 & .55470 & 0 & 0 \\ -.55470 & .83205 & 0 & 0 \\ 0 & 0 & 1 & 0 \\ 0 & 0 & 0 & 1 \end{pmatrix}$$

When applied to P and P_1 this transformation matrix generates new points in homogeneous coordinates $(-.27735, 2.21880, 4, 1)$ and $(0, 3.60555, 3, 1)$, respectively. P_0 remains at the origin.

3. To compute the matrix needed to rotate the new point P_1 around the x axis to place it on the z axis, we need the cosine and sine of the angle ϕ_2 shown in Figure 7.13c. Call the rotation matrix $\mathbf{R}_2$. The reader can verify that the cosine and sine of ϕ_2 are approximately .63960 and .76871, respectively, resulting in the transformation matrix

$$\mathbf{R}_2 = \begin{pmatrix} 1 & 0 & 0 & 0 \\ 0 & .63960 & .76871 & 0 \\ 0 & -.76871 & .63960 & 0 \\ 0 & 0 & 0 & 1 \end{pmatrix}$$

When applied to P and P_1 this transformation matrix generates new points in homogeneous coordinates $(-.27735, -1.65567, 4.26401, 1)$ and $(0, 0, 4.69042, 1)$, respectively. P_0 remains at the origin. The effect of this rotation is shown in Figure 7.13d.

4. Rotate the point P an angle $\theta = 60$ degrees around the z axis. The required matrix to accomplish this is

$$\mathbf{R}_3 = \begin{pmatrix} .5 & .86602 & 0 & 0 \\ -.86602 & .5 & 0 & 0 \\ 0 & 0 & 1 & 0 \\ 0 & 0 & 0 & 1 \end{pmatrix}$$

This transforms the point P to the $(1.29512, -1.06803, 4.26401, 1)$ as shown in Figure 7.13e.

5. Undo the translation in step 1 and the rotations in steps 2 and 3. This requires reversing the effects of the matrix $\mathbf{TR_1R_2}$ given (approximately) by

$$\mathbf{TR_1R_2} = \begin{pmatrix} .83205 & .35479 & .42640 & 0 \\ -.55470 & .53218 & .63960 & 0 \\ 0 & -.76861 & .63960 & 0 \\ -.27735 & -.11826 & -1.70561 & 1 \end{pmatrix}$$

The inverse of this matrix is

$$(\mathbf{TR_1R_2})^{-1} = \begin{pmatrix} .83205 & -.55470 & 0 & 0 \\ .35479 & .53218 & -.76871 & 0 \\ .42640 & .63960 & .63960 & 0 \\ 1 & 1 & 1 & 1 \end{pmatrix}$$

When applied to P from the preceding step, we obtain the final, rotated point $(3.51691, 2.44045, 4.54827, 1)$, as shown in Figure 7.13f.

Finally, we note that the entire series of transformations can be reduced to the multiplication by a single matrix given by

$$\mathbf{TR_1R_2R_3}(\mathbf{TR_1R_2})^{-1} = \begin{pmatrix} .59091 & .69027 & -.41755 & 0 \\ -.41755 & .70455 & .57382 & 0 \\ .69027 & -.16473 & .70455 & 0 \\ .13636 & -.23009 & .13918 & 1 \end{pmatrix}$$

7.7 PARAMETRIC AND NONPARAMETRIC CURVES

The most common way to represent a curve in mathematics is in *nonparametric* form. In two dimensions, nonparametric curves can be represented with explicit functions of the form $y = f(x)$.

Not all curves of interest can be represented as explicit functions. For example, the equation for a circle of radius r centered at the point (a, b) is $(x - a)^2 + (y - b)^2 = r^2$. The full circle cannot be expressed as a simple function because functions require that there be at most one value of y for any value of x. For this reason, most graphics methods for representing curves do not use explicit functions.

While nonparametric functions have some uses, it is often more convenient to use functions in *parametric* form. By this we mean that the values of x and y are each a function of some other variable, which we shall denote as t. Thus, the points on a parametric curve would be computed with the functions

$$x = x(t)$$

$$y = y(t)$$

for some range of t.

Note that any nonparametric curve can also be represented in parametric form. If the nonparametric form is $y = f(x)$, the equivalent parametric form is simply

$$x = x(t) = t$$

$$y = y(t) = f(t)$$

As an example of parametric representation, consider a line segment that joins points $P_1 = (x_1, y_1)$ and $P_2 = (x_2, y_2)$. The parametric form for a segment connecting these two points would be

$$x(t) = x_1 + (x_2 - x_1)t$$

$$y(t) = y_1 + (y_2 - y_1)t$$

where $0 \le t \le 1$. Similarly, if we wanted to represent the entire line passing through P_1 and P_2 rather than just the segment, we would use the same parametric equations but allow $-\infty \le t \le \infty$.

Consider as another example the equations for a circle. One parametric representation for a circle of radius r centered at the point (x_r, y_r) is

$$x(t) = x_r + r\cos(t)$$

$$y(t) = y_r + r\sin(t)$$

for $0 \le t \le 2\pi$.

Yet another interesting set of interesting parametric curves are the *Lissajous figures*. These are defined by the parametric functions

$$x(t) = a\cos(bt)$$

$$y(t) = c\sin(dt)$$

These equations reduce to the representation of a circle of radius 1 centered at (0,0) when $a = b = c = d = 1$. However, for different values of a, b, c, and d, the Lissajous figures produce a rich variety of interesting shapes. For example, if $b = d$, then the parametric equations yield an ellipse.

It is worth noting that the parametric representation for a curve is not unique. For example, a circle could also be represented in parametric form by the following equations:

$$x(t) = x_r + r\cos(\sqrt{t})$$

$$y(t) = y_r + r\sin(\sqrt{t})$$

for $0 \le t \le 4\pi^2$. As we will discuss in the next subsection, some possible parametric representations may have better properties than others.

7.7.1 Drawing Curves

We now turn to the problem of drawing curves represented by parametric functions on a raster display. As in the discussion of coordinate transformations, we assume that there is a layer of software that allows us to work in world coordinates rather than device coordinates. We assume that this software layer provides a function for drawing a line segment in world coordinates. This function, which we shall call **world_line()**, has four arguments:

- **double x1**—the x coordinate of the beginning point (in world coordinates) of the line segment
- **double y1**—the y coordinate of the beginning point (in world coordinates) of the line segment
- **double x2**—the x coordinate of the endpoint (in world coordinates) of the line segment
- **double y1**—the y coordinate of the endpoint (in world coordinates) of the line segment

The function **world_line()** will be assumed not to return a value. Thus, the prototype for the function is

```
void world_line(double, double, double, double);
```

We can use the function **world_line()** to code a general-purpose function to draw a curve in parametric form. The algorithm will simply compute $x(t)$ and $y(t)$ at equally spaced values of t. The curve drawing function, called **pdraw()**, will have the following arguments:

- **double (*x)(double)**—a pointer to a function that computes $x(t)$
- **double (*y)(double)**—a pointer to a function that computes $y(t)$
- **tlow**—the smallest value of t to use in drawing the curve
- **thi**—the largest value of t to use in drawing the curve
- **deltat**—the increment of t to use

The function simply draws successive line segments for each increment of t. The C code is as follows:

```
/*  function to draw a parametric curve  */

void world_line(double, double, double, double);

void pdraw(
    double (*x)(double),  /* function to compute x(t) */
    double (*y)(double),  /* function to compute y(t) */
    double tlow,          /* minimum value of t */
    double thi,           /* highest value of t */
    double deltat)        /* increment of t   */
{
    double xold,yold, xnew, ynew;
    xold = x(tlow); /* initial x */
    yold = y(tlow); /* initial y */
/* loop through steps in increments of deltat */
    for (tlow+=deltat; tlow < thi ; tlow+=deltat ) {
```

```
        xnew = x(tlow);
        ynew = y(tlow);
        world_line(xold, yold, xnew, ynew);
        xold = xnew;
        yold = ynew;
    }
}
```

The implementation of **pdraw()** stores values of $x(t)$ and $y(t)$ in local variables in order to avoid having to call these functions more than once per point.

Because **pdraw()** uses fixed increments of t to approximate the actual curve with a series of line segments, different (but mathematically equivalent) parametric representations of a curve can produce different drawings. For example, two alternative parametric forms for a circle will produce a different series of line segments. The first

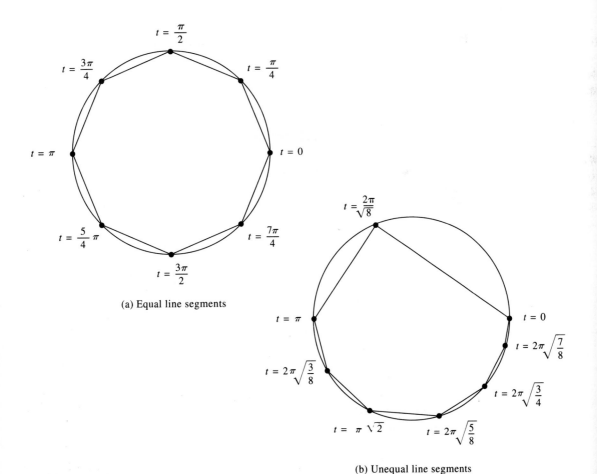

(a) Equal line segments

(b) Unequal line segments

Figure 7.14 Drawing circles with different parametric representations.

form,

$$x(t) = x_r + r \cos(t)$$

$$y(t) = y_r + r \sin(t)$$

$$0 \leq t \leq 2\pi$$

results in segments of equal length. Figure 7.14a illustrates the segments produced by this form when eight segments are used. A second representation,

$$x(t) = x_r + r \cos(\sqrt{t})$$

$$y(t) = y_r + r \sin(\sqrt{t})$$

$$0 \leq t \leq 4\pi^2$$

produces the drawing shown in Figure 7.14b when eight segments are used. In this example, the first parametric representation will produce a more accurate rendering of the circle since it spaces the points defining the line segments at equal intervals along the curve.

7.8 ELEMENTARY GEOMETRIC ALGORITHMS

Many graphics applications require functions that can detect various geometric conditions. For example, it is often important to be able to determine if two line segments intersect or whether a given point is inside some polygon.

The range of geometric problems is enormous. Rather than attempt to present this full range, we will give algorithms for four problems that illustrate some of the interesting techniques that can be applied. The specific problems we will consider are:

1. Is a point above or below a line defined by two points?
2. Do two line segments intersect?
3. Is a point inside a polygon?
4. Given a set of points, what subset, when connected by line segments to form a polygon, enclose the remaining points? The set of points which does this is called the *convex hull*.

Each of these questions is considered in a subsection below.

In all the algorithms, we will define a point in two dimensions as a **struct** of type **Point2D** using the following declarations:

```
/* struct template and typedef for point */
struct point2D_struct {
  double x;
```

```
   double y;
};
```

```
typedef struct point2D_struct Point2D;
```

7.8.1 Is a Point Above or Below a Line?

The first question we will consider is given a line defined by two points, whether a third point is above, below, or on the line. The algorithm we use for this will be incorporated in later algorithms.

Assume that the line is determined by points $P_a = (x_a, y_a)$ and $P_b = (x_b, y_b)$, and the point being tested is $P^* = (x^*, y^*)$. We can determine the position of P^* relative to the line through P_a and P_b by computing the point along the line with $x = x^*$ and determining whether the y value for that point is greater than, less than, or equal to y^*. If the y value of the interpolated point is less than y^*, then the point P^* is above the line; if it is greater than y^*, then P^* is below the line. If the interpolated value of y equals y^*, then P^* is on the line.

The point on the line where $x = x^*$ is given by

$$y = y_a + \frac{x^* - x_a}{x_b - x_a}(y_b - y_a)$$

Here $(y^* - y)$ is positive if P is above the line, negative if P is below the line, and 0 if P is on the line. The function **above_or_below()** given below computes this quantity.

```
/* function to check if point is above, below or
        on a line defined by two points */

double above_or_below(
    Point2D pa,    /* first point on line */
    Point2D pb,    /* second point on line */
    Point2D p)     /* point being tested */
{
/* check if slope of line is infinite */

  if( (pb.x-pa.x) == 0.0)
    return(p.x-pa.x);
  else
    return(p.y-pa.y-(p.x-pa.x)/(pb.x-pa.x)*(pb.y-pa.y));
}
```

The sign of the value returned by the function **above_or_below()** indicates the position of P with respect to the line. Note that the code for the function first checks if the slope of the line is infinite. If so, it returns a positive value if the point P lies to the right of the line, a negative value of P lies to the left of the line, and 0 if P is on the line.

Figure 7.15 illustrates some possible arrangements of points and lines and gives the respective values returned by **above_or_below()** in each of these cases.

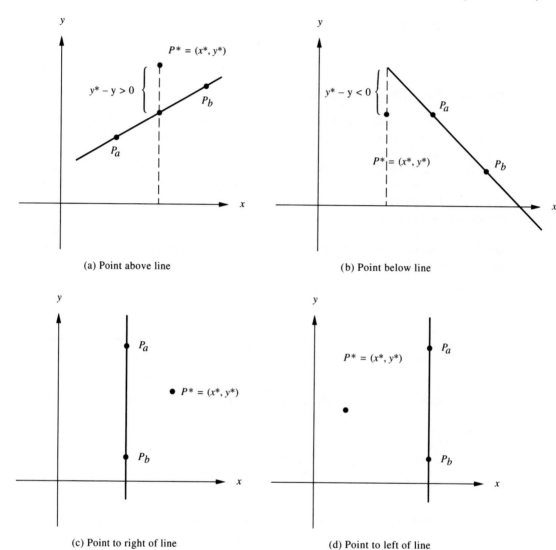

(a) Point above line   (b) Point below line

(c) Point to right of line   (d) Point to left of line

Figure 7.15 Is a point above or below a line?

7.8.2 Do Two Line Segments Intersect?

We now consider two line segments, the first connecting points P_1 and P_2, and the second connecting points P_3 and P_4. The coordinates of the respective points are as follows:

$$P_1 = (x_1, y_1)$$

$$P_2 = (x_2, y_2)$$

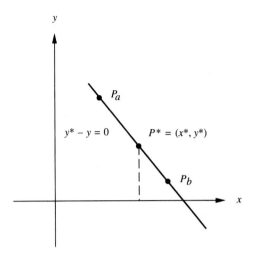

(e) Point on line

Figure 7.15 (continued)

$$P_3 = (x_3, y_3)$$

$$P_4 = (x_4, y_4)$$

The most straightforward way to detect whether these two segments intersect is to note that they must intersect if the following two conditions *both* hold:

- Points P_1 and P_2 lie on opposite sides of the complete line (not the line segment) through points P_3 and P_4.
- Points P_3 and P_4 lie on opposite sides of the complete line (not the line segment) through points P_1 and P_2.

These two conditions can be checked using the function **above_or_below()** from the preceding section. However, there is one special case that must be treated separately. This is when the two segments are collinear. In this situation, we must make a separate check as to whether any point on one segment is contained within the other segment. This can be done by checking if either endpoint on one segment is contained within the other segment. If so, the segments intersect. (They may intersect only at an endpoint or for an entire line segment.)

The function **lines_intersect()** below implements this algorithm. This function takes four arguments, each of which is **Point2D**. The arguments **p1** and **p2** define the endpoints of the first line segment, and the arguments **p3** and **p4** define the endpoints of the second segment. **lines_intersect()** returns an integer constant defined as TRUE or FALSE, indicating whether or not the lines intersect.

lines_intersect() calls the function **above_or_below()** and the function **inside()**, which returns a value of TRUE if a point known to be on the line connecting two points lies inside the line segment connecting those points. **inside()** calls two simple functions, **max()** and **min()**, that compute the maximum and minimum of two values.

inside() tests whether the *y* value of the point is between the values bracketed by the endpoints of the line segment. Note that the function **inside()** deals separately with the special case where the lines are collinear and parallel to the *x* axis. In this case, it tests whether the *x* value of the point is in the interval defined by the endpoints of the line.

The code for **lines_intersect()** given below assumes that the appropriate definitions of the **Point2D** structure and the code for **above_or_below()** is available.

```
/* function determines whether lines can intersect */

#define TRUE 1
#define FALSE 0

/* function prototypes */
double above_or_below(Point2D, Point2D, Point2D);
int inside(Point2D, Point2D, Point2D);
double max(double, double);
double min(double, double);

/* function to test if two segments intersect */
int lines_intersect(
    Point2D p1,    /* (x,y) coordinates of P1 */
    Point2D p2,    /* (x,y) coordinates of P2 */
    Point2D p3,    /* (x,y) coordinates of P3 */
    Point2D p4)    /* (x,y) coordinates of P4 */
{
  double test1, test2, test3, test4;
  test1 = above_or_below(p1,p2,p3);
  test2 = above_or_below(p1,p2,p4);
  test3 = above_or_below(p3,p4,p1);
  test4 = above_or_below(p3,p4,p2);


 /*check if lines are collinear */
  if(test1 == 0.0 && test2 == 0.0) {
    if(inside(p1,p2,p3) || inside(p1,p2,p4) ||
       inside(p3,p4,p1) || inside(p3,p4,p2) )
      return(TRUE);
    else
      return(FALSE);
  }

/* check cases where lines are not collinear intersect */
  if(test1*test2 <= 0.0 && test3*test4 <= 0.0)
    return(TRUE);
  else
    return(FALSE);
}
```

```
/* function returns true if c is inside segment joining
      Points a and b */
int inside(Point2D a, Point2D b, Point2D c)
{
  if(a.y != b.y) { /* check if line is parallel to y axis */
    if(c.y <= max(a.y,b.y) && c.y >= min(a.y, b.y))
      return(TRUE);
  }
  else if(c.x <= max(a.x,b.x) && c.x >= min(a.x, b.x))
    return(TRUE);
  return(FALSE);
}
/* function to take the maximum of two doubles */
double max(double t1, double t2)
{
  if(t1>t2)
    return(t1);
  return(t2);
}

/* function to take the minimum of two doubles */
double min(double t1, double t2)
{
  if(t1<t2)
    return(t1);
  return(t2);
}
```

One of the properties of `lines_intersect()` that we will exploit in the next subsection is that it can be used to detect whether a point lies on a segment. To do this, simply define one of the segments as having the same start and end coordinates as the point being tested. For example, if we wanted to know whether **pc** lies on the segment connecting **pa** and **pb**, a simple call to `lines_intersect()` as follows could be used:

```
if(lines_intersect(pa, pb, pc, pc))
  printf("Point on segment\n");
else
  printf("Point not on segment\n");
```

7.8.3 Is a Point in a Polygon?

The third geometric problem we will consider is determining whether a particular point (x, y) is inside or outside a polygon. We will define any point that is on one of the line segments that form the polygon as *inside* the polygon.

We define a polygon as a series of line segments connecting an ordered series of n points $P_0, P_1, P_2, \ldots, P_{n-1}, P_0$. Each of the points is a vertex of the polygon. Figure

7.16 illustrates one possible polygon. We are interested in whether a particular point such as P_a or P_b in the figure lies inside or outside the polygon.

The approach we will use is to construct a line segment called the *test segment* which begins at the point of interest and ends at some other point known to be outside the polygon. The segment we will use will be drawn horizontally from the point being tested to a point with a "very large" x coordinate. We assume that this x coordinate is large enough so that the test segment goes outside the polygon. In most (but not all) situations, if we count the number of times the test segment crosses one of the segments that make up the polygon, we will get an odd number if the point is inside the polygon and an even number if the point is outside the polygon.

This approach can fail when the test segment we choose passes through one of the vertices of the polygon. For example, in Figure 7.16, the test segment drawn from point P_e intersects the polygon at two places, the vertex P_5 and along the segment joining P_3 and P_4. For our odd/even intersection rule to work, the intersection at P_5 should not be counted (or should be counted twice). However, the test segment drawn from P_a intersects the polygon at vertex P_3; this intersection should be counted for the odd/even rule to work correctly.

The other case where the odd/even rule can fail is if the point lies exactly on the polygon. For example, points P_c and P_d are both inside the polygon even though a test segment drawn horizontally from P_c intersects the polygon twice while a test segment drawn similarly from P_d intersects the polygon only once.

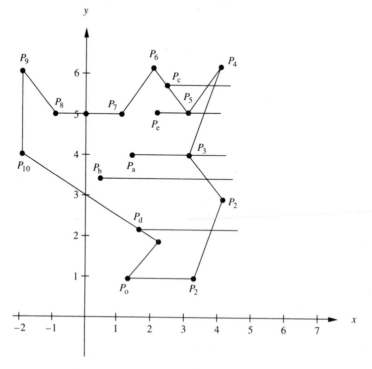

Figure 7.16   Is a point within a polygon?

The case where the test segment intersects the polygon at a vertex can be handled correctly by keeping track of the endpoint of the polygon segment which last intersected the test segment. We initialize this "saved point" at P_0. Suppose we now find that the side of the polygon described by the segment connecting P_i and P_{i+1} intersects the test segment. If the intersection point is not a vertex, then we add one to the count of intersections and set the saved point to P_{i+1}. If the intersection between the test segment and the polygon is a vertex, we perform a check on that intersection before counting it. The check makes sure that P_{i+1} and the saved point are on *opposite sides of a line through the test segment*. If so, then the vertex should be counted, and P_{i+1} becomes the new saved point. Otherwise, we ignore the vertex in counting intersections.

For example, if we consider point P_e in Figure 7.16, the test segment will pass through the vertex P_5 as well as the segment joining P_3 and P_4. If we check the segments starting at point P_0, then the first segment in the polygon that crosses the test segment is the one joining P_3 and P_4. Point P_4 would be saved as the endpoint of the last segment that crossed the test segment. When checking the segment from P_4 to P_5 we discover that vertex P_5 intersects the test segment. However, since P_5 does not lie on the opposite side of the line through the test segment from P_4, we would not count this intersection. Similarly, we would not count the point where the segment joining P_5 and P_6 intersected the test segment at vertex P_5 because P_4 and P_6 are not on opposite sides of the test segment.

The case where the test point is on one of the segments of the polygon needs to be tested separately. If this is the case, the test point is by definition inside the polygon and we need not check for any other intersections.

The function `point_in_polygon()` given below implements the algorithm described above. Its arguments are the point being tested, an array of points defining the vertices of the polygon, and the number of points in the polygon. The value returned by `point_in_polygon()` is TRUE if the point is inside or on the polygon, and FALSE if the point is not inside the polygon. The implementation is as follows:

```
/* prototypes for functions used */
int lines_intersect(Point2D, Point2D, Point2D, Point2D);
double above_or_below(Point2D, Point2D, Point2D);
int inside(Point2D, Point2D, Point2D);
double max(double, double);
double min(double, double);

#define TRUE 1

/* check if point inside polygon */

int point_in_polygon(
   Point2D p,        /* point being tested */
   Point2D poly[],  /* vertices of polygon */
   int n)            /* number of points in polygon */
{
 int i,flag,nextp,count;
```

```
    Point2D psave,out;
    count = 0;
    out.y = p.y;
/* find x value outside polygon */
    out.x = poly[0].x;
    for(i=0; i<n; i++)
       out.x = max(out.x, poly[i].x);
    out.x++;

/* start checking at P0 */
    psave = poly[0];
    for(i=0; i<n; i++)   {
       nextp = (i+1)%n;

/* check if point is on segment. If so, return true */
       if(lines_intersect(poly[i],poly[nextp],p,p))
          return(TRUE);   /* return TRUE */

/* set flag if intersection is a  vertex*/
       flag = lines_intersect(poly[i], poly[i], p, out) ||
         lines_intersect(poly[nextp], poly[nextp], p, out) ;

       if(lines_intersect(poly[i], poly[nextp], p, out))
          if (!flag || above_or_below(p,out,psave) *
                 above_or_below(p,out,poly[nextp]) < 0.0) {
             psave = poly[nextp];
             count++;
          }
    }
    return(count
}
```

The **Point2D out** in the above code is the endpoint of the test segment. Its x coordinate value is set one greater than the largest x value in the polygon's vertices. **point_in_polygon()** uses many of the functions developed in the previous subsections. For example, it makes extensive use of **lines_intersect()** and **above_or_below()**. The value **nextp** is used to index the point after the one being examined; it is assigned the value $(i+1)\%n$ so that the segment connecting P_{n-1} and P_0 gets checked. The variable **flag** indicates if either of the vertices of the segment being examined are intersection points. The variable **psave** stores the endpoint of the last side of the polygon which intersected the test segment.

The implementation was coded assuming that P_0, the first point in the array of points that define the vertices of the polygon, does not lie on the test segment. This assumption can be relaxed by having the algorithm first search through the vertices of the polygon to find one not on the test segment, and then reordering the segments so that found vertex is the first in the array of vertices. This is left to the reader as an exercise.

7.8.4 Convex Hulls

The last geometric problem we consider is the formation of what is called a *convex hull*. Given a set of points $P_0, P_1, P_2, \ldots, P_{n-1}$, their convex hull is an ordered subset of those points which, when connected to form a polygon, contain all the other points. Figure 7.17a and b show a set of points and a polygon connecting a subset of those points which is their convex hull.

The conceptually simplest method for finding a convex hull is called *package wrapping*. We start with a point known to be on the hull. This can be found simply by identifying the point with the smallest y coordinate. We will call this point H_0. We then search through the remaining points in the set and find the one which makes the smallest angle with the line from H_0 parallel to the x axis. This point, which we denote as H_1, is also on the convex hull. We proceed by finding the point H_{i+1} as the point in the original set that creates the smallest angle between the line connecting it and point H_i and the line connecting H_i and H_{i-1}. This process continues until we return to point H_0.

For example, Figure 7.17c shows a partial hull. The points P_0, P_1, and P_2 have already been added to the hull. The point P_4 would be the next added to the hull because the line formed by connecting it to P_2 makes the smallest angle of the remaining points with the line connecting P_1 and P_2.

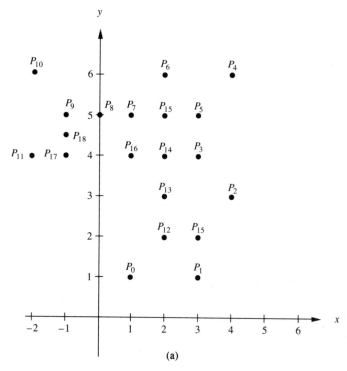

(a)

Figure 7.17   Convex hull of a set of points.

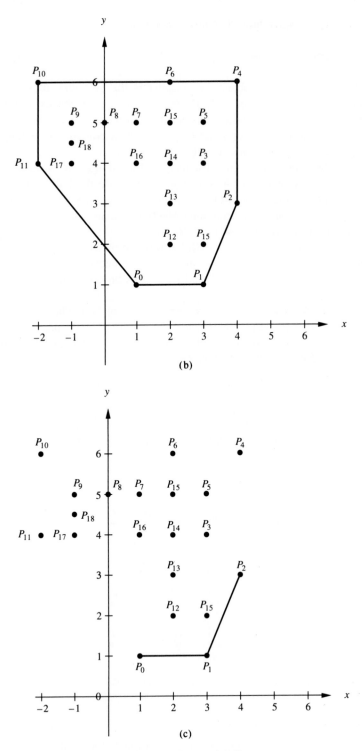

Figure 7.17 (continued)

One way to visualize how this algorithm works is to imagine that the (x, y) plane is a board, and that a nail is driven into each point in the set. The package-wrapping algorithm ties the string to the first point H_0, and then wraps the string counterclockwise starting parallel to the x axis. When the string hits a nail, that nail joins the convex hull, the string is tied to that nail, and the wrapping moves in the counterclockwise direction. Eventually, the string gets wrapped around H_0 again, and the algorithm terminates.

To implement this algorithm we will need a function that computes the angle formed by the x axis and a line between two points. The geometry of this is shown in Figure 7.18a. The angle denoted as θ in that figure is simply the arctangent of dy/dx corrected for the quadrant in which the points lie. The function **atan()** in the C math library computes the arc tangent in radians, returning a value between $-\pi/2$ and $\pi/2$. The following function, called **c_atan()**, has as its arguments two points, and returns the angle between the line connecting the point and the origin and the x axis. The angle returned by **c_atan()** is between 0 and 2π.

```c
#include <math.h>
#define PI 3.14159

/* function to compute angle for a point */
double c_atan(Point2D p1, Point2D p2)
{
  double t;
  double dx,dy;
  dx = p2.x-p1.x;
  dy = p2.y-p1.y;
  /* check if line is vertical */
  if(dx == 0.0) {
    if(dy > 0.0)
      t = PI/2;
    else if(dy < 0.0)
      t = 1.5*PI;
```

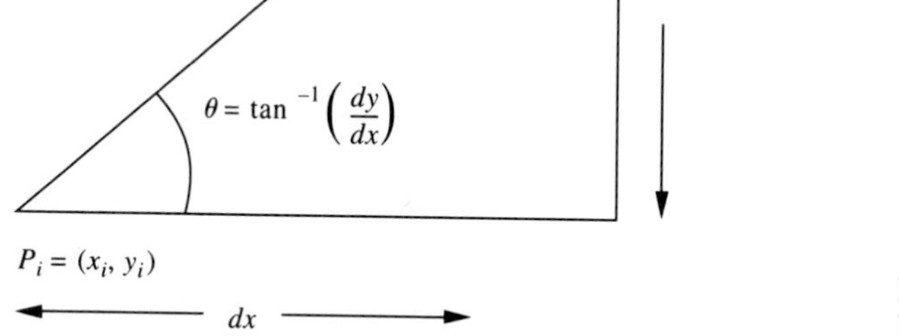

$P_{i+1} = (x_{i+1}, y_{i+1})$

dy

$\theta = \tan^{-1}\left(\dfrac{dy}{dx}\right)$

$P_i = (x_i, y_i)$

dx

Figure 7.18 Computing the angle between two segments.

```
      else
        t = 0.0;
    }
    else {
      t = atan(dy/dx); /* use atan() in math library */
      if(dx < 0.0)
        t = PI + t;
      else if( dx > 0.0 && dy < 0.0)
        t = 2*PI + t;
    }
    return(t);
}
```

Our implementation deals with the case where more than one point can enter the convex hull. This can happen when two or more points lie on a line from the point last entered into the convex hull. The approach we use is to add the point that is farthest from the current point. The hull created by our algorithm will automatically exclude all the closer points that are collinear. We use the function **dist()** to compute the squared distance between two points. This function is as follows:

```
double dist(Point2D p1, Point2D p2)
{
return((p1.x-p2.x)*(p1.x-p2.x)
       +(p1.y-p2.y)*(p1.y-p2.y));
}
```

Given the functions **c_atan()** and **dist()**, we can now implement the package-wrapping algorithm for finding the convex hull. The function, called **find_hull()**, has as its arguments an array of structures representing the complete set of points and the number of points in the array. It returns a pointer to an array of integers that is allocated by the function. The entries in the array of integers correspond to the entries in the original array of points. Each integer in the array contains a zero if the corresponding point is not in the convex hull or a positive integer from 1 to the number of points in the hull. The positive integer shows the order in which points entered the hull. Connecting the points in that order produces a polygon that defines the convex hull.

For the sake of clarity in exposition, the implementation developed below assumes that point P_0 is the one with the smallest value of y. This assumption can be relaxed by modifying the code to search for the point with the smallest y. The code for find_hull() is as follows.

```
#include <stdio.h>
#include <stdlib.h>
#include <float.h>

double c_atan(Point2D, Point2D);
double dist(Point2D, Point2D);
```

```
#define PI 3.14159

/* This routine finds convex hull of a set of points.
   It returns an array with integer entries showing
   order of points in the hull. */

int *find_hull(
  Point2D p[],        /* set of points */
  int n)              /* number of points */
{
  int i,j,curmin;
  double testh,mint;
  double lastt=-DBL_MIN; /* #defined in float.h */
  int counter=1;
  int *hull;

/* Allocate array using calloc. This
   array is initially zeros. */

  hull = calloc(n, sizeof(int));
  if(hull == NULL) {
    printf("Unable to allocate hull array.\n");
    exit();
  }
  /* initialize point with minimum angle */
  curmin = n;
  i = 0;

/* Find next point on hull until
   you reach starting point */

  while(curmin != 0) {
    mint = 2*PI;
    /* search through points */
    for(j=0; j <n; j++) {
      if(j != i) {
      testh = c_atan(p[i], p[j]);
        if(testh > lastt &&  testh < mint ||
           (testh==mint &&
           dist(p[i],p[j]) > dist(p[i],p[curmin]))) {
          curmin = j;
          mint = testh;
        }
      }
    }
  }
/* add point to hull*/
    *(hull+curmin) = counter++;
    lastt = mint;
    i = curmin;
```

```
    }
  return(hull);
}
```

In the above code, the variable **curmin** is array index for the point that at any given time currently makes the smallest angle with the last segment on the hull. **mint** is the value of that angle. Note that the implementation adds the starting point, P_0, to the hull last.

As an example, suppose that **find_hull()** is called with the following array of (x, y) points:

x	y
1	1
3	1
4	3
3	4
4	6
3	5
2	6
1	5
0	5
−1	5
−2	6
−2	4
2	2
2	3
2	4
2	5
3	2
1	4
−1	4
−1	4.5

The function **find_hull()** would identify the following subset of these points on the convex hull:

x	y
3	1
4	3
4	6
−2	6
−2	4
1	1

These points are listed in the order in which they would be connected to form the convex hull.

7.8.5 Improving the Package-Wrapping Algorithm

The function `c_atan()` requires more computation than is required for the package-wrapping algorithm. This is because the algorithm does not really need to compute the actual angle between two segments; instead, it simply needs to know which candidate point to enter the convex hull produces the smallest angle. Any function that puts points in the same order as the arctangent would work for our purposes. For this reason, many graphics algorithms compute what might be termed a *pseudo-angle*, defined as simply $\Delta y/(\Delta x + \Delta y)$ appropriately corrected for the quadrant. This avoids having to invoke the relatively slow `atan()` function in the C math library.

The function `theta()` below computes the pseudo-angle value with the appropriate correction for quadrants. It can be used in place of `c_atan()` in the package-wrapping algorithm.

```
#include <math.h>
#define PI 3.14159

/* function to compute a pseudo-angle */
double theta(Point2D p1, Point2D p2)
{
   double dx,dy,ax,ay,t;
   dx = p2.x - p1.x;
   ax = fabs(dx);
   dy = p2.y - p1.y;
   ay = fabs(dy);
/* check if line is vertical */
   if(dx==0.0 && dy==0.0)
      t=0;
   else
      t = dy/(ax+ay);
/* correct for quadrant */
  if(dx < 0.0)
      t = 2-t;
   else if (dy < 0.0)
      t = 4+t;
   return(t*PI/2);
}
```

A second improvement in the performance of `find_hull()` can be achieved by first finding a subset of points that are known to be on the hull and then restricting the search for other points on the hull to those known to be outside the polygon formed by the known points. The simplest way to do this is to note that the following points must be in the convex hull:

- The point with the largest value of x
- The point with the smallest value of x
- The point with the largest value of y
- The point with the smallest value of y

These points define a polygon with as many as four sides. (It is possible that one or more points satisfies more than one of the conditions above.) Only points outside this initial polygon are candidates for being on the convex hull. Points in the interior of the polygon need not be checked, thereby reducing the number of points searched at each iteration of the hull-finding algorithm.

7.9 SUMMARY OF CHAPTER 7

In this chapter we introduced some of the central concepts in computer graphics. The three major categories of graphics output devices—*storage tubes*, *vector refresh displays*, and *raster devices*—were described. Most computer displays in use now are raster devices, which display a grid of rectangular areas (most often squares) called *pixels*. At any given instant, each pixel on a display is a uniform color. Any drawing is made up of a pattern of pixels. Pixel colors are stored in an area of the computer's memory called the *frame buffer*, which is frequently scanned by the display hardware, making it possible to change drawings very quickly.

Display systems that can simultaneously display 2^{24} or more colors are usually called *true color* displays. However, in many frame buffers, the number of colors which can be displayed at any given moment is limited. This limitation is imposed to reduce the amount of memory needed for the frame buffer and to reduce the complexity (and consequently the cost) of the display hardware. When the number of possible pixel values is restricted in this way, the translation of the values in the buffer into actual colors is usually managed by a translation table called a *color map*. Various graphical input devices, including a *mouse*, a *trackball*, *data tablet*, a *joystick*, *lightpen*, and *touch screen*, were also described.

Raster displays generally use *device coordinates*, where each pixel is given an absolute pair of integer coordinates. One of the major issues in drawing pictures on such systems is that any figure must ultimately be reduced to a series of pixels. *Bresenham's algorithm* for drawing line segments and circles in device coordinates on monochrome displays was described in detail. This efficient algorithm uses a mathematical measure of the extent to which any potential pixel in a figure deviates from the ideal figure to determine which pixels should be drawn.

The idea of *coordinate transformations* was then explored. The concepts of *normalized device coordinates*, where the coordinates of anything on the screen are expressed in normalized values between zero and one, and *world coordinates*, where the coordinates reflect the natural units of the objects being displayed, were described. In these coordinate systems, floating-point numbers, rather than integers, can be used for coordinate values.

The three operations of *translation*, *scaling*, and *rotation around the origin* were described for two- and three-dimensional points. These three basic operations can be expressed in matrix algebra. They can be used in combination to perform more complex transformations. The concept of *homogeneous coordinates*, where an extra, artificial dimension is added to any point, was used so that any coordinate transformation can be expressed as a series of matrix multiplications. This greatly increased the efficiency of combined transformations, particularly when the same transformation must be applied to a large number of points. Homogeneous coordinates allow a combination of transformations to be expressed by a single matrix. Any point is transformed by multiplying it by this composite matrix. Moreover, transformations can be undone by multiplying the transformed point by the inverse of the original composite matrix.

Methods for drawing various mathematical curves in world coordinates were then discussed. The idea of *parametric representation*, where the x and y values for some figure are both expressed as functions of some third variable, was described and some examples of specific curves, including circles and *Lissajous figures*, were shown.

Some important two-dimensional *geometric algorithms* were then introduced. Algorithms for testing whether a point is above or below a line, whether two line segments intersect, and whether a point is inside or outside a polygon were described. A method for finding the subset of points which, when connected by line segments, completely enclose a larger set of points was developed. This subset of points is called a *convex hull*.

7.10 EXERCISES

Many of the exercises below require plotting points on a display. The computer system you use may have a graphics library that implements an equivalent of the function **plot_pixel()** *used in this chapter. If not, you may implement* **plot_pixel()** *simply by using* **printf()** *to output the coordinates of the point to be plotted.*

7-1. As presented in Section 7.3, the restricted version of Bresenham's algorithm draws a line segment that is one pixel wide. Develop and implement an extension Bresenham's algorithm that draws lines that are n pixels wide, where n is an integer argument to the line drawing function.

7-2. Write a function that will draw a dashed line segment. The function should have as arguments the start and end points of the segment, the length of each dash (in pixels), and the space between dashes (in pixels). Test your function by drawing a dashed line from (1,2) to (10,12) using dashes that are two pixels long with one pixel between successive dashes.

7-3. Suppose that you wanted to draw a circle in device coordinates. Assume that the circle is centered at pixel (10,10) and has radius 5. Use Bresenham's algorithm to compute by hand which pixels in the first 45 degrees of the circle should be colored.

7-4. Write a function that will draw a "filled" circle in device coordinates. Your function should have as arguments the coordinates of the center of the circle and its radius. Think about modifying Bresenham's algorithm by using straight lines to fill all the pixels between the center of the circle and the pixels defining the edge of the circle.

7-5. Consider a point in two dimensions. Without using homogeneous coordinates, compute by hand the complete transformations that will translate this point 2 units in the x direction and -4 units in the y direction and rotate the point 45 degrees around the point (1,2).

7-6. Consider a point in two dimensions represented in homogeneous coordinates. Give the transformation matrices for each of the following separate transformations:
   (a) Rescale the x axis by 3 and the y axis by 2.
   (b) Rotate the point 180 degrees around the point (2,2).
   (c) Translate the point 6 units in the x direction and 3 units in the y direction.
        Now compute the single composite matrix that does all these transformations in a single matrix multiplication. Apply the separate steps one at a time and the composite matrix to the point (1,1) and verify that they result in the same transformed point.

7-7. Consider the point (1,2,3) in three-dimensional space. Find the following:
   (a) The coordinates of the point if rotated 30 degrees around the x axis.
   (b) The coordinates of the point if rotated 45 degrees around the y axis.
   (c) The coordinates of the point if rotated -60 degrees around z axis.
   (d) The coordinates of the point if rotated 45 degrees around the line connecting the points (1,1,2) and (2,2,2). You may present your result as the product of matrices to avoid having to compute a matrix inverse.

7-8. Write a function that creates a reflected image of a line drawing in two dimensions. The function should have as its arguments the number of line segments in the drawing and an array of line segments, with each segment defined by a pair of points. It should output the coordinates of the segments that make up the mirror image of the line segments. You should assume that all the points in the original drawing are in the first quadrant and that the mirror is placed along the y axis. The points are reflected into the fourth quadrant as shown in Figure 7.19.

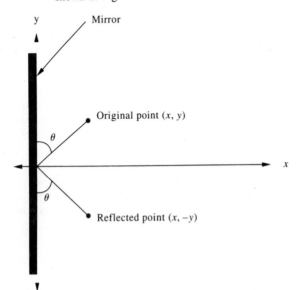

Figure 7.19 Reflection Process

7-9. In Exercise 4-14 we introduced the game of Life. Write a function that will draw a "map" on the screen showing the evolution of the organisms' world. You can indicate a cell containing an organism by drawing a special graphic symbol in the cell.

7-10. Write a set of routines to draw capital block lettering using a series of straight-line segments on a display. These routines should be written such that the letters can be drawn anywhere, in any orientation, and of any size. You might want to do this by creating an array of lists where each row of the array points to a list containing the coordinates of the points (relative to (0,0)) to connect in order to draw a single character. Write a `main()` function that uses your function to draw your first name in four different places rotated 30 degrees, 90 degrees, 150 degrees, and 280 degrees from vertical.

7-11. Many scientific applications require the use of graphs to present data. These graphs are such that the independent variable is on the horizontal axis and the dependent variable is on the vertical axis.
   (a) Write a C function that has as arguments the ranges of the horizontal and vertical axes and draws appropriate x and y axes. The function should mark values on the x and y axes in fixed intervals. (These values are called *tic* marks.)
   (b) Write a C function that has as its arguments a `struct` containing an (x, y) pair and a 3 by 3 transformation matrix in homogeneous coordinates. The function should place the point in the correct position in the graph. This transformation matrix must take into account the space on the display taken up by the x and y axes.
   (c) Write a C function that plots a series of points. This function should have as its arguments two arrays containing the x and y values to be plotted and the number of these values.
   (d) Write a `main()` program that uses the functions in parts (a), (b), and (c) above to plot 10 data points you make up.

7-12. A *histogram* displays the frequency with which values occur in a series of observations of some process. The values of the variable, shown on the x axis of the histogram, are generally discrete or ranges of a continuous value, and the frequencies are indicated by the height of lines or bars parallel to the y axis. Write a C function that draws a histogram for the case where a variable x takes on only discrete values. The arguments to the function should be the number of discrete values of x, an array containing those discrete values, and an array containing the counts indicating the frequency with which the corresponding values of x occurred in the data. Your function should scale the x and y axes appropriately and show the frequency with a vertical line. Then develop a `main()` function that uses your histogram function on some data you invent.

7-13. The *cycloid* function depicts the path a point on a wheel will follow when the wheel moves along a horizontal surface. This function can be represented parametrically as

$$x(t) = a(t - \sin t)$$

$$y(t) = a(1 - \cos t)$$

for $-\infty < t < \infty$. Write a C function that draws this figure for two complete rotations of a wheel.

7-14. Write a `main()` function that uses the function `pdraw()` described in Section 7.7.1 to draw the *rose function*, which in polar coordinates is given by

$$r = a \sin 2\theta$$

Test your program with the following values for **deltat**: .01, .001, and .0001. What do you notice about the differences in resolution and processing time?

7-15. Rewrite the C function **point_in_polygon()** given in Section 7.8.3 so that it returns 1 if the point is in the interior of the polygon, 0 if the point lies on one of the segments that make up the polygon, and -1 if the point is outside the polygon.

7-16. The implementation of the package-wrapping algorithm shown in Section 7.8.4 identifies points that define the hull, but it may miss a point that falls exactly on the hull but is not a vertex of the hull. Rewrite the C function **find_hull()** so that it locates *all* the points that fall on the convex hull.

7-17. Rewrite the C function **find_hull()** so that it first identifies the points with the largest and smallest values of x and y, and then restricts the search for additional points to those outside the polygon formed by those initial points.

7-18. It is often useful to be able to fill a convex polygon drawn in device coordinates with a particular color. Suppose that a convex polygon is described by an array of n vertices. A simple algorithm begins by drawing the segments of the polygon, keeping track of the plotted pixels in an array. A rectangular box that completely encloses the polygon can then be found. The polygon can then be filled by scanning each row of pixels in the bounding box and plotting all the pixels in the interior of the polygon row by row. Write a function that has as its arguments an array of pixels that are the vertices of a polygon and the number of vertices. You will find it useful to allocate an array in memory that reflects the contents of the frame buffer inside the bounding box.

Write a **main()** program that reads the number of vertices of a polygon and the coordinates of those vertices from a file, invokes the polygon filling function, and outputs the coordinates of the filled pixels.

7-19. A general region in device coordinates is "enclosed" if, starting from any point in the interior of the region, no series of vertical or horizontal moves can be made without crossing a pixel of a different color. For example, the region in Figure 7.20a is enclosed, while the region shown in Figure 7.20b is not. Filling an enclosed region with a single color is a standard operation in computer graphics.

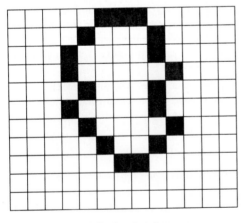

(a) Enclosed region

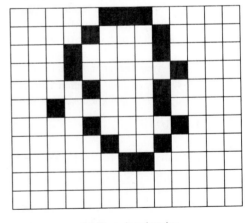

(b) Unenclosed region

Figure 7.20 Enclosed and Unenclosed Regions

Assume that the display is black and white only and that the contents of the frame buffer are represented by an array `pixel` where `pixel[i][j]` is zero if the pixel at (i, j) is white and one if the pixel is black. A simple algorithm, adapted from Esakov and Weiss [Esakov, J. and Weiss, T. 89] for filling a region starts with a point P known to be in the interior of the enclosed region. Assuming that the interior of the region is entirely white and the enclosing figure is drawn in black, the algorithm is as follows:

- Setp 1. Push P on a stack.
- Step 2. If the stack is empty, exit. Otherwise, go to step 3.
- Step 3. Pop the stack, calling the point popped from the stack Q.
- Step 4. If Q is white, set the color of Q to black and push the north, west, east, and south neighboring pixels (if they exist) on the stack. Go to step 2.

Implement this algorithm in a C function. Your function should have the array `pixel` and the coordinates of the point P as arguments. Then write a `main()` function that tests your region-filling function starting at `pixel[5][5]` using a 10 by 10 array of pixels as follows:

```
0 0 0 0 0 0 0 0 0 1
0 0 0 1 1 1 0 0 0 1
0 0 1 0 0 0 1 0 0 1
0 1 0 0 0 0 0 1 0 0
0 1 0 0 0 0 0 1 0 0
0 0 1 0 0 0 0 1 0 0
0 0 0 1 0 0 0 1 0 0
0 0 0 1 0 0 1 0 0 0
0 0 0 1 0 0 1 0 0 0
0 0 0 0 1 1 0 0 0 0
```

7-20. Raster graphics displays can be used to generate animations of moving objects. In general, the way to make an object appear to move is to draw it at its initial point on the screen, "undraw" it by overwriting the original figure using the background color, and redraw it in a new, updated position. If this is done very rapidly (faster than 20 or so times per second), one can create the illusion of smooth motion. Even if such rapid redisplay is infeasible, simple animations done in the way described above can illustrate motion.

Write a C program that animates the motion of a ball that is dropped from some height, simulating the rebounding of the ball off a rigid surface. You can assume the existence of a function `unplot_pixel()` that draws a pixel in the background color.

8

PROBABILISTIC SIMULATION

8.1 INTRODUCTION

There are many physical and social systems that are subject to some degree of randomness. These systems range from the subatomic phenomena of quantum theory to the large-scale effects of climate changes induced by increased carbon dioxide in the atmosphere. Random processes of importance in science, engineering, and management are often so complex that they cannot be analyzed using the mathematical tools of probability theory. In such cases, it is often useful to use computer simulation.

Consider, for example, a city where police cars are dispatched in response to calls for assistance. The time and location of the calls are inherently random, making the distribution of the patrol cars at any instant random as well. In addition, the length of time to travel from any given point in the city to a call will vary, both because the locations of the cars will change over time and because the level of traffic will fluctuate. Moreover, the amount of time needed to service any single call will vary widely depending on the type of call and the actions the police must take. From the perspective of the person responsible for deciding how many cars should be available during various shifts and how those cars should be prepositioned, most of the factors affecting the decision are intrinsically random.

The inherent randomness and complexity of many large systems has led to the development of *probabilistic simulation* as a tool for making design and operating decisions. The basic approach is to use the speed of the computer to "step through" the events that can occur in probabilistic systems. By simulating a sufficiently large number of such events and keeping statistics on important measures of the system's performance, we can obtain a good approximation of how the real system might behave.

The tools of probabilistic simulation are applicable to many problems where other analysis methods fail. They can provide predictions of important performance indicators such as the expected waiting time for services, the percentage of parts that will be defective in a manufacturing process, or the odds that some complex game of chance will be won. In this chapter we introduce some of the computational tools that can be used to understand these systems. Because these methods provide a natural way of analyzing games of chance, they are often called *Monte Carlo methods*.

We begin with a quick introduction to the ideas, terminology, and notation of random variables and processes in Section 8.2. This is followed by Section 8.3, which describes the random number generation function provided in the standard C library. Sections 8.4 and 8.5 show two programming projects. The first illustrates how simulation can be used to approximate an integral, and the second models a simple queue of people waiting in a line for service. These examples show the basic concepts behind Monte Carlo simulation. The techniques for *random number generation* are then described in Sections 8.6 and 8.7.

Section 8.8 introduces a data structure called an *ascending heap*. This data structure provides a flexible way of organizing pending events in a simulation, making it computationally efficient to find the next pending event and to add new events as they arise during a simulation's execution. This idea is used in a third programming project to simulate the operation of a *modem pool*, a bank of communications devices that allows users to connect via telephone lines to a computer. Such pools are used by various dial-up services, such as airline reservation systems or bulletin boards. They allow users to phone a single number and be connected to the central computer through any one of the available modems in the pool. In Section 8.10 we explore some of the important considerations in designing simulations, particularly large simulation programs. The chapter is summarized in Section 8.11.

8.2 RANDOM VARIABLES AND PROCESSES

The idea of randomness in certain phenomena is central to simulation, and it is important to understand what such randomness implies. It means that it is impossible to predict whether or not an event will occur with certainty. For example, in a bank we do not know the time the next customer will arrive or when a customer being served will be finished. Instead, all we can make are statements about the *probability* that something will happen. For example, we can predict the *probability* that a customer will arrive at or before some time.

Most people have an intuitive sense of randomness in the case of discrete phenomena such as coin flips or lottery games. For example, everyone recognizes that it is impossible to know whether the next flip of a coin will come up as a head or a tail; all that can be stated is that if the coin is fair, the probability of a head or a tail is .5. Similarly, we can compute that the probability of the next three tosses all being heads is .125. In the case of continuous variables such as time, we need to think about the probability that the outcome of the random process will be in some interval, for example t_1 to t_2.

Figure 8.1 illustrates the behavior of two random variables. Figure 8.1a shows a discrete variable such as the sum of the values on two six-sided dice. This random process can produce values between 2 and 12. The height of the bars is the probability of the corresponding outcome. In the discrete case, this graph illustrates what is called the *probability mass function*.

The case of a continuous variable is shown in Figure 8.1b. Here, the function is continuous, and the area under the curve for some interval $[x_1, x_2]$ corresponds to the probability that the variable will fall in that interval. This function is called the *probability density function*.

The standard convention in probability theory is to use capital letters such as X or Y to denote random variables and to use the corresponding lowercase letters for specific values those variables can take. For example, the notation Prob[$X = 1$] would be read as "the probability that in one particular event the random variable X will be 1." Similarly, the notation Prob[$y \leq Y \leq y + \Delta y$] would be read "the probability that in one particular event the random variable Y will be in the interval $[y, y + \Delta y]$."

Probability mass functions are generally denoted in the form $p_X(x)$, which would be read "the probability mass function for the discrete random variable X evaluated at some value x." Similarly, probability density functions are generally written with the notation $f_Y(y)$, which would be read "the probability density function of continuous random variable Y evaluated at some value y."

Probability mass and density functions both have the property that they have no values less than zero. In the discrete case, the values of the probability mass function sum to 1; in the continuous case, the integral of the entire probability density function equals 1.

The simplest discrete random variable is generated by the *Bernoulli process*. In this case, only two possible outcomes are allowed. By convention the two feasible outcomes are coded as a random variable that can have values of one or zero, with corresponding probabilities of p and $1 - p$. If we define X as a Bernoulli random variable, the probability mass function for this process is

$$p_X(x) = \begin{cases} p, & x = 1 \\ 1 - p, & x = 0 \end{cases}$$

For example, we could define the toss of a coin such that a head corresponded to a value of 1 and a tail corresponded to a value of zero. In this case, p would be $\frac{1}{2}$. Similarly, if a manufacturing process produced 1 defective part per 100, a value of 1 might be used to represent a defective part and a value of zero would correspond to a good part; p would be .01.

Another standard random process is described by the *uniform density function*. This is used to represent continuous variables where the outcomes of the process

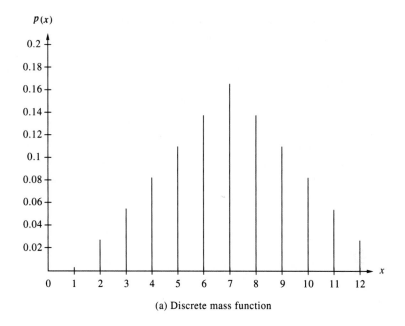

(a) Discrete mass function

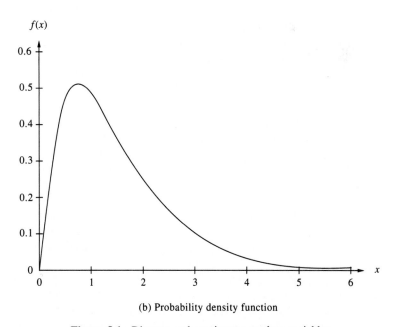

(b) Probability density function

Figure 8.1 Discrete and continuous random variables.

are equally likely over some interval. For example, if a variable T corresponded to measurements of the length of time between successive arrivals of customers, and people are equally likely to arrive anytime between 0 and 30 seconds apart, then the probability density function for T would be uniform. The probability density function would be written as follows:

$$f_T(t) = \begin{cases} \frac{1}{30}, & 0 \le t \le 30 \\ 0, & \text{otherwise} \end{cases}$$

The uniform density function can be used to compute the probability that the time between customer arrivals will be in some interval. For example, if arrivals are uniformly distributed between 0 and 30 minutes apart, then the probability of a customer arriving between 10 and 20 minutes is

$$\int_{10}^{20} f_T(t)\, dt = \int_{10}^{20} \frac{1}{30}\, dt = \frac{1}{3}$$

We will explore several other commonly used probability mass and density functions further in Section 8.7.

8.3 RANDOM NUMBER GENERATION FUNCTIONS IN C

Since computers are deterministic devices, it is somewhat odd to think of them as capable of generating random numbers. In fact, without creating some specialized device which in effect tosses a coin or measures some intrinsically random phenomenon such as the decay of atomic particles, computers cannot generate truly random values. Instead, methods that generate a series of values which *appear* to be random are generally used. Such methods are called *pseudo-random number generators*. If the pseudo-random number generation method is selected appropriately, the difference between the values provided by such methods and truly random numbers is usually not a practical problem.

One of the key distinctions between true random values and those generated by pseudo-random number generators is that the series of pseudo-random numbers will always have some cycle. That is, if we call the function a sufficient number of times, the sequence of values returned will eventually be repeated. In general, well-designed and carefully implemented pseudo-random number generators have cycle lengths which are very long, and the outcome of a simulation that uses these values is virtually indistinguishable from what would be obtained with real random values.

In Chapter 2 we introduced the standard C library function **rand()**, which generates pseudo-random numbers. In particular, it creates integer values which, to a very close approximation, have equal probability of taking on any value between 0 and some value **RAND_MAX**. The function **rand()** returns an **int** and has no arguments.

The function prototype for **rand()** and the value of **RAND_MAX** are provided in the standard header file **stdlib.h**. The ANSI C standard requires that **RAND_MAX** be at least 32767, although many implementations have values of **RAND_MAX** that are considerably larger.

Because it returns only discrete values, the function **rand()** simulates a probability mass function. As a technical matter, since computers always use a finite number of digits to represent variables which may be continuous, it is technically impossible to simulate random variables that are described by probability density functions. However, much in the same spirit as we use floating-point representation for real numbers, we often treat transformations of the values generated by **rand()** as if they yielded continuous values.

For example, to transform the values returned by a call to **rand()** into values which are uniformly distributed between 0 and 1, we can convert the returned **int** to a **double** and rescale it appropriately. The following function accomplishes this:

```
/* function to generate pseudo-random
   number between 0 and 1 */

#include <stdlib.h>
double simple_uniform(void)
{
   return( (double) rand() / RAND_MAX);
}
```

This **return** statement casts the **int** returned by **rand()** to a **double**. This forces the conversion of **RAND_MAX** to a **double** before the division is performed, producing a **double** between zero and one.

We will consider how pseudo-random-number generators such as **rand()** are implemented and how their outputs can be used to simulate a wide range of probability mass and density functions in Sections 8.6 and 8.7, respectively.

8.4 PROGRAMMING PROJECT: MONTE CARLO INTEGRATION

One application of probabilistic simulation is *Monte Carlo integration*, where random number generators are used to approximate complicated integrals. While numerical integration problems are more usually solved by the methods shown in Section 3.7, they provide an interesting first application of Monte Carlo methods. We consider the simple example of approximating the value of π.[1]

Consider the problem of integrating the first quadrant of the unit circle. We know that the area under the curve shown in Figure 8.2 is $\pi/4$. If we can approximate the area under the curve, we can multiply the resulting value by 4 to estimate π.

Figure 8.2 illustrates how Monte Carlo integration works. The figure shows the first quadrant of the unit circle and a rectangular box that is 1 unit on each side enclosing the quadrant of the circle. Monte Carlo integration proceeds by generating points within the bounding box that are uniformly distributed and computing the fraction of those randomly generated points which fall under the curve being integrated. In the

---

[1] As Exercise 8-1 shows, this is not a particularly good method for computing a value for π. However, it does serve as a good illustration of how simulation can be used.

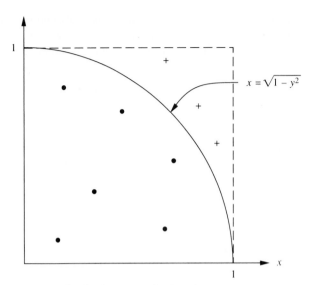

$$x = \sqrt{1 - y^2}$$

+ Randomly generated points above curve

• Randomly generated points below curve   **Figure 8.2** Monte Carlo integration.

figure, these random points are shown as small crosses and dots. Those points under the curve are illustrated with dots, and those above the curve are shown with crosses. If we generate a sufficiently large number of random points, the fraction falling under the curve will, in the probabilistic sense, come closer and closer to approximating the integral of interest.

The C code for implementing this procedure is shown below. It uses the function **simple_uniform()** developed in Section 8.3 to draw (x, y) values which are uniformly distributed inside the square enclosing the curve.

```c
/* program to use Monte Carlo integration
   to approximate PI */

#include <stdlib.h>

/* simple uniform 0,1 generator */
double simple_uniform(void);

main()
{
   int i;          /* a loop counter */
   int count=0;    /* counter of draws under curve */
   int maxdraws;   /* maximum number of draws */
   double x,y;     /* values drawn in rectangle */

/* get number of draws */
   printf("Enter number of points to be drawn: \n");
   scanf("%d", &maxdraws);
```

```
/* loop through draws */
  for (i=1; i<=maxdraws; i++) {
    x = simple_uniform();   /* draw x value */
    y = simple_uniform();   /* draw y value */
    if(x*x + y*y < 1.0)   /* check if point */
      count++;             /* is inside circle */
  }

  printf("Estimate of PI is %lf\n", 4.0*count/maxdraws);
}


/* function to generate pseudo-random
   number between 0 and 1 */

double simple_uniform(void)
{
  return( (double) rand() / RAND_MAX);
}
```

The logic of the program is straightforward. The test for whether a point is below the unit circle simply checks whether the value of **x*x + y*y**, the square of the distance between the point and the origin, is less than 1. If so, the point must lie below the circle. The program iterates until a user-specified number of trials is reached and then outputs the estimate of π.

8.5 PROGRAMMING PROJECT: A SIMPLE QUEUEING SYSTEM

Simulation can also be used to model what are called *queueing processes*. In this section we consider a service such as a bank teller or a grocery checkout line where people arrive for service at random times. If the bank teller or checkout clerk (more generally called the *server*) is available, the customer is served immediately. The time required to serve the customer is also random. If the server is busy, the customer joins a line which operates as a *first in, first out queue*.

If we know the random properties of the time between successive arrivals of new customers and the time it takes to serve customers, the behavior of such systems can be simulated quite easily. For now, we assume that there are two functions **draw_arrival()** and **draw_service()** which, when called, return a pseudo-random value for the next interarrival time between customers and the next service time, respectively.

The queue simulation executes by keeping track of the state of the system between events. In this case, the only two events that can occur are the arrival of a new customer or the completion of service for a customer. Each time an event occurs, we use the appropriate random number generator to predict the time of the next event of its type. The simulation steps through time, moving in jumps from the current event to the next event. At each of these discrete jumps, statistics about the number of people in the queue, the average waiting time and the total service time are maintained. After a sufficiently large number of events have been simulated, the simulation stops and outputs the summary statistics.

Figure 8.3 illustrates how the state of this simple queueing system might change. Figure 8.3a shows the queue at time 2534, where there are three people in the queue and the server is busy. The next event to occur will either be the server finishing with the current customer, allowing the person at the head of the line to be served (thus reducing the length of the queue to 2), or another customer arriving for service, increasing the queue length to 4. In the situation shown in Figure 8.3a, the next simulated completion of service is at $T = 2589$, while the next customer arrival is at $T = 2595$, so the next event will be the completion of service, as shown in Figure 8.3b. Summary statistics on the total time people spend in the system are updated and the time clock is updated to 2589. In addition, the function **draw_service()** is called to find when the next customer will be finished by the server. In this example, the time the next customer's service will be completed is 2634. Since a customer will arrive before that time, the next event to be simulated will be the arrival of another customer at time 2595, increasing the queue length back to 3. This is shown in Figure 8.3c.

We will assume that the time between successive arrivals of customers is uniformly distributed between 0 and 50 seconds and that the time it takes to serve a customer is uniformly distributed between 15 and 25 seconds. The two probability density functions

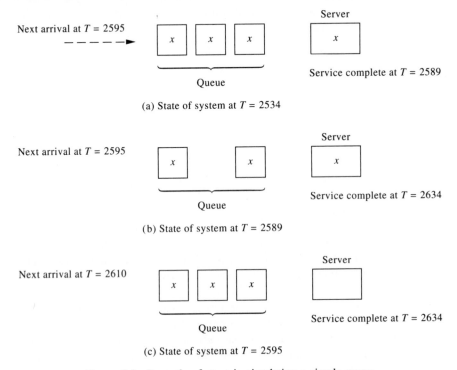

Figure 8.3 Example of steps in simulating a simple queue.

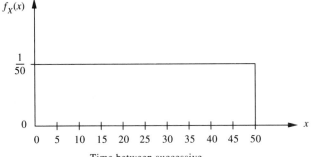

Time between successive
arrivals of customers (sec)

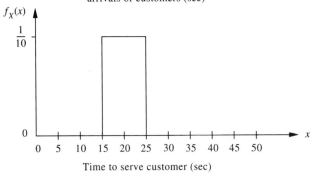

Time to serve customer (sec)

Figure 8.4 Probability density functions for simple queue.

for these random processes are shown in Figure 8.4. For simplicity, our simulation will keep track of only two summary statistics, the number of total minutes spent by all customers in the system and the total number of customers served.

Virtually all simulations of random processes over time, including the simple queueing system defined above, have a set of common elements. These elements may vary greatly in complexity for different simulation programs. In the simple queueing system, the elements and how they are implemented are as follows:

- A set of variables that describe the *state* of the system. In the simple single-server queue, the state of the system is summarized by a variable **in_system**, which is an **int** that stores the number of people either in the queue or currently being served.
- The *simulation clock*. The **double** variable named **time** will be used to keep track of the simulated time in seconds.
- The pending events. These include all the events which could occur next. In the case of the simple queue, the next event is either the arrival of a new customer or the completion of service for a current customer. The times for these events will be stored in the **double** variables **ta** and **tf**, respectively. However, when there is no one in the system, the next event will always be the arrival of the next customer. We will indicate this situation by setting the time at which the next service will be completed, **tf**, to the largest representable **double**, **DBL_MAX**. This value is set in the standard header file **float.h**.

- Summary statistics. The total number of minutes spent by all customers and the total number of customers served will be stored in the integer variables `total_sec` and `total_cust`, respectively.
- Initialization of system. The simulation will be initialized with `time` set to zero and with an empty queue. Because there is no one being served when the simulation starts, the first event will always be the arrival of a customer rather than the completion of service. The initial state of the system is established through the following variable definitions:

```
double time = 0.0;       /* simulated time = 0 */
double total_sec = 0.0; /* total customer time */
int total_cust = 0;  /* total customers served*/
int in_system = 0;  /* no one in system */
double tf = DBL_MAX;    /* from header <float.h> */
double ta = draw_arrival(); /* next arrival time */
```

- A method to select the next simulated event. In this case, the next event will be determined by finding the minimum of `ta` and `tf`. If `ta` is less than `tf`, then the next event is an arrival of a new customer; otherwise, the next event is a service completion.
- Event actions. Each time an event of a particular type occurs, the simulation program must modify the state of the system, update the summary statistics, and, in some cases, determine the time at which the next event of that type will occur. In the simple queue, event actions for the arrival of a new customer and the completion of service for a current customer are needed.

When the service of a customer is completed, the following actions must be taken:

1. The summary statistics being maintained by the simulation must be updated.
2. The simulation clock must be advanced to the time when the completion of service occurs.
3. The total number of customers in the system should be decremented by one to reflect the departure of the served customer.
4. If there are customers in the queue waiting for service, then the completion time for service of the next customer in the queue needs to be simulated.

On the other hand, if the next event is the arrival of a new customer, the simulation program must do the following:

1. The summary statistics being maintained by the simulation must be updated.
2. The simulation clock must be advanced to the time when the arrival occurs.
3. The total number of customers in the system must be incremented by one to reflect the arrival of the next customer.
4. If there is no one currently being served, then the time at which the arriving customer will complete service should be simulated.
5. The time at which the next customer arrives should be simulated.

- Report generation. We will use simple `printf()` statements to report the simulation results. In a larger simulation program, the report generation may be quite complicated.
- Control of simulation. Some way of determining when the simulation is completed needs to be established. We will define a variable `tfinish` as the total number of seconds to be simulated. The value of `tfinish` will be input by the user of the simulation.

Once the foregoing components of a simulation are defined, the actual implementation is usually straightforward. The following `main()` program simulates the simple queue.

```c
/* program to simulate simple queue */
#include <stdio.h>
#include <stdlib.h> /* header file for rand() */
#include <float.h> /* floating point header file */

/* function prototypes */

double draw_arrival(void); /* arrival drawing */
double draw_service(void); /* service completion */

main()
{

   double time = 0.0; /* simulated time = 0 */
   double total_sec = 0.0; /* total customer time */
   int total_cust = 0; /* total customers served*/
   int in_system = 0; /* no one in system */
   double tf = DBL_MAX; /* from header <float.h> */
   double ta = draw_arrival(); /* next arrival time */
   double tfinish; /* total simulated time */

 /* read in total simulation duration */
   printf("Enter time to be simulated in seconds: ");
   scanf("%lf", &tfinish);

 /* main event loop of simulation */
   while(time < tfinish) {
     if(tf <= ta) { /* next event is service completion*/
       total_sec += in_system * (tf-time);
       total_cust++; /* increment customers served*/
       time = tf;    /* update clock */
       in_system--;  /* decrement no. in system */
       tf = DBL_MAX;
       if(in_system > 0) /* draw next service time */
         tf = time + draw_service();
     }
```

```
              else {  /* next event is an arrival for service */
                total_sec += in_system*(ta-time);
                time = ta;
                in_system++;
        /* if no one is being served, draw service
           completion time for new customer*/
                if(in_system == 1)
                   tf = time + draw_service();
                ta = time + draw_arrival();
              }
          }

        /* output results of simulation */
          printf("Total customer-seconds in system = %lf\n",
                 total_sec);
          printf("Total customers served = %d\n", total_cust);
          printf("Time per customer served = %lf\n",
                 total_sec/total_cust);
        }
```

The implementations of **draw_arrival()** and **draw_service()** are minor modifications of the transformation used in creating the function **simple_uniform()** shown in Section 8.3. The key difference is that the values returned by the library routine **rand()** must be both scaled and shifted. In general, if some random value is uniformly distributed between a and b, then its value can be simulated by starting with a simple uniformly distributed value between zero and one, multiplying it by $(b - a)$ and adding a to the result. This method is used in the following implementations of **draw_arrival()** and **draw_service()**.

```
        /* draw arrival time for next customer */
        double draw_arrival()
        {
        return( (double) rand()/RAND_MAX  * 50.0);

        }

        /* draw service time for customer */
        double draw_service()
        {

        return( (double) rand()/RAND_MAX  * 10.0 + 15.0);

        }
```

8.6 RANDOM NUMBER GENERATORS

Note to Reader: This section can be skipped without loss of continuity.

In Section 8.3 we introduced the standard library function **rand()**, which generated a pseudo-random integer uniformly distributed between zero and some upper value **RAND_MAX**. In this section we explore the most widely used techniques for creating such functions. The two approaches we illustrate are the *linear congruential* and *additive congruential* methods.

8.6.1 Linear Congruential Method

The linear congruential method begins with a starting value called the *seed*. Each time the method is invoked, it uses the most recently generated value to create the next value. If r_i is the value generated from the ith invocation of the linear congruential method, the value of r_{i+1} is found from the following formula:

$$r_{i+1} = (a\,r_i + b)\%m$$

where a, b, and m are fixed values.

To see how this technique works, consider the simple case where $a = 13$, $b = 3$, and $m = 17$. If we select the value of the seed (defined as r_0) to be 1, the first four values we would obtain would be

$$r_0 = 1$$
$$r_1 = (13 * 1 + 3)\%17 = 16$$
$$r_2 = (13 * 16 + 3)\%17 = 7$$
$$r_3 = (13 * 7 + 3)\%17 = 9$$
$$r_4 = (13 * 9 + 3)\%17 = 1$$

Note that after four values are generated the next value of r in this sequence will repeat the cycle that began with r_0. Thus, in this simple example, the values will cycle very quickly, resulting in poor pseudo-randomness. More generally, because the linear congruential method uses only the most recently generated value to create the next value, the method can *at best* have a cycle of m values. All else equal, we would like to select values of a, b, and m so that the cycle length is as long as possible.

Long cycle length is only one of the desirable properties of a pseudo-random-number generator. We would also like a sequence of numbers which have subsequences that have the same properties as true independent random numbers. For example, a long cycle in which the first half of the values generated were less than $m/2$ and the second half were greater than $m/2$ would not be desirable. While such a sequence could occur with truly random values, it would be extremely unlikely.

Unfortunately, there is no absolute set of rules for selecting the values of a, b and m so as to produce a good linear congruential generator. The methods that seem to work the best rely on a combination of some theory that is beyond the scope of this book and a great deal of empirical trial and error. Some of the rules of thumb that can be applied are as follows:

- The value of a should be equal to $8x + 5$, where x is a positive integer.
- When a and m are expressed as binary numbers, a should be one digit shorter than m.
- The value of b should be odd.
- The value of m should be large, ideally the largest representable integer value on the machine for which the linear congruential generator is being implemented.
- There should be no obvious pattern in the digits of a and b.
- The value of b should be selected to be approximately $.21132m$.

Even with the guidelines above, creating efficient implementations of good linear congruential generators is somewhat of an art. Aside from the problems of selecting the parameters of the generator, implementation of the foregoing function in a way that executes efficiently and correctly on many different computers is quite difficult. For example, the computation of $a * r_i$ can result in a value which exceeds the largest representable integer, producing an integer overflow. When this occurs, some computers keep only the lower-order bits that can fit in an integer, while others keep as many bits as can be represented in an unsigned integer. Given this lack of standardization, we urge most programmers to rely on the professionally created random number generators.

8.6.2 Implementation of rand() in the C Library

The ANSI C standard [American National Standards Institute 88] recognizes that implementations of **rand()** will often be optimized for specific computers. Rather than impose a single implementation, the standard provides an example, leaving it to individual C library developers to either use that example or create their own. The ANSI example is implemented assuming that the size of the largest random number, **RAND_MAX**, is set to 32767. The code is given below.

```
/* example implementation of rand()
   given in ANSI C specification */

static unsigned long int next=1;

int rand(void)
{
  next = next * 1103515245 + 12345;
  return (unsigned int) (next/65536) % 32768;
}
```

Because the linear congruential method requires that each new value generated make use of the most recently generated value, C code implementing the method requires some way to specify storage which is not automatically allocated and reused each time the function is invoked. Rather than pass the previously generated value to the function as an argument each time it is invoked, the implementation above uses an external variable, **next**, to store the most recently generated value. This external variable is defined as **static**, a storage class that we have not until now introduced.

In the C language, any external variable can be accessed from any part of a C program, including parts in separately compiled source files. When creating a library function such as **rand()**, it is important to avoid the possibility that a user of your library function will accidentally use the same name for an external variable as the library uses. Defining an external variable as **static** limits the *scope* of the definition to the source file, thus avoiding the possibility of an unintended *name conflict*. Any variable defined by the programmer with the name **next** in a different source code file will be a variable with separate storage from the static variable **next** in the implementation of **rand()**. In effect, the use of the storage class **static** hides the variable from any function that is not in the same source code file.

The effect of declaring an external variable **static** parallels the use of **static** functions discussed in Section 5.8. The effect of the **static** declaration on functions is to hide the function, limiting the scope of its declaration to the source file in which it is defined.

When applied to a variable defined inside a function (i.e., internal variables), the **static** storage class has a slightly different meaning. Unlike internal, automatic variables, where memory is allocated when the function is invoked and then freed after the function returns, **static** variables inside functions are persistent. Memory for internal **static** variables is allocated and initialized when the program is compiled, and it is never reallocated or reused.

Note that the ANSI example version of **rand()** shown above uses the **unsigned long** integer data type to represent the value **next**. This forces all the integer arithmetic in the function to be done in **unsigned long** form, avoiding the possibility of an integer arithmetic overflow occurring. The computations in the **return** statement then reduces **next** to a value which can be stored in an **int** between zero and 32767.

In actual applications, we often want random number generators with cycle lengths that are considerably longer that the ANSI-required minimum of 32767. Implementations of such generators in an efficient way may require code that is not portable across different computer architectures. Such implementations will have to be rewritten to take into account how different computer systems represent integer values and how they handle overflows resulting from integer arithmetic operations.

One common case we consider here is computer processors that:

- Represent **int**s in 32 bits, where the high-order bit represents the sign of the integer value
- Discard the higher-order bits when integer operations cause an overflow

For such systems, the following implementation of **rand()** will provide pseudo-random numbers between 0 and **INT_MAX**, the largest representable positive **int**. **INT_MAX** is defined in the standard header file **limits.h**.

```
/* nonportable implementation of rand() that
   will work on many computer systems that
   use 32 bits to represent an int */

#include <limits.h>

static int next=1;

int rand(void)
{
/* generate next value */
   next = next * 843314861 + 453816693;
   if(next < 0) /* reduce to value that can be an int */
      next += INT_MAX + 1;
   return(next);
}
```

The statement

```
next = next * 843314861 + 453816693;
```

will often generate a value which is too large to be represented by an **unsigned int**, and will thus often cause an integer overflow. This overflow may set the highest-order bit of **next**, resulting in a value which in many integer representations will be *negative*. This can be converted back to a positive value on most machines by adding **INT_MAX+1**, as in the statement

```
next += INT_MAX + 1;
```

8.6.3 Setting the Seed in the C Library

Another function provided in the standard C library allows the programmer to reset the seed value of the random number generator. This function, **srand()**, has an **int** containing the new seed value as its sole argument. For example, the invocation

```
srand(1);
```

will reset the value of **next** to 1, having the effect of restarting the series of the random numbers generated by **rand()** from the beginning. This feature of the standard random number generator in the C library can be used to "replay" a simulation or begin a new simulation starting at the last random number generated.

The implementation of **srand()** resets the value of **next** as follows:

```
void srand(int seed)
{
   next = seed;
}
```

Note that since **next** is a **static** variable, the source code for **rand()** and **srand()** must be in the same file.

8.6.4 Additive Congruential Method

The second technique of generating linear methods we will demonstrate is the *additive congruential method*. This method begins with a table of random integers and generates a new random number by adding two entries in the table, ignoring any high-order bits that overflow as a result of the integer addition. The new number is then inserted into the table, replacing the oldest entry.

Implementing the additive congruential method requires that we initialize the table. One simple way is to use the linear congruential method to load entries into the table. We will use this approach here, creating a function **rinit()** that loads the initial table. This function would be invoked before the additive congruential random number generator is used. The version we present here uses a table with 55 entries. The size of the table, however, will be set with a **#define** preprocessor directive to a value **TSIZE**, making it easy to change. The function **rinit()** has no arguments and no return value. The implementation is as follows:

```
/* initialization of additive congruential table */
#include <stdlib.h>
#define TSIZE 55

static int table_index;
static unsigned int table[TSIZE];

void rinit(void)
{
   for(table_index=0; table_index<TSIZE; table_index++)
      table[table_index] = rand();
}
```

Note that we use the **static** storage class for the array **table** and the integer **table_index**. As in the case of the linear congruential generator, this is done to avoid the possibility that these two variables will be accessed from other source code files.

The function that actually generates the random numbers will be called **rand_add_cong()**. It will have no arguments and will return a pseudo-random

int. In order to implement this function, we will have to select an algorithm for deciding which two numbers in the table should be added to produce the next number.

In the implementation below, the table will be treated as though it wrapped around on itself, much in the same way as we did in creating a hash table in Section 6.6. Knuth [Knuth, Donald E. 73b] recommends using values which are 24 entries apart, starting with entry zero in the table. Thus, the first random number we generate will be the sum of entries of the most recently generated value, **table[54]**, and element 24 items "in front" of the last element, or **table[23]**. This first invocation will replace the oldest entry, **table[0]**, with the newly generated value. The next invocation of the function will use the sum of entries 0 and 24 and would replace entry 1. This process would continue, replacing the oldest entry on the list with the sum of the entry last added and the item 24 entries ahead of that item.

Assuming that the code is in the same source file as the code for **rinit()**, the implementation of **rand_add_cong()** is as follows:

```
/* implementation of additive congruential
   random number generator */

#include <limits.h>

#define B 23
#define D 54

int rand_add_cong(void)
{
   table_index = (table_index+1)%TSIZE;
   table[table_index] = (table[(table_index+B)%TSIZE] +
               table[(table_index+D)%TSIZE]) % INT_MAX;
   return(table[table_index]);
}
```

This code assumes that the function **rinit()** was invoked to initialize both the table of random values and the variable **table_index**.

Note that the implementation above uses **unsigned int**s to represent entries in **table** so that the addition of two values represented as **int**s does not generate an overflow. This relies on an assumption that the largest **unsigned int** is at least twice the largest signed **int**. While this is true in many cases, C does not guarantee it. Thus, the version of **rand_add_cong()** given above needs to be checked when it is used on a specific computer.

8.7 CREATING NONUNIFORM RANDOM NUMBERS

Functions such as **rand()** serve as the basic building blocks for generating random variables with different probability density or mass functions. We have already seen how to use **rand()** to create uniformly distributed values. In this section we show some more general ways of creating pseudo-random values.

We consider three different methods for generating random numbers with different distributions. Each of these techniques is described in a subsection below.

8.7.1 Inverse Cumulative Method

Whether a random variable is continuous or discrete (or some combination), it is always possible to construct what is called the *cumulative distribution function* for that variable. For any random variable X, the cumulative function, denoted by $F_X(x)$, is defined as the probability that X is less than or equal to some value x. In conventional mathematical notation the cumulative distribution function is written as

$$F_X(x) = \text{Prob}[X \leq x]$$

For example, suppose the random variable X is uniformly distributed between three and five. The probability density function for this variable is illustrated in Figure 8.5a. The cumulative distribution function for that variable is the area underneath the

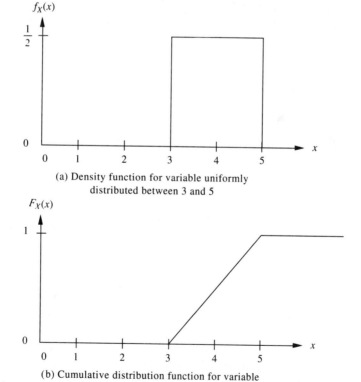

(a) Density function for variable uniformly
distributed between 3 and 5

(b) Cumulative distribution function for variable
uniformly distributed between 3 and 5

Figure 8.5   Simple probability density function and its cumulative distribution function.

density function, which can be computed as follows:

$$F_X(x) = 0 \quad \text{if} \quad x < 3$$

$$F_X(x) = \text{Prob}[X \le x] = \int_3^x dx = \frac{x-3}{2} \quad \text{if} \quad 3 \le x \le 5$$

$$F_X(x) = 1 \quad \text{if} \quad x > 5$$

This function is depicted in Figure 8.5b.

Note that every cumulative distribution function is by definition bounded between zero and one. It is also monotonically increasing, though not necessarily strictly so. It is often possible to solve for a closed-form equation for the *inverse cumulative function*, denoted by $F_X^{-1}(x)$. The inverse cumulative function can be used to generate random values with any probability distribution that has an invertible cumulative distribution function $F_X(x)$ by using the following procedure:

- Step 1. Draw a random value u which is uniformly distributed between zero and one.
- Step 2. Compute $x = F_X^{-1}(u)$ the value of the inverse cumulative evaluated at u.

Values generated by this procedure will have the cumulative distribution function $F_X(x)$. As an example, consider the *exponential* probability density function

$$f_X(x) = \lambda e^{-\lambda x}, \quad x > 0$$

where λ is some positive value. This probability density function is often used to represent random arrival or service processes, where X is the time between successive arrivals. Figure 8.6a shows a graph of this function for the case where $\lambda = 2$. The cumulative distribution function for the exponential density function can be found as follows:

$$F_x(x) = \int_0^x \lambda e^{-\lambda x} dx = 1 - e^{-\lambda x}$$

This cumulative function is shown for the case $\lambda = 2$ in Figure 8.6b.

If we define u as the argument of the cumulative distribution function, the inverse cumulative is given by

$$F_X^{-1}(u) = \frac{-\log[1-u]}{\lambda}$$

Figure 8.6c illustrates the inverse exponential cumulative function for the case $\lambda = 2$.

Given the inverse cumulative for the exponential function, we now can write a C function named **expon()** that generates exponentially distributed pseudo-random numbers. This function has one argument, **lambda**, a **double** value equal to the parameter λ in the exponential density function. It returns a pseudo-random value as a **double**. The implementation is as follows:

```
/* generate an exponentially distributed random value */
```

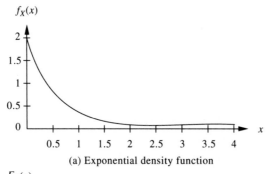

(a) Exponential density function

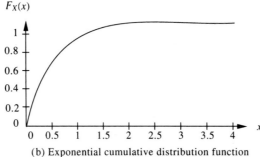

(b) Exponential cumulative distribution function

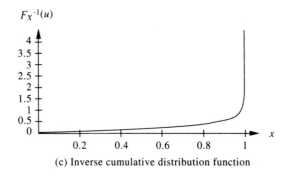

(c) Inverse cumulative distribution function

Figure 8.6 Exponential density function, cumulative distribution function, and inverse cumulative function.

```
#include <stdlib.h>
#include <math.h>      /* needed for log function */

double expon(double lambda)
{
   return(-log( 1.0 -(double) rand()/RAND_MAX)/lambda);
}
```

This version of **expon()** can be improved by noting that the value
1.0 - (double) rand()/RAND_MAX
will be uniformly distributed between zero and one, and can therefore be replaced by
(double) rand()/RAND_MAX.

The inverse cumulative method can be used on discrete-valued random variables as well. For example, suppose that we wanted to create a random number generator to simulate the outcome of tossing a six-sided die. In this case the probability mass function for the die toss is

$$P_X(x) = \begin{cases} \frac{1}{6}, & x = 1, 2, 3, 4, 5, 6 \\ 0 & \text{otherwise} \end{cases}$$

The cumulative distribution function for the die toss would be

$$F_X(x) = 0, \qquad x < 1$$

$$F_X(x) = \frac{1}{6}, \qquad 1 \le x < 2$$

$$F_X(x) = \frac{1}{3}, \qquad 2 \le x < 3$$

$$F_X(x) = \frac{1}{2}, \qquad 3 \le x < 4$$

$$F_X(x) = \frac{2}{3}, \qquad 4 \le x < 5$$

$$F_X(x) = \frac{5}{6}, \qquad 5 \le x < 6$$

$$F_X(x) = 1, \qquad x \ge 6$$

We can use the inverse of this function to create a C function named **die_toss()** that returns an **int** between 1 and 6. An implementation of **die_toss()** is given below.

```
/* generate a die toss */

#include <stdlib.h>

int die_toss(void)
{
   int die;
   die = (double) rand()/RAND_MAX *6 + 1.0;
   if(die == 7)
     die = 6;
   return(die);
}
```

Note that the implementation must deal with the case where **rand()** returns the largest possible value, **RAND_MAX**. In this case, the computation
(double) rand()/RAND_MAX *6 + 1.0
will produce a value of 7, which is clearly not allowed. We deal with this case here by simply resetting the value to 6. This will skew the simulated die toss slightly. An additional small source of error is that the value of **RAND_MAX** may not be evenly divisible by 6. Exercise 8-10 explores a method for correcting these biases.

Another way to implement the outcome of the toss of a die is to use modulo arithmetic on the integer value produced by **rand()**. More specifically, the expression

```
rand()%6 + 1
```

is guaranteed to yield a value between 1 and 6. While this approach seems simpler than the method given above, it will often produce values which are not randomly distributed. This is because the least significant digits of the values produced by many random number generators are often not particularly random. It is far safer to use transformation methods that use the entire value generated by **rand()** rather than the approach above, which uses only the least significant digits.

8.7.2 Construction Method

A second method for generating random variables with different density or mass functions exploits known mathematical relationships among different random variables. In this approach we begin by generating values for a random variable X with a known probability density or mass function. These values are then transformed by computing a function $Y = g(X)$, where g is selected so that Y has the probability mass or density function we want.

For example, if some random variable X is uniformly distributed between zero and one, then it is straightforward to show the variable

$$Y = g(X) = a + (b - a)X$$

will be uniformly distributed between a and b. This result is used below to create a C function that generates a uniformly distributed variable.

```
/* generate a uniform from a to b */

#include <stdlib.h>

double uniform(double a, double b)
{
   return( (double) rand()/RAND_MAX * (b-a) + a);
}
```

Use of the construction method requires some knowledge of how various functions $g(X)$ transform the distribution of random variables. This topic is called the study of *derived distributions* and is covered in most introductory courses in probability theory. We limit our discussion here to two common cases, one discrete and one continuous.

The discrete case is where we are making successive drawings of a Bernoulli distributed variable (See Section 8.2). In each Bernoulli drawing, the probability $X = 1$ is p, and the probability $X = 0$ is $1 - p$. We are frequently interested in random processes that count the results of a series of independent Bernoulli trials. For example, we might be interested in simulating a system of elevators in a building, where each elevator holds 10 people. As a component of such a simulation, we might need to simulate the number of people going to the top floor of the building. If each person has a probability p of going to the top floor, we can treat the total number (out of 10 elevator users) who go to the top floor as the sum of 10 different Bernoulli drawings. In this case, if we define Y as the number going to the top floor, we can construct Y as follows:

$$Y = X_1 + X_2 + X_3 + X_4 + X_5 + X_6 + X_7 + X_8 + X_9 + X_{10}$$

Variables such as Y that are the sum of independent, identically distributed Bernoulli variables are said to be *binomially distributed*. The following code illustrates the implementation of functions that simulate both Bernoulli and binomially distributed variables.

```
/* generating a Bernoulli variable
   and a binomial variable */

#include <stdlib.h>

/* use inverse cumulative method to
   generate Bernoulli outcome */
int bernoulli(double p)
{
  if((double) rand()/RAND_MAX < p)
    return(1);
  else
    return(0);
}

/* prototype for Bernoulli function */
int bernoulli(double);

/* generate binomially distributed value */

int binomial(double p,  /* Bernoulli probability */
             int n)     /* number of Bernoulli trials */
{
  int i;                /* variable to control loop */
  int count=0;          /* counter */
  for(i=0; i < n; i++)
    count += bernoulli(p);
  return(count);
}
```

A useful example with continuous variables is the *Gaussian* or *normal* distribution described in Section 3.7. The standard form of this function is

$$f_X(x) = \frac{1}{\sqrt{2\pi}} e^{-x^2/2}$$

This function can be used as a probability density function. In the form given above, the distribution is centered around zero. Many processes studied in statistics and other fields produce random outcomes that, appropriately normalized for shifts in their central tendency and spread, have this distribution.

The density function of a Gaussian-distributed random variable can be shifted by adding a constant value. This has the effect of sliding the entire density function left or right along the x axis, centering it at any other value. The form above also has what is called *unit standard deviation*. In qualitative terms, the standard deviation of a random variable measures the degree of "spread" of its distribution. If we multiply a Gaussian-distributed variable by a constant, its standard deviation is multiplied by that constant.[2]

It is possible to show that we can generate values whose distribution closely approximates the Gaussian distribution by summing a number of uniformly distributed values. This approximation is accurate enough for most purposes when we use ten or twelve uniformly distributed values. We generally need to transform the sum of the uniformly distributed values to obtain the correct average and standard deviation. More specifically, it can be shown that if $X_1, X_2, \cdots, X_n$ are independent random variables that are uniformly distributed between $-1/2$ and $1/2$, then the variable

$$Y = \sum_{i=1}^{n} X_i$$

is approximately Gaussian distributed with mean zero and standard deviation $\sqrt{n/12}$. The accuracy of this approximation improves as n gets larger.

The result above leads to the set of C functions shown below. The function **standard_gaussian()** generates a Gaussian-distributed value with mean zero and standard deviation 1. It has no arguments and returns a pseudo-random number as a **double**. The function **general_gaussian()** has two **double** arguments, the mean **m** and the standard deviation **sigma**, and returns a **double** containing a Gaussian-distributed random number with the corresponding mean and standard deviation.

```
/* generate standard gaussian drawing */

double standard_gaussian(void)
{
   int i;                  /* counter for loop */
   double sum = 0.0; /* sum of uniform (0,1) variates */
   for(i=1; i<=12; i++)
     sum += (double) rand()/RAND_MAX;
   return(sum-6.0);
}
```

---

[2]In mathematical terms, the standard deviation is the square root of $\int_{-\infty}^{\infty} (x - m)^2 f_X(x)dx$, where m is the mean of the random variable.

```
/* generate Gaussian drawing with mean
   m and standard deviation sigma */

double general_gaussian(
    double m,                  /* mean of distribution */
    double sigma)              /* standard deviation */
{
    return(standard_gaussian()*sigma + m);
}
```

Since **standard_gaussian()** uses values which are uniformly distributed between zero and 1 (rather than $-1/2$ and $1/2$), the value of **sum** is shifted by subtracting 6 before it is returned. Also, using the value $n = 12$ in **standard_gaussian()** avoids the need to normalize the resulting sum of uniform variables to correct the standard deviation in order to have a standard deviation of 1. It also gives resulting random values that very closely approximate the Gaussian distribution.

8.7.3 Rejection Method

The last technique of pseudo-random-number generation we present is the *rejection method*. This approach uses the same idea as Monte Carlo simulation, creating potential values and deciding which values should be counted and which should be rejected. This method can be used when the cumulative distribution function has no closed form or when it cannot be inverted. For example, suppose that we have a continuous random variable which has a complicated density function $f_X(x)$ such as the one shown in Figure 8.7. Further, suppose that there is no closed-form solution for the cumulative distribution function corresponding to this density function.

In the example shown in Figure 8.7, the density function is nonzero over the interval from 0 to 6. In cases such as this, the algorithm for the rejection method is as follows:

- Step 1. Find the largest value of $f_X(x)$ which can occur. Call this value f^{max}. Also, find the interval $[x^{min}, x^{max}]$, where the density function is nonnegative.[3]
- Step 2. Draw a uniformly distributed value x^* in the interval $[x^{min}, x^{max}]$.
- Step 3. Draw a uniformly distributed random value y^* in the interval $[0, f^{max}]$.
- Step 4. If $y^* \leq f(x^*)$, then return x^*. Otherwise, go to step 2.

This method works by selecting potential values for the random variable and then accepting or rejecting them with probability $f_X(x^*)/f^{max}$ and $1 - f_X(x^*)/f^{max}$, respectively. Those values x where the density function is small will be rejected relatively frequently, while those for which the density function is large will be accepted more often. Overall, the set of accepted values will have a density function identical to $f_X(x)$.

---

[3]There may be more than one interval where the density function is positive. The rejection method generalizes to this case with only minor modifications. See Exercise 8-9.

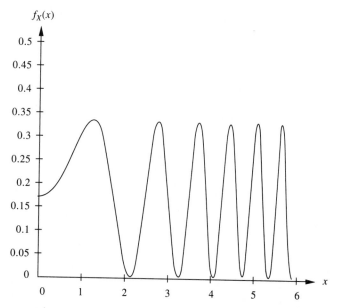

Figure 8.7 Example of a complicated density function.

The core of the rejection method can be implemented in a straightforward way. The density function $f_X(x)$ (or more exactly, a pointer to that function), the interval $[x^{min}, x^{max}]$ and f^{max} will be arguments to the function. The implementation is based on the assumption that function prototypes and implementations for **bernoulli()** and **uniform()** are provided elsewhere. The C code is as follows:

```
/* general-purpose rejection method simulator  */

double rejection(
   double (*f)(double), /* density function */
   double fmax, /* largest value of f */
   double xmin, /* minimum value of random variable */
   double xmax) /* maximum value of random variable */
{
/* initial trial value */
   double xstar = uniform(xmin, xmax);

   /* loop until value is accepted */
   while (bernoulli(f(xstar)/fmax) == 0)
     xstar = uniform(xmin, xmax);
   return(xstar); /* return simulated value */
}
```

Note that the function **rejection()** uses the function **bernoulli()** to determine whether or not to reject the trial value of **xstar**. The rejection or acceptance of any particular value of x is in fact a Bernoulli process, where the probability of acceptance, p, is given by

$$\frac{f_X(x^*)}{f^{\max}}$$

8.8 USING HEAPS IN SIMULATIONS

While the example of a simple queueing system in Section 8.5 illustrated some of the major concepts in computer-based simulation, the structure of that problem made keeping track of pending events very straightforward. The only possible events in the simple queuing model are the arrival of a customer or the completion of service for a customer already in the system. The number of pending events in most simulations is much larger, and it is usually desirable to create some systematic data structure for keeping track of them and determining which event will occur next. The data structure should operate as what is called a *priority queue*, allowing the user to find the next event easily. The ideal data structure for implementing a priority queue would not only allow efficient access to the next pending event but would also make adding new events to the queue straightforward.

Storing the pending events as an unsorted list has the advantage of making it easy to add new events to the list, but makes it very time consuming to find the next pending event. The alternative of using a sorted list makes finding the next event simple but imposes the relatively high overhead of keeping the list in sorted order each time a new pending event arrives in the course of the simulation. A third alternative, the use of a data structure called an *ascending heap*, is a compromise between these two extremes that balances ease of adding new elements against ease of finding the next pending event in a way that is well suited for use in large simulations.

An ascending heap is defined as a complete binary tree (or one that is as complete as possible given the number of entries in it) in which the key value for every node is greater than or equal to the key value for its parent node. Thus, the root node of an ascending heap will always contain the entry with the smallest key value.

For example, suppose that there are 11 pending events in a simulation, and that these events are scheduled to occur at the following times: 2340, 2349, 2467, 2890, 2045, 2219, 2195, 2187, 2765, 2235, and 2934. Figure 8.8 illustrates one possible ascending heap that uses these event times as key values. Note that in general there is more than one possible ascending heap for any set of key values.

When the pending events in a simulation are organized into an ascending heap, it is trivial to find the next pending event. *The root node will always contain the next event to be simulated.* In most simulations, each entry in the heap will include information about the event (such as a code indicating the event type) as well as the time at which it is scheduled to occur. This data can be placed in a **struct**.

In order to use heaps in simulations, we will need to develop algorithms and corresponding implementations in C to perform the following operations:

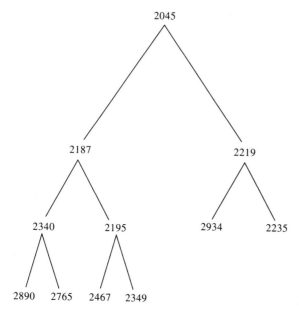

Figure 8.8 Ascending heap.

- Create an initially empty heap.
- Add an event to the heap by placing it in the correct position to preserve the heap's properties.
- Remove the next pending event, and adjust the heap to preserve its properties.

The particular properties of a heap make these operations reasonably straightforward. In the implementation below we will use a very simple heap that stores only the event times. This can easily be extended to hold more information about simulation events.

The elements of the heap will be stored in an array, where the positions in the array implicitly define a complete binary tree. In this *implicit tree* form, position zero in the array stores to the root of the tree, positions 1 and 2 hold the left and right child of the root respectively, positions 3 and 4 store the children of position 1, etc. Figure 8.9 illustrates how the positions in the array map to positions in the tree. In the general case, if i is the array index of some node in an implicitly stored tree, then the elements $2i + 1$ and $2i + 2$ (if they exist) hold the left and right child nodes of i. In addition, the parent of a node with index $i > 0$ will be stored in element $(i - 1)/2$ of the array, where the computation of $(i - 1)/2$ is done using the standard rules in C for integer arithmetic.

Following the approach used in Chapter 5, we will begin by declaring a template for a **struct** to hold the basic information about the heap. This **struct** will include the maximum size of the heap, how many entries are in the heap, and an array used to store the values in the heap in an implicit binary tree. For convenience, we will use a **typedef** statement to define a data type called a **Heap**. We will also need to

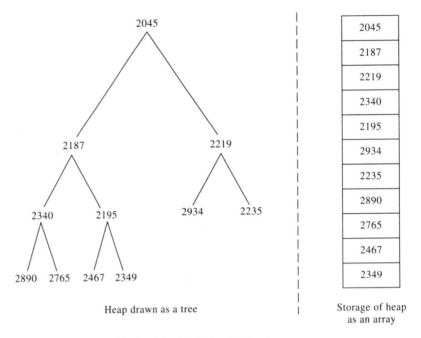

Figure 8.9 Storing a tree in an array.

#include some standard header files and #define some values for later use. The C preprocessor directives and structure templates that will begin the implementation are as follows:

```
/* initial statements for heap implementation */

#include <stdio.h>
#include <stdlib.h>

#define TRUE 1
#define FALSE 0

/* struct template for a heap */
struct heap_info {
    int last_used;        /* last used node in heap */
    int capacity;         /* max entries in heap */
    int * event_times;    /* times of pending event */
};

/* typedef for Heap */

typedef struct heap_info * Heap;
```

A function called **make_heap()** will allocate memory for a heap and return a pointer to it. It will have as its sole argument an **int** setting the maximum size of the heap. (See Exercise 8-17 for extensions of the heap implementation which allow the maximum size to increase when needed.) The function **make_heap()** returns either the **Heap** that was created or the **NULL** pointer if the attempt to allocate memory for the heap failed. The implementation is given below.

```
/* make an empty heap */

Heap make_heap(int max_size)
{
  Heap h;
/* allocate heap */
  h = malloc(sizeof(struct heap_info));
  if(h == NULL)               /* check memory allocation */
    return(NULL);

/* allocate storage for array of event times */
  h->event_times = calloc(max_size, sizeof(int));
  if(h->event_times == NULL) {
    free(h);
    return(NULL);
  }

/* initialize heap values */
  h->last_used = -1;
  h->capacity = max_size;
  return(h);

}
```

make_heap() uses a convention that the value of the structure member **last_used** is set to -1 when the heap is empty. This will make it easy to check whether or not the heap has elements in it. Note also that if the attempt to allocate memory for the array of event times is unsuccessful, **make_heap()** uses the standard library function **free()** to release the memory for the heap before returning the **NULL** pointer. The practice of always freeing memory that has been allocated but which will not be used should be followed whenever feasible.

The next function, **add_to_heap()**, adds a new element to the heap. The algorithm for this operation begins by placing the new value at the "bottom" of the heap (i.e., in the next available position in the array used to store the heap's values). The algorithm then begins swapping this new element with its parent node until either the new element becomes the root of the tree or its parent's value is less than its own. Once this swapping is completed, the new element is in a position that preserves the heap's properties.

Figure 8.10 illustrates this process. The heap begins with the 11 entries originally shown in Figure 8.8. Figure 8.10a shows the first step in the addition of the value 2198 to the heap, placing that value in the next available node at the bottom of the tree. This value is then compared with its parent's value of 2934, and because the new value is less than its parent, the two are exchanged as shown in Figure 8.10b. This process is repeated again, resulting in the exchange of the new value with 2219 as shown in Figure 8.10c. At this point, 2198 is in a position that preserves the heap, and the algorithm terminates.

This algorithm for adding a new element to the heap is implemented in the C function **add_to_heap()** provided below. The function has two arguments, the **Heap** to operate on and the **int** to be added. It returns an **int** which is **TRUE** if the addition is successful and **FALSE** if the heap is already full.

```
/* function to add new entry to heap. Returns
   TRUE if addition is successful, FALSE if
   there is no space on heap */
```

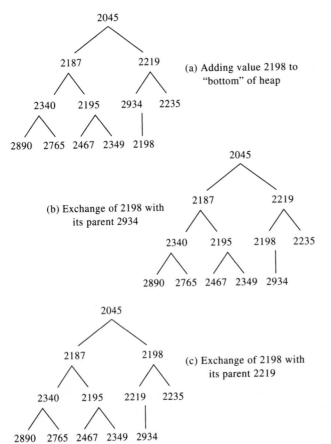

(a) Adding value 2198 to "bottom" of heap

(b) Exchange of 2198 with its parent 2934

(c) Exchange of 2198 with its parent 2219

Figure 8.10   Adding 2198 to a heap.

```
int add_to_heap(
  Heap h,                         /* heap to add entry to */
  int time)                       /* time of event */
{
  int index;                    , /* subscript for insertion */
  int parent;                     /* parent node of index node */

/* check if there is space for insertion */
  index = h->last_used + 1;
  if (index == h->capacity)
    return(FALSE);

/* add node to bottom of heap and swap it with parent
   until correct place is found */
  parent = (index-1)/2;
  while(index>0 && h->event_times[parent] > time) {
    h->event_times[index] = h->event_times[parent];
    index = parent;
    parent = (index -1)/2;
  }

/* put new entry into place found */
  h->event_times[index] = time;
  h->last_used++;
  return(TRUE);
}
```

The last of the heap functions will delete the root of the heap, which by definition is always the smallest entry. The algorithm works by removing the root node and then relocating the element that was at the bottom of the heap to an appropriate place that preserves the heap. The search for the appropriate place begins at the root node. At each step in the search, either the element that was at the bottom is inserted or the node being examined is replaced by the *smaller* of the node's children. This process continues until the smaller of the child nodes exceeds the value from the bottom of the heap or a leaf node of the tree is reached. In either case, the node that was at the bottom of the heap is inserted where the algorithm stops.

Figure 8.11 illustrates the removal of the root node from the heap shown in Figure 8.8. The root node is deleted and the node at the bottom of the heap, 2349, needs to be placed in its correct position. This is shown in Figure 8.11a. The question mark in the figure denotes the now empty root node, and the circle around the value 2349 indicates that this is the node to be relocated. The two children of the root node are examined, and the smaller of the two, 2187, is compared with 2349. Since the smaller child is less than the node we are trying to put in its correct place, the root is replaced by its smaller child, and that child's position becomes the next candidate spot for 2349 as shown in Figure 8.11b. Again, the smaller child node is less than 2349, so the heap is adjusted to the configuration shown in Figure 8.11c. Finally, the smaller of the child nodes (in this

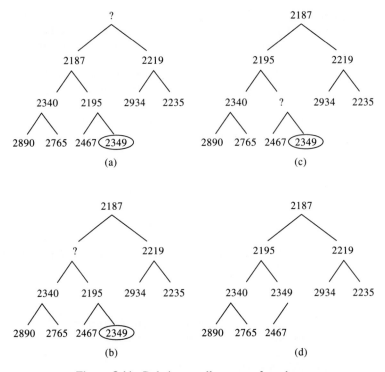

Figure 8.11 Deleting smallest entry from heap.

case, there is only one child) is greater than 2349, so the original bottom node is placed as shown in Figure 8.11d.

To implement the algorithm above we will need a function to find the smallest child of any node in the heap. We will call this function **small_child()**. It will have two arguments: the **Heap** being used and an **int** indicating the index number of the parent node in the array in which the heap is stored. It returns the index number of the smaller child node or -1 if the parent node is a leaf of the tree. The C code for **small_child()** is given below.

```
/* function to find small child node in heap */
int small_child(
  Heap h,                 /* heap to use */
  int index)              /* index of parent node */


{
/* indices of right and left children */
  int rchild, lchild;

  lchild = 2*index + 1; /* compute left child index */
  rchild = lchild + 1;  /* compute right child index */
```

```
/* check if the node index has any children at all */
  if(lchild > h->last_used)
    return(-1);

/* check if there is a right child and if so,
   if it is the smaller of the two child nodes */

  if(rchild <= h->last_used &&
       h->event_times[lchild] > h->event_times[rchild])
    return(rchild);
  else
    return(lchild);
}
```

Given `small_child()`, the heap deletion algorithm is implemented in the function `delete_from_heap()` shown below. This function has two arguments, the **Heap** to delete from and a pointer to an **int** where the deleted value is to be stored. It returns an **int** which is **TRUE** if the deletion was successful or **FALSE** if the heap was empty to start with.

```
/* function to delete smallest value from heap.
   Returns TRUE if deletion is successful, FALSE
   if heap is empty. Time of deleted event is
   returned through pointer argument. */

int delete_from_heap(
  Heap h,               /* heap to delete entry from */
  int *time)            /* pointer to time of event */
{
  int value;   /* value of last heap entry */
  int parent, child; /* parent and child nodes */

/* check if there are any entries on heap */
  if(h->last_used < 0)
    return(FALSE);

  *time = h->event_times[0]; /* set next event time */
  value = h->event_times[h->last_used];
  h->last_used--;

/* adjust heap by swapping smaller of children
   with parent until correct place for bottom
   node on heap is found */

  parent = 0;                     /* start at root */
  child = small_child(h, parent); /* get smaller child */
  while(child >= 0 && value > h->event_times[child]) {
```

```
        h->event_times[parent] = h->event_times[child];
        parent = child;
        child = small_child(h, parent);
    }

    /* insert value from bottom of heap */
      h->event_times[parent] = value;
      return(TRUE);


}
```

The complete code for the heap implementation can be placed in a separate source code file and a header file can be created with the function prototypes for the heap operations, preprocessor directives and the **struct** templates. This would create a small library of heap functions that could be useful to other programmers, particularly if the heap structure were augmented as discussed in Exercise 8-17.

8.9 PROGRAMMING PROJECT: SIMULATING A MODEM POOL

8.9.1 Description of a Modem Pool

In this section we develop a simulation of a *modem pool*. A *modem* is a hardware device used to convert digital information to a form suitable for transmission on standard phone lines. Such devices are widely used in telecommunications to connect computer terminals (or personal computers running software that emulates standard terminals) to a computer that is often shared by many potential users. Commercial information services make extensive use of modems to allow their customers to access their databases and other services. In large computer installations, it is common to have a bank of modems connected to a sequence of phone lines. Users can dial a single number and they are automatically connected to the computer through any one of the available modems in the pool. If there are no modems available, they receive a busy signal.

The advantage of a modem pool is that it allows potential users to share the available modems. Service is provided on a first come, first served basis. In addition, the users need only remember a single telephone number.

One of the major questions facing someone installing a modem pool is how many incoming phone lines and modems should be installed. It is usually economically impractical to have one line for every potential user. On the other hand, if too few modems are installed, many people requesting service will have to wait, potentially for long periods of time. In this programming project we will construct a simulation of a hypothetical modem pool and explore the tradeoffs in selecting the number of modems to install.

We begin with a set of assumptions about the patterns of use of the modem pool.

- For each potential user of the system, the number of minutes between successive first requests for service is exponentially distributed with parameter $\lambda = .001$.
- When someone calls the modem pool and receives a busy signal, they then redial the number after waiting a time that is uniformly distributed between zero and 20 minutes later. If they receive a busy signal again, they redial again after a wait that is uniformly distributed between zero and 25 minutes. This pattern continues so that each time they receive their nth busy signal, the distribution of the time until their next call is uniformly distributed between zero and $15 + 5n$ minutes.
- Once a person is connected to the computer through the modem pool the time they use that modem is uniformly distributed between 50 and 200 minutes.

Note that the assumptions above are entirely hypothetical. In a real application of simulation to this problem we would have to collect data about the actual pattern of times between phone calls for service and the durations of computer sessions.

8.9.2 Major Variables Used in Simulation

The simulation of the modem pool will need variables that collectively define the state of the system, the simulation parameters, and summary statistics for use in making a decision about the number of modems. For convenience, the system state will be stored in external variables, making it possible for all the functions to access them.

Below are the variables we will use:

```
/* system state variables */
Heap h;                       /* the event heap */
double time = 0.0;            /* simulated time */
int modems_in_use = 0;        /* number of lines in use */

/* simulation parameters */
double time_limit;            /* simulation duration */
int nlines;                   /* number of lines in pool */
int nusers;                   /* number of users */

/* summary statistics */
int failed_requests=0;     /* number of failed requests */
int requests = 0;          /* number of requests served */
double user_minutes = 0.0; /* minutes lines are used */
```

The **Heap h** will be used to store all pending events in the simulation. The heap functions will be identical to those presented in Section 8.8 except that each event will consist of two values: the time at which the event will occur (stored as a **double**) and a code indicating the type of event, stored as an `int`. The coding system for event types will follow the convention below.

- A code value of 1 will indicate the end of a terminal session currently in progress.
- A code value of 2 will indicate a first request for service (i.e., an initial call by a user).
- A code value of $i+2$ will indicate a repeated call after receiving i consecutive busy signals.

To make this coding system easier to use, we will use the following **#define** statements:

```
/* code for end time of session */
#define END_SESSION    1

/* code for terminal session request */
#define BEGIN_SESSION 2
```

The simulated time is stored in the variable `time` and the number of modems being used at any time during the simulation is stored in the integer `modems_in_use`.

The simulation parameters are mostly self-explanatory. They describe the total simulated time, the total number of phone lines serving the modem pool, and the number of potential users. These parameters will be set by reading inputs from the user of the simulation when the program starts.

The final three variables are summary statistics. The variable `requests` counts the total number of calls to the modem pool, and `failed_requests` counts the number of calls that received busy signals. Finally, the variable `user_minutes` holds the number of minutes in total that the modems in the pool are used. They will be used to summarize the fraction of times the average modem is in use during the simulation.

8.9.3 Functions Used in Simulation

The heap management functions we use are straightforward extensions of those presented in Section 8.8. We will therefore not show their implementation. Instead, we will assume that the extended versions of these functions are in a separate source code file and that a header file `heap.h` provides the function prototypes for the heap functions. In this case, the `add_to_heap()` and `delete_from_heap()` functions will have three arguments. For both functions, the first argument is the `Heap` to operate on. In the case of `add_to_heap()` the remaining arguments are a `double` containing the event time and an `int` with the event type code. For `delete_from_heap()` the two arguments are pointers to a `double` and an `int` in which the event time and code respectively are put.

The simulation will consist of seven functions plus `main()`. The first two functions were described earlier in the chapter. They are random number generators for the uniform and exponential density functions. Their function prototypes are given below.

```
/* function prototypes for random number generation */
double uniform(double, double);
double expon(double);
```

The remaining five functions besides the **main()** correspond to specific actions during the execution of the simulation. These functions are as follows:

- **initialize()** sets up the starting conditions for the simulation, including reading the simulation parameters from the user.
- **new_session()** is invoked whenever an event requesting use of a modem arrives. Its arguments are the time of the event and the type code of the event. This function determines whether or not a modem is available. If there is one available, it updates the system state and generates a completion time, putting the session completion event on the heap. If no modem is available, then the time of that user's next call is generated and a repeat call event is placed on the heap.
- **complete_session()** handles the completion of a session. As with **new_session()**, its arguments are the time of the event and the type code of the event.
- **print_statistics()** outputs the summary statistics after the simulated period is over.
- **heap_error()** is invoked whenever an error in the heap manipulation occurs. It has a character string as its argument. This string is output before the simulation is aborted due to the error.

None of these functions return values. Their function prototypes are given below.

```
/* function prototypes for simulation */
void initialize(void);
void new_session(double, int);
void complete_session(double, int);
void print_statistics(void);
void heap_error(char *);
```

8.9.4 Implementation of Simulation

We now turn to the implementation of the modem pool simulation. The **main()** function contains the overall event loop. It begins by invoking **initialize()** and then starts a **while** loop. Each iteration of the loop involves taking the next event off of the heap and updating the state of the simulation depending on the event type. If the event is a call for service, **new_session()** is invoked; otherwise, **complete_session()** is called. Once the simulation is complete, the function **print_statistics()** is invoked to report on the simulation results.

The implementation is given below.

```
/* main() function for simulation */

main()
{
  int test;           /* flag for failed heap use */
  int type;           /* type of next event */
  double t;           /* time of next event */

/* initialize simulation */
  initialize();

/* start main event loop */
  while(time < time_limit) {
    test = delete_from_heap(h, &t, &type);
    if(!test)
      heap_error("Unable to delete from heap\n");
    user_minutes += modems_in_use *(t-time);

/* check if start of a new terminal session */
    if(type >= BEGIN_SESSION) /* start of new session */
      new_session(t, type);
/* if event not start of new session,
          it is a completion */
    else
      complete_session(t, type);
    time = t;
  }
  print_statistics();
}
```

The code for `initialize()` begins with a series of `printf()` and `scanf()` statements to prompt users for appropriate inputs and read them in. (A more elaborate version might check those inputs to determine whether they have appropriate signs and magnitudes.) The function then makes the heap and generates the first calling event for each of the potential users, placing each event on the heap. Note that the heap is created with a capacity equal to the number of potential modem users. This is because every potential user can have only one pending event, either a request for a new session or the end of a current session. The complete implementation is as follows:

```
/* function to initialize simulation */
void initialize(void)
{
  int i;                     /* variable used to control loop */

/* get number of lines, users, and simulation length */
```

```
    printf("Enter number of lines in modem pool: ");
    scanf("%d", &nlines);
    printf("Enter number of users: ");
    scanf("%d", &nusers);
    printf("Enter duration of simulation: ");
    scanf("%lf", &time_limit);

/* make the heap */
  h = make_heap(nusers);
  if(h == NULL)
    heap_error("Unable to allocate heap\n");

/* initialize first request times */
  for(i=0; i<nusers; i++)
    add_to_heap(h, expon(.001), BEGIN_SESSION);


}
```

The function **new_session()** is invoked whenever a call to the modem pool arrives. It tests whether there is an available modem, and if so, generates the ending time for that session. If no modem is available, then **new_session()** generates the time that user will call again. The implementation of **new_session()** is

```
/* function to initiate new session */
void new_session(
    double t,            /* time of event */
    int type)            /* type code of event */

{
  int test;        /* test value for heap operations */

  requests++;    /* update number of service requests */
  if(modems_in_use < nlines) {      /* lines free */
    test = add_to_heap(h, t+uniform(50.0, 200.0),
                        END_SESSION);
    if(test)
      modems_in_use++;
    else
      heap_error("Unable to add event to heap\n");
  }
  else {                            /* no lines free */
    test = add_to_heap(h, t+uniform(0.0, 10.0+type*5.0),
                        type+1);
    if(test)
      failed_requests++;
    else
      heap_error("Unable to add event to heap\n");
  }
}
```

The third function is `complete_session()`. This function must update the number of modems in use and generate the next calling time for the user whose session just ended. The C code is as follows:

```c
/* function to handle completion of session event */
void complete_session(
   double t,              /* time of event */
   int type)              /* type code of event */
{
   int test;       /* test value for heap operations */
/* completion of service */
   test = add_to_heap(h, t+expon(.001), BEGIN_SESSION);
   if(test)
     modems_in_use--;
   else
     heap_error("Unable to add event to heap\n");
}
```

The remaining two functions are straightforward. `print_statistics()` simply outputs the average modem utilization, the number of served requests, and the number of failed requests. The function `heap_error()` outputs the error message contained in the string passed to it and exits. The code for these two functions is given below.

```c
/* function to output simulation statistics */
void print_statistics(void)
{
   printf("Utilization was %lf\n",
           user_minutes/(nlines*time));
   printf("Total requests was %d\n", requests);
   printf("Number of failed requests was %d\n",
           failed_requests);
}

/* function to handle error in heap */
void heap_error(char *message)
{
   printf("%s", message);
   exit(1);
}
```

8.9.5 Using the Modem Pool Simulation

As a last part of the programming project, we explore how the simulation might be used to aid in guiding some decision. Suppose, for example, that a modem pool serves 50 users. One possible design question is, "How many modems would we need so that on average no more than 1 in 10 of the people dialing in receive busy signals?" Alternatively, we might be interested in how the average utilization of modems varies

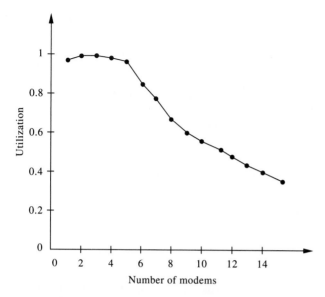

Figure 8.12 Graph of modem utilization vs. number of modems.

with the size of the modem pool. For example, we might design the pool so that the average modem utilization is 50%.

Figures 8.12 and 8.13 illustrate the predictions of the simulation model. They reflect results from running the program for 50,000 simulated minutes with different numbers of modems ranging from 1 to 15.

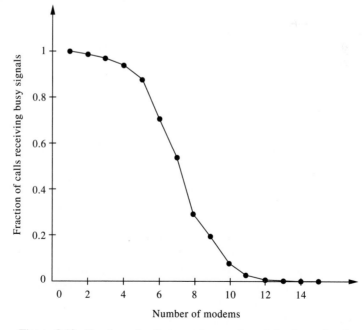

Figure 8.13 Fraction of calls to modem pool receiving busy signals.

Figure 8.12 graphs the size of the modem pool versus the fraction of the total of modem time actually used servicing calls. Utilization is very high when the pool is small because there are many pending requests. Once one session is completed, very little simulated time elapses until the arrival of the next request for use of the pool. The utilization drops off to about 50% when there are 11 modems.

Figure 8.13 depicts predictions from the same set of simulations but shows the fraction of all calls for use of the pool that received busy signals. The graph shows that when there are more than 13 modems, there are no calls during the simulation which receive busy signals. Thus, at least in the simulated period, additional modems beyond 13 are never used. Additional modems beyond this level serve to reduce the utilization of the average modem without improving any aspect of the pool's performance.

8.10 MAJOR ISSUES IN LARGE SIMULATIONS

Monte Carlo simulation can be a powerful tool for building quantitative models of complex systems with random behavior. However, as with many such tools, there are a number of potential pitfalls that need to be avoided if the resulting simulations are to be useful and not misleading. We consider some of these in this section.

The first issue is the need for what is often termed a *warm-up period* in a simulation. Simulations often start with an empty system, thus producing misleading statistics in the early time periods. Unlike the simple examples shown in this chapter, it is common practice to run the simulation for some amount of simulated time before beginning the collection of any summary statistics. This avoids skewing the summary statistics by mixing data from the startup phase with the more representative steady state of the system. The decision of how long the warm-up period should be is most often based on experiments with the simulation program, looking for the point in the simulation where the startup effects have largely been eliminated.

A second issue is how long a simulation should run. Because the process being simulated is random, any simulation produces just one possible series of events. If the simulated period is too short, it is possible for a chance series of unusual events to give an unrepresentative set of summary statistics. For example, in the simple queueing simulation, there is always a chance that there will be a series of very quick arrivals, increasing the average time in the queue to a value which is much greater than the true steady state. Running the simulation for a longer period decreases the probability that such unlikely sequences will dominate the summary statistics. In general, simulations should be run a number of times with different starting seed values. If these different runs yield very different results, a longer simulation period is likely warranted.

A related issue is the need to understand what the summary statistics from a simulation really mean. Most often, the summary statistics of a simulation are used to decide among alternative designs or operating procedures. For example, an airline might use a simulation to determine how different operating schedules might affect their on-time arrival rates. Because the process being simulated is random, the summary statistics will also be random variables. Different runs of the simulation with different seed values for the random number generator should yield different numerical results.

In deciding what course of action to take based on simulation summary statistics, one should exercise care not to overemphasize small differences which may be due to randomness rather than any systematic performance differences among the alternative designs. Differences in summary statistics due to intrinsic randomness are said to be *statistically insignificant*. The theoretical and practical issues in testing whether or not observed differences are truly meaningful is a topic considered in most statistics texts but is beyond the scope of this book.

A fourth potential pitfall in using simulation has to do with how detailed a simulation model should be. There is a tendency to build simulations that capture every imaginable aspect of the process being studied, often resulting in simulations which are extremely difficult to implement correctly. Simulation modeling projects often fall behind schedule because they try to capture too much detail, and even when these efforts produce working computer codes, the programs are often so computationally intensive that they become unwieldy tools for real decision making. While each simulation effort is different, some thought should be given as to whether the decision being made using the simulation requires that any particular detail of the system be included.

It is often possible to ignore small effects in building a simulation if those factors will have little bearing on the final decision. Judgments on such matters require a good understanding of both the system being studied and the potential decisions being considered. In large projects, the people developing the simulation should make sure they work closely with people who understand the system and have experience with its operation.

The last potential problem with simulation modeling is that the results it produces are often given *too* much attention. Because a simulation model closely parallels the actual operation of a system, simulation developers often forget that the goal is to predict the behavior of a *real system*. As with any model, it is crucial to compare the simulated results with the real-world experience before any decisions are made based on the model's predictions. It is amazing that this validation effort is often given short shrift in many studies, resulting in reams of simulation results of questionable accuracy. When planning any simulation, there should always be a clear plan for collecting data about real systems and comparing that data with the simulation as part of a complete validation effort.

8.11 SUMMARY OF CHAPTER 8

In this chapter we explored the development and application of Monte Carlo simulation. It began with an introduction to simple random variables and the processes that generate them. Processes with discrete outcomes are characterized by *probability mass functions*, while those with continuous outcomes are described by *probability density functions*. The Bernoulli process and the uniform density functions are examples of discrete and continuous processes, respectively.

The idea of random number generators was then introduced, and the function **rand()** in the standard C library was presented. This function returns an integer value between zero and the value **RAND_MAX** defined in the standard header file **stdlib.h**.

The value returned by **rand()** is called a *pseudo-random number*. Because such numbers are created by an entirely deterministic process, they are not truly random. However, as a practical matter, with some care they can be used as though they were random, and virtually all Monte Carlo simulations are based on such values.

Two different examples of simulation were then presented. The first uses pseudo-random numbers to approximate the value of an integral. This method generates a rectangle around the portion of the function to be integrated. Some number of (x, y) points in the rectangle are then drawn and the fraction that fall under the function of interest is found. The simulated fraction is an approximation to the actual fraction of the bounding box's area that is under that curve. This technique is called *Monte Carlo integration*.

The second example simulated a single-server queue, where customers arrive for service by some known random process and are served on a first come, first served basis. Variations of such processes arise very often in the service sector of the economy.

The question of how pseudo-random number generators are implemented was then explored. The *linear congruential method* was introduced along with some discussion of the problems of creating completely portable implementations of such functions. A second, less frequently used technique for random number generation, the *additive congruential method*, was also described.

Methods by which the results of integer-valued functions such as **rand()** can be used to generate pseudo-random numbers with other distributions were then presented. The three basic techniques shown are the *inverse cumulative method*, the *construction method*, and the *rejection method*. These approaches were used to create random number generators for the *exponential* distribution, the *binomial* distribution, the *Gaussian* distribution, and the *uniform* distribution.

The creation and use of a data structure called an *ascending heap* were then described. An ascending heap is a complete binary tree in which each node has a key value which is smaller than the corresponding values in its child nodes. Such data structures are often used to store pending events in a simulation because they balance the computational effort needed to retrieve the next pending event and the difficulty of adding new events. C functions for creating a heap, adding a new node to a heap, and deleting the smallest value in a heap were explained.

A programming project that simulated the operation of a modem pool was then shown. This simulation modeled a bank of modems in which incoming phone calls are routed to any one of the available modems in the pool. This project illustrated how a simulation can be used to explore the design tradeoffs in creating a service. In particular, the tradeoff between the costs of adding more lines and the improvement in service provided was illustrated.

Finally, in Section 8.10 we discussed some of the potential pitfalls in using simulation. These included the need to be careful in interpreting the significance of summary statistics from simulations and the danger of trying to create simulations which are too detailed. The need to validate simulation programs against actual experience with the real-world systems they simulate was also discussed.

8.12 EXERCISES

8-1. Modify the Monte Carlo integration program shown in Section 8.4 so that it computes the value of π ten times for a given value of **maxdraws** and computes the average sum of squared differences between the estimated value and the true value of π for each set of estimates. To do this, you can use the following formula:

$$S^2 = \frac{1}{10} \sum_{i=1}^{10} (\pi_i - 3.14159)^2$$

where S^2 is the average squared error and π_i is the estimate of π obtained in the ith set of trials. Run this new program using 1000, 2000, 5000, and 10,000 draws. Graph how the value of S^2 varies with the number of trials.

8-2. Modify the simple simulation presented in Section 8.5 so that when the queue has more than three people waiting for service, the next arriving customer decides not to join the line. This behavior is called *balking*. Your simulation should keep track of the number of people who decide to forego the service rather than wait in line. Run your program and compare the number of people served and the total number of minutes spent per customer in the system with the values obtained from the same process without balking.

8-3. Modify the simple simulation presented in Section 8.5 so that there are two servers rather than one. Assume that there is a single line, and that the next customer always goes to the first available server. Assume that the probability density function for the time needed to serve a customer is the same for the additional server as for the original one. Run the simulation and compare the predicted number of minutes spent per customer in the system with the values from the program described in Section 8.5.

8-4. Modify the simple simulation presented in Section 8.5 so that there are two servers rather than one, but make each new server only half as fast (on average) as the original server. Thus, the server time for each of the new servers should be uniformly distributed between 30 and 50 seconds. Assume that there is a single line, and that the next customer always goes to the first available server. Run the simulation and compare the results with the original simulation. Discuss whether one server provides better or worse service than two servers each half as fast. Provide an intuitive explanation for your result.

8-5. Consider a manufacturing process which produces three-dimensional rectangular objects. Each item is X centimeters by Y centimeters by Z centimeters. Because of imperfections in the materials used and the manufacturing process, the values of X, Y, and Z are random. Suppose that X is uniformly distributed in the interval [1.9, 2.1], Y is distributed in the interval [2.8, 3.2], and Z is uniformly distributed in the interval [3.9, 4.1]. Answer the following:

   (a) What are the smallest and largest values the volume of the object can have?

   (b) Write a function in C that simulates values for the volume.

   (c) Write a **main()** function that simulates 10,000 objects, computes their volumes, and creates a histogram of the frequency of volumes from the smallest to the largest values in increments of .5 cubic centimeter. The program should use your answers to parts (a) and (b) and output the fraction of manufactured products in each volume range.

8-6. Suppose we encode the faces on a deck of playing cards so that each card is represented by a unique integer between 1 and 52. Propose a possible coding system and then write a function that returns an array of cards which is shuffled so that the order of the cards is random. Write a **main()** function that invokes your shuffling function and then outputs the values in the simulated, shuffled deck.

8-7. Imagine a situation where two types of customers arrive for service, one who requires t_1 minutes to serve and a second who requires t_2 minutes to serve. Assume that customers arrive with an exponential distribution and that each customer is of type 1 with probability p and type 2 with probability $1 - p$. Write a function that generates customer arrivals from this process. The function should have as arguments the overall arrival rate for the exponential process, the value of p, and a pointer to an **int**, where the function places either a 1 or a 2, depending on the type of the simulated customer. The function should return a **double**, which is the simulated interarrival time between successive customers.

8-8. Define a random variable Z as the number of successive Bernoulli trials until the first event in which Bernoulli variable is a 1. This might be used, for example, to represent the number of coin tosses until the first head comes up. Variables defined by this process have a *geometric* distribution. Develop a function that uses the construction method to generate a random variable which has the geometric distribution. The function should have a **double** representing the probability p for the Bernoulli process that generates the zeros and ones and should return an **int**, which is the simulated value of Z.

8-9. Modify the function **rejection()** developed in Section 8.7.3 so that it accepts a linked list of intervals where the density function is non-zero rather than just a pair of **double** values that establish the interval for the density function. Each entry on the list should be a **struct** that contains the lower and upper values for an interval on the x axis and a pointer to the next interval on the list.

8-10. Use the idea of the rejection method developed in Section 8.7.3 to correct any bias in the function **die_toss()** so that each face of the die has equal probability of coming up. You will want to divide the range of possible integer values into six equal intervals. Since **RAND_MAX** may not be evenly divisible by 6, you will need to reject some outcomes of **rand()** to eliminate any bias.

8-11. Generalize the function you created in answering Exercise 8-10 so that it will generate integer outcomes between 1 and some integer argument **n** with equal probability.

8-12. Suppose that we have a river valley where the level of the river varies directly with the amount of rainfall. Storms in this valley arrive at exponentially distributed intervals with parameter $\lambda = .05$, where the time between storms is measured in days. The intensity of storms (measured in inches of rainfall) is uniformly distributed between .25 and 2.5 inches. Assume that the level of the river rises 1 foot for each .5 inch of rainfall.

Write a C function that simulates the level of the river at its highest point in a 20-year period. This is called the *20-year flood*. Then code a **main()** program that generates the 20-year flood level for 1000 intervals of 20 years. The function should compute and output the average height of the 20-year flood level.

8-13. A *random walk* is the path resulting from a series of randomly chosen steps from an initial starting point. Write a simulation that generates a series on n random steps. Each step should go in a direction that is drawn from a uniform distribution of angles between zero and 360 degrees and should be of length uniformly distributed between zero and 1 unit. You should simulate 10 random walks of 10, 100, and 1000 steps and output the average Euclidean distance between the beginning and ending points of the walks for each of these cases.

8-14. Consider a situation where n people are meeting at a given time. Suppose that the people arrive independently and that each person is late by a random amount of time that is exponentially distributed with parameter $\lambda = .2$ minute. Assume that the meeting does not start until all n people arrive. Write a simulation program that finds the average amount of time the meeting will start after the scheduled start time for $n = 3$, 5, and 10 people. Simulate 1000 meetings to compute this value. Then rewrite your simulation so that the meeting starts whenever $n - 1$ people arrive and rerun the same simulated situations.

8-15. The *trapezoidal* density function for a random variable X is as shown in Figure 8.14. The density function increases linearly between values a and b, is flat between b and c, and decreases linearly between c and d. The density function is zero outside the interval $[a, d]$.

    (a) Find the value of the height of the trapezoidal density function at its maximum value $f^{\max}$ shown in Figure 8.14.

    (b) Graph the cumulative distribution function corresponding to the trapezoidal density function.

    (c) Graph the inverse cumulative distribution function for the trapezoidal density function.

    (d) Write a C function that uses the inverse cumulative method to generate a trapezoidally distributed value. The arguments to the function should be the values of a. b, c, and d. The function should return the generated value in a **double**.

8-16. In the version of roulette played in U.S. casinos, the wheel has 38 slots, a set numbered 1 through 36, and two slots labeled 0 and 00. The odd-numbered slots are black and the even slots (other than 0 and 00) are red. Create a simulation program that plays a simplified version of roulette that has the following rules:

    • Players may bet on any number, including 0 and 00. If the ball falls on that number, the bet pays 36 to 1.

    • Players may bet on black or red. This bet pays 2 to 1. Entries 0 and 00 on the wheel are neither black nor red, so if the ball falls into these two entries, bets on black and red both lose.

    • Players may bet on numbers 1–12, 13–24, or 25–36. If the ball falls within the appropriate range, the bet yields 3 to 1.

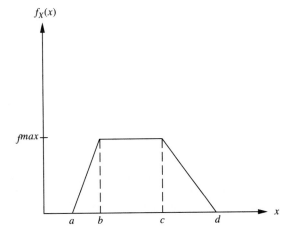

Figure 8.14 Trapezoidal density function.

Your simulation should give the player an initial stake of $100. It should allow the player to place any series of bets they can afford and then simulate the spin of the roulette wheel. The player should then be informed of which bets won and which lost, and the total value of the player's stake should be updated.

8-17. Modify the heap functions shown in Section 8.8 to add the following improvements:

- The heap should grow automatically when there is no more space in it for new entries. The function `make_heap()` should have an additional argument that is the increment by which the heap should grow when it is filled. You should also modify the `struct` used to store the heap so that the increment is included.

- Each new addition to a heap should be a `struct` of some new type `event_info`. The array allocated in creating the heap should be an array of this structure type. The first entry in this `struct` should be the key value, and the remaining entries should be additional information about the event. The function `add_to_heap()` should be modified to accept one of these `struct`s as an argument and the function `delete_from_heap()` should have a pointer to one of these `struct`s as one of its arguments.

8-18. A heap can be used to sort items. Write a function that reads in a series of integer values and places them into a descending heap. The function should then take items off the heap one at a time and place the items sequentially in an array. When the heap is empty the resulting array should have the integers in sorted order. Call your function `heap_sort()`. Write a `main()` function that reads 30 values, sorts them and outputs the resulting, sorted array.

8-19. Consider a circular bus route that is 8 kilometers in length with two stops spaced at equidistant locations around the circle. There are two buses which, at the beginning of the day, are positioned initially at the bus stops. Assume that the buses travel deterministically at 30 kilometers per hour when they are moving. At each stop, passengers arrive at time intervals which are exponentially distributed with parameter $\lambda = 4$, where time is measured in minutes. Once a bus reaches a stop, it requires 10 seconds per passenger for boarding. Assume that the time needed to discharge passengers is always 30 seconds. Write a program that simulates this system. Your simulation should output the average waiting time per passenger and the average distance between the pair of buses. *Note*: You can assume that all passengers get off the bus at each stop. If passengers are boarding one bus when a second bus arrives, assume that all the boarding passengers get on the first bus, allowing the second bus to drop off passengers without picking up others.

8-20. Magnetic disk drives that are used to store computer files generally read and write data in units called *sectors* or *blocks*. These sectors are organized in concentric rings often called *tracks* or *cylinders*. This organization is illustrated in Figure 8.15. When the computer makes a request for a particular sector, the *read/write head* of the disk drive is positioned to the correct track and then the data is read as the appropriate portion of the rotating disk passes by the head. Thus, the delay in getting reading or writing a sector consists of two parts: the time needed to move the disk head to the appropriate track (the *seek time*), and the time needed for the disk to rotate to where the sector is located (the *rotation time*).

Suppose that a particular disk has 1024 tracks, with each track holding 64 sectors. The sectors in the first track are numbered from 0 to 63, those in the second track are numbered from 64 to 127, etc. Develop a simulation model of the disk drive under the following assumptions:

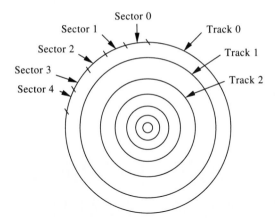

Figure 8.15 Organization of information on typical disk drive.

- Requests for reading or writing sectors arrive with exponentially distributed times between arrivals. If the time between successive requests is measured in milliseconds, then the parameter of the exponential density function is $\lambda = .05$.
- The sector numbers all have equal probability of being requested.
- The seek time (measured in milliseconds) from any track i to another track j is $|i - j|/25$.
- The disk rotates at 3600 revolutions per minute.
- If a request for a sector arrives and no current request is being serviced, then that request is handled immediately. Otherwise, the request is put in a first in, first out queue for service.

The simulation should output the average wait time for service by the disk, the average seek time, and the average rotational time. It should also output the longest time required to service a request. Run the program for 10,000 sector requests.

8-21. Some software systems attempt to improve the performance of disk drives by examining the queue of waiting requests and servicing the one on the track that is nearest to the current position of the read/write head. Modify the simulation you created in answering Exercise 8-20 so that it uses this strategy. Run the simulation for 10,000 sector requests and compare the results to those obtained in answering Exercise 8-20.

OBJECT ORIENTED PROGRAMMING AND C++

9.1 INTRODUCTION

In this final chapter we examine an important new trend in software design and development called *object-oriented programming*, or OOP. This approach is motivated by the need to reduce the costs of creating and maintaining computer software, particularly large, complex systems. It is leading to the evolution of an extension of the C language called *C++* (pronounced as "C plus plus") which extends the capabilities of C to provide a new set of powerful features which directly support object-oriented software development.

The basic philosophy of the object-oriented approach is to view parts of a large program as abstract "objects." This way of thinking was introduced in Chapter 6, where we developed abstract representations for data structures such as stacks, queues, lists, and trees. Object-oriented programming takes this philosophy still further by encouraging a style of software development in which *everything* is represented as an object and where objects contain not only data, but also the functions which operate on that data.

Consider, for example, a software system to aid engineers and architects in designing a new building. The various components of the building, such as the structural steel support, the floor assemblies, the foundation, and the exterior facade, might each be an object. These objects in turn may be made up of still other objects, such as steel beams, joints, or precast concrete members. Each object might contain data such as its physical dimensions and a distinct set of things it "knows" how to do, such as compute the stresses and strains under known loading conditions, compute its volume or cost, or draw itself on a graphics display.

Object-oriented software design offers a number of useful advantages over conventional approaches. The most significant of these are as follows:

- By organizing a program into discrete units such as objects, we can easily divide the programming of the entire system among several teams or individuals. Each object has its own internal representation and a well-defined interface. As long as programmers are careful to define the interfaces and implement them correctly, each team can construct the internal object representation of the parts of the program it is responsible for without consulting any of the other teams. As we shall see, the extensions to the C language provided in C++ facilitate this type of programming by allowing the programmer to "hide" the internal representation of an object from other objects, thereby restricting the access and manipulation of the object to the well-defined interface.
- Once we create an object that works well in one program, we can often reuse the implementation of that object in other software development projects. This ability to reuse parts of programs can vastly reduce the costs of software development. In addition, companies now sell *object libraries* that provide a set of general-purpose objects for functions such as computer graphics or numerical problem solving. It is generally cheaper to buy a tested and documented implementation than to create a new one.
- Languages such as C++ provide facilities that make it easy to adapt existing objects to meet new needs. These languages allow you, for example, to make new objects that have all the properties of some existing objects but have additional features as well.
- Creating programs that consist of objects often makes the overall structure of the complete software system clearer. Even though the objects are not real in the physical sense, their organization and structure provides a natural way of communicating how the software is organized to future generations of programmers who will have to maintain and upgrade the program.

Our goal in this chapter is to introduce some of the important ideas in object-oriented programming and C++. We stress that our treatment of this topic is entirely introductory. Readers interested in this subject should refer one of the many books that deal exclusively with this topic. Our intention is to give the reader a foundation upon which further study can be based. Readers interested in just the main ideas in object-oriented programming may wish to read only Sections 9.2 and 9.3.

9.2 KEY IDEAS IN OBJECT-ORIENTED PROGRAMMING

There are several key concepts that virtually all object-oriented software systems draw upon. In this section we describe the most important of these concepts. In later sections we show how these ideas are reflected in the C++ language.

The most significant concept is the idea of a *class*. An object class is analogous to the template for a **struct** in C. It defines the organization of a type of object, but does not allocate storage or create an object of that type. For example, we might define a class named **Polygon**. We can create any number of objects of this class. The declaration of the class defines the variables and functions that all objects of the class possess. A class named **Polygon** might have as its members a list of vertices and functions that draw the polygon on a display, determine whether points are inside or outside the polygon, or compute the area of the polygon. The variables and functions that comprise any class are often called the class' *members*.

The functions associated with a class which are intended to be invoked by other objects are called the class's *methods*. A subset of the methods associated with a class constitutes the public interface of that class.

The names of methods and variables of a class are local to that class. By this we mean that it is permissible to have a member in one class with the same name as a member in another class without any conflict. For example, a class named **Ellipse** and a class named **Triangle** might each have a method named **find_area()** which computes their respective areas and a variable named **centroid** that contains their centers of gravity. The two methods will have entirely different implementations but they are allowed to have identical names; the two variables are entirely distinct.

The members of a given class can be objects of other classes. For example, if the class **Polygon** contains a list of vertices, we might also define a **List** and a **Vertex** as separate classes, each with its own variables and its own methods.

Any particular object of a class is referred to as an *instance*. For example, a program might create many different instances of the class **Polygon**. Each instance is a distinct object with its own storage. The values of the variables inside one instance of a class will generally differ from the values in other instances.

For example, suppose that we had a drawing consisting of four polygons as shown in Figure 9.1a. In object-oriented programming, we would represent this set of polygons by first creating a class for all polygons. This class would provide a template for describing any polygon and would include among other things variables to hold the coordinates of a polygon's vertices and a method to draw a polygon. The coordinates themselves might be objects of some other class. Once the polygon class is created, each of the four polygons in Figure 9.1a could be an instance of that class, as shown in Figure 9.1b.

Instances can be created or destroyed as a program executes in the same way as we used dynamic memory allocation to create new data structures in Chapter 6. They can also be used as elements of arrays or as arguments to functions.

One of the most useful ideas in object-oriented programming is the concept of *inheritance*. Any new class can be declared to inherit the variables and methods of an already declared class. This means, for example, that we could declare a class called **RegularPolygon** which inherited the properties of the class **Polygon**. All the methods already created for the class **Polygon** would automatically be available to instances of the class **RegularPolygon**. In object-oriented terminology, **Polygon** is the *superclass*, or *base class*, of **RegularPolygon**, and **RegularPolygon** is a *subclass*, or *derived class*, of **Polygon**.

(a) Original drawing

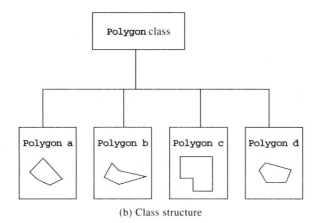

(b) Class structure

Figure 9.1 Example of classes and instances.

Inheritance allows the programmer to create new classes that are very similar to existing ones without having to reprogram any of the existing methods of the original class. In a sense, the methods of the base class come for free as a result of declaring that a derived class inherits the properties of an existing class. This can greatly reduce the effort in implementing or enhancing object-oriented programs. In creating the new class **RegularPolygon** we need only add variables and methods that are appropriate to the class **RegularPolygon** but are not supplied by the class **Polygon**. Object-oriented languages generally allow an arbitrary number of levels of inherited classes. For example, a class named **Square** could inherit the properties of **RegularPolygon**, which in turn inherited the properties of **Polygon**. The inheritance relationships are often called the *class hierarchy*.

Object-oriented languages support either *single inheritance* or *multiple inheritance*. In a language that provides only single inheritance, each class can have at most one base class. Thus, we cannot have a class such as **Square** that inherits all of the properties of the classes **RegularPolygon** and **Quadrilateral** unless one of these two classes was the base class (either directly or through a chain of single inheritance relationships) of the other.

Languages that permit multiple inheritance allow a class to inherit variables and methods from more than one base class. In such a language, a class **Square** could inherit all of the properties of the classes **RegularPolygon** and **Quadrilateral** even though these two classes had no inheritance relationship with each other.

Object-oriented programs use the idea of *encapsulation*, or *data hiding*. This means that some or all of the members of a class can be made inaccessible to methods that are not part of the class. One can think of such members as being local to the class but global to all the methods of that class. One advantage of allowing the programmer to hide some of the variables or functions in a class from other parts of the program is that it makes the class more modular. The creator of the class can force other programmers (and by implication, other members of the programming team) to access the object *only* through the well-defined interface for the class. The programmer of the class is free to implement that interface any way he or she chooses without affecting the work of any of the other programmers.

Object-oriented programming languages support the idea of *overloading*. The simplest form of this is called *function overloading*, where there may be several distinct implementations of a function for different argument types. For example, we might have a function which computes the average of a list of numerical values. This function might have several different implementations depending on whether the values being averaged are **int**s, **float**s, **double**s, etc. In a language that allows function overloading we could give each of these implementations the same name. The correct version would be automatically invoked depending on the type of the arguments.

A second type of overloading is *operator overloading*. In this case, operators such as addition, subtraction, and modulo arithmetic can be given new meanings. In a very limited way, C already has a form of operator overloading. For example, the division operator in the expression **6/5** has a completely different meaning than in the expression **6.0/5.0**. Evaluation of the former expression requires integer division and has a value of **1**, while the second expression calls for floating point division and has the value **1.2**. Many object-oriented languages permit operators to be given a much wider range of meanings.

For example, if **poly1** and **poly2** are both instances of the class **Polygon**, we might want the expression **poly1 && poly2** to evaluate to true if **poly1** and **poly2** intersect, and false otherwise. Object-oriented languages such as C++ allow us to do this. To the extent that certain operators "make sense" when applied to members of various classes, the ability to overload operators makes it feasible for the programmer to write understandable and easier-to-maintain programs.

Another key concept in object-oriented programming is *late*, or *dynamic, binding*. In most computer languages, the branching implied by the invocation of a function is resolved before the program is executed. This is called *static binding*, and is typically done by a *linker* when the executable version of the program is created. Because with static binding all references to other functions are resolved before execution of the program, every invocation of a function must be unambiguously determined before the program executes. In object-oriented programs, we often write function calls which are applied to many different types of objects. The resolution of which specific function to invoke depends on the class of the arguments, which may only be known when the program is executing. To allow this, object-oriented languages have a *run time environment* that can resolve which version of a function should be invoked when the program executes the function call.

The last important feature of object-oriented languages is that they often allow the programmer to write methods that are automatically invoked whenever a member of a class is created or destroyed. For example, in C++, each class can have functions called *constructors* which execute when a class member is created. Constructor methods are often used to initialize variables in the class. Similarly, classes can have a method called a *destructor* that executes when the member is deleted. This method can, for example, be used to free memory allocated by the class instance that will no longer be used after the instance is destroyed.

9.3 A SIMPLE CLASS IN C++

There are many existing computer languages that were designed to aid in the development of object-oriented software. The language Smalltalk,[1] designed by the Palo Alto Research Center of Xerox, pioneered this field. Common Lisp has a series of functions that facilitate the creation of object-oriented software. Given the widespread use of C, however, it is not surprising that one of the most popular languages for object-oriented programming is a direct extension of C called C++. It was developed by Bjarne Stroustrup of AT&T Bell Laboratories and described in his definitive 1986 book [Stroustrup, Bjarne 86].[2]

C++ was designed to be an evolutionary step in the development of the C programming language. As is appropriate for an evolutionary development, virtually all C code is valid in C++. In fact, the majority of C++ "compilers" are really translators that convert C++ programs into C code, which is then input to the C compiler for compilation.

C++ provides a set of features that makes it easy to write code in an object-oriented style. C++ does not *force* you to write object-oriented code. You can take advantage of some of C++'s features and write programs much as you did using C. However, the real power and utility of C++ derives from its ability to construct and use classes. In this section we show how a point in two dimensions can be implemented as a class.

9.3.1 Declaration of the Class Point2D

Most C++ classes are coded in two parts. The first part is the *class declaration*, which is usually placed in a header file with a **.h** suffix. This file declares the variables and functions that are members of the class. The class declaration file is then included in any programs that rely on the class. The second part of a class is the implementation of the methods. These functions can be compiled and provided to users of the class as part of a *class library*. The class users never need to see the implementation; they work exclusively with the interface to the class as described in the class declaration.

---

[1] Smalltalk is a trademark of Xerox, Inc.

[2] The name C++ is an obscure pun. The **++** operator in C means "increment by one unit." Thus, C++ represents the next version of C.

The following is the declaration for a class named `Point2D`. An explanation of this declaration is provided below.

```
//  This is the header file for class Point2D.
//  This would typically be placed in a header
//  file such as Point2D.h

#include <stdio.h>

//  class declaration for Point2D

class Point2D {
  double x;        // x coordinate
  double y;        // y coordinate

public:
  Point2D(double, double);     // standard constructor
  Point2D(void);               // default constructor
  void show(FILE *f=stdout);   // display point
  Point2D operator+(Point2D);  // overload of + operator
  Point2D operator=(Point2D);  // overload of = operator
  friend double length(Point2D *, Point2D *);  // length
  };
```

Comments in C++ begin with two backslashes, `//`, and continue to the end of a line. C++ also accepts the standard syntax for comments in C. The declaration of `Point2D` begins with the **class** keyword followed by the name of the class and an opening curly bracket (`{`). The variables declared immediately after this opening bracket and before the **public** keyword are by convention the *private* members of the class.[3] In this example, two variables **x** and **y**, corresponding to the x and y coordinates of a point, are declared. Any functions declared in this section would also be private to the class. These private variables and functions cannot be accessed by any code outside the class.

The functions declared after the **public** keyword are the **public** members of the class. Any variables that are to be public should be declared here. Five functions are declared in this section. The first two of these are *constructors* for the class. Any function member with the same name as the class is a constructor function. The reason there are two of these functions rather than just one is that the constructor function in this example is *overloaded*. Note that every C++ class must have at least one constructor function.

Which of the two constructor functions get invoked when a new instance of the class is created depends on how the new instance is declared. For example, if in a program that uses the class we defined a variable with the statement

---

[3]You can also declare private members explicitly by prefacing their declarations with the **private** keyword followed by a colon.

```
// definition of an instance of Point2D
Point2D p1(1.0, 2.0);
```

the class constructor that has two **double**s as its arguments would be used. This would initialize the members **x** and **y** of **p1** to 1.0 and 2.0, respectively. Conversely, if the declaration

```
Point2D p2;      // definition of an instance
                 // with default constructor
```

is used, then the constructor with no arguments would be applied. A constructor that does not require any arguments is called a *default constructor*.

The third public function is named **show()**. This function will print out the coordinates of a point. The declaration of **show()** illustrates another feature of C++, the ability to declare *default values* for arguments. In this case, the default output file is declared as **stdout**, the standard output device. Default values for arguments are used when a member function is invoked without any value for that argument. C++ requires that any of the arguments with default values are listed *after* any arguments without default values. Put another way, the arguments with defaults must be the *rightmost* arguments to the function.

Member functions are invoked using the same dot operator(**.**) or member access operator(**->**) as is used to access members of a **struct** in C. Thus, if **p1** and **p2** are declared as instances of the class **Point2D**, the fragment

```
// fragment showing use of default function values
FILE *fout;
fout = fopen("my_result", "w");

p1.show();         // use default output device
p2.show(fout);     // override default output device
```

would invoke the function **show()** on the points **p1** and **p2**. The values for **p1** would be written to the standard output file because the invocation of **show()** has no arguments. The value of **p2** would be written to the file **my_result**. Similarly, if a variable **q** was declared as a *pointer* to an instance of the class **Point2D**, then the statement

```
q->show(fout);
```

would invoke **show()** on whatever instance of **Point2D q** was pointing to, writing the output to the file named **my_result**.

The remaining two functions, **operator+()** and **operator=()**, show how a standard operator in C can be overloaded in C++. By convention, any function member with the name **operator** followed immediately by a standard C operator is an overloading function for that operator. Any use of that operator on members of the class will use the overloaded function. For example, if we declared the variables

```
Point2D p1(1.0,2.0), p2(3.0,4.0);
```

then the expression **p1+p2** would be interpreted as the function invocation

```
p1.operator+(p2)
```

In this case the **operator+()** member of **p1** would be invoked using **p2** as its argument. Similarly, the expression **p2=p1** would be interpreted as

```
p2.operator=(p1)
```

This would invoke the member **operator=()** of object **p2** with **p1** as its argument.

The last function listed in the class declaration is **length()**. This function is declared as a **friend** function. This means that the function is not a member of the class, but is allowed to access private members of the class. In this case, the function **length()** will compute the Euclidean distance between two **Point2D**s. It has 2 pointers to instances of **Point2D**s as its arguments. To perform this computation, it needs access to the class's private members **x** and **y**. The **friend** declaration grants permission for a nonmember function to use members that it normally would not be allowed to access.

The function **length()** has two pointers to instances of the class **Point2D** as its arguments. It returns a **double** which is the Euclidean distance between the two points.

friend functions should be used with some care. While they can sometimes simplify software design, their overuse violates the spirit of object-oriented design. At the extreme, if every function is declared as a **friend** function, the ability to separate the interface to a class from the internal representation of the class is lost.

9.3.2 The Implementation of the Class Point2D

Given the declaration of the **Point2D** above, we now turn to the implementation of the member functions of that class. The class that a function belongs to is indicated by the *scope resolution operator*, denoted by **::** (two semicolons without any white space between them). For example, one of the constructors for **Point2D** would be written as follows:

```
#include "Point2D.h"

// constructor
Point2D::Point2D(double a, double b)
{
  x=a;
  y=b;
}
```

The **#include** statement is used because we have assumed that the implementation of the class is in a source code file that is distinct from the class's declaration. In this case we assume that the declaration of the class is in the file **Point2D.h**. The operand before the scope resolution operator denotes the class to which the function belongs. In this case, the notation **Point2D::** at the beginning of this function means that the function is a member of the **Point2D** class. This is followed by the name of the function and the function's arguments. In this case, the constructor function assigns the value of its two arguments to the class's private members **x** and **y**.

Note that the function **Point2D()** references the private members of the class. This is allowed because the function is part of the class. Functions outside the class are not allowed to access the class's private members directly unless they are declared as **friend** functions of that class.

The second function in the class is the default constructor. As a convention, we will set the default values for a **Point2D** to the origin, (0,0). The implementation of this function is as follows:

```
// default constructor
Point2D::Point2D(void)
{
   x=0.0;
   y=0.0;
}
```

The third public member of the class is the function **show()**. It uses the C library function **fprintf()** to output the coordinates of a point. The C++ code for this function is

```
// show a point
void Point2D::show(FILE *f)
{
   fprintf(f, "Point is (%lf,%lf)\n", x, y);
}
```

Recall that if no argument is given when the function is invoked, the value of **f** will default to the standard output device, **stdout**.

The fourth function is the addition operator. This function returns an instance of the class **Point2D** which is the coordinates of the sum of two points. Its implementation is as follows.

```
// addition operator
Point2D Point2D::operator+(Point2D b)
{
   Point2D total;
   total.x = x + b.x;
   total.y = y + b.y;
   return(total);
}
```

The **operator+()** function uses a local instance of **Point2D** named **total** to store the sum. In C++, instances of a class are declared in the same way as are variables in C. The instance **total** is created when the function is executed and destroyed when the function exits. Because **total** is not given an explicit initialization, the default constructor is used when it is created, resulting in initial values of zero for **x** and **y**. Note also that objects can be returned from functions. As with **return** statements in C, the object is copied into memory provided by the calling function. Further details of the behavior of the **return** statement are provided in Section 9.4.

The last member function is **operator=()**, the assignment operator. This function copies the values in one object to another object. The assignment operator returns the value on the left-hand side of the assignment. This is done so that assignment statements for member of the **Point2D** class such as **a=b=c** will follow the same semantics as assignments in C, assigning the value of **c** to **b**, producing the new value of **b** as a result, and then assigning that new value to **a**.

The implementation of **operator=()** is given below.

```
// assignment operator
Point2D Point2D::operator=(Point2D b)
{
   if(this != &b){ // check if left side is same as right
     x = b.x;
     y = b.y;
   }
   return(b);
}
```

The **operator=()** function introduces an important new concept. Note the variable **this** in the expression **this != b**. The variable **this** is *created automatically by the C++ compiler* in every member function. It is a pointer to the object to which the member function is being applied. For example, in the expression **a=b**, the value of **this** is a pointer to the object **a**. The value of **&b** is the address of the argument **b**, which is the object on the right-hand side of the assignment. These two are compared in the **if** statement to test if the assignment statement is of the form **c=c**, in which case the assignment of members **x** and **y** is unnecessary.

The last function, **length()**, is a **friend** function and is therefore not a member of the **Point2D** class. Its implementation in C++ does not begin with a scope resolution operator (**::**) because it is not a member of a class. The C++ code for **length()** is as follows:

```
// friend function to compute
// distance between 2 Point2D's

#include <math.h>
double length(Point2D *p0, Point2D *p1)
{
```

```
    double temp = (p0->x - p1->x)*(p0->x - p1->x) +
                  (p0->y - p1->y)*(p0->y - p1->y);
    return(sqrt(temp));
}
```

The header file **math.h** is included in this function because **length()** makes use of **sqrt()**, the square root function in the standard math library.

9.3.3 Using the Simple Class Library

Given both the declaration and implementation of **Point2D**, we can now use the class in a C++ program. The program we will show is trivial, but it illustrates the central ideas of using classes, constructors, and member functions. The C++ code is as follows.

```
// main function for Point2D example

#include "Point2D.h"

main()
{
  Point2D a, b(1.5,2.5);  // instances of Point2D
  Point2D c=b;  // another type of initialization
  FILE* fout;  // file for output

// open file
  fout = fopen("my_result", "w");

// display initial values and find length
  a.show();
  b.show();
  c.show();
  printf("Distance from a to c is %lf\n",
         length(&a, &c));

//test assignment
  a=b;
  a.show();

// test addition and assignment
  c = a+b;
  c.show();
  a=b=c;
  a.show();
  b.show();
  c.show(fout);
}
```

The example creates three instances of **Point2D**. The first instance, **a**, uses the default constructor, while the second, **b**, gives explicit initial values for **x** and **y**. The third instance, **c**, uses the equals sign for initialization in the same way as variables in C can be initialized when they are declared.

The example also illustrates how the default argument for the function **show()** works. An invocation of **show()** that uses the default has an empty argument list [as in the statement **a.show()**], while invocations that override the default use a **FILE** pointer as their argument [as in the statement **c.show(fout)**].

9.4 BUILDING A MORE COMPLICATED CLASS

Note to Reader: The remaining sections of this chapter can be skipped without loss of continuity.

In this section we build on the ideas presented in Section 9.3 to illustrate some additional features in C++. We will create two new classes, named **Polygon** and **Square**. These classes will show how the ideas of destructors and inheritance work. We will also show some new C++ operators for dynamic memory management and a feature that allows you to relax C's strict call-by-value protocol for function invocation.

9.4.1 Declaration of the Polygon Class

The class **Polygon** will be used to represent any closed series of line segments connecting points in two dimensions. The private members of **Polygon** will be an integer to store the number of vertices in the **Polygon** and a pointer to an array of **Point2D** objects. Since the **Polygon** class uses the **Point2D** class, we will assume that their class declarations are in the same header file named **Polygon.h**. (We could alternatively **#include** the file containing the declaration for **Point2D** in the declaration of **Polygon**.) The class declaration for **Polygon** is as follows.

```
//  class declaration for Polygon

class Polygon {
  int n;                             // number of sides
  Point2D * vertices;                // array of vertices

public:
  Polygon(void);                     // default constructor
  Polygon(int, Point2D *);           // array constructor
  Polygon(Polygon&);                 // copy constructor
  void show(FILE *f=stdout);         // display Polygon
  double side_length(int);           // finds length of side
  Polygon operator+(Point2D&);       // addition operator
  Polygon operator=(Polygon&);       // assignment operator
```

```
double perimeter(void);         // finds perimeter
~Polygon(void);                 // destructor
};
```

Note that the private member **vertices** is a *pointer* to an instance of the class **Point2D**. In this case the member **vertices** will contain the address of the beginning of an array of **Point2D** instances.

The first two member functions are both constructors for the class. The first of these has no arguments; it is the default constructor. The second constructor has two arguments, an **int** that equals the number of vertices and an array of **Point2D**'s that are the vertices of the **Polygon**. Thus, a triangle with its vertices at points (2,3), (2,5) and (5,6) could be declared with statements such as

```
Point2D s[3] = {Point2D(2.0,3.0),
                Point2D(2.0, 5.0),
                Point2D(5.0,6.0)};
```

```
Polygon pb(3, s);
```

The first of these statements defines an array of three instances of **Point2D** and initializes the values in that array. Note the use of a constructor function for the class **Point2D** in the list of initial values for the array **s**. The second statement defines an instance of a **Polygon** with three sides that has the values in the array **s** as its vertices.

A new feature of the class declaration is the use of the ampersand (**&**) after the argument type in three of the public member functions. This is used in one of the constructor members and in the function **operator+()**. Following an argument type by an ampersand indicates that the argument is passed as a *reference* rather than as a value. This corresponds to what is termed *call by reference* argument passing rather than the usual *call by value* used in C. The use of reference arguments in C++ avoids some of the messiness of passing pointers as arguments that appears in many C programs. It also eliminates a common source of programming errors, such as accidentally passing a variable to a function such as **scanf()** that expects a pointer instead.

To see how references are used in C++, consider the function **interchange()** presented in Section 2.13. This function exchanged the values of two **int**s by passing the pointers to the two values and using the dereferencing operator ***** to exchange their respective values. The C version for this function is repeated below.

```
/* C function to interchange two integers */
void interchange(int *i, int *j)
{
  int temp;    /* define temporary variable */
  temp = *i;
  *i = *j;
  *j = temp;
}
```

This function could be written in C++ in a much more straightforward fashion using reference arguments as follows:

```
//   C++ version of interchange

void interchange(int& i, int& j)
{
  int temp;
  i=temp;
  i=j;
  j = temp;
}
```

The C++ compiler automatically handles the dereferencing of the reference arguments passed to **interchange()**, avoiding the complicated use of pointers in the implementation. References make it easier to work with pointers to classes in member functions. For example, the function **operator+()** in the **Polygon** class does not require a complete copy of its argument; it only needs to know the contents of the **Polygon**.

The function labeled as a *copy constructor* illustrates another new concept. A copy constructor is invoked whenever a new instance of the class is initialized to the value of an existing instance. For example, we might have the C++ fragment

```
Point2D s[3] = {Point2D(2.0,3.0),
                Point2D(2.0, 5.0),
                Point2D(5.0,6.0)};
Polygon pb(3, s);
Polygon pa=pb;
```

In this example, the **Polygon pa** is defined as a new instance and initialized to the value of **pb** by invoking the copy constructor. This initialization is *not* an assignment even though the = sign is used.

In many classes, we do not need an explicit copy constructor function because C++ automatically provides a default copy constructor, which simply makes an exact, bit-by-bit replica of the existing instance. We have used this fact without explaining it earlier in the program shown in Section 9.3.3 in the declaration **Point2D c=b**.

If the default copy constructor is used for the **Polygon** class, it would result in the instance **pa** having the same values of **n** (the number of vertices) and **vertices** (a pointer to an array of vertices) as **pb**. The problem with this default copy constructor is that some of the constructors for **Polygon** will allocate memory dynamically to store the array of vertices. The instances **pa** and **pb** need to have *separate* areas of memory allocated for this array. The default constructor will result in the pointer member **vertices** for instances **pa** and **pb** having the same value, and therefore pointing to the same section of memory. In this case, if we later changed one of the vertices in **pb**, that change would automatically alter the vertices in **pa**. This is clearly not what we intend by the initialization **pa=pb**.[4]

The member function **show()** will output the number of vertices and their coordinates. It has a **FILE** pointer as its argument and sets the value of that pointer to **stdout** as a default.

The member function **side_length()** computes the length of a side of the **Polygon**. Its integer argument is the number of the side. We assume that sides of the **polygon** are numbered from 1 through **n**, where a side is a line segment between adjacent vertices.

We will define the addition operator, when applied to a **Polygon** and a **Point2D**, as the translation of the entire **Polygon**. The coordinates of the **Point2D** are added to the corresponding coordinates of each vertex in the **Polygon**. (See Section 7.4.2 for further details on this operation.)

The assignment operator, **operator=()**, will be similar to the assignment operator we created for the class **Point2D**. The member function **perimeter()** returns the perimeter of the **Polygon**.

The last function is the *destructor* for the class. Destructor functions are denoted with a tilda sign,~, followed by the class name. We need a destructor function for this class because the constructor functions will allocate memory dynamically, and that memory needs to be explicitly freed whenever an instance is destroyed. An object can have at most one destructor function.

9.4.2 Implementation of the Polygon Class

We now turn to implementation of the nine member functions for the **Polygon** class. Each of the nine functions is considered in turn.

Assuming that the class declaration is in a separate file from the implementation, the first statement in the class implementation should be an **#include** directive referencing the class header file. All the function definitions below rely on this file.

The default constructor for the class **Polygon** is straightforward. It must set the number of sides of the **Polygon** to zero and set the pointer to the array of vertices to **NULL**. The implementation is as follows:

```
#include "Polygon.h" // header file
// default constructor

Polygon::Polygon(void)
{
```

[4]A still more subtle reason why an explicit copy constructor is required for the **Polygon** class is shown in Section 9.4.2.

```
        n = 0;
        vertices = NULL;
    }
```

The constructor that allows initialization of a **Polygon** is a little more complicated than the default constructor. It must allocate an array of **Point2D**s and copy the array of **Point2D** instances passed as an argument into that array.

We introduce the C++ operator **new** to allocate an array of **Point2D** instances. This operator is a more general version of the dynamic memory allocation function **calloc()** described in Section 5.4. The **new** operator returns a pointer to a specified object and ensures that the default constructor is executed on that object. For example, the fragment

```
        Polygon *q;
        q = new Polygon;
```

will allocate memory for an instance of the class **Polygon** and invoke the default constructor on that instance. It will return a **NULL** pointer if the memory allocation fails.

The **new** operator can also allocate memory for an array of instances. For example, the fragment

```
        Polygon *qarray;
        qarray = new Polygon[10];
```

would allocate an array of 10 **Polygon**s, invoking the default constructor on each of them. The **new** operator can also be used to allocate standard C variables, arrays, and structures.

The complete implementation of the constructor must allocate an array of **Point2D** objects, copy the points initializing the vertices to the allocated storage, and set the value of **n** to the number of points defining the **Polygon**. The complete code for this function is given below. Note that **n**, the private member of the class indicating the number of points in the **Polygon**, gets set correctly as a result of the **for** loop.

```
    // point constructor for Polygon
    Polygon::Polygon(int npoints, Point2D *v)
    {
      vertices = new Point2D[npoints];
      for(n=0; n<npoints; n++)
        *(vertices+n) = *v++;   // copy array to class
    }
```

For the sake of brevity we have omitted checking whether the pointer returned by the **new** operator is **NULL**. We will follow this practice throughout the remainder of this chapter. *However, the reader is cautioned that fully functional implementations of* *classes, particularly those which are going to be used by other programmers, should include verifications that any memory allocation is successful.*

Note the use of pointers to instances of objects in the implementation above. C++ extends the use of pointers to any valid object. The address operator, **&**, and the dereferencing operator, *****, can be applied to objects in the same way as in C. The code also makes use of the assignment operator for instances of the class **Point2D**. We provide this code below.

The copy constructor for the class must allocate memory for the new array of vertices and copy the values in the argument into that array. It must also initialize the number of vertices in the new **Polygon**. The implementation is as follows.

```
//   copy constructor
Polygon::Polygon(Polygon& poly)
{
  int i;

//   set number of vertices and allocate new array
  n = poly.n;
  vertices = new Point2D[n];

// set pointers to beginning or arrays and copy
  Point2D *p = vertices;
  Point2D *q = poly.vertices;
  for(i=0; i<n; i++)
    *p++ = *q++;
}
```

The fourth member function outputs the number of sides and the vertices of a **Polygon**. Its implementation uses the **show()** function for the class **Point2D** to output the vertices. The C++ code is as follows.

```
//output a Polygon
void Polygon::show(FILE *f)
{
  Point2D *p;
  fprintf(f, "Polygon has %d sides\n", n);
  for(p=vertices; p<vertices+n;p++)
    p->show(f);
}
```

The **side_length()** function makes use of the **length()** function described in the preceding section. Its implementation is as follows:

```
// compute length of side i
double Polygon::side_length(int i)
{
```

```
    if(i < n)
      return(length(vertices+i-1, vertices+i));
    else
      return(length(vertices+n-1, vertices));
}
```

The `operator+()` member makes use of several features of C++, including the `this` pointer and the overloaded addition operator created in Section 9.3 that adds two points. It returns an instance of a `Polygon` which is the translated object. The code is as follows:

```
// addition of a Point to a Polygon
Polygon Polygon::operator+(Point2D& point)
{
  Polygon result = *this;
  Point2D *p;
  for(p=result.vertices; p<result.vertices+n;p++)
    *p =  *p + point;
  return(result);
}
```

The statement

```
Polygon result = *this;
```

initializes to the `Polygon result` to the `Polygon` pointed to by `this`, the left operand of the addition. The initialization relies on the variable `this`, which points to the instance to which the member function is being applied. Since `this` is a pointer to a `Polygon`, the expression `*this` is itself a `Polygon`. The copy constructor function would be invoked to perform this initialization. The function then loops through all the vertices, using the overloaded addition operator for instances of the class `Point2D`. Thus, the statement

```
*p =  *p + point;
```

is the addition of two `Point2D`s as defined in Section 9.3. The `Polygon result` is returned by the addition operator.

The addition function for `Polygon` illustrates another, less obvious use of the copy constructor function. To understand this subtlety, the reader must recall that, as in C, local objects in C++ are automatic variables. Thus, *when a function defines a local variable that is a class instance, that instance is destroyed automatically when the function exits*. The instance `result` will therefore be destroyed when the function `operator+()` exits. Part of the destruction of any instance includes the invocation of the destructor function for that class. In the case of the `Polygon` class, the destructor function will deallocate the memory for the array of vertices that was allocated by the constructor function.

Since memory for the array of vertices is allocated when **result** is created, that memory will be deallocated when the function ends. One of the purposes of the copy constructor function is to make a separate copy of the array of vertices for the function that invoked **operator+()** so that when the original memory for **result** is deallocated, a valid copy of the array of vertices will still exist. In C++, the copy constructor is used automatically by the **return** statement to copy the returned object into memory provided by the calling function. This ensures that in the calling function, any pointers will point to valid parts of dynamic memory even after **result** is destroyed.

The assignment operator for a **Polygon** must perform several functions. First, as in the case of the **Point2D** class, it should detect trivial assignments of the form **a = a**. In the usual case, where a real assignment is needed, it must first deallocate the memory holding the previous vertices stored in the left side of the assignment, and then allocate sufficient memory for the number of vertices in the **Polygon** on the right side of the assignment. It must then copy all the vertices' values from the right side of the assignment to the left, and return a **Polygon** as the value of the assignment expression. This is accomplished in the code that follows.

```
// assignment operator
Polygon Polygon::operator=(Polygon& poly)
{
    int i;
    if(this != &poly){   // check if assignment of form a=a
      delete[n] vertices;
      n = poly.n;
      vertices = new Point2D[n];

// copy array of vertices
      Point2D *p = vertices;
      Point2D *q = poly.vertices;
      for(i=0;  i<n;  i++)
        *p++ = *q++;
    }
    return(poly);          // return a Polygon
}
```

The implementation above uses the C++ **delete** operator. This operator is the inverse of the **new** operator. The syntax

```
        delete[n] vertices;
```

indicates that **n** objects pointed to by **vertices** are to be deleted. The square brackets and the integer they enclose can be omitted when a single object is to be deleted.

The function **perimeter()** will loop through the sides of the **Polygon**, invoking the function **side_length()** on each of the pairs of adjacent vertices. The code for **perimeter()** is given below.

```
// function to compute perimeter of a Polygon
double Polygon::perimeter(void)
{
  int i;
  double temp = 0.0;
  for(i=1; i<=n; i++)
    temp += side_length(i);
  return(temp);
}
```

The implementation assumes that a **Polygon** with only two vertices consists of two line segments, one from vertex 0 to vertex 1 and another from vertex 1 to vertex 0.

The last function in the **Polygon** class is the destructor. It simply deallocates the memory allocated by the constructors. The code for the destructor is as follows:

```
// destructor function
Polygon::~Polygon(void)
{
  if(vertices != NULL)
    delete[n] vertices;
}
```

9.4.3 Using the Polygon Class

The **Polygon** object can be used in a complete program just like any other object. For example, the following **main()** function creates some **Polygon**s, outputs their values, performs a translation of one of the **Polygon**s, and computes the perimeters.

```
// main function for Polygon example

#include "Polygon.h"

main()
{

  Point2D a(1.5,2.5);    // instance of Point2D

  // declare an array of points
    Point2D sides[3] = {Point2D(1.0,1.0),
                        Point2D(1.0,2.0),
                        Point2D(3.0,5.0)};
  // create a polygon
    Polygon pa(3,sides), pb;

  // output pa and pb

    pa.show();
    pb.show();
```

```
    pb = pa;
    printf("Perimeter of pa is %lf\n",pa.perimeter());


    pa = pb + a;    // translation to a new origin
    pa.show();
    printf("Perimeter of a perimeter of b is %lf\n",
            pa.perimeter()+pb.perimeter());

}
```

9.5 INHERITANCE: CREATING A DERIVED CLASS

The last example we will explore is the creation of a *derived class*, or *subclass*, from an existing class. In this case we will create an object class named **Rectangle**. This class will have **Polygon** as its base class and will inherit the methods of that class.

The major advantage of inheritance is that we can often create a derived class with very little work. Most of the capabilities already embodied in the base class will be immediately useful, and we will not have to recode them. An additional benefit is that over time, as we add new methods to the base class, these features will be immediately useful in all the derived classes.

C++ allows for two options when creating a derived class. In the default case, the public members of the base class are private, *not* public, members of the derived class. For example, the declaration

```
class Derived_class_name :  Base_class_name {
{
// derived class declaration goes here
};
```

will have the effect of making the public members of **Base_class_name** *private* members of **Derived_class_name**. The class name following the colon is the name of the base class.

The other option is to explicitly declare the public members of the base class as public members of the derived class, as in the declaration

```
class Derived_class_name :  public Base_class_name {
{
// derived class declaration goes here
};
```

We will declare **Rectangle** so that it has all the public members of **Polygon** as public members. The complete declaration for the class **Rectangle** is as follows:

```
//  class declaration for Rectangle
```

```
class Rectangle: public Polygon {
public:
  Rectangle(void);                // null constructor
  Rectangle(Polygon&);            // copy constructor
  Rectangle (Point2D,Point2D,
     Point2D,Point2D);            // point constructor
  Rectangle operator=(Rectangle&);  // assignment
  double perimeter(void);  // perimeter for rectangle
};
```

The **Rectangle** class has five public members. The first three are constructors. As we will show later, most of the work of the constructor functions for derived classes can be done by using the constructors from the base class.

The copy constructor defines how to copy a **Polygon** into a **Rectangle**. This will be used in the implementation of the derived class to permit us to use any of the base class functions from **Polygon** that produce an instance of a **Polygon** as their result. Once these base class functions create a **Polygon**, the copy constructor for changing a **Polygon** to a **Rectangle** can be used to create an instance of a **Rectangle**. This copy constructor will be invoked automatically by the C++ compiler in most situations.

C++ uses a well-defined set of rules in constructing new instances of a derived class. A constructor for a derived class can pass some or all of its arguments to a constructor in its base class. The constructor for the base class will be invoked *before* the constructor for the derived class. This rule is applied recursively when the base class is itself a derived class of some other base class. For example, if **Polygon** was itself a derived class of another class named **Figure**, then the constructors would be invoked for **Figure**, then for **Polygon**, and then for **Rectangle**. Destructors are applied in the *opposite* order from constructors. In this example, **Rectangle** has no destructor because it relies on the destructor for **Polygon** to deallocate memory for its array of vertices.

Note that the third constructor function has four instances of the class **Point2D** as its arguments. Unlike the corresponding constructor for the **Polygon** class, the constructor for a **Rectangle** does not need to know how many vertices the figure has; all rectangles have four sides.

The two other functions in the class are an overloading function for the assignment operator and a function to compute the perimeter of a **Rectangle**. These functions closely parallel the corresponding operators for the **Polygon** class.

In this example, the **Rectangle** class has no explicitly declared private members. However, the private members of its base class, **Polygon**, are in fact private members of the **Rectangle** class.

9.5.1 Implementation of the Derived Class Rectangle

The implementation of the member functions of **Rectangle** is remarkably short. We begin with the default constructor, coded as follows:

```
// default Rectangle constructor
Rectangle::Rectangle(void)
{ };
```

Note that this is a null function. *This is because the constructor for* **Polygon** *will do all the work necessary to initialize a new instance of* **Rectangle**. If a derived class relies on its base class to initialize an instance, C++ requires that a constructor function be defined even though that function does not do anything.

The copy constructor for **Rectangle** converts a **Polygon** to a **Rectangle**. Its implementation is given below.

```
// copy Rectangle constructor
// passing arguments to base class

Rectangle::Rectangle(Polygon& poly) : Polygon(poly)
{ };
```

This implementation uses a new piece of C++ syntax. The constructor for **Rectangle** uses the notation **:Polygon(poly)** to pass values of its arguments to the base class constructor. In this case, the constructor for the **Rectangle** passes an instance of a **Polygon** to the **Polygon** copy constructor. When a constructor for a **Rectangle** that has a **Polygon** as its argument is initialized, the C++ compiler will first invoke the **Polygon** copy constructor.

The third constructor has the four vertices of the rectangle as its arguments. The C++ code is as follows:

```
// four-point constructor
Rectangle::Rectangle(Point2D a,
                     Point2D b,
                     Point2D c,
                     Point2D d)
{
  Point2D *q =  new Point2D[4];

  *q++ = a;
  *q++ = b;
  *q++ = c;
  *q   = d;
  *this = Polygon(4,q);
}
```

This implementation copies the four vertices passed as arguments to an array of **Point2D**s. It then invokes one of the constructors for the **Polygon** class. The resulting **Polygon** is then assigned to the **Rectangle** being constructed by the assignment

```
*this = Polygon(4,p);
```

This can be done because the class includes a copy constructor that converts a **Polygon** to a **Rectangle** and an overloaded assignment operator for assigning an instance of one **Rectangle** to another.

The assignment operator function is also brief but requires careful use of the **Polygon** assignment operator defined in Section 9.3.1. The implementation is as follows:

```
// assignment operator for Rectangles
Rectangle Rectangle::operator=(Rectangle& r)
{
//  use Polygon assignment function
  *(Polygon *) this = (Polygon) r;
  return (r);
}
```

The key to this function is a clever use of casts to convert instances of **Rectangle**s to instances of **Polygon**s. This conversion is essential because the assignment operator for **Polygon**s requires that both the left side and the right side of the assignment be of class **Polygon**. The casting of the right side in the statement

```
*(Polygon *) this = (Polygon) r;
```

is straightforward. However, the left side, ***(Polygon *) this**, requires some explanation. The variable **this** is a pointer to the instance being operated on (in this case, the left side of an assignment statement involving two rectangles). Therefore, **this** is a pointer to an instance of a **Rectangle**. The cast **Polygon *** casts **this** to a pointer to a **Polygon**, and the indirection operator, *****, then finds the **Polygon** at the address pointed to. The complete statement therefore converts both the left and right sides of the assignment to instances of **Polygon**s, allowing use of the overloaded assignment operator on **Polygon**s.

The casting of a **Rectangle** to a **Polygon** is allowed because the former is a derived class of the latter. C++ treats any instance of a derived class as if it contained an instance of its base class, making casts from the derived class to the base class permissible automatically. The conversion from the base class to the derived class generally requires that an explicit function member for such a conversion be provided by the programmer as one of the member functions of the derived class.

The last function, **perimeter()**, is implemented to take advantage of the special geometry of the class **Rectangle**. While we could simply use the **perimeter()** function from the class **Polygon** to compute the perimeter of a **Rectangle**, some of the computation needed to compute the perimeter of a general **Polygon** is unnecessary in the case of a **Rectangle**. In particular, we need only compute the length and width of the rectangle, not the lengths of all four sides. To take advantage of this geometric property, we can create a member function named **perimeter()** for the derived class **Rectangle**. C++ searches for member functions of derived classes by first looking for a public member of the derived class. If it finds a function member in the derived class, it will not look in the base class. Thus, the **perimeter()** function appropriate to **Rectangle**s will be used for instances of that class, while the more general **perimeter()** function for **Polygon**s would be used for other derived classes of **Polygon**s that do not have their own **perimeter()** function member.

The implementation of **perimeter()** is given below.

```
// function to compute perimeter of a rectangle
double Rectangle::perimeter(void)
{
   return( 2 *( side_length(1)+side_length(2)));
}
```

The function **perimeter()** uses the function **side_length()**, which is inherited from the **Polygon** base class.

9.5.2 Using the Rectangle Derived Class

The following program uses the **Rectangle** class and the functions in that class. The program defines two instances of **Rectangle**s and an instance of a **Point2D**. It uses the overloaded addition operator to translate one of the **Rectangle**s and assigns the result to the other **Rectangle**. It also illustrates the use of the **perimeter()** function member.

```
//  program to use Rectangle class
#include "Polygon.h"

main()
{
   Point2D a(1.5,2.5);      // instance of Point2D
// create an initial array of four points
   Rectangle ra;
   Rectangle rb(Point2D(1.0,1.0), Point2D(2.0, 1.0),
     Point2D(2.0,2.0), Point2D(1.0,2.0));
   rb.show();         // output rb
   ra = rb + a;       // translation of rectangle
   ra.show();         // output ra
   printf("Perimeter is %lf\n", rb.perimeter() );
}
```

9.6 OTHER FEATURES IN C++

C++ provides many additional features, some of which are beyond the scope of this introductory-level overview. We consider some of the more useful features briefly in this section.

9.6.1 Function Prototypes Are Required in C++

Unlike ANSI C, C++ *requires* that every function have a prototype. In addition, functions that do not have arguments need not use the keyword **void** for their argument lists. They can simply have nothing between the parentheses that normally define the argument list. For example, the prototype

```
int show(void);
```

could also be written as

```
int show();
```

9.6.2 Inline Functions

In general, object-oriented programs make a very large number of function calls. Object constructors, operator overloads, and the reliance on public function members to access and manipulate objects all impose the overhead of a function call. Many of these functions are very short, and the computer time required to pass arguments and return values may well exceed the time required to perform some of the functions. C++ provides a mechanism called *inline functions* to eliminate this computational overhead.

The code for an inline function is inserted by the C++ compiler directly into the invoking function. Rather than copying arguments, executing the function, and returning a value, a complete copy of an inline function is created at each place in the program where the function is invoked. The tradeoff is that rather than having a single, compiled copy of each function in a program, a distinct copy of each inline function is made everywhere the function is used. This will generally increase the amount of memory required by the executable program.

Inline functions are declared and defined as part of a class definition. For example, we could modify the declaration of the class **Point2D** described in Section 9.3.1 to make both of the constructor functions and the function **show()** inline functions. This is illustrated below.

```
#include <stdio.h>

//   class declaration for Point2D

class Point2D {
    double x;        // x coordinate
    double y;        // y coordinate

public:
    Point2D(double a, double b)      // standard constructor
        {x=a; y=b;}
    Point2D(void) {x=y=0.0;}         // default constructor
```

```
void show(FILE *f=stdout)        // display point
  { fprintf(f, "Point is (%lf,%lf)\n", x, y);}
Point2D operator+(Point2D); // overload of + operator
Point2D operator=(Point2D); // overload of = operator
friend double length(Point2D *, Point2D *);   // length
};
```

Inline class members are written as part of *header* files, not as part of the implementation of the class. This is because the code for inline functions must be available whenever any part of the C++ program using that function is compiled. In addition, when you change any inline function, you need to recompile all parts of that program that make use of the header file containing the function.

C++ also allows you to declare functions that are not members of any class as inline by using the **inline** keyword as part of the function's declaration. For example, the function **square_x()** is declared as inline.

```
inline square_x(double x) {return(x*x);}
```

Functions that are declared inline are similar to preprocessor macros in C. However, unlike macros, inline functions enforce type conversions on their arguments, making them much safer than standard macros.

9.6.3 The iostreams Class Library

While C++ continues to provide the standard input and output library supported by the C language, it also provides a more flexible, easier-to-use set of input/output operators. These features are implemented as a set of C++ classes named **istream**, for input streams, and **ostream**, for output streams. A class derived from these two classes, called **iostream**, provides for both input and output. Other derived classes provide for file input and output and other variants. We provide only a cursory introduction to these classes here.

The declarations for these classes are provided as part of C++ in the file **iostream.h**, which must be included in C++ programs that use these facilities.

The **iostream** classes rely on two operators. The first, called *insertion* (denoted by the operator **<<**), is used for output. The second, called *extraction* (denoted by the operator **>>**), is used for input. These are most often used in conjunction with two standard instances of streams. **cin** is an instance of **istream** which is tied to the standard input device (usually the keyboard), while **cout** is an instance of **ostream** tied to to the standard output device (usually the display). In addition, the **ostream** instance **cerr** is tied to the standard error device.

The insertion and extraction operators are used with **cin**, **cout**, and **cerr** to replace the functions **printf()** and **scanf()**. For example, the C++ statement

```
cout <<  "Hello world\n";
```

is equivalent to

```
printf("Hello world\n");
```

What makes **cout** and the other **iostream** objects useful is that the extraction and insertion operators can by applied to any data type. For example, the C++ fragment

```
// fragment showing use of insertion operator
int i=3;
int j=6;
cout << "The sum is "  << i+j  <<".\n";
```

would generate the output

```
The sum is 9.
```

The **cin** instance can be used with the extraction operator in the same way. For example, the C++ fragment

```
// fragment showing use of extraction operator
int i;
double y;
cin >> i >>y;
```

would read an integer value from the standard input device into **i** and a floating-point value into **y**.

The streams classes in C++ do far more than just simplify the input and output of values. Because insertion and extraction are implemented as operators, you can implement overloaded versions of **>>** and **<<** operators for classes you create. This allows you to extend the simple syntax of **cin** and **cout** to *any* class in your program.

9.6.4 Protected Class Members

In Section 9.5 on inheritance, we discussed how the declaration **public** could be used to declare that the public members of a base class are public members of a derived class. The alternative was to omit the **public** keyword. In this case the public members of the base class would be private members of the derived class. C++ provides a third option for controlling access to members of a base class. You can declare members of a base class to be **protected**. This means that they can only be accessed by members or friends of the base class, or members or friends of any of their derived classes.

Protected members are often used when you create groups of related classes to be used by other programmers. Some of the classes in such libraries are often designed for "internal use." You might, for example, have a general class called **GeometricObject** which is the base class for more specific classes such as **Polygon**s, **Ellipse**s, etc. The

`GeometricObject` class might have some simple class members that report errors when they are called. These functions might be useful as part of the class library, but you probably do not want to allow the library's users to create instances of such objects. To limit such access, you could declare that the constructors for `GeometricObject`s are `protected`. Other classes in the library could still use those functions because they are all derived from `GeometricObject`, but the users of the library could not access the constructors.

The `protected` members are declared as part of the class declaration. For example, if we wanted to make the constructor for `GeometricObject` protected, we would declare the class as follows:

```
class GeometricObject
{
//  private members would be declared here

protected:
  GeometricObject(void);  // protected constructor
//  other protected members be declared here

public:
//  public members would be declared here
};
```

9.6.5 Multiple Inheritance

C++ allows a class to inherit the members of more than one class. This is called *multiple inheritance*. For example, suppose that the class `Rectangle` was to be derived from both the class `Polygon` and a class `Quadrilateral`. The `Quadrilateral` class might provide additional methods such as the ability to determine quickly if a point is inside or outside a given instance. The class definition for `Rectangle` would begin as follows:

```
// class Rectangle inheriting
// from Polygon and Quadrilateral

class Rectangle: public Polygon, public Quadrilateral {

  // class definition would go here

};
```

In this example the public members of both `Polygon` and `Quadrilateral` are declared to be public members of `Rectangle`. Omitting the keyword `public` before either of the base class names would result in the public members of that base class being private members of the derived class.

9.6.6 Dynamic Binding and Virtual Functions

In all of the examples shown in this chapter so far, it was possible to determine before the program was executed the exact type of each object. However, C++ also allows for the type of object (and therefore the methods applied to that object) to be resolved when the program is running. This feature is called *dynamic*, or *late, binding*.

To motivate why this might be useful, imagine that we extended our geometric example to create other classes derived from the base class **Polygon**. For example, we might have derived classes **Triangle**, **Hexagon**, and **Octogon**. Some of these derived classes of **Polygon** might have a member function that provided a method for efficiently computing the perimeter of their instances; other of these derived classes might rely on the method provided with the **Polygon** class. Suppose that we wanted to declare an array containing instances of the different derived classes of **Polygon** and compute the sum of the perimeters of the instances in that array. When the program is compiled, we will not in general know which element in the array belongs to which derived classes. In order to apply the version of **perimeter()** tailored specifically for each derived class, we need to postpone the binding of the function call to **perimeter()** until the program is actually running and the types of each member of the collection of geometric figures are known.

A member function that is going to be resolved during the program's execution is called a *virtual* function; its declaration is modified using the **virtual** keyword. For example, if the function **perimeter()** was to be used as a virtual function, its declaration in the **Polygon** class would be

```
virtual perimeter(void);    // virtual class member
```

Since all instances of the different derived classes of **Polygon** by definition are instances of the **Polygon** class, we can store a collection of these geometric objects by having an array of pointers to **Polygon**s. For example, the array **poly_collection** declared as

```
Polygon *poly_collection[1000];
```

could be used to store a collection of pointers to 1000 different **Polygon**s, some or all of which might in fact be instances of one of the derived classes of **Polygon**. If the function **perimeter()** is declared as **virtual** in the base class **Polygon**, we could then use the following C++ code fragment to compute the sum of the perimeters of the objects pointed to by the array **poly_collection**:

```
double sum = 0.0;
int i;

for(i=0; i<1000; i++)
  sum += poly_collection[i]->perimeter();
```

In this example, the version of the function **perimeter()** that would be invoked would be determined when the program is executed. When the object pointed to by **poly_collection[i]** was an instance of one of the derived classes of **Polygon** that had its own **perimeter()** member, the C++ runtime system would invoke that specific version. If the derived class did not have a tailored version of **perimeter()**, the C++ runtime environment would automatically use the general-purpose member from the base class **Polygon**.

9.7 SUMMARY OF CHAPTER 9

In this chapter we described the central concepts in *object-oriented programming*. Using this approach the programmer is able to structure elements of a computer program as abstract objects, each of which has a series of methods. The C++ language provides extensions to C that support an object-oriented programming style. Some of the major features of C++ were introduced in this chapter.

The central idea of object-oriented programming is the *class*. A class is similar to a **struct** in C. However, unlike a **struct**, a C++ class can have *members that are functions* as well as data. A class declaration establishes a name, or tag, for a class and describes the template for that class. Any object is an *instance* of some class.

Classes have special function members called *constructors*. These create new instances of the class. A class may have many constructors, each defining how an instance of the class is created from different types of initial values. A constructor that has no arguments is called the *default constructor*.

A class may also have a *destructor* function member. If a destructor is declared, this function is invoked whenever an instance of the class is destroyed. For example, local instances of a class are often created when a function is invoked. When the function invocation ends, each created instance is destroyed automatically, resulting in the destructor function being invoked on each destroyed instance. Destructors are often used to free memory allocated by constructors.

Instances of classes are accessed in C++ using the *dot operator* (.) and *member access operator* (->). These two operators work on class instances in exactly the same way as they do on **struct**s in C.

The idea of *encapsulation* is central to object-oriented programming. This means that instances of a class can be accessed only through an interface created by the programmer of that class. In C++, members of any class can be *public, private* or *protected*. Private members can be accessed only by functions that are members of the class. This provides the mechanism for encapsulation. Public members can be accessed by any part of a C++ program.

C++ allows specified functions to be declared as *friends* of a class. Such functions also have access to private class members.

C++ provides two memory allocation operators called **new** and **delete**. The **new** operator allocates memory, returning a pointer to whatever was allocated; the **delete** operator deallocates memory previously allocated by **new**. In addition to allocating and deallocating memory, **new** and **delete** invoke the default constructor and destructor for the class.

Object-oriented programming provides for *operator and function overloading*. Function overloading allows the programmer to provide implementations of a function that vary with the argument types. All the implementations have the same function name. The C++ compiler determines which version to use, depending on the number and types of the function arguments. Operator overloading allows you to give meanings to the standard C++ operators that apply to instances of classes you create. For example, you can create a class to store a matrix and define the multiplication operator * to mean matrix multiplication when that operator has two instances of the matrix class as operands.

Object-oriented programs often rely on *inheritance*. This means that some classes can be declared as derived from other classes. Such classes *inherit* the members of the class from which they are derived. Inherited members that are public in the base class can be declared either public or private in the derived class. C++ allows classes that are derived from one class also to be base classes for some other class. It also supports *multiple inheritance*, allowing a class to inherit members from more than one base class.

C++ also allows functions to be declared as *inline*. This eliminates the overhead involved in the function's invocation by inserting the code for the function directly into any C++ expression that would normally invoke the function. Functions that are very short are excellent candidates for inlining. Functions that are members of classes as well as functions that are not can be made inline.

C++ implementations come with a standard library of classes for input and output. These classes, called *streams*, simplify the input and output of the standard variable types. These classes implement two operators, extraction (denoted by >>), and insertion (denoted by <<), for reading and writing to standard input and output. Because input and output are implemented as overloaded operators, new C++ classes can create their own versions of the extraction and insertion operators, allowing them to generalize the streams classes.

As with any programming paradigm, object-oriented design of software can be misused. It is important to create classes that match some characteristics of the problem at hand. For example, in modeling physical processes, one might create classes that correspond to physical objects. Creating classes that are hard to describe may make programs difficult to maintain. Similarly, operator overloading should be used only when the operation on the classes matches the normal meaning of the operator. For example, declaring the multiplication operator as overloaded for matrix multiplication makes sense. Creating obscure meanings for standard operators is generally considered poor program design.

9.8 EXERCISES

Note: Most of these exercises require use of a C++ complier.

9-1. Create a new class named **Complex** that holds the real and imaginary parts of a complex number. In creating your class you should code a class declaration and an implementation of the class. Write a `main()` function that creates some instances of `Complex` and uses each of the member functions. Your class should include a default constructor that sets the real and imaginary parts to zero, a constructor that accepts two `doubles` corresponding to the values of the real and imaginary parts, and overloaded operators for the addition, subtraction, and multiplication of instances of the `Complex` class. All the function members of the class should be public.

9-2. Modify the `Point2D` class described in Section 9.3 to provide two additional, public functions that return the coordinates of a point in polar coordinates. Values of the angles should be computed in radians with a point on the positive x axis defined as zero radians. Modify the class's declaration and implementation to add these functions. Modify the example `main()` function shown in Section 9.3.3 to demonstrate that these additional functions work.

9-3. Modify the implementation of the class `Point2D` described in Section 9.3 to use reference variables whenever possible.

9-4. The implementation of the class `Polygon` described in Section 9.4 does not perform any error checking. Examine the code in detail and identify the places where error checks are appropriate. Implement those error checks. Your revised version of `Polygon` should include a new, private function member named `poly_error()` which is invoked whenever an error in the `Polygon` class is found. `poly_error()` should output an appropriate error message and invoke the `exit()` function in the standard library to terminate the program.

9-5. Add a new constructor to the implementation of the class `Polygon` described in Section 9.4 which has as its arguments an `int` for the number of sides in the `Polygon` and a character string containing the (x, y) coordinates of the vertices. Each of the coordinate values can be separated by one or more blanks. For example, the definition

```
Polygon triangle(3, "0.0 0.0 1.0 0.0 0.0 2.0");
```

would define an instance of a three-sided `Polygon` with vertices at (0,0), (1,0), and (0,2).

You may want to use the standard library function `sscanf()`. This function works like `scanf()` except that its first argument is a character string from which values are to be read. For example, the C fragment

```
char cf[80];
sscanf(cf, "%lf %lf", &x, &y);
```

would read values from the character string `cf` into the addresses of `x` and `y`. The function prototype for `sscanf()` is in `stdio.h`. Your implementation need not do error checking on the inputs.

9-6. Create a class named `Square` as a derived class of the class `Rectangle` in Section 9.5. This new class should provide all the member functions in `Rectangle` and should implement a version of the function `perimeter()` that requires finding the length of only one side of the square.

9-7. Modify the implementation of the class `Point2D` described in Section 9.3 to add public function members for uniform scaling and rotation. Both of these functions should have a `double` as their argument and both should return an instance of `Point2D`. The argument to the scaling function should be the amount by which the original coordinate system is scaled; the argument to the rotation function should be the angle (in radians) the point is to be rotated by around the x axis. Write a `main()` function to test your new functions. (You may want to reread Sections 7.4.3 and 7.4.4 to review these operations.)

9-8. Design a class `StackInt` to hold a stack of `int`s. This class should hold an arbitrary number of integers. It should provide three member functions: `push()` and `pop()`, to push and pop the stack, and `show()`, which outputs all the values in the stack. The class should have a default constructor that creates an empty stack, a constructor which puts a single value on the new stack (specified as an argument), and a destructor which frees any memory required by the stack. Your answer should include a class declaration, a file implementing all the function members of the class, and a `main()` function that loads a series of values on a stack, outputs the values in the stack, pops all the values from the stack, pushes them onto another stack, and outputs the values in the second stack.

9-9. Examine the implementation of the `Rectangle` class described in Section 9.5. Explain why you cannot access the x and y coordinates of the vertices of an instance of a `Rectangle` in a function that is a member of the class.

9-10. Create a class named `Circle` that contains the center of a circle as an instance of the `Point2D` class and the radius of the circle as private members. Provide a default constructor, a constructor that has three `double` values as arguments corresponding to the (x, y) coordinates of the circle's center and its radius, and a constructor that has an instance of class `Point2D` and a `double` as arguments corresponding to the center and radius of the circle. Create public member functions that return the perimeter and area of the circle. Write a `main()` function that shows how your class works.

APPENDIX

OTHER PARTS OF THE C LANGUAGE

The presentation of C in the various chapters of this book omitted reference to parts of the language that are infrequently used in the programs we have presented. Many of these features are quite valuable, however, in other types of programming. For example, developers of operating systems often need to manipulate information on a bit-by-bit basis. In this appendix we provide a summary description of "the rest of C."

A.1 OTHER REPRESENTATIONS FOR CONSTANTS

In addition to decimal notation, C allows integer constants in either octal form (as a base 8 number) or in hexadecimal form (as a base 16 number). An octal integer constant is written with a leading zero. For example, the constant **0154** in a C program means the number 154 in base 8, or 108 as a decimal constant. Hexadecimal constants are written with a leading zero followed by the letter **X** (either lower or upper case). In hexadecimal notation, the letters **A**, **B**, **C**, **D**, **E**, and **F** are used for the hexadecimal digits greater than 9. Thus, decimal constant 108 written in hexadecimal is **0X6C**.

Constants of type **char** can be written in octal form by using a leading backslash (\) before three digits. The notation **'\013'** means the character constant 13 in base 8, or 11 in base 10. Similarly, constants of type **char** can be written in hexadecimal by using a leading backslash followed by an **X** (lower or upper case), followed by two hexadecimal digits. Thus, the notation `'\x0D'` means the character constant in D in base 16, or the decimal constant 13.

A.2 MIXED ARITHMETIC WITH UNSIGNED QUANTITIES

In Chapter 2 we discussed how C promotes values of a lower type to a higher type before performing mixed arithmetic operations. Since we make little use of the **unsigned** integer types, we did not discuss how the rules apply to operations involving various unsigned integers.

When unsigned integer types are involved in operations, C applies the following rules for promoting values:

- If one of the two integers is a **long unsigned int**, then the other is converted to a **long unsigned int**.
- Otherwise, if one of the two values is an **unsigned int** and the other is a **long int**, the result is dependent on the implementation. Specifically, if a **long int** can hold all possible values taken by an **unsigned int**, the **unsigned int** is converted to a **long int**. Otherwise, both are converted to **unsigned long int**.
- Otherwise, if either integer operand is an **unsigned int**, the other is converted into an **unsigned int**.

A.3 STORING VARIABLES IN REGISTERS

Most central processing units have a number of *registers*. These are portions of the central processing unit that can store variables. Data in registers can be operated on much faster than comparable operations performed on data stored in regular memory. For this reason, a program may execute much faster if variables that are frequently used are stored in registers rather than in memory.

In many cases, the C compiler automatically uses registers in an efficient way. However, C also provides a way for the programmer to advise the compiler on which variables should be put into registers. This is done by adding the **register** prefix in the declaration of a variable, as in the examples

```
register int i;
register char c;
```

C compilers are not required to put a variable declared as **register** in a register. In fact, the compiler can ignore such advice entirely. However, some compilers do attempt to use the advisory information from **register** declarations. Indices for loops are good candidates for **register** variables.

There are a few restrictions on the use of **register** variables. Because the registers of a processor are not part of the computer's regular memory, variables stored there do not have addresses. Use of the address operator (**&**) on **register** variables is therefore not permitted, and any attempt to reference such variables through a pointer will generally fail. Only automatic variables can be declared to be stored in a **register**. Variables which are **static** or **external** may not be stored in a **register**. Finally, some processors may restrict the types of values that can be stored in registers. These restrictions are machine dependent.

A.4 THE const AND volatile QUALIFIERS

C allows you to qualify the declaration of a variable to specify that its value will not change. For example, the declaration

```
const double sqrt2=1.4142136;
```

initializes the variable **sqrt2** and declares that its value will not be altered during the program's execution.

Declaring an array as **const** indicates that none of the values of the array's elements will be changed. For example, the declaration

```
const char str[]="Hello World\n";
```

shows that the characters in the array **str** will not be altered.

The **const** qualifier can be used for function arguments to indicate that the function uses the variable as an input but does not alter its value. Many library functions use this qualifier. For example, the header file **stdlib.h** includes the prototype for a library function named **system()** in the form

```
int system(const char *s);
```

This function is used to pass a complete operating system command from a C program to the command line interpreter of the computer for execution. It has as its argument a character string containing the command. The **const** qualifier for this string argument indicates that the function **system()** does not alter the character string.

How a C implementation treats variables declared as **const** is entirely implementation specific. A C implementation can ignore the declaration entirely or place such variables in areas of memory which, during a program's execution, can only be read, not written to.

C provides a second qualifier, **volatile**, that is used less frequently. The **volatile** qualifier tells the C implementation not to do certain types of optimization that it might normally perform. It is used in special circumstances where the programmer knows that the optimizations may be inappropriate.

A.5 OTHER PARTS OF CONTROL STRINGS IN printf() AND scanf()

In addition to allowing all the various special markers in control strings described
in Chapter 2, **printf()** and **scanf()** provide for output and input in octal and
hexadecimal. The two control string codes for this are:

- **%o** —for input and output of integers in unsigned, octal notation
- **%x** or **%X**—for input and output in unsigned, hexadecimal notation

These format codes can be used with all the modifiers that apply to the integer format
code **%d**.

A.6 CHARACTER INPUT AND OUTPUT

The standard C library provides several functions for input and output of characters.
The headers for these functions are part of **stdio.h**.

The functions generally work with characters stored in **int**s. This is because
pre-ANSI C did not provide function prototypes, and in the absence of a function
prototype, any function argument of type **char** is automatically converted to an **int**.

A.6.1 Character Input

The function **getchar()** has no arguments. It returns an **int** containing the next
character on the standard input device. The character is represented as an **unsigned
char** and then converted to an **int**. Note that newlines, tabs, etc. are all treated as
distinct characters by **getchar()**. The function returns the end-of-file indicator when
the end of file is reached or when an error is encountered in reading the next character.

The function **fgetc()** is used to get the next character from a file. It has a
pointer to a **FILE** [as returned by **fopen()**] as its argument. The function **getc()** is
identical to **fgetc()** except that it may be implemented as a preprocessor macro. As
with **getchar()**, both **getc()** and **fgetc()** return the end-of-file indicator, **EOF**,
if the end of file is reached or an error is encountered.

Note that the expression **getc(stdin)** is equivalent to **getchar()**.

A.6.2 Character Output

The functions for character output parallel those for character input. For example,
the function **putchar()** writes a single character to the standard output device. It
has one argument, an **int** containing the character to be written (converted from an
unsigned char). It returns an **int** containing either the character it wrote or the
value **EOF** if an error is encountered.

The function **fputc()** outputs a character to a file. Its two arguments are an **int**
containing the character to be written and a pointer to a **FILE** as returned by **fopen()**.
The function **putc()** is identical to **fputc()** except that it may be implemented as a

preprocessor macro. Both return an **int** containing either the character written or **EOF** if an error is encountered.

The expression **putc(c, stdin)** is equivalent to **putchar(c)**.

The last character output function is **ungetc()**. It pushes a character back onto an input stream pointed to by a **FILE** pointer, ensuring that the pushed character will be the next one read. Its arguments are an **int** containing the character to be pushed and the **FILE** pointer. The ANSI C standard requires that only one character may be pushed onto the stream before another read operation from that stream is performed. **ungetc()** returns an **int** containing the character pushed or **EOF** if an error is encountered.

A.7 STRING INPUT AND OUTPUT FUNCTIONS

The standard C input and output library provides functions for reading and writing character strings. The prototypes for these functions are contained in the header file **stdio.h**, which should be included whenever these functions are used.

Unlike the **%s** control string option in **printf()** and **scanf()**, these functions read and write strings that can include white space. They are typically used to read or write a complete line that ends in a newline character. For example, the C fragment

```
char string1[80];
scanf("%s", string1);
```

will read a series of characters terminated by any whitespace character from the standard input, but it will not read a complete line that has embedded spaces or tabs. In contrast, the library function **gets()** reads characters from the standard input until either the end of the file is encountered or a newline is read. The function returns the string read if it is successful, replacing the newline character or the end of file encountered at the end of the input string with the null character. Thus the fragment

```
char string2[80];
if(gets(string2) != NULL)
    printf("String is %s\n", string2);
```

will read a string from the standard input into **string2**. If the end of file is encountered before any characters are read, **gets()** returns a **NULL** pointer, leaving its argument unchanged.

Note that **gets()** will read as many characters as are in the input stream until a newline or end of file is found, regardless of whether there is enough space in the array provided as its argument for those characters. This can produce programs that fail on execution when the input string is too long. An alternative function, **fgets()**, is a more general version. It allows you to limit the number of characters to be input and has an **FILE** pointer argument to read from files other than standard input. A typical use of this function is

```
char *fgets(char *s, int n, FILE *stream);
```

The first argument of **fgets()** is the character array into which the string is to be read. The second argument, **n**, is one greater than the largest number of characters to be read. [The last character is reserved for the **NULL** character automatically appended to the input string by **fgets()**.] The last argument is a pointer to a file from which the read operation is to be performed. A possible usage of **fgets()** is shown in the following code fragment.

```
FILE *s_in;
char buf[80];
s_in = fopen("my_file", "r");
if(s_in != NULL && fgets(buf,80,s_in) != NULL)
 printf("String is %s\n", buf);
```

This would read up to 79 characters from the file **my_file** into the character array **buf**.

The function **puts()** *writes* a string to the standard output device. The null character at the end of the string is not output, and the function adds a newline character to the output stream. **gets()** returns the value **EOF** if a write error occurs when it is called; otherwise, it returns a positive integer value. A typical usage would be

```
puts("Hello world");
```

The function **fputs()** is a more general version of **puts()**. It has a pointer to the **FILE** as its second argument. For example, the fragment

```
FILE *s_out;
char buf[80];
s_out = fopen("output_file", "r");
if(s_out != NULL)
   fputs(buf, s_out);
```

outputs whatever string is in **buf** up to the first **NULL** character to the file named **output_file**. As with **puts()**, the function **fputs()** returns **EOF** if an error is encountered when writing and a positive integer value otherwise.

A.8 THE MATH LIBRARY

Chapter 3 introduced many of the functions provided in the standard C mathematics library. The table below gives the complete list of functions required by the ANSI standard.

MATH FUNCTION LIBRARY

Function	Arguments	Value Returned
`acos()`	`double x`	arc cosine
`asin()`	`double x`	arc sine
`atan()`	`double x`	arc tangent
`atan2()`	`double y, double x`	arc tangent of `y/x`
`ceil()`	`double x`	smallest **double** >= **x** that can be represented as an **int**
`cos()`	`double x`	cosine
`cosh()`	`double x`	hyperbolic cosine
`exp()`	`double x`	exponential function
`fabs()`	`double x`	absolute value
`floor()`	`double x`	largest **double** <= **x** that can be represented as an **int**
`frexp()`	`double x, int *p`	splits **x** into fraction and exponent
`fmod()`	`double x, double y`	see text below
`ldexp()`	`double x, int n`	computes $x*2^n$
`log()`	`double x`	natural logarithm
`log10()`	`double x`	logarithm base 10
`modf()`	`double x, int *p`	splits **x** into fractional and integer parts
`pow()`	`double x, double y`	x^y
`sin()`	`double x`	sine
`sinh()`	`double x`	hyperbolic sine
`sqrt()`	`double x`	square root
`tan()`	`double x`	tangent
`tanh()`	`double x`	hyperbolic tangent

Some of the functions in the mathematical library are used to convert values in floating-point representation to other forms. For example, the function **frexp()** returns a value **f** which is the fractional part of its first argument **x**. **f** has absolute value between .5 and 1.0. **frexp()** puts the exponent of **x** into the **int** pointed to by its second argument **p**. The value of **f** and the value pointed to **p** are such that **x** equals **f** times 2 to the power of the value pointed to by **p**. If the value of **x** is zero, then the value returned by **frexp()** and the value pointed to by **p** are both 0.

The function **ldexp()** is the inverse of **frexp()**. It returns a **double** which is the value $x * 2^n$.

The function **modf()** returns a value **f** and sets the value of the **int** pointed to by **p**. These values are such that the absolute value of **f** is less than 1 and **x** is equal to **f+n**.

The function **fmod()** has the following characteristics:

- It returns a value **f** that has the same sign as **x**.
- The absolute value of **f** is less than the absolute value of **y**.
- There exists some integer **k** such that **k*y+f** is equal to **x**.

A.9 THE CHARACTER LIBRARY

C provides a group of functions to test a value containing the numerical representation of a character to determine whether it belongs to a particular class. These functions are defined in the standard header file **ctype.h**. They all have a single **int** argument that must contain either the value defined as **EOF** (the end-of-file indicator) or a value which is representable as an **unsigned char**. Most of these functions return a value which is TRUE (i.e., nonzero) if the character belongs to a given class and FALSE (i.e., zero) otherwise. The following classes of character types can be tested.

- Decimal digits (**'0'** through **'9'**)
- Uppercase letters (**'A'** through **'Z'**)
- Lowercase letters (**'a'** through **'z'**)
- Punctuation characters
- Control characters
- A *printable* character, (i.e., one that corresponds to a single character that can be output, including punctuation characters)
- White space: blank, formfeed, new line, carriage return, tab, and vertical tab
- Hexadecimal digits (**'0'** through **'9'**, **'A** through **'F'**, and **'a'** through **'f'**)

The functions provided include the following:

CHARACTER CLASS LIBRARY

Function	Value Returned by Function
isdigit(c)	TRUE if c is decimal digit, FALSE otherwise
isxdigit(c)	TRUE if c is hexadecimal digit, FALSE otherwise
islower(c)	TRUE if c is lowercase, FALSE otherwise
isupper(c)	TRUE if c is uppercase, FALSE otherwise
isalpha(c)	TRUE if c is uppercase or lowercase, FALSE otherwise
isalnum(c)	TRUE if c is uppercase, lowercase, or digit, FALSE otherwise
iscntrl(c)	TRUE if c is control character, FALSE otherwise
isgraph(c)	TRUE if c is printable but not a space, FALSE otherwise
isprint(c)	TRUE if c is printable including space, FALSE otherwise
ispunct(c)	TRUE if c is punctuation character, FALSE otherwise
isspace(c)	TRUE if c is white space, FALSE otherwise
tolower(c)	if c is uppercase, returns c as lowercase, otherwise returns c
toupper(c)	if c is lowercase, returns c as uppercase, otherwise returns c

In many cases the character library is implemented as a set of macros in **ctype.h**. When macros are used, the standard library also provides a corresponding set of functions with the same names as the macros. These can be accessed by enclosing the name of the function in parentheses, as in the form

```
(isupper)('A')
```

The parentheses result in surpressing substitution of the macro form of **isupper()** because macros with arguments are expanded by the preprocessor only when the left parenthesis that begins the argument list is not separated by any character from the name of the macro.

A.10 SORTING AND SEARCHING FUNCTIONS
IN THE C LIBRARY

The standard C library has general-purpose searching and sorting functions named **bsearch()** and **qsort()**. The prototypes for these functions are part of the header file **stdlib.h**.

qsort() sorts an array of entries that may be simple values or structures. The items are sorted "in place," reorganizing the entries in the array passed in as an argument. The function has four arguments, as follows:

- The array to be sorted. This is a pointer to the first array element. The function prototype for **qsort()** casts this argument to a pointer to **void**.
- An integer containing the number of elements in the array.
- An integer which is the size of each array element as provided by the **sizeof** operator.
- A pointer to a function that compares two items in the array. This function has as its arguments pointers to two items in the array. It must return an integer which is negative if the first item pointed to is less than the second in the sorting order desired, zero if the two items are equal in sorting order, and positive if the first item is greater than the second item. In most cases, the user of **qsort()** will write this function.

qsort() has no return value.

The second function, **bsearch()**, searches a sorted array which may have been sorted by **qsort()**. Its arguments are:

- A pointer to the key being searched for. This is cast in the function prototype for **bsearch()** to a pointer to **void**.
- The array to be searched. This argument is the same as the first argument to **qsort()**. The function assumes this array is sorted.
- An integer containing the number of elements in the array.
- An integer which is the size of each array element as provided by the **sizeof** operator.
- A pointer to a function that compares two items in the array. This function should have the same properties as the fourth argument to **qsort()**.

bsearch() returns a pointer to **void** which points to the item in the array if it was found or is **NULL** if the item was not found.

A.11 OTHER PARTS OF THE STANDARD C LIBRARY

The standard C library includes many other functions not covered in detail in this book. We list here some of the broad categories of these functions.

- In addition to the file input and output functions covered in Chapter 6, the standard input and output library includes functions to position the reads and writes on a file to different parts of a file and functions to read and write on a file without formatting the output into characters. The headers for these functions are part of the file **stdio.h**.

- There are functions for conversion of numbers between character and numeric representations, and communicating between the command interpreter (or shell) and the program. The headers for the collection of diverse functions are in the file **stdlib.h**.

- There are functions for obtaining the time and date and for representing that information in various forms. The headers for these functions are in the file **time.h**.

- The library includes functions that adapt to the output standards for currency, date, and time of a particular locale. These functions are useful in making programs portable to different countries. The headers for these functions are in the file **locale.h**.

- There is a part of the library for handling *signals* that are generated by a program when exceptional conditions such as arithmetic overflow, illegal instructions, or user-generated interrupts occur. The headers for these functions are in the file **signal.h**.

- There are functions for handling situations when the number of arguments to a function can vary. (The standard functions **printf()** and **scanf()** are examples of functions that use this feature.) The headers for these functions are in the file **stdarg.h**.

- There are functions to detect the occurrence and cause of various error conditions, including some that may vary across different C implementations. The headers for these functions are in the file **errno.h**.

- There are functions that allow programs to jump from one point in their execution to a point in an entirely different function. This is called a *nonlocal jump*. The headers for these functions are in the file **setjmp.h**.

Readers interested in more details about these parts of the C library should examine the ANSI standard ([American National Standards Institute 88]) or Kernighan and Ritchie [Kernighan, Brian W. and Ritchie, Dennis M. 88].

A.12 SPECIAL TYPES size_t AND ptrdiff_t

Because different implementations of C are free to use different numbers of bytes to store **unsigned int**s and pointers, the ANSI C standard requires that implementations create special types for storing quantities such as amounts of memory or the differences between two pointers. If this were not the case, a programmer might try to assign the difference between two pointer values to an **int** using a C implementation in which the difference between two pointers can exceed the maximum allowed value of an **int**. The two special variable types are called **size_t** and **ptrdiff_t**. These two variable types are created using **typedef** statements in the header file **stddef.h**.

The type **size_t** can store an unsigned integer value. The operator **sizeof** yields a value of this type. In addition, many functions in the standard C library such as **malloc()**, **calloc()**, and **realloc()** have values of type **size_t** as one of their arguments. For example, the correct function prototype for **malloc()** (as it would appear in the header file **stdlib.h**) is

```
void *malloc(size_t);
```

Because the function prototype will cause a conversion of any expression that appears as an argument to **malloc()** to the type **size_t**, you can generally think of such functions as having unsigned integers as their arguments.

The difference between two pointers is of type **ptrdiff_t**. Technically, any variable that is assigned to the difference between two pointers should be defined as type **ptrdiff_t** rather than type **int**. This assures that the range of values in the variable storing the difference can always accommodate all possible outcomes of the pointer subtraction.

A.13 ENUMERATIONS

There are many situations where the values a variable can take are confined to a well-defined set of possibilities. For example, logical values are either true or false, the days of the week range from Sunday through Saturday, and the months range from January through December. C allows for the definition of *enumeration constants* to represent these situations.

For example, in Section 4.11 we used the preprocessor directives to define names for the possible instructions a simple robot could execute. The preprocessor statements used in that example are repeated below.

```
#define FORWARD      1
#define IN_MAZE      2
#define WALL_AHEAD   3
#define COND_BRANCH  4
#define RIGHT        5
#define DISPLAY      6
#define BRANCH       7
#define HALT         8
```

We could also use an enumeration as follows:

```
enum code {FORWARD=1, IN_MAZE, WALL_AHEAD, COND_BRANCH,
    RIGHT, DISPLAY, BRANCH, HALT};
```

Note that we have explicitly assigned a value to the constant **FORWARD** but have not done so for the remaining values. This is because when an explicit value is omitted, the **enum** statement generates the next integer for each constant in the enumeration. If the first constant is not given a value, then it is assumed to be zero.

In this example, the name **code** is a tag that can be used much like a **struct** tag to define variables. For example, after the enumeration **code** is defined, we could have a declaration such as

```
enum code instruction;
```

that would declare the variable **instruction** to be an enumeration of type **code**. This would allow assignment statements such as

```
instruction = HALT;
```

As with tags for structures, a variable may be defined as an enumeration without using an **enum** tag. For example, the variable **instruction** could have been defined with the statement

```
enum  {FORWARD=1, IN_MAZE, WALL_AHEAD, COND_BRANCH,
    RIGHT, DISPLAY, BRANCH, HALT} instruction;
```

You may also define a tag for an enumeration in the same statement as a variable declaration, as in

```
enum  code {FORWARD=1, IN_MAZE, WALL_AHEAD, COND_BRANCH,
    RIGHT, DISPLAY, BRANCH, HALT} instruction;
```

The C compiler will automatically generate integer values for elements in an enumeration if none are provided. For example, if we had

```
enum flavors {VANILLA, CHOCOLATE, STRAWBERRY, PEACH};
```

the compiler would begin numbering the constants with consecutive integers starting at 0.

If any enumeration constant is given a value, then the default for the next constant in the list is one greater than the previous value. For example, if the example above were changed to

```
enum flavors{VANILLA, CHOCOLATE=2, STRAWBERRY, PEACH=5};
```

then the constant **VANILLA** would be zero and the constant **STRAWBERRY** would be 3. C also allows a number of enumerated constants to have the same value, in effect providing a synonym for a constant.

C implementations do not check when a program is running to ensure that the value of a variable that is an enumeration remains in the allowed set. For example, if the variable **ice_cream_type** were an enumeration of type **flavors**, the following C statement would still be executed:

```
ice_cream_type = PEACH + 1;
```

even though the integer 6 does not correspond to any of the values in the **enum flavors**.

The advantage of using an enumeration over a series of **#define** preprocessor directives is that the compiler can often use the information that a particular variable has a restricted set of values to detect coding errors. For example, if a variable were an enumeration of type **flavors**, then assigning it a constant value which is a day of the week would be detectable. This would not be the case if **#define** statements were used. For this reason, many programmers argue that enumerations should be used instead of **#define** preprocessor directives whenever possible. We have avoided introducing enumerations in the body of the book because they were not essential to the algorithmic material being presented. We nevertheless encourage the use of them.

A.14 OTHER PREPROCESSOR FEATURES

While the most commonly used preprocessor directives are **#define** and **#include**, the standard C preprocessor supports many other features as well. Some of the more useful of these are described here.

The **#if** directive allows you to test the value of a preprocessor macro and to pass through different source code to the compiler, depending on the outcome of that test. This feature allows what is called *conditional compilation*, where different segments of code are used depending on defined preprocessor values.

For example, we might have a C program intended to be compiled on three different computers, one running the MSDOS operating system, one running an older version of the UNIX operating system and some default system.[1]   These operating systems have different rules about naming files. In MSDOS, file names are restricted to eight characters plus a three-character extension, some older versions of UNIX restrict file names to 14 characters, and other versions of UNIX have no restrictions on file lengths. If a program is going to have a function to read a file name from the user and check it for validity, then there will have to be different versions of that function for different computer systems. An example of how this might be done is as follows.

```
#define MSDOS 1
```

[1]MSDOS is a trademark of Microsoft, Inc. UNIX is a trademark of ATT Laboratories.

```
#define UNIX 2

#if OP_SYSTEM == MSDOS

...code for MSDOS implementation goes here

#elif OP_SYSTEM == UNIX

...code for UNIX goes here

#else
...code for default option goes here

#endif
```

When the program is compiled on a computer with a particular operating system, you would only have to add a single **#define** statement of the form

```
#define OP_SYSTEM MSDOS
```

or

```
#define OP_SYSTEM UNIX
```

before the **#if** statement. Depending on which operating system was chosen, the preprocessor would pass on only those lines of source code that satisfied the **#if** or **#elif** conditions. The **#if**, **#elif**, and **#else** directives are used in the same way as are the **if...elseif...else** statements in C. The **#endif** denotes the end of the **#if** preprocessor clause.

The preprocessor has two special forms of the **#if** statement. The **#ifdef** directive tests whether a preprocessor name has been defined; it evaluates to true (nonzero) if the name is defined and false (zero) otherwise. The **#ifndef** directive does the opposite; it tests if a preprocessor name has *not* been defined. The example above with different versions of the source code for different operating systems could also have been coded as follows:

```
#ifdef MSDOS

...code for MSDOS implementation goes here

#endif

#ifdef UNIX

...code for UNIX goes here

#endif
```

```
#ifdef OTHER_OS

...code for default option goes here

#endif
```

The particular version compiled would be controlled by putting a single **#define** statement at the beginning of the source code file that **#define**d one of the three names: **MSDOS**, **UNIX**, or **OTHER_OS**.

Another common use of **#ifdef** statements is to conditionally compile code that is used for debugging purposes. This code often includes **printf()** statements that output values of variables. Rather than maintaining two separate versions of a program, with and without the debugging code, all the debugging statements can be placed inside **#ifdef** statements, as in the example

```
#ifdef DEBUG

....put debugging statements here

#endif
```

When the program is to be compiled with the debugging statements, you need only add the preprocessor directive

```
#define DEBUG
```

at the beginning of the source file. This defines the name **DEBUG** without any corresponding value. If this statement is deleted, then the debugging statements will not be compiled.

A preprocessor directive may span across more than one line in the source file. When this is the case, all the lines except the last should have a backslash (\) as their last character. (This backslash really isn't the last character since every line ends with a newline character. The backslash is simply the last visible character.)

The preprocessor has a set of predefined names that can be used to produce useful information. These names all begin and end with two underscores (_ _). They are as follows:

- _ _**DATE**_ _—a string constant set to the date of the compilation.
- _ _**FILE**_ _—a string constant set to the name of the file currently being compiled.
- _ _**LINE**_ _—a constant set to the current line number in the source file.
- _ _**STDC**_ _—a constant set to 1. This can be used to test whether the compiler is ANSI-compliant since it will not be defined for pre-ANSI compliers.
- _ _**TIME**_ _—a string constant set to the time of the compilation.

The reader should remember that the C preprocessor is not truly part of the C compiler. It only modifies the C code, which is in turn passed to the actual compiler. In some of the examples above, the modifications consist of deciding which subset of the source code to pass on to the compiler. Also, the preprocessor can only evaluate and test expressions that are constants.

A.15 THE do. . .while STATEMENT

Chapter 2 introduced **while** and **for** loops. C provides a third looping syntax that has the property that the body of the loop is always executed at least once. The basic form of this loop is

```
do
   statement;
   while(exp);
```

where **statement** is either a single or a compound statement (enclosed in curly braces) and **exp** is a valid C expression. The **statement** is always executed at least once. Then **exp** is evaluated. If **exp** is true (i.e., not zero) then the loop is executed again; otherwise, the loop is exited.

This type of loop is used less often than are **while** and **for** loops. However, it can be convenient when you are reading from a file and must test if the end of file has been reached. For example, the following function counts "words" in a file, where a word is a series of consecutive characters separated by any white space. It has a file pointer (type **FILE ***) as its argument and returns an **int** with the count of the number of "words" in the file.

```
#include <stdio.h>

/* function to count words in a file */
int word_count(FILE *f)
{
   int count=-1;        /* number of words */
   char buffer[100];    /* place to read strings into */
   int flag;            /* value returned from fscanf */

   do {
     flag=fscanf(f, "%s", buffer);
     count++;
   }
     while(flag != EOF);   /* loop until EOF reached */
   return(count);          /* return word count */
}
```

A.16 THE switch AND break STATEMENTS

There are many cases where some expression must be tested to determine which of several situations applies. For example, after reading a character from an input file, one might test whether that character was a blank, a number, a letter, or some other character. In this book we used `if...elseif...else` statements for such situations. When the value to be tested needs to be compared with integer possibilities, C provides a more compact form called the `switch` statement.

The general form of the `switch` statement is as follows:

```
/* general form of the switch statement */
switch(exp) {
  case cons_0: statements_0
  case cons_1: statements_1
  case cons_2: statements_2
      .
      .
      .
  case cons_n: statements_n
  default: statements
  }
```

where `exp` is an integer expression and `cons_0`, `cons_1`, `cons_2`, ..., `cons_n` are all integer constants or *integer constant expressions*. A constant expression is one which can be evaluated prior to the program's execution. For example, the expression `'A'+1` is an integer constant expression because its value is an integer and it can be computed before the program executes. `statements_0`, `statements_1`, `statements_2`, ..., `statements` are all one or more normal C statements.

The `default` clause can be omitted. If it is omitted and the value of the expression does not match any of the cases, then the entire `switch` statement has no effect.

The `switch` statement has the property that once the expression matches any case, the execution of the program proceeds as though all subsequent cases were matched unless the programmer explicitly states otherwise. The most common ways of taking explicit action to exit from the `switch` is for one of the statements in a clause to be a `return` statement or through the use of the `break` statement. The `break` statement causes the execution to exit immediately from the `switch` statement. (The `break` statement also causes immediate exit from a `while`, `do`, or `for` loop.)

In the robot simulator given in Section 4.11 we used a series of `if` statements to test which direction the robot should be moved when interpreting the instruction to move forward one step. The relevant fragment of C code from that example could have been written using a `switch` as follows:

```
switch(direct) {
  case NORTH:
    y++;
```

```
        break;
    case SOUTH:
      y--;
      break;
    case EAST:
      x++;
      break;
    case WEST:
      x--;
      break;
    default:
      printf("Illegal direction--Program halted\n");
      return;
  }
```

A.17 THE continue STATEMENT

There are some situations inside a loop when it is useful to be able to skip to the end
of a loop, causing the next iteration of the loop to occur. For example, we might have
a function that counts the number of times each letter in the alphabet appears in a long
text string. The counts could be stored in an array of integers with 26 elements, one for
each letter in the alphabet. The loop would go through each character in the string and
first test whether the character was a letter. Entries in the string which are not letters
need not be examined further, while entries which are letters must be examined to test
for whether they are upper or lower case. An example of a function which uses the
continue statement to simplify the logic of this test would be as follows:

```
/* function to count letters in a string */
void char_count(
  char *s,        /* string to be counted */
  int counts[])   /* array of counts */
{
/* loop through entire string */
  for(; *s!= '\0'; s++) {

    if(!isalpha(*s)) /* if not a letter, continue loop */
      continue;
    else {
      if(isupper(*s))
        counts[*s - 'A']++;
      else
        counts[*s-'a']++;
    }
  }
}
```

A.18 STATEMENT LABELS AND goto

Many languages such as BASIC and FORTRAN make extensive use of statements that cause execution within a function to jump from one place to another. The abuse of this capability is often cited as a reason many programs are difficult to read and maintain, particularly when a function is long and complicated. Many programmers argue that such jumps should never be used. However, consistent with the C philosophy that a computer language should give the programmer wide latitude by not forbidding constructs even if they can lead to obscure programs, the C language includes the ability to label any C statement with a symbolic name and a **goto** statement to jump to that statement as long as the statement label and the **goto** statement are in the same function.

Any sequence of characters that would be a valid variable name can be used as a statement label. A label precedes the statement and is separated from it by a colon. For example, the statement

```
add_one : a = a+1;
```

gives the label **add_one** to the statement **a = a + 1**.

Given that **add_one** is a valid statement label, the statement

```
goto add_one;
```

within the same function will transfer control of execution to the statement **add_one**. **goto** statements cannot be used to transfer control of execution to a statement outside the function in which the **goto** appears.

One possible use for a **goto** statement is to exit from a deeply nested loop. This ability is often useful for handling errors detected inside the loop, where the error-handling code is entirely outside the loop. In such situations, selective use of the **goto** statement may lead to code that some would argue is clearer than the alternatives. However, we urge programmers to be very cautious in using **goto** statements.

A.19 UNIONS

A **union** in C is a variable that can be used to store objects which may be of different types and sizes. Consider, for example, a program where inputs can be generated from a keyboard, a light pen, or a mouse with two buttons. We might want to have a single variable to store the code of the key that was pressed, the (x, y) pixel coordinate where the light pen was activated, or the (x, y) pixel coordinate where the mouse button was pressed and a character code indicating which of the two buttons (**'L'** for left and **'R'** for right) was pressed. We could define a **union** type called **input_event** that could store the three possible inputs as follows:

```
/* template declaration for a union */
union input_event {
```

```
    char keycode;        /* key press */
    struct {             /* light pen press */
       int x;
       int y;
    } pen_coord;
    struct {             /* mouse button press */
       int x;
       int y;
       char button;
    } mouse_info;
};
```

A variable which is a **union** of this type could be used to store a key code *or* the coordinates of a light pen *or* information about a mouse button.

The name **input_event** is a *union tag* which can be used in the same way as a structure tag. For example, with the foregoing declaration of the template **input_event**, we could define a variable named **inp** to store an event with as follows:

```
union input_event inp;   /* variable which is a union */
```

As with structures and enumerations, a variable which is a **union** can be declared without first declaring a union tag. C also allows a union tag to be declared in the same statement as the definition of a variable.

At any one time, a **union** can be used to hold only a single type of value. However, a variable which is a **union** can first be used to hold one type of value and later to hold another type.

Members of a **union** are referenced in using the same notation as members of a **struct**, using either the dot operator (**.**) or the arrow operator (**->**). For example, all of the following are legal references to members of the variable **inp**.

```
union input_event * pinp; /* pointer to an input_event */

inp.keycode = 'A';        /* sets keycode */
inp.pen_coord.x = 300;    /* sets x coord. of light pen event*/

pinp = &inp;     /* assigns address of inp to pointer */

pinp->mouse_info.button = 'L'; /* set button pressed */
```

In using a **union** it is up to the programmer to keep track of what type of information has been stored there. It is often convenient to have a variable that all elements of the union have in common that stores a code indicating the use to which the **union** was last put.

The storage occupied by a **union** is always large enough to hold its largest member. In the example above, the **mouse_info** member requires the most memory, so any variable defined as a **union** of type **input_event** will be large enough to store the **mouse_info** structure regardless of whether it is ever used for that purpose.

The example above shows that a **union** may include one or more **struct**s. C also allows a **struct** to contain one or more **union**s.

A.20 THE CONDITIONAL OPERATOR

C has a special operator for *conditional* expressions. The basic form of this operator is as follows:

```
exp0 ? exp1 : exp2;
```

where **exp0**, **exp1** and **exp2** are all valid C expressions. This complete expression is evaluated by first evaluating **exp0**. If **exp0** is true (i.e., not zero), then **exp1** is evaluated as the value of the complete expression. Otherwise, **exp2** is evaluated and is the value of the complete expression. For example (taken from Kernighan and Ritchie [Kernighan, Brian W. and Ritchie, Dennis M. 88]), the statement

```
z = (a>b) ? a : b;
```

is completely equivalent to the statements

```
if(a>b)
    z = a;
else
    z = b;
```

While the conditional operator can produce very compact code, it often produces hard-to-read programs. For that reason we discourage its use.

A.21 BIT OPERATORS

C provides a group of *bit operators*. These operators manipulate the individual 1's and 0's in C variables. The operators include the following:

CHARACTER CLASS LIBRARY

Operator	Explanation
&	bitwise logical AND
|	bitwise logical OR
^	bitwise exclusive OR
<<	left shift
>>	right shift
~	one's complement

These operators can be used on integer values, including the signed and unsigned versions of **char**, **short**, **int**, and **long**.

Bitwise logical AND, OR, and exclusive OR perform logical operations on a bit-by-bit basis. The left-shift and right-shift operators take the binary representation of their first operand and move the bits left or right by the number of places indicated by the second operand, filling the vacated places with zeros. For example, **a << 4** shifts the binary numbers in **a** left four binary places, filling the rightmost four bits with zeros. The one's complement operator has a single operand; it converts each 0 to a 1 and each 1 to a 0. For example, **~a** reverses all the bits in the variable **a**.

The reader should be careful to avoid confusing the bitwise operators **&** and **|** with their logical counterparts **&&** and **||**. Bitwise operators work on each bit in their operands separately, while the normal logical operators work on the entire value.

C also provides versions of the bitwise operators that include an assignment. Thus, the statement

```
a = a << b;
```

can also be written as

```
a <<= b;
```

Similarly, C provides the operators **>>=**, **|=**, **^=**, and **&=**. All of these evaluate from right to left and have the same precedence as the other assignment operators.

With these additional operators, the complete table of operator precedence and associativity for the C language is as given below.

OPERATORS IN DECREASING PRECEDENCE

Operator	Association
{} () [] -> .	left to right
! + - ~ ++ -- * & *(type)* sizeof	right to left
* / %	left to right
+ -	left to right
<< >>	left to right
< <= > >=	left to right
== !=	left to right
&	left to right
^	left to right
|	left to right
&&	left to right
||	left to right
? :	right to left
= += -= *= /= %= &= ^= |= <<= >>=	right to left
,	left to right

A.22 BIT FIELDS

All of the variables discussed in this book occupy storage that is organized in *bytes*, which in the C language is a unit large enough to hold all possible values of a character. C also allows you to pack variables into adjacent portions of storage units. Variables packed in this way are called *bit fields*; they are useful when storing integer values that are small when memory is limited. Bit fields are also useful when programming for data communications or in situations where one must access and manipulate the binary representation of small values.

The syntax for declaring bit fields uses a generalization of C **structs**. For example, we might want to have a series of bit fields that each occupy a single bit to indicate the classes to which a particular character belongs. (See Section A.9.) The following **struct** template would define such bit fields:

```
/* struct with bit fields for character classes */
struct char_classes {
    unsigned int decimal : 1; /* 1 if decimal, else 0 */
    unsigned int upper : 1; /* 1 if upper-case, else 0 */
    unsigned int lower : 1; /* 1 if lower-case, else 0 */
    unsigned int punct : 1; /* 1 if punctuation, else 0 */
    unsigned int control : 1; /* 1 if control,  else 0 */
    unsigned int printable : 1;/* 1 if printable, else 0 */
    unsigned int white : 1; /* 1 if white space,  else 0 */
    unsigned int hex : 1; /* 1 if hexadecimal,  else 0 */
};
```

The integer after the colon denotes the number of bits for the field. Bit fields may only be declared as **int**s.

Bit fields should be used with extreme caution. Many aspects of bit fields are left up to the implementation of the C compiler, so writing programs that use bit fields in a portable way is extremely difficult. We suggest that they be used only as a last resort.

A.23 BACKWARD COMPATIBILITY WITH EARLIER VERSIONS OF C

This entire book was written assuming that the reader is using a compiler that is based on the ANSI C specification. Even though developers of compilers are all adopting the ANSI standard, there is still a large base of C code that was written prior to the standard's development. This section highlights some of the most significant differences between ANSI C and prior versions.

The most notable distinction is that pre-ANSI C does not provide for function prototypes. This has two significant effects on programs. First, there is no way in pre-ANSI C to tell the compiler the type and number of arguments required to invoke a function. Given this, pre-ANSI C compilers cannot check the number and types of arguments for consistency. They also cannot automatically convert arguments to the types expected by a function. It is up to the programmer to ensure that arguments match in type and number.

The second distinction is in how the arguments of a function are written in the definition of the function. In pre-ANSI C, the types of function arguments are declared in separate statements rather than in the argument list. For example, the function **average_ints()** in Chapter 2 was written in ANSI C as

```
double average_ints(int i, int j, int k)
{
   return ( (i + j + k) / 3.0);
}
```

In pre-ANSI C this would be coded as follows:

```
double average_ints()
   int i;
   int j;
   int k;
{
   return ( (i + j + k) / 3.0);
}
```

Pre-ANSI C also does not use the keyword **void**. Thus, functions without arguments are indicated simply by not listing any variable declarations before the body of the function. Also, the concept of **void** pointers does not exist. Programmers often used pointers to **char** as generic pointers.

Versions of C before the ANSI standard also had different rules for passing arguments to functions. All arguments that were declared **short** or **char** were "promoted" to **int**s before they were passed. Similarly, all **float**s were converted to type **double**. For this reason, most functions written in pre-ANSI C rely on arguments of type **int** and **double**.

Pre-ANSI C has slightly different rules for evaluating numerical expressions. The most notable of these is that any value which is a **float** is always converted to a **double** before an expression is evaluated. On most computers this makes performing numerical operations of **float**s more computation-intensive than the same operations on **double**s, leading many programmers to avoid using **float**s unless their lower storage requirements were needed.

Some pre-ANSI C implementations did not allow **struct**s to be passed as arguments, assigned to other **struct**s, or returned from functions. This restriction was relaxed by most compilers even before the ANSI C specification was formulated.

ANSI also extended the rules for initialization of variables. These changes were upwardly compatible. In particular, pre-ANSI C did not allow automatic arrays, structures, or unions to be initialized.

There are many other, less significant changes. Readers are referred to either the ANSI specification [American National Standards Institute 88] or Kernighan and Ritchie [Kernighan, Brian W. and Ritchie, Dennis M. 88] for a more detailed list. The most common specification of pre-ANSI C is provided in Kernighan and Ritchie [Kernighan, Brian W. and Ritchie, Dennis M. 78].

REFERENCES

[**Abelson, H., Sussman, G. and Sussman, J. 85**]   Abelson, H., Sussman, G. and Sussman, J., *Structure and Interpretation of Computer Programs.* MIT Press, Cambridge, Massachusetts, 1985.

[**Abramowitz, Milton 64**]   Abramowitz, Milton, and Stegun, Irene A., *Handbook of Mathematical Functions, Applied Math Series, Volume 55.* National Bureau of Standards, Washington, D.C., 1964.

[**American National Standards Institute 88**]   American National Standards Institute. Draft Proposed American Standard for Information Systems–Programming Language C. Jan., 1988 Document Number X3J11/88-001.

[**American National Standards Institute 89**]   American National Standards Institute. American National Standard for Information Systems–Programming Language C. Dec., 1989 Document Number X3.159-1989.

[**Bertsekas, Dimitri P. 89**]   Bertsekas, Dimitri P. and Tsitsiklis, John N., *Parallel and Distributed Computation; Numerical Methods.* Prentice Hall, Inc., Englewood Cliffs, New Jersey, 1989.

[**Brassard, G. and Bratley, P. 88**]   Brassard, G. and Bratley, P., *Algorithmics: Theory and Practice.* Prentice Hall, Englewood Cliffs, New Jersey, 1988.

[**Esakov, J. and Weiss, T. 89**]   Esakov, J. and Weiss, T., *Data Structures.* Prentice Hall, Englewood Cliffs, New Jersey, 1989.

[**Foley, James D. 90**] Foley, J. D., van Dam, A., Feiner, S. K. and Hughes, J. F., *Computer Graphics: Principles and Practice.* Addison-Wesley Publishing Company, Reading, Massachusetts, 1990.

[**Hoare, C. A. R. 62**] Hoare, C. A. R. Quicksort., *Computer Journal* 5(1), 1962.

[**Horowitz, Ellis and Sahni, Sartj 78**] Horowitz, Ellis and Sahni, Sartaj. *Fundamentals of Computer Algorithms.* Computer Science Press, Inc., Rockville, Maryland, 1978.

[**Institute of Electrical and Electronics Engineers 85**] Institute of Electrical and Electronics Engineers. *ANSI/IEEE Standard 754-1985.* Institute of Electrical and Electronics Engineers, Inc, Piscataway, New Jersey, 1985.

[**Kernighan, Brian 78**] Kernighan, Brian W. and Ritchie, Dennis M., *Prentice Hall Software Series: The C Programming Language.* Prentice Hall, Inc., Englewood Cliffs, New Jersey, 1978.

[**Kernighan, Brian 88**] Kernighan, Brian W. and Ritchie, Dennis M., *Prentice Hall Software Series: The C Programming Language.* Prentice Hall, Inc., Englewood Cliffs, New Jersey, 1988.

[**Knuth, Donald E. 73a**] Knuth, Donald E., *Addison Wesley Series in Computer Science and Information Processing: The Art of Computer Programming. Volume 1 Fundamental Algorithms.* Addison-Wesley Publishing Company, Reading, Massachusetts, 1973.

[**Knuth, Donald E. 73b**] Knuth, Donald E., *Addison Wesley Series in Computer Science and Information Processing: The Art of Computer Programming. Volume 2 Seminumerical Algorithms.* Addison-Wesley Publishing Company, Reading, Massachusetts, 1973.

[**Pattis, R. E. 81**] Pattis, R. E., *Karel the Robot: A Gentle Introduction to the Art of Programming.* Wiley, New York, New York, 1981.

[**Press, William H. 88**] Press, William H., et al., *Numerical Recipes in C.* Cambridge University Press, Cambridge, England, 1988.

[**Rivest, R. 78**] Rivest, R., A. Shamir, and L. Adelman. A Method for Obtaining Digital Signatures and Public-Key Cryptosystems. *Communications of the ACM* 21(2):120–126, 1978.

[**Sedgewick, Robert 90**] Sedgewick, Robert. *Algorithms in C.* Addison-Wesley, Reading, Massachusetts, 1990.

[**Stroustrup, Bjarne 86**] Stroustrup, Bjarne. *The C++ Programming Language.* Addison-Wesley, Reading, Massachusetts, 1986.

[**von Neumann, John 63**] von Neumann, John. *Collected Works.* Pergamon Press, New York, 1961–1963.

INDEX